DATE DUE		
ILL			
10-15-97			
Salida			

BREAKING
— THE —
MAYA CODE

MICHAEL D. COE

BREAKING — THE — MAYA CODE

with 112 illustrations

THAMES AND HUDSON

To Yuri Valentinovich Knorosov
ah bobat, ah miatz, etail

© 1992 Michael D. Coe

First published in the United States of America in 1992
by Thames and Hudson Inc.,
500 Fifth Avenue, New York, New York 10110
Reprinted 1993

First paperback edition 1993

Library of Congress Catalog Card Number 91-65312

Printed in the United States of America

Contents

Preface

The history of the American continent does not begin with Christopher Columbus, or even with Leif the Lucky, but with those Maya scribes in the Central American jungles who first began to record the deeds of their rulers some two thousand years ago. Of all the peoples of the pre-Columbian New World, only the ancient Maya had a complete script: they could write down anything they wanted to, in their own language.

In the last century, following the discovery of the ruined Maya cities, almost none of these records could be read by Western scholars. Except for the Maya calendar, which has been understood for over a hundred years, the situation was not much better than this when I was a student at Harvard in the 1950s. Today, thanks to some remarkable advances made by epigraphers on both sides of the Atlantic, we can now read most of what those long-dead scribes carved on their stone monuments.

I believe that this decipherment is one of the most exciting intellectual adventures of our age, on a par with the exploration of space and the discovery of the genetic code. This is the story that I wish to tell in these pages. I have been lucky enough to have known personally many of the protagonists in the more recent part of my tale; it will soon become apparent to the reader, as it has to me, that the course of this decipherment has involved not just theoretical and scholarly issues, but flesh-and-blood individuals with strongly marked characters.

If one wants, one can find both heroes and villains in my history, yet let me say here that there are really no "bad guys" in these pages, just well-meaning and determined scholars who have sometimes been impelled by false assumptions to take wrong turns, and had their posthumous reputations suffer as a consequence. And if you must find a villain, remember that even John Milton's fallen angel, Satan himself, had his heroic side.

I have had help from many quarters in writing this book, but it must be emphasized that its facts and interpretations, for better or for worse, are my own. Deserving of special thanks is George Stuart, whose unpublished manuscript on the history of the decipherment has often guided me to new clues and insights. I owe a heavy debt to Linda Schele, Elizabeth Benson, David Stuart, Floyd Lounsbury, and David Kelley for their patience and forbearance during lengthy taped interviews, often by long-distance telephone. With her usual ebullient generosity, Linda provided me with copies of the voluminous correspondence which had passed between the "Young Turks" described in Chapter 10.

I wish to thank Y.V. Knorosov and his colleagues of the Institute of Ethnography, Russian Academy of Sciences, for their warm hospitality during the visit of my wife and myself to St. Petersburg (then Leningrad) in 1989, and especially the young Mayanists Galina Yershova and Anna Alexandrovna Borodatova.

The early chapters of the book were written while I was on triennial leave from Yale, in the neoclassical splendor of the British School at Rome; I am grateful to the School's Director, Richard Hodges, and to Valerie Scott, the Librarian, for making this a most rewarding experience. For valuable editorial comments, I would also like to express my appreciation to James Mallory, Andrew Robinson, and the staff of Thames and Hudson. Lastly, my thanks go to all those former Yale students, particularly Steve Houston, Karl Taube, and Peter Mathews, who have kept me in touch with much that is old and new in the world of Maya decipherment.

In this book, I have followed the transcription first devised in Colonial times by Spanish friars for writing the Yucatec Maya language, and revised in modern times. It should be noted that this differs somewhat from the more linguistically-oriented orthography used by many epigraphers, but it conforms to the way place-names and the names of archaeological sites appear on modern maps.

The vowels are generally pronounced as they are in Spanish. However, *u* preceding another vowel is pronounced like English *w*; thus, *ui* sounds like English *we*. Most of the consonants have the same values as in Spanish. An exception is *c*, which is always hard (like English *k*), even before *e* and *i*. As it had in sixteenth-century Spain, *x* has the sound of English *sh*. In addition, the Mayan languages make an important distinction between glottalized and non-glottalized consonants; the former are pronounced *fortis*, with constricted throat. In the orthography followed here, these would be as follows:

Non-glottalized	Glottalized
c	k
ch	ch'
tz	dz
p	p'
t	t'

The glottal stop (') is also a consonant, and is similar to the way a Cockney Englishman might pronounce the *tt* in *little*.

Stress in Mayan words is almost always on the final syllable.

Prologue

It was 12 cycles, 18 katuns, 16 tuns, 0 uinals, and 16 kins since the beginning of the Great Cycle. The day was 12 Cib 14 Uo, and was ruled by the seventh Lord of the Night. The moon was nine days old. Precisely 5,101 of our years and 235 days had passed since the creation of this universe, and only 23 years and 22 days yet remained until the final cataclysm that would destroy it. So the ancient Maya scribes and astronomers would have calculated, for the day was 14 May 1989, and we were in Leningrad.

"Gostini Dvor!" As the disembodied voice announced the Metro station, the car doors opened, and my wife and I were swept along with thousands of morning passengers up the escalator, and into the bright sunshine of Nevsky Prospekt, the great avenue and artery of Tsarist St. Petersburg and post-Revolutionary Leningrad. Crossing the bridges over the Griboyedov and Moika Canals – Peter the Great had built his capital along the lines of his beloved Amsterdam – we turned right through the huge structure of the General Staff building and emerged onto Palace Square. Beyond the granite column commemorating Alexander I's victory over Napoleon lay the immense, green-and-white, baroque façade of the Winter Palace, the whole vast space conjuring up the terrific events which led to the 1917 revolution and the overthrow of the tsars. To the left, gleaming gold in the morning light, rose the needle-like spire of the Admiralty, celebrated in Pushkin's poetry.

Passing between the Winter Palace and the neoclassical splendor of the Admiralty, we stood on the embankment, as the main branch of the Neva with its tumbling waters flowed southwest towards the Baltic. Leningrad/St. Petersburg is one of the very few great European cities that has maintained a low skyline, not disfigured by the hideous skyscrapers and glass boxes that have destroyed the beauty of such capitals as London and Paris, and wherever we looked stood buildings that Pushkin himself would have recognized. Directly opposite us was Vasilievski Island, with the old (capitalist!) Stock Exchange at its point and the brick-red Rostral Column. It was on the Neva embankment of the island that Peter built his great university: this was where Russian science had flourished in all its glory.

Right on the waterfront itself, the great reforming tsar had established his Kunstkammer, at what is now Universitetskaya Naberezhnaya 4, a

9

somewhat silly, blue-green baroque structure with white trim and a bell
tower: an early eighteenth-century fantasy designed by Italian architects
to house his somewhat sinister collection of monsters, oddities, and
other disjuncta from the world of nature. His curiosities are still there on
display, but the principal function of the Kunstkammer today is to
house the Institute of Ethnography of the Academy of Sciences.

This was our destination today, for I was a Visiting Scholar from the
U.S. National Academy of Sciences to the Institute. After a short walk
across the Palace Bridge, dodging the electric trams, we were at the
entrance door. The Kunstkammer has three floors, mostly devoted to
archaic exhibits containing astonishing ethnographic collections from
all over the world, but it was the offices on the first floor that drew us, for
in one of these worked our principal host, Dr. Yuri Valentinovich
Knorosov, the man who, against all odds, has made possible the modern
decipherment of Maya hieroglyphic writing.

Our friend Yuri Valentinovich, along with four other colleagues, is
affiliated with the American (New World) branch of the Institute, and all
five scholars are housed in an astonishingly cramped room near the end
of the first-floor hallway. Inside the room, there is a clutter of desks,
books, papers, along with paraphernalia to concoct the endless teas
which make up a vital part of Russian life and conversation. Privacy, as
elsewhere here, is at a minimum. When we first entered this sanctum, on
a private visit twenty years ago, it was January, and in the dim winter
light, from the two tall windows of the room, could be seen the frozen
Neva, although at that time the ever-active samovar had so steamed up
the glass that very little was visible.

Over the decades that he has occupied this veritable warren of
ethnologists, linguists, and assistants, Knorosov has managed to
establish a very cozy corner, near the window on the far left. Here we
gathered every day, along with his scientific protégées Galina Yershova
("Galya") and Anna Alexandrovna Borodatova, for long, wide-ranging
talks about Maya hieroglyphs and a host of other matters.

Let me now describe Yuri Knorosov, for even among his compatriots
he is considered something of an original. Short and lean, a trim man in
his late sixties, I suppose the most striking thing about him is his
extraordinary eyes: they are a deep sapphire blue, set beneath beetling
eyebrows. If I were a nineteenth-century physiognomist, I would say that
they express a penetrating intelligence. Above his brow his iron-grey hair
is brushed straight back, although when we first met him in 1969, it was
parted in the middle and much darker. In spite of what seems to be an
almost perpetual scowl on his face, Yuri Valentinovich has an ironic,
almost impish sense of humor, and allows fleeting smiles to cross his
face, like proverbial rays of sunshine breaking out from dark clouds.

Like many Russians, Knorosov is a chain smoker, and his fingers are
deeply stained with nicotine; this is a habit which he shares with that
other great Russian (albeit American) pioneer of Maya decipherment,
the late Tatiana Proskouriakoff. Unlike most tobacco addicts in my own
country, he is a very considerate man, and always steps outside the door
to indulge in his favorite weed.

Altogether, Yuri Valentinovich, always conservatively dressed in a
brown double-breasted suit, a white shirt, and dark tie, is a very
impressive figure; even more so to foreigners like ourselves, with his war
medals pinned to his jacket (he leaves one of them at home, since it bears
the likeness of Stalin, not exactly a popular subject in today's Russia).
What is not apparent to those who know him only through his writings
is that Knorosov has an encyclopedic knowledge of a host of subjects,
above all of the history and architecture of St. Petersburg. According to
our friend, just about everything that goes on today in the city, for better
or worse, can be ascribed to Peter I and his corrupt henchman
Menshikov, whose splendid palace still rises above the embankment
further downstream. One day, while we were as usual drinking tea and
eating biscuits from one of the innumerable caches which he keeps in his
nook, the subject was brought up of Captain Bligh and his amazing open-
boat journey after the famous mutiny. Knorosov turned out to be an
expert on the subject! But, with his innate sense of what is right, he wears
his learning lightly, in both speech and writing.

What is truly astonishing is that until the recent Gorbachev
revolution this man never once saw a Maya ruin, or stood in the plazas
and courts of Copán, Tikal, Palenque, or Chichén Itzá; or even touched a
real Maya inscription. Only once had he ever been outside the borders
of his own country, and that was briefly in the summer of 1956, when he
was permitted to attend the Congress of Americanists in Copenhagen. In
the history of decipherment, Knorosov ranks with the great Jean-
François Champollion, the French genius who "cracked" the Egyptian
script in the early nineteenth century. The conditions under which Yuri
Valentinovich and his colleagues work have to be seen to be appreciated,
and those of us who enjoy such benefits as free access to any part of the
world, to foreign meetings and institutes, and even to personal
computers and copy machines (modern glyphic research is almost
inconceivable without xerographic copiers, which are practically
nonexistent in Russia) should count our blessings.

This man, Yuri Valentinovich Knorosov, clearly has a mind inured to
adversity: a veteran of the terrible battles of the World War II, his first
pioneering article on the decipherment appeared the year before Stalin
died, and much of his subsequent research was carried out during the
grim, Cold War period under Leonid Ilyich Brezhnev – the "years of

stagnation," to use current. terminology. To me it represents the triumph of the human spirit that one determined, dedicated scholar was able through sheer brain power to penetrate the mental world of an alien people who had lived over one millennium before, in the tropical forests of a distant land.

To those far-off Maya, writing was of divine origin: it was the gift of Itzamná, the great creator divinity whom the people of Yucatán on the eve of the Conquest considered to be the first priest. Each year in the month Uo – the same month in which we found ourselves on the Neva embankment – the priests invoked him by bringing out their precious books and spreading them out on fresh boughs in the house of the local lord. Sacred *pom* incense was burned to the god, and the wooden boards which formed the covers of the books were anointed with "Maya blue" pigment and virgin water. Let us now take leave of the Neva and Peter's city, and of the man who helped disclose the secret of those books and Itzamná's gift. It is time, before the Maya Great Cycle runs its inexorable course, to see how these ancient writings have finally been read by modern mortals.

1 The Word Made Visible

Writing is speech put in visible form, in such a way that any reader instructed in its conventions can reconstruct the vocal message. All linguists are agreed on this, and have been for a long time, but it hasn't always been this way. In the Early Renaissance, when scholars began to take an interest in these matters, very different ideas were proposed, most of them erroneous and some of them based on quite fantastic reasoning, however ingenious. It has taken a very long time in the history of decipherment to clear away some of these notions: ingrained preconceptions can be as ferociously guarded by scholars and scientists as a very old bone by a dog.

Writing as "visible speech" was first invented about five thousand years ago, by the Sumerians in lower Mesopotamia, and almost simultaneously by the ancient Egyptians. Being totally dependent upon writing ourselves, we would say that this was one of the greatest human discoveries of all time; Sir Edward Tylor, who virtually invented modern anthropology in the mid-Victorian age, claimed that the evolution of mankind from "barbarism" to "civilization" was the result of literacy.[1] Yet a few of the thinkers of the Classical world were not so sure that writing was all that great a boon.

Plato, for example, definitely felt the written word was inferior to the spoken. In his *Phaedrus*,[2] he makes Socrates recite an old myth about the Egyptian god Theuth (i.e., Thoth) inventing writing, along with arithmetic, geometry, and astronomy, not to mention "various kinds of draughts and dice." Theuth came with his innovations to the king of the country, one Thamus, claiming that they should be made known to all Egyptians. Thamus examined each in turn. As for writing, Theuth declared, "Here is an accomplishment, my lord the king, which will improve both the wisdom and the memory of the Egyptians. I have discovered a sure receipt for memory and wisdom." Thamus was skeptical: "you, who are the father of writing, have out of fondness for your offspring attributed to it quite the opposite of its real function. Those who acquire it will cease to exercise their memory and become

13

forgetful; they will rely on writing to bring things to their remembrance by external signs instead of on their own internal resources. What you have discovered is a receipt for recollection, not for memory." People will receive a quantity of information from script, but without proper instruction: they will look knowledgeable, when in fact they will be ignorant.

Socrates makes the point in Plato's dialogue that writing will not help in the search for truth. He compares writing to painting – paintings *look* like living beings, but if you ask them a question, they are mute. If you ask written words a question, you get the same answer over and over. Writing cannot distinguish between suitable and unsuitable readers: it can be ill-treated or unfairly abused, but it cannot defend itself. In contrast, truths found in the art of dialectic *can* defend themselves. Thus, the spoken is superior to the written word!

Socrates was undoubtedly right – nonliterate peoples are capable of astonishing feats of memory, as ethnologists can testify. Immense tribal histories have been committed to memory by bards and other specialists; one has only to think of the *Iliad* and the *Odyssey*, which were recited with line-for-line accuracy by Greek bards in that Dark Age when Mycenaean (Linear B) script had been forgotten, and before the alphabet had appeared. I myself can bear witness to such feats of memory. Late one chilly afternoon during the great Shalako ritual of Zuñi pueblo, in New Mexico, my friend Vincent Scully and I were in the Council House of the Gods; seated around the walls were the impassive priests, chanting the immensely long Zuñi Creation Myth, hour upon hour of deep, unison droning, in which not one word or syllable could be gotten wrong. And all that without benefit of written text. One mistake in recitation would have meant disaster for the tribe.

And my wife reminds me that by the time our own children (all five of them) had reached First Grade and knew how to read and write, they had lost the incredible capacity for remembering things that they had when younger. So William Blake's optimistic lines in *Jerusalem*,

> ... God ... in mysterious Sinai's awful cave
> To Man the wond'rous art of writing gave ...

may not be entirely justified.

After Plato and the Classical Age, the first to think seriously about writing systems were the humanists of the Renaissance. Unfortunately, it is on them that the blame must fall for perpetuating misconceptions that have dogged the subject ever since those glorious days.

Visitors to the historic center of Rome may have run across a very curious yet charming monument in the Piazza della Minerva, standing before the ancient church of Santa Maria. This monument, designed by the great Bernini himself, consists of an inscribed Egyptian obelisk, sustained by the back of a somewhat baroque little elephant with a twisted trunk. On the pedestal supporting this strange combination is a Latin inscription, which says in translation:

> The learning of Egypt
> carved in figures on this obelisk
> and carried by an elephant
> the mightiest of beasts
> may afford to those who look on it
> an example
> of how strength of mind
> should support weight of wisdom.[3]

Now in the mid-seventeenth century, when the pope Alexander VII ordered this odd amalgam of ancient Egyptian and Italian Baroque (the obelisk is actually a sixth-century BC monument of the pharaoh Psammetichus) to be placed in the square, there was not one person in the world who could actually read the strange signs carved on the four facets of the obelisk. Then how did the composer of the inscription know that the obelisk dealt with "wisdom"?

For the answer to this, we must go back to Classical antiquity, the memory of which was being actively revived among European humanists. Thanks to the work of the decipherers of the early nineteenth century, in particular Champollion, the Egyptian script can now be read pretty much in its totality. The principles on which it operates are a complex combination of phonetic and semantic ("meaning") signs – as in all ancient writing systems, as we shall see. Due to the Macedonian and Roman conquests of Egypt, and eventual Christianization, after having flourished for over three millennia, Egyptian civilization gradually died out, as did knowledge of its marvelous writing system (the last inscription in the system dates to shortly before AD 400).

The Greeks, with their insatiable curiosity, were fascinated by the civilization of the Nile. In the fifth century BC, Herodotus, father of anthropology as well as history, visited Egypt and questioned its priests about many things; he flatly – and rightly – stated that the script was mainly used for the writing of historical records, especially royal achievements, and was written from right to left. As Egyptian culture dwindled under the onslaught of the Classical world, information transmitted by the Greeks about Egyptian writing made less and less sense. Perhaps they were deliberately misled by the native priesthood. Consider the influential Diodorus Siculus, who wrote in the first century BC that "their script does not work by putting syllables together to render an underlying sense, but by drawing objects whose metaphorical meaning is impressed on the memory." For example, a picture of a falcon stood for "anything that happens suddenly," a crocodile meant "evil," and an eye symbolized both "body's watchman" and "guardian of justice."[4] We are a long way from Herodotus.

It was Horapollon (Horus Apollus or Horapollo), in the fourth century AD, who gave us the word *hieroglyphic* for Egyptian writing; in fact, he penned two books on the subject, claiming that the symbols carved on the walls, obelisks, and other monuments of the Nile were "sacred carvings," which is what "hieroglyph" means in Greek. If it were not that Horapollon's nonsensical explanations were to be echoed among twentieth-century Maya epigraphers, they would be laughable. Two examples will suffice. According to him, the hieroglyph *baboon* can indicate the moon, the inhabited world, writing, a priest, anger, and swimming. "To indicate a man who has never traveled they paint a man with a donkey's head. For he never knows or listens to accounts of what happens abroad."[5]

Horapollon's *Hieroglyphics* was published in two editions in sixteenth-century Italy, and was enthusiastically read by humanists such as Athanasius Kircher. Even more influential on Renaissance thinking was the Egyptian-born religious philosopher Plotinus, the inventor of Neoplatonism in the third century AD. Plotinus greatly admired the Egyptians, because they could express thoughts directly in their script, without the intervention of "letters, words, and sentences." "Each separate sign is in itself a piece of knowledge, a piece of wisdom, a piece of reality, immediately present."[6] Published in Florence in the year that Columbus discovered the New World, such notions were to give rise to the Renaissance view of Egypt as the spring of wisdom: here was a people who could express their thoughts to others in visual form, without the intervention of language. Here was truly ideographic writing.

Now Athanasius Kircher (1602–80) must make a proper entrance onstage, proclaiming his doctrine of hieroglyphic wisdom.[7] Today, this German Jesuit priest hardly rates a paragraph in any encyclopedia, but he was the most extraordinary polymath of his age, revered by princes and popes alike. There was hardly a subject on which he did not write, hardly a science in which he had not experimented. Among his various inventions was the magic lantern, precursor of the cinema, and if one needed a fountain that played music, Kircher was your man. Rome, where he taught mathematics and Hebrew, was his home for much of his life. The seventeenth-century Eternal City under popes like Sixtus V had obelisk fever: as part of a massive reordering of the capital, obelisks were strategically placed at the nodal points of a new network of avenues, as well as in the center of Bernini's great arcade at St. Peter's. All of these obelisks had been removed by the ancient Romans from Egypt, and most, like the Minervan Obelisk, were covered with Horapollon's supposed "hieroglyphs."

Kircher claimed to be able to read them, and he devoted an enormous effort to their study and publication. He had read the Greek sources with great care: obviously, these hieroglyphic signs transmitted thought directly. He completely accepted the Neoplatonic nonsense of Plotinus. Here is his "reading" of a royal cartouche on the Minervan Obelisk, now known to contain the name and titles of Psamtjik (Psammetichus), a Saite pharaoh of the Twenty-Sixth Dynasty:

The protection of Osiris against the violence of Typho must be elicited according to the proper rites and ceremonies by sacrifices and by appeal to the tutelary Genii of the triple world in order to ensure the enjoyment of the prosperity customarily given by the Nile against the violence of the enemy Typho.[8]

Kircher's fantasies of decipherment were to go down in history as a *reductio ad absurdum* of scholasticism, the equal in futility to Archbishop Ussher's calculations of the date of Creation. As the Egyptologist Sir Alan Gardiner once put it, they "exceed all bounds in their imaginative folly."[9]

Yet the notion that non-alphabetic writing systems mainly consisted of *ideographs* – signs conveying metaphysical ideas but not their sounds in a particular language – was to have a long life, in the New World as well as the Old.

We are told that even a stopped clock is right every twelve hours, and not all of our polymath's endeavors were wasted. Kircher was also a polyglot, and fascinated by languages. One of these was Coptic, an Egyptian tongue, as "dead" as Latin, but which remained in use for the liturgy of the Christian Coptic Church in Egypt. It had been the language of the peoples of the Nile before Greek began to replace it, and before the Arab invasion of the seventh century AD. Kircher was one of the first serious students of Coptic, and one of the first to insist that it was descended from the ancient language of the pharaohs. Thus, while on the one hand he paved the way for the decipherment that was made much later by Champollion, on the other, by his stubbornly mentalist attitude towards the hieroglyphs, he impeded their decipherment for almost two centuries.

It would be a mistake to condemn Kircher for his irrationalities: he was a man of his time. Other Jesuits were returning from China, and they described a kind of writing which contained tens of thousands of different "characters" directly expressing ideas (in hindsight we now know this to be wildly off target). This merely confirmed what intelligent scholars *knew* to be true. So did the sketchy accounts of "Mexican" hieroglyphic writings which were being brought to Europe by missionaries such as the Jesuit Joseph de Acosta.

Is it at all possible, as Kircher believed, to construct a writing system out of symbols that have no necessary connection with language, or with any particular language? and that express thoughts directly? The British linguist Geoffrey Sampson evidently thinks so: in his book *Writing Systems*,[10] he divides all possible scripts into *semasiographic* ones, in which symbols are unrelated to utterances, and *glottographic* ones, in which writing reflects a particular language, such as English or Chinese. He is just about alone among members of his profession in making such claims for semasiographic "writing" as a complete system, since he can only propose it as a theoretical possibility, without being able to point to an actual example of such a script.

Yet, admittedly, some degree of semasiography plays a part in all known writing, even in alphabetic ones. Consider written English, and the electronic typewriter on which I am composing this book. The Arabic numerals 1, 2, 3, and so forth are mathematical constructs which are read "one, two, three" in English, but "uno, due, tre" in Italian, and "ce, ome, yei" in Nahuatl (Aztec). The bar-and-dot numbers that were in use among the ancient Maya, Zapotec, and other peoples of Mexico and Central America before the Spaniards are likewise semasiographic (or ideographic, to use the old, confusing terminology). But how divorced are they in reality from spoken language? I challenge any native English speaker to avoid thinking of the word "twelve" when looking at "12," or an Italian to avoid the utterance "dodici" when going through the same performance.

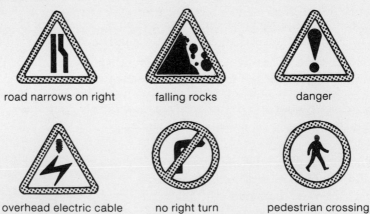

road narrows on right   falling rocks   danger

overhead electric cable   no right turn   pedestrian crossing

1 *The international road sign system.*

A linguist, Archibald Hill, tells us that "all writing represents speech, either audible or silent, and can never represent ideas which have not yet been embodied in speech."[11] In books on writing, the international road-sign conventions are often pointed to as a "languageless" system that communicates with drivers no matter what their native tongue, but the driver still "says" something mentally, such as "No!" when confronted by a red circle with a diagonal slash by the side of the road. On my typewriter, the symbols $ and £ are just as related to language as the letter sequences "dollars" and "pounds." In every culture in which such purportedly "languageless" symbols or even pictures have been used for communication, their meaning still has to be learned through the medium of spoken or written language. Thus, semasiography, "writing" by such signs, has little or nothing to do with the origin of writing, or even its evolution. That major step in the development of human culture has to do with the representation of the actual sounds of a particular language.

Nevertheless, some very curious and interesting semasiographic systems have existed in history, apart from the above-mentioned road signs. All of them are codes, dependent upon a specific set of visual marks which have previously been agreed upon by encoder and decoder. Paul Revere's semimythical "one if by land, two if by sea" lantern signal to warn of the coming of the Redcoats is a very simplified example of this sort of arrangement. Some systems have been very complex, imparting across space and time a great deal of information; the trouble is that without a key to the code it is impossible for us to decipher such a system. Even the best cryptographer could not do it.

Consider the famous *quipu* of Inca Peru (fig. 2), on which the administration of the Inca Empire depended.[12] This kind of knot record was crucial to the Inca bureaucracy, for the mighty Inca state was almost unique in the history of the world in having no true writing. Each *quipu* is made up of a number of connected, color-coded cords on which various kinds of knots are tied at intervals. Internal, structural evidence led twentieth-century scholars to conclude that the knots and cords were in a decimal system of counting. Frustratingly, nothing further has been discovered about them, in spite of the statements by early Spanish and native sources that they recorded not only census and economic data, but also history, mythology, astronomy, and the like. Quite probably, like Plato's Egyptians before writing was invented, the memories of specialists trained to remember everything of importance were called into play at crucial moments. In other words, as in other semasiographic systems that we know about, the visual signs were mnemonic records – *aides-mémoires* to jog the recollections of the *quipu*-keepers.

Even more complexity can be found in a remarkable script invented in

2 *An Inca accountant with* quipu, *from a drawing by Guaman Pomo de Ayala.*

the early part of this century by an Apache shaman in Arizona named Silas John.[13] To transmit prayers received by him in a dream, he devised a series of signs which were painted on buckskins and "read" by his followers; needless to say, they were "read" in Apache, but they transmit no phonetic data. However, encoded into the system are detailed instructions for ritual behavior during the performances, suggesting that other semasiographic systems which are known to archaeologists and ethnologists may not be as primitive as some have made out.

Now, what about "picture writing"? Don't pictures speak to us "directly"? Doesn't the old saw say, "one picture is worth a thousand words"? Kircher, his fellow Jesuits, and the whole intellectual world of Rome in the sixteenth and seventeenth centuries were enormously impressed by the pictorial symbols on those wise obelisks, and even by the animals, plants, and other objects which they saw delineated in the exotic screenfold books from Mexico which had been deposited in the Vatican Library. This was the world of the Counter-Reformation, reeling from the attacks being made by Protestant theologians on religious iconography, and anxious to fight back. "Picture writing," or "pictography," took on a life of its own, not to die out even in our own day. To these Jesuit thinkers, pictures were a great and good thing.

It is true that representations of objects in the natural world *do* enter into some writing systems: even our own alphabet, derived from the Phoenicians, is based on pictures, for example the letter A began as an ox head, and N as a snake. And a very small percentage of Chinese characters are derived from the "real" world, such as the character *shan*, "mountain," which began as a representation of a three-peaked mountain. Pictures have been used by scribes in many ways to form scripts, but there is not now, nor has there ever been, a real pictographic writing system. Why not? Because as the linguist George Trager has put it,[14] pictures alone cannot pass the test of being able to depict all possible utterances of a language (try to write in pictures an English sentence like "I find metaphysics impossibly dull"); and there is no way to be sure a picture will be interpreted in the same way (in the same words) by two successive observers.

We cannot really talk about writing until we talk about spoken language. To understand how a writing system can be put together so as to make possible the writing of any utterance of the language, and the reading of it without too much ambiguity, we must see how spoken languages work.

One of the very few honors that has ever come my way was when I was a student in a church school, and actually won a prize for Sacred Studies. It was a book which I still treasure to this day, called *The Book of a Thousand Tongues*, put out by the American Bible Society.[15] It not only named and described all the spoken languages into which the King James Bible has been translated, but gave facsimile examples of the first verses of the Gospel According to St. Mark, in the appropriate printed orthography. It was probably my first approach to anything resembling a subject of anthropological interest, and it kindled in me a lifelong interest in foreign languages and scripts.

There are many more than a thousand languages in the world: not counting dialects, the usual estimate is between 2,500 and 4,000. The Tower of Babel was a very large place! To a linguist, languages are mutually unintelligible communication systems. Each language is made up of dialects which *are* mutually intelligible, although sometimes with difficulty. Now, this word "dialect" has been badly manhandled in the public press and in popular usage. The worst example of this relates to the various tongues spoken in China, such as Mandarin, Shanghai, and Cantonese: these are quite mistakenly called "dialects." Although closely related tongues, spoken Mandarin is quite as incomprehensible to a Cantonese-speaking taxi driver in Hong Kong as Dutch would be to his counterpart in New York. One more example: for years, the *New York Times* insisted that the native peoples of the New World, whether Hopi, Aztec, or Inca, spoke only "dialects." Presumably, the editors felt that American Indians were incapable of communicating in languages as mature as those of Europe.

Some sort of order was imposed on the Tower of Babel by eighteenth-
and nineteenth-century scholars when they discovered that certain
groups of languages had descended from a common ancestor. An
example commonly given is the English word *father*. In Greek this is
pater, in Latin *pater*, in French *père*, in German *Vater*, all clearly
"cognates" or related words. We have known from philologists for over
two centuries that most of the languages of Europe go back to a single,
ancestral tongue; other descendants of the same ancient progenitor,
called "Proto-Indo-European," are Sanskrit in India, and Persian. It was
not long before American scholars such as the amazing John Wesley
Powell, one-armed hero of Shiloh and founder of the U.S. Bureau of
American Ethnology, were finding that native American languages could
be similarly combined into families. Aztec or Nahuatl, to give just one
example, was discovered to be part of the widespread Uto-Aztecan
family, spread all the way from Oregon to Panama in pre-contact times.

While the philologists were busy classifying languages into larger
groupings, the linguists were pulling them apart to see how they worked.

On the lowest level of analysis, a language consists of a set of sounds;
the study of these is called "phonetics" or "phonology" – as fans of
Shaw's *Pygmalion* will recall. The *phoneme* is defined as the smallest unit
of distinctive sound in spoken language. To illustrate this, let us take the
hackneyed example of the three English words *pin*, *bin*, and *spin*. The
bilabial stop or consonant at the beginning of *pin* is clearly different from
that of *bin* – one is unvoiced and the other is voiced, and the meaning
changes depending on which is used. Thus *p* and *b* are separate
phonemes. On the other hand, the *p* in *spin* and the *p* in *pin* actually
sound somewhat different to a trained phonetician; but it is clear from
their distribution that they vary according to their environment (that is,
to the neighboring sounds), and are thus members of one and the same
phoneme.

Languages vary widely in the number of phonemes they contain.
Professor DeFrancis tells us that English has about 40, in the middle
range.[16] At the lower end of the range are Hawaiian and Japanese, with 20
each, while at the upper end are some minority languages of Southeast
Asia such as White Meo, with 80 phonemes (57 consonants, 15 vowels,
and 8 tones).

As anyone who has had to learn Latin or French can testify, languages
not only consist of meaningful sound patterns, or pronunciation, they
also have a grammar: the rules by which words and sentences are put
together. *Morphology* deals with the internal structure of words, and
syntax with relations between words in a sentence structure. The smallest
meaningful unit of speech is the *morpheme*, consisting of one or more
phonemes. Consider the English word *incredible*: *in-*, *-cred-*, and *-ible* are

the morphemes of which it is made up. Or the word *trees*, which can be morphologically analyzed into the basic noun *tree* and the plural *-s*.

Back in the days when linguists mistakenly thought that the spoken languages of the world could be arranged in some sort of developmental order, from "primitive" to "civilized," they started to classify them according to their morphology and syntax. Although the idea that languages could be put on an evolutionary scale is tommyrot on a par with the discredited "science" of phrenology, the classification is still useful. Here are the categories, for better or for worse:

Isolating or *analytic* languages are those in which words are morphologically unanalyzable, and in which sentence structure is expressed by word order, word grouping, and use of specific grammatical words or particles. The Chinese languages are isolating, and so is Vietnamese.

Agglutinative languages string together, or agglutinate, successive morphemes, each with a single grammatical function, into the body of single words. Turkish is a fine example of this, with ever more complex words being built up like a train in a railroad yard from a root (the locomotive) followed by a string of suffixes (the carriages). For instance, the word *evlerda*, meaning "to the houses," can be broken down into *ev*, "house"; *-ler*, the plural suffix; and *-da*, the dative suffix. Nahuatl, the lingua franca of the Aztec Empire, is another such: take the word sentence *nimitztlazohtla*, constructed from *ni-*, "I," *mitz*, "you" (object), *tlazohtla*, unpluralized verb root "to love" – "I love you!" Sumerian, for which the earliest writing in the world was devised, was agglutinative.

Inflectional languages change the form of a word to mark all kinds of grammatical distinctions, such as tense, person (singular, plural, and so forth), gender, mood, voice, and case. The Indo-European languages tend to be highly inflectional, as anyone who has studied Latin can testify, with its cases, declensions, and conjugations. Indo-European is unusual among the language families of the world in the prominent place it gives to gender distinctions; languages that insist not only on giving the sex of those referred to in pronouns, but also on jamming all nouns into such unreal categories as masculine, feminine, and even neuter are rare or unheard-of elsewhere. Sexism of this kind is unknown in Aztec and the Mayan languages.

Few languages fit perfectly into any one of these categories. In English, all three are represented. English can be isolating in its use of word order alone to express grammatical differences (for instance, *John loves Mary* vs. *Mary loves John*); it shows agglutination in words like *manliness* (*man*, basic noun, plus *-li-*, adjectival formative, plus *-ness*, abstract noun formative); and it is inflectional (as in forming the plurals *man/men*, *goose/geese*). Although the Mayan languages are predominantly agglutinative, they show a similar potpourri of linguistic types.

Cultures borrow from each other, and so do languages, for a variety of reasons, some of which are compelling in their own right: conquest is the best of all. Who can forget the discussion in Sir Walter Scott's *Ivanhoe* of the influx of French words that were added to Anglo-Saxon after 1066 to form the basic English tongue? Words can be borrowed through emulation as well as outright conquest; a glance at the business, science, and entertainment pages of any Italian newspaper will find a host of words taken lock, stock, and barrel from English, such as *manager*, *personal computer*, *stress*, and *lifestyle*, all absorbed into perfectly good Italian syntactical structures. English itself through the centuries has been remarkably open to this kind of borrowing, even from the "dead" languages of antiquity. Other languages are highly impervious to lexical borrowing, above all Chinese, which prefers to concoct new words from old ones for unfamiliar, introduced items; when the steam railroad appeared in China, it was dubbed *huo-che*, or "fire-cart."

The study of borrowings is a science in its own right, and an extremely interesting one, for it can describe culture contacts which took place in the past, and linguists can even reconstruct something of the cultures and societies that impinged upon each other in remote periods. If the languages have been recorded in visible form, so much the better. But sometimes this produces mysteries as well as solutions – in the oldest script of all, Sumerian writing on clay tablets, the names of their cities (including "Ur of the Chaldees"), and of most of the important professions practiced almost thirty centuries ago in southern Mesopotamia, are not in the Sumerian language or in any of the rival Semitic languages, but in an unknown tongue. This suggests that the Sumerians were not really native to that region, but had moved in and borrowed these words from some shadowy people who had been truly autochthonous to the Land Between the Rivers.[17]

The serious study of writing systems, as opposed, say, to the study of particular kinds of writing or of calligraphy, is relatively recent, a kind of step-child to linguistics. I suppose that this is because in the last century there were just not enough different scripts known, or at least understood, to make sensible comparisons. One would have thought that linguists would have become interested in writing early on, but an entire generation of them, especially in the United States, adopted the view that it was spoken, rather than written, language that was important; scripts were really unworthy of their attention. Perhaps the acknowledged lack of "fit" between modern spoken and written English played a part. Luckily, things have changed.

But there was another roadblock to understanding much about

writing: evolutionism. The Darwinian view of nature which gradually triumphed in Western science following the publication of *The Origin of Species* in 1859 had its repercussions in the nascent field of anthropology, dominated by Sir Edward Tylor and the American lawyer Lewis Henry Morgan, scientific titans of the nineteenth century. Morgan and Tylor thought that all societies and cultures had to pass, like the creatures and plants of the natural world, through a rigidly ordered sequence of stages. These began with "savagery" (read "hunting and gathering"), through "barbarism" (read "agriculture and animal husbandry, with clan organization"), to "civilization" (ourselves, naturally, with state or territorial organization). Some peoples, like the Aborigines of Australia, are still bogged down in "savagery," and others, like the Pueblos of the American Southwest, in "barbarism," but given enough time all will eventually emerge into our enlightened world. What a pleasantly smug, Victorian view!

Unhappily, this hyperevolutionism has fettered with theoretical chains all sorts of scholars who have written about writing, in spite of the fact that linguists themselves long ago discarded the hoary notion of "primitive" versus "civilized" languages. The Mayanist Sylvanus Morley, under Tylorian influence, proposed three evolutionary stages for the supposed development of writing.[18] Stage 1: writing is *pictographic*, the object or idea being given by a drawing, painting, or some such; nothing is meant by the picture itself except what is depicted. Stage 2: *ideographic* writing appears, in which the idea or object is given by a sign having no resemblance or only a distant similarity to it; Chinese script is the example given by Morley – the worst possible one that he could have picked. Stage 3: *phonetic* writing appears, in which signs lose all resemblance to the original images of objects and denote only sounds; syllabic signs appear first (Morley invoked another wrong example, Egyptian), with alphabetic ones appearing later (Phoenician, Greek). So said Morley.

Onward and upward! Long live progress! *We* have phonetic writing and the alphabet and *they* (all those savages, barbarians, and Chinese) don't. A comforting idea, and one that continues to grip the twentieth-century mind. Now, there are so many things wrong with this scheme, it is hard to know where to begin. In the first place, we have already seen that there is no such thing as a purely pictographic writing system, nor has there ever been, even though pictures of real objects, and parts of them, are used in some scripts. Point two, there is no such thing as an ideographic script, either. And finally, *all known writing systems are partly or wholly phonetic, and express the sounds of a particular language.*

A far more sophisticated and linguistically informed scheme has come from the pen of Ignace Gelb, whose book *A Study of Writing*[19] was for long the only detailed work on the subject. Gelb, a specialist in the languages and scripts of the Near East at the University of Chicago's Oriental Institute, was one of the decipherers of Anatolian ("Hittite") Hieroglyphic, which would entitle him to a place in any Epigraphic Hall of Fame. But he had his intellectual blind side, too. Just as hyper-evolutionist as many others, Gelb's scheme, like Morley's, begins with that will-o'-the-wisp "picture writing," and proceeds from that through systems like Sumerian and Chinese (more about these later), to syllabic writing, to the alphabet. "The alphabet's conquest of the world" is how Gelb introduces this subject – even the Chinese, with their old-fashioned and clumsy script, are going to have to bow to the inevitable some day and write alphabetically.

Having met Gelb but once, many years ago in the halls of the Oriental Institute, I cannot really call him a racist. His book, however, is very definitely infected with that sinister virus of our century. It appears to have been inconceivable to him that a non-White people could ever have invented on their own any kind of script with phonetic content. On one side, he refuses to allow the Chinese the invention of their own writing, claiming on totally non-existent grounds that it was derived from his beloved Near East (i.e., from the Sumerians); and on the other, he insists that no New World peoples, including the Maya, had the intellectual capacity for writing phonetically, except on rare occasions to express names (like the place-names of the Aztec manuscripts). The Maya are, in effect, suspended from the lowest branches of the evolutionary tree. Such attitudes held up the decipherment of Maya script for almost a century.

What kinds of writing systems have been devised, and how do they work? Setting aside semasiography, which we have seen cannot by itself constitute a workable script, we are left with systems which really do express the utterances of a spoken language, be it Chinese or Greek. These writing systems may be categorized as logographic, syllabic, and alphabetic, as we shall shortly see.

Jane Austen once wrote a book called *Sense and Sensibility*; a book on the true scripts of the world might be called *Sense and Sound*. For purposes of analysis, every speech-dependent, visual system of communication has two dimensions: the *semantic*, the dimension of "sense" or meaning, and the *phonetic*, the dimension of sound. Scripts vary in the amount of emphasis which they give to one or the other of these dimensions. Modern alphabetic scripts, for instance, lean heavily towards the phonetic, but the earliest form of the most ancient script in the world, the Sumerian of southern Iraq, is strongly semantic.

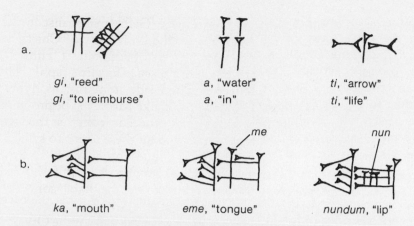

a.

gi, "reed"   a, "water"   ti, "arrow"
gi, "to reimburse" a, "in"   ti, "life"

b.

ka, "mouth"   eme, "tongue"   nundum, "lip"

3 Some principles of Sumerian cuneiform writing: a. Use of the rebus principle to express abstract concepts; these signs were originally pictographic. b. Use of phonetic complements to express Sumerian words conceptually related to the logogram ka, "mouth."

Sumerian, which was written on clay tablets, is *logographic*, as are Chinese and Egyptian. This term indicates that its semantic element is expressed by *logograms*, a word derived from the Greek *logos*, "word," and *gramma*, "something written"; a *logogram* is a written sign which stands for a single morpheme, or (rarely) a complete word. If written sentences consisted only of logograms, which they never do, this would be pure semasiography, but the would-be reader would never get the message right. Accordingly, some five thousand years ago a Sumerian scribe hit upon a way to take out the ambiguity inherent in semasiography: he decided to supplement, or help out, the logograms by means of signs of a purely phonetic nature.

Now, Sumerian was a strongly monosyllabic language, and thus was filled with *homonyms* – words of different meaning but with the same pronunciation. Once the scribe began to use phonetic signs to write words, the possibility of misunderstandings lay there, too. To solve this dilemma, he supplemented such signs with logograms called *determinatives*, which are silent characters indicating or *determining* the general class of phenomena to which the thing named belongs; this is tantamount to saying that out of all the things that have the sound *x*, this is the specific one in the meaning-class *y*. As an example, the names of all Sumerian deities on the tablets are accompanied by an asterisk or star sign, telling the reader that such a name is indeed that of a supernatural.

An examination of Sumerian writing shows that logographic systems are a complex mixture of logograms and phonetic signs. Where did the scribes get the latter? They did this by discovering the *rebus* principle.

What is a rebus? I have discovered in the Oxford English Dictionary that the word comes to us from France, and that originally it was Latin for "concerning things." Once upon a time lawyers' clerks in French Picardy gave satirical performances called *de rebus quae geruntur*, "concerning things that are taking place," which contained riddles in picture form. For the last two centuries it has been used in English and American children's books as a test of wits. Rebus or puzzle-writing can be seen in such lines as "I saw Aunt Rose" expressed by pictures of an eye, a saw, an ant, and a rose-flower. What has happened is that for something that is hard to picture, such as the female sibling of one's parent, a homonymous but easily pictured word from the "real" world has been expressed visually, in this case, an ant. This is what the early Sumerian scribes did, and this is what all ancient scribes everywhere have done.

The second major type of writing system is *syllabic*. As some of us may remember when we were asked to "spell our name in syllables" in grade school, all languages have a syllabic structure. Most common are consonants followed by vowels (CV, in linguistic shorthand) and consonant-vowel-consonant (CVC) combinations. Consider the English word *syllabary*; this may be analyzed into a string of CV syllables, as *sy-lla-ba-ry*. The English word *pin* is an example of a single CVC syllable. In many parts of the world and in various time-periods, purely syllabic scripts have been devised, each sign of which stands for a particular syllable (often for a CV syllable). Until the decipherment of Mycenaean Linear B, the earliest Greek writing, the best-known example of a complete syllabary was put together by the Cherokee Indian leader Sequoyah, in part inspired by the alphabetic literacy of his White American neighbors. Sequoyah's system has eighty-five signs, and is highly praised by linguists for its accurate representation of Cherokee phonology; it is still in use among the Cherokee for newspapers and religious texts.

CV-type syllabaries have been invented many times, most recently by missionaries to write the native tongues of northern North America, such as Inuit (Eskimo).[20] Some languages are amenable to such visual treatment, some less so, and some not at all. At the upper end of the amenability scale is Japanese, with its predominantly CV syllabic structure (*sa-shi-mi, Yo-ko-ha-ma*, etc.), and such a script was devised by the Japanese back in our Dark Ages. At the other end are languages like our own, with dense consonant clusters. For instance, the city of Scranton in Pennsylvania might have to be written syllabically as *Su-cu-ra-na-to-n(o)*, with the final o suppressed in speaking.

Let us turn now to the third system of writing, the *alphabet*. Theoretically, or ideally, in alphabetic scripts the utterances of the

a	e	i	o	u	A
ga	ge	gi	go	gu	gA
ha	he	hi	ho	hu	hA
la	le	li	lo	lu	lA
ma	me	mi	mo	mu	
na	ne	ni	no	nu	nA
gwa	gwe	gwi	gwo	gwu	gwA
sa	se	si	so	su	sA
da	de	di	do	du	dA
dla	dle	dli	dlo	dlu	dlA
dza	dze	dzi	dzo	dzu	dzA
wa	we	wi	wo	wu	wA
ya	ye	yi	yo	yu	yA

	ka
	hna
	nah
	s
	ta
	ti
	tla

4 *Sequoyah's Cherokee syllabary.*

language are broken down into phonemes, the individual consonants and vowels that make up the sounds of the language. Like many other things important in our civilization, this system was invented by the Greeks: in the ninth century BC, they took over a Phoenician system which had been used by those seafaring merchants for representing the consonants. Being Semites, the Phoenicians had ignored the vowels, since in Semitic tongues (including Arabic and Hebrew), the consonants are more important than the vowels in forming words. For the Greeks, this was not enough – they *had* to have vowels to make their writing understandable to the reader as well as to the writer, so they appropriated some Phoenician letters standing for consonantal sounds absent in Greek, and had them stand for vowels.[21]

Thus, the alphabet was born. From the Greeks, alphabetic writing spread to the Etruscans and Romans of Italy, and then to the rest of Europe and the Mediterranean. With the rise of European colonialism in the modern age, it was destined to extend around the globe. But this was hardly the "conquest" that some scholars have claimed: logographic writing continues in vigorous use among the Chinese and Japanese, who represent a major segment of humanity.

A hyperevolutionist like Ignace Gelb saw the alphabet as the acme of scripts, and could not understand why the Chinese have clung to their supposedly cumbersome and outmoded mode of writing. Yet, no script other than highly technical ones invented by modern professional linguists is perfect, in the sense that it represents everything important in the language. What is omitted in a script can often be "filled in" by the reader from the context. Take written English for example; this generally ignores stress and intonation, even though they are highly significant in English speech. Compare "I love you" with "I love *you*" (and not somebody else), or with "*I* love you" (I'm the one who loves you).

Another feature of English alphabetic writing which some critics and would-be reformers like George Bernard Shaw have seen as a deficiency is that one and the same sound is often represented by more than one letter or letter group. Consider a contrasted group of words with identical pronunciation, such as *wright:write:right:rite*. When this kind of thing occurs in a script, linguists call it *polyvalence*, "many values"; it is, in fact, remarkably common in writing systems around the world, in logographic, syllabic, and even alphabetic ones like ours.

Logographic, syllabic, alphabetic: these are the three great classes of writing systems. It is important to keep this typology in mind, because it was grasped badly or not at all by most of the early scholars who tried to explain or decipher ancient scripts. By claiming that Egyptian hieroglyphs were "ideographs," Kircher and his contemporaries confused logographic writing with semasiography; while a century earlier, Fray Diego de Landa, Bishop of Yucatán, was misled into thinking that Maya writing was alphabetic rather than logographic. Real decipherment of these logographic systems came only when the complex intertwining of the semantic and phonetic elements inherent to them became fully understood.

If only Athanasius Kircher had received some inkling of the true nature of the Chinese script from his fellow Jesuits who had been missionaries in the Celestial Kingdom, he might have avoided the "myth of the ideograph" that so fettered his inquiring mind. Like the Egyptian hieroglyphs on which his posthumous reputation has foundered, written Chinese is logographic, and not "ideographic" or alphabetic. But Europeans of the Renaissance and Enlightenment persisted in viewing written Chinese as another marvelous, ideographic system, full of ancient wisdom, which communicated ideas directly without the intervention of language.

Because the Chinese script,[22] and its Japanese derivative, are living writing systems, in daily use among hundreds of millions of people, they provide excellent examples of how the principles of logographic writing work in actuality. Spoken Chinese is in fact a collection of closely related

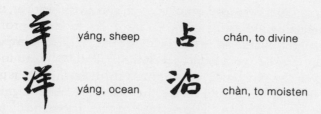

5 The formation of Chinese compound characters. The "water"
determinative has been added to a phonetic.

languages, mistakenly called "dialects." These languages are isolating,
with a minimum of grammar, and words always consist of one, or at the
most two, single-syllable morphemes, plus morphemic particles which
are sometimes used as suffixes. Matching every individual morpheme in
spoken Chinese is a written sign or "character," of which there are a
large number. Since tones are phonemic in China – there are four in
Mandarin, the language of three-quarters of the population, and as many
as nine in Cantonese – there are a great many morphemes to be matched.

How many signs are there? The great Kang Hsi dictionary, finished in
AD 1717, has no fewer than forty thousand characters, but thirty-four
thousand of these are "monstrosities and useless doubles, generated by
ingenious scholars." While larger Chinese dictionaries still have about
fourteen thousand such signs, it is generally agreed that only about four
thousand are in widespread use.

Now, how do millions of Chinese children manage to file away in their
brains so many different signs? After all, alphabet-using English speakers
have only to learn 26 letters. The answer lies in the fact that Chinese, like
all other logographic scripts known to scholarship, is actually highly
phonetic; at the same time, it has a strongly semantic component.

The vast majority of characters are formed by combining a semantic
with a phonetic element. Sinologist John DeFrancis calculates that, by
the eighteenth century, some ninety-seven percent were of this type.[23]
Let's take the phonetic element first. These make up a large and
occasionally inconsistent syllabary, each syllabic sign corresponding to a
morpheme. In one modern Chinese–English dictionary, there are 895 of
these elements, usually occupying the right-hand or the bottom two-
thirds of the character. To the left or the top is a silent, semantic
determinative (called "radical" by Sinologists). Whereas the phonetic
gives the general sound of the syllable in spoken Chinese, the
determinative (as in Sumerian and Egyptian) tells one the general class of
phenomena to which the thing named belongs. There is a determinative
which applies to plants in general, one for things connected with water,

another dealing with things made of wood, and so on. Altogether, there are 214 determinatives.

The remaining characters are pure logograms, and include those signs – originally pictorial, if one goes back to the beginning of Chinese history – from which the phonetics were derived through the rebus principle. Many such signs are scratched on the "oracle bones" of the Shang Dynasty, at the dawn of Chinese civilization, and because they depict things in the real world (the sign for "horse" looks like a horse, the sign for "moon" or "month" like a crescent moon, and so forth), it has been assumed that the script originated as picture-writing or pictographs. Quite the contrary: right from the beginning, Chinese scribes were exploiting these pictorial signs for their sound value.

The system is thus far simpler, and far easier to learn, than it looks at first glance. Of course, the Chinese languages have changed considerably over the many centuries that have elapsed since the script was devised and elaborated, and the phoneticism sometimes presents problems for the modern reader; but DeFrancis still estimates that if one memorized the pronunciation of those 895 elements, it is possble in sixty-six percent of the cases to guess the sound of a given character one is likely to encounter in reading a modern text.[24]

For a student of Maya civilization, a study of the logographic Japanese script[25] is even more instructive; I will anticipate by revealing here that while there is no possible connection between Japanese and Maya writing, they are remarkably similar in structure.

Chinese influence in Japan began in the fifth century AD, when China was an empire and Japan a land of tribes and small chiefdoms. The previously illiterate Japanese began to write all their political and religious documents in Chinese, using Chinese characters. Since spoken Japanese is totally unrelated to Chinese – it is a highly polysyllabic, inflected tongue – the scribes of Japan were faced with a huge problem in adapting the foreign script to their language.

Their solution was reached about one thousand years ago, when they selected a few dozen Chinese logograms or characters on the basis of their sounds, and, in linguist William S.-Y. Wang's vivid phrase, "stripped them down graphically."[26] These 46 signs stand for 41 CV syllables and the five vowels, and so make up a complete syllabary.

Logically, one would have thought that the Japanese would have abandoned Chinese characters completely, and written everything with their new syllabary (called *kana*), but cultural conservatism and the enormous prestige of Chinese culture overruled this impulse. Chinese characters which had been used to write Chinese morphemes, some of

Initials / Finals	—	k	s	t	n	h	m	y	r	w		g	z	d	b	p
a	あ	か	さ	た	な	は	ま	や	ら	わ	ん n	が	ざ	だ	ば	ぱ
i	い	き	し shi	ち chi	に	ひ	み		り	ゐ i		ぎ	じ ji	ぢ ji	び	ぴ
u	う	く	す	つ tsu	ぬ	ふ fu	む	ゆ	る			ぐ	ず	づ zu	ぶ	ぷ
e	え	け	せ	て	ね	へ	め		れ	ゑ e		げ	ぜ	で	べ	ぺ
o	お	こ	そ	と	の	ほ	も	よ	ろ	を o		ご	ぞ	ど	ぼ	ぽ

6 *The Japanese syllabary.*

which had been taken wholesale into the language, were employed to write Japanese root morphemes of the same meaning but different sound. It was not long before polyvalence ran wild, which is the case today: often various Chinese-derived characters are used to represent the same sound, and sometimes a character will have a Chinese as well as a native Japanese pronunciation.

The Japanese syllabic signs are used in two ways: firstly, to write out the sometimes lengthy grammatical endings which follow the word roots (these given by means of Chinese characters), and secondly, written in minuscule besides the root-characters, to help the reader in their pronunciation.

The Japanese thus managed to swallow the Chinese writing system whole, and reshape it to their language by extracting their own phonetic syllabary from it. In other words, a syllabary can effectively coexist with logograms in a complex yet viable writing system. This is exactly what we are to find inscribed on the monuments of the abandoned cities of the ancient Maya.

Maurice Pope, who has written the best general book on decipherment, has said this: "Decipherments are by far the most glamorous achievements of scholarship. There is a touch of magic about unknown writing, especially when it comes from the remote past, and a corresponding glory is bound to attach itself to the person who first solves its mystery."[27] But it is not just a mystery solved, it is also a key to further knowledge, "opening a treasure-vault of history through which for countless centuries no human mind has wandered" – poetic, but true.

Strange to say, cryptologists – those makers and breakers of codes from the world of espionage and counter-intelligence – have played little role in the great decipherments of ancient scripts. In fact, I remember the announcements in the American press that the famous husband-and-wife team of Col. William Friedman had received foundation support to decipher Maya hieroglyphic writing. The Friedmans having achieved well-deserved fame by cracking the Japanese naval code on the eve of the war,[28] it was a foregone conclusion that the ancient Maya were going to be a pushover for them. Nothing resulted from this doomed project, and they went to their graves without having deciphered a single Maya hieroglyph.

One has only to look at the dictionary definition of cryptology to find out why these people get low grades as archaeological decipherers. Based on the Greek words *kryptos*, "secret," and *logos*, "word," cryptology is the science dealing with secret communications. In an encrypted communication, the message is meant to be unintelligible, and ever since the Italian Renaissance, trained cryptologists have been around to invent ever more ingenious methods making these messages as unreadable as possible, except to those with special keys or codebooks. By contrast, very few secret communications are found in the pre-Renaissance past — scribes were interested only in making their messages legible and unambiguous, and if they had to hide them, they took other means to make their communication channels secure.

Quite another reason why cryptology has been an absent handmaiden to decipherment is the nature of the raw material on which it traditionally works. The "plaintext," to use the appropriate jargon, which is to be enciphered or encoded, is usually in a language written alphabetically (see, for instance, the alphabetic transposition cipher used in Poe's *The Gold Bug*, or the substitution cipher solved by Sherlock Holmes in *The Dancing Men*), while most really ancient scripts are not alphabetic, but logographic, such as Egyptian, Sumerian, and Anatolian Hieroglyphic. In the world of telegraphy and cryptology, the living logographic scripts of China and Japan, morphemic characters are turned into four-digit code groups, using conventional Arabic numerals. I will run ahead of myself by saying that none of these procedures has worked, or would ever work, on Maya.

We left the writing of the ancient Egyptians still buried in the absurdities of Athanasius Kircher and his predecessors. This prestigious script was finally deciphered largely due to the labors of one man, Jean-François Champollion (1790–1832), who in the space of an incredibly short time brought the civilization of the Nile from obscurity into history. It would be instructive to see how this came about, and how this brilliant young Frenchman overcame intellectual and human obstacles finally to achieve success. The story is an object lesson in how to go about things the right way, when faced with a writing system of some complexity, a lesson that would-be decipherers of the Maya script ignored (to their detriment) for over a century.

I will reverse the usual romantic history of Champollion and the Rosetta Stone by putting the cart before the horse – revealing the solution before the problem.[29]

As Kircher had correctly surmised, Coptic is a very late descendant of the language of the pharaohs, and both are distantly related to the Semitic languages of the Near East and to Hamitic ones of Africa. Like Semitic, the consonants carry far more weight in word formation than the vowels, and it is no cause for surprise that hieroglyphic writing virtually ignores vowels, as in Hebrew and Arabic scripts. In fact, we have only the sketchiest idea of how the vowels sounded in any Egyptian written words.

The invention of hieroglyphic writing took place in the Nile Valley about 3100 BC, along with the rise of the state, and appears to have been contemporaneous with the appearance of writing in Mesopotamia. The system was entirely logographic from the outset, and did not change in its essential character until it died out early in the Christian era. It thus lasted for thirty-four centuries, far longer than the alphabet has been in use, and almost as long as the span covered by the Chinese logographic system. Exponents of the wonders of alphabetic writing enjoy denigrating the hieroglyphs as clumsy, but the Egyptologist John Ray[30] reminds us that the system is far better adapted to the structure of the Egyptian language than is the alphabet: the Greek alphabet was used to write Egyptian in Hellenistic and Roman times, but the results are often extremely difficult to follow. Further, even though the script was pretty much a monopoly of the scribes, it is far easier to learn than, say, Chinese.

There are three forms of Egyptian writing.[31] First of all, there are the mistakenly-named (and misinterpreted) "hieroglyphs" themselves, which are most often seen in monumental, public inscriptions. Developed in parallel with these was a cursive script used chiefly for everyday purposes, usually in papyrus manuscripts; one of these is known as *hieratic*, mainly used in priestly texts, while the other, developed somewhat later, is *demotic*, a popular script employed in business transactions. Apart from general appearance, there is no essential difference between the three.

There are about 2500 individual signs in the Egyptian corpus, but only a small percentage of these were in common use. The experts divide these into *phonograms*, or signs representing phonemes (or clusters of them), and *semagrams*, signs with wholly or partly semantic reference.

Let us now consider the phonograms. Twenty-six of these are monoconsonantal, giving the sound of a single consonant; we will pick these up later in the famous royal cartouches on the Rosetta Stone. Suffice it to say that this is *not* an alphabet, since ordinary vowels are missing; what one gets are a few weak vowels or semiconsonants like *y*, but even these are often omitted by the scribe. Although Gelb insisted that this was a syllabary,[32] in line with his theories about the evolution of writing, I know of no Egyptologist who follows him. Added to this are eighty-four signs expressing two consonants each, and even some tri- and quadri-consonantal signs. Now, Egyptian scribes probably could have managed to write everything using just the monoconsonantal signs (as they did with outlandish foreign names like "Cleopatra" and "Tiberius Caesar" in late times); but they didn't try, any more than literate Japanese have abandoned Chinese characters for purely syllabic writing (*kana*), except to write foreign names and words.

Many of the semagrams ("meaning signs") are actually logograms, that is, words are indicated by a picture of the object denoted – a sun disk, for example, is *Re'*, "the sun" or "Sun God"; a plan of a house is *pr*, "house." Often placed after phonetic signs are determinatives. There are about one hundred of these, and they tell one what class of things a word falls into – so, a seated profile god indicates that the word is a deity name, a tied-up papyrus scroll that it is an abstract idea, a circle divided into four quarters that it is a town or country, and so forth. As with their counterparts in Chinese and in the cuneiform writing of Mesopotamia, the determinatives were silent partners of the spoken phonetic signs. And finally, there are small vertical bars with important roles to play: a single bar below the sign means that it is a logogram, two bars indicate duality, and three that it is in the plural.

There is, as in all such systems, a degree of polyvalence (a sign can be used both as a phonogram *or* as a semagram, for instance, the "goose" sign, which can be biconsonantal *z* or the determinative "bird"), but the script is remarkably down-to-earth and free from ambiguity. One big help along these lines is that multiconsonantal signs are often reinforced by phonetic complements drawn from the monoconsonantal list – for instance, the word *hetep*, "offering," which consists of the sign for *htp* plus *t* and *p*.

So, in structure, we once again have a complex duet involving sound and meaning, as we did with the Far Eastern scripts. But other, extralinguistic factors played a role among the scribes of the Nile. Calligraphic considerations – in other words, concepts of script beauty – often resulted in words and individual signs being changed from their usual order (as we learnt from Herodotus, the script was usually written from right to left, but not invariably so). There was always an intimate relation between picture and text to a degree that is unique in the Old World. And public texts, at least those which appear on monuments like granite

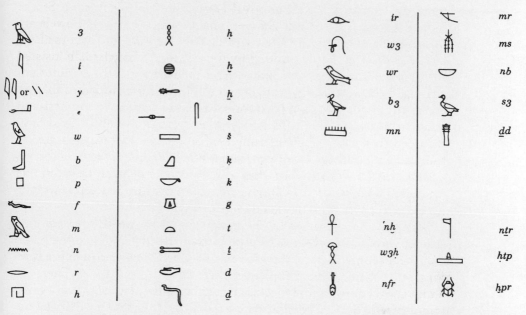

7 Egyptian phonograms:
monoconsonantal signs.

8 Egyptian phonograms: some
biconsonantal and triconsonantal signs.

obelisks, are remarkably terse in what they say, and often quite formulaic. The Nile traveler comes across the equivalent of Shelley's "I am Ozymandias, king of kings" over and over and over!

Champollion was a virtual Hercules of the intellect.[33] It is an amazing fact that most of his great decipherment was carried out within the short space of two years. Born at Figeac in southern France, by the age of seventeen he was already an expert in Oriental languages, especially Coptic, and went on to Paris to perfect his knowledge of Persian and Arabic. By 1814, when he was only twenty-four, he had brought out two volumes on Coptic place-names in the Nile Valley – which, by the way, he never saw until long after his great decipherment.

In the mid-eighteenth century, the French Abbé J.J. Barthélemy had guessed (rightly) that the rope-like ovals – the so-called "cartouches" – on the Egyptian monuments might contain the names of kings, but there was no proof then extant. Then, in 1798, what must be the most famous piece of rock in the world, the Rosetta Stone,[34] was discovered by the Napoleonic army which had swept into Egypt accompanied by an extraordinary group of scientists. On its face were three parallel texts: one in Greek (stating among other things that the inscription was the same in all three texts), one in demotic, and a badly damaged one on top in hieroglyphs. Copies were immediately made and circulated among

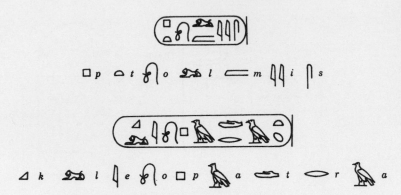

9 Royal cartouches of Ptolemy (top) and Cleopatra (above).

interested scholars, a remarkable example of scientific cooperation when one considers the turbulent times.

The great race to the decipherment had begun, in some ways reminiscent of the highly competitive research of the 1950s which led to the discovery of the double helix of the DNA molecule, or of the race to the Moon. It was generally considered that the demotic inscription must be in some kind of alphabet, while the hieroglyphs were surely "symbolic" only – the dead hand of Kircherian thought once again. By 1802, two first-rate Orientalists, Count Silvestre de Sacy in France, and the Swedish diplomat Johan Åkerblad, had managed to read the names "Ptolemy" and "Alexander" in the demotic, as well as the remaining non-Egyptian names and words in the same text. The Ptolemies were foreigners, Macedonian Greeks left in charge of Egypt by Alexander the Great, and the decree recorded on the Rosetta Stone as it subsequently transpired had been put forth in 196 BC by Ptolemy V, who probably did not even speak Egyptian.

The next to try his hand with the Rosetta Stone was the polymath Englishman Thomas Young. Physician and physicist, in 1801 he discovered both the cause of astigmatism and the wave theory of light. Young's involvement with Egyptian script is a somewhat depressing mishmash of correct hits and inexcusable misses, and he himself, as a human being and scholar, was far from admirable. Nevertheless, Young realized that the demotic text was full of signs which could not be purely phonetic or "alphabetic," and he also grasped that demotic and hieroglyphic were but two forms of the same writing system. He also took the reading for "Ptolemy" in the demotic, and found its equivalent inside Barthelemy's cartouches; perhaps due to Lady Luck, he got five out of seven of the monoconsonants right (p, t, m, i, and s). Yet he never

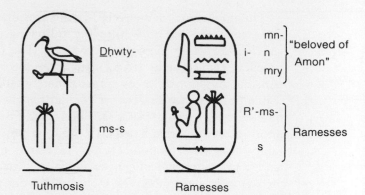

10 *Royal cartouches of*
Tuthmosis and Ramesses.

advanced much beyond this; until his death in 1829, he stubbornly clung
to the delusion that while the names in the cartouches were beyond
doubt phonetic, this was probably only because this was the way
Egyptians wrote foreign names – the rest of the hieroglyphs were
Kircherian symbols.

Ironically, this is exactly what Champollion himself once believed.
But beginning with the red-letter year of 1822, a real revolution in his
thinking began to take shape. By then, an immense amount of new
material, most of it from the Napoleonic campaign, had been published
in great and accurate detail. And now this happened: in January of that
year, he saw a copy of an obelisk which had been brought to Kingston
Lacy in Dorset, England. The Greek inscription on the pedestal on
which it had once stood showed that it had been dedicated to Ptolemy
and Cleopatra, and he soon found "Cleopatra" spelled out in
monoconsonantal signs in one of the obelisk cartouches as well as on the
Rosetta Stone. Armed with these new readings, Champollion was then
able to read a large number of late names and titles (including those of the
Roman emperors) on other monuments, such as some of the obelisks set
up in the squares of Renaissance Rome.

But what about pharaonic Egypt before its subjugation by the armies
of Greece and Rome? By 14 September 1822, Champollion had
recognized the names of the early rulers Ramesses the Great and
Tuthmosis, both spelled out phonetically. Again, in that year the Abbé
Rémusat had brought out the very first study of Chinese writing which
was not hampered by mentalist fantasy, and it showed to our young
Egyptologist that even Chinese script was heavily phonetic in its very
structure, and not a mere string of "ideographs." With this in mind,
Champollion published his immortal *Lettre à M. Dacier*, in which he
showed why he had changed his mind about the hieroglyphs *outside* the
cartouches – phoneticism must be important there, too.

The intellectual dam erected by his precursors, from Greco-Roman times on, had burst. Within the following two years, Champollion cracked Egyptian hieroglyphic writing. The product of this towering intellect came out in 1824: *Summary of the Hieroglyphic System of the Ancient Egyptians.* In its approximately 400 pages and 46 plates, Champollion proved (1) that the script was largely but not entirely phonetic; (2) that alternative spellings could be used for the same sound (polyvalence); (3) that based on Coptic grammar, the hieroglyphic forms of the masculine, feminine, and plural could be read, as well as pronouns and demonstrative adjectives (such as "my," "his," etc.); (4) the existence of determinatives, including the one for gods; (5) the names of all the important deities; and (6) how scribes could play around with the script by giving alternative spellings for the same god's name – sometimes written purely morphemically, sometimes phonetically. As if that were not enough, Champollion demonstrated how royal cartouches worked (each king had two – take a look at the nearest obelisk, and you will see that this is so).

Lest anyone doubted the correctness of the decipherment, Champollion produced an Egyptian alabaster vase with a bilingual inscription in hieroglyphs and in the wedge-shaped cuneiform signs of the Old Persian syllabary, which had only recently been partially deciphered; both gave the same name, Xerxes (*Khschearscha* in Persian).

Acclamation was not long in coming from the scholarly world – and so were the usual brickbats. The Comte de Sacy and the German linguist Wilhelm Humboldt, among others, were high in their praise. Thomas Young, ever the sourpuss wedded to his untenable theory about the ideographic nature of the hieroglyphs, on the one hand claimed Champollion's discoveries as his own, and on the other did all he could to discredit them. The grumbling among the specialists, most of them probably with noses bent far out of shape by Champollion's feat of intellect, went on for more than four decades following the publication of the *Summary.* It was only stifled once and for all by the discovery in 1866 of the Decree of Canopus, another self-serving Ptolemaic decree conferring honors on Ptolemy III and his queen, Berenice. Cut, like the Rosetta Stone, in Greek, hieroglyphic, and demotic, it furnished stunning proof that Champollion had been completely right.

There is bitter truth in the old adage that the good die young. After having finally had the chance to visit Italy and the ruins of the Nile, Champollion succumbed to a series of premature strokes in 1832, at the age of forty-one. Looking out at us in his portrait by Cogniet, he seems the embodiment of a hero in a tale by his compatriot and contemporary Stendahl. Champollion's achievement only leads me to regret that those eyes never studied a Maya hieroglyphic inscription, for I doubt whether under the right circumstances this script would have failed to yield to him some of its secrets. John Lloyd Stephens, the early nineteenth-century discoverer of the Maya civilization, on contemplating the fallen monuments of one of its forest-buried cities, lamented: "No Champollion has yet brought to them the energies of his enquiring mind. Who shall read them?"[35]

Champollion opened up the world of ancient logographic writing systems to eventual decipherment. Of greatest importance to the history of the Western world was the decipherment of the cuneiform records of the Near East, for these held the histories, religions, and mythologies of peoples known to the Old Testament Hebrews. The word *cuneiform* is based on the Latin *cuneus*, "nail," from the shape of the wedge-like strokes with which the Mesopotamian scribes impressed their wet clay tablets. The first step in the decipherment was the cracking of a late cuneiform syllabary employed by the scribes of the Persian Empire. It was through a trilingual inscription boasting of the achievements of Darius and Xerxes that the earlier Babylonian script – logographic like all other ancient systems known – began to be deciphered, during the first half of the last century.

Now the Babylonians and Assyrians, who also wrote in cuneiform, were Semites. In the course of time, even earlier cuneiform tablets were unearthed which proved to be in another, totally unrelated language, named "Sumerian" by the Semites; this was in use among the temple-dominated city-states of southern Mesopotamia from around 3100 BC on, and many scholars believe that it is the oldest writing in the world.[36] Similar to all other ancient scripts with respect to the employment of the familiar rebus-transfer to invent phonetic signs, these earliest examples of visual language are also aberrant in another way: while in the rest of the world's civilizations writing developed as an aspect of the religious and political power of the royal *persona*, here in the irrigated deserts of the Tigris and Euphrates it was basically a form of bookkeeping – this was a civilization of accountants.

Decipherers have also laid siege to other logographic scripts, sometimes coming off with flying colors, sometimes not. In the plus column, one of the most impressive successes was the decipherment of so-called Hittite Hieroglyphic (which actually turned out to be in another Indo-European tongue, Luvian), the script in which the Bronze Age rulers of what is now central Turkey trumpeted their warlike deeds.[37] Between the two world wars, helped by the discovery of a few cuneiform/hieroglyphic bilingual seals, and by the identification of determinants for things like "country," "god," and "king," a remarkable collection of scholars from a number of countries (including Gelb in America) was finally able to read the script. It consisted of about five hundred signs of which most were pictorially-derived logograms and contained a fairly complete syllabary of sixty signs.

Next to Champollion's triumph with Egyptian, certainly the world's best-known decipherment was that announced by the young British architect Michael Ventris in a radio broadcast of 1952. In June of the next year, a leader in *The Times*, which brought this discovery to the attention of the world, significantly coincided with the conquest of Everest by Hillary and Tensing.[38] Ventris' achievement was the cracking of Linear B, a kind of Everest of the mind, if there ever was one, and made even more poignant by the brilliant decipherer's untimely death at the age of thirty-four in a car accident. The script is known only from economic records incised on clay, and kept in the archives of the Bronze Age palaces of Mycenaean Greece and Crete.

As Ventris discovered, against the considered judgment of his elders and betters – and even against his own inclination – Linear B records an early form of Greek. It is a fairly pure syllabary, primarily CV, of eighty-seven signs; in addition, there are some pictorial logograms, such as signs for "horse" (both male and female), "tripod," "boat," and other items of interest to palace accountants. What makes this decipherment of such immediacy to us is that for the very first time we can read the records (mundane though they are) of the people and society talked about in the Homeric epics. These Bronze Age people were our own cultural ancestors.

How did Ventris do it? It must be kept in mind that this is an almost completely phonetic script – in fact, a syllabary – so that the methodology in solving the puzzle is not completely divorced from cryptography (or for that matter, from crossword puzzles). In a CV syllabary – and Ventris had every reason to believe that this is what it was – each sign will share a consonant with other signs, and its vowel with still others. Ventris thus began to construct experimental grids, with the possible consonants listed in the lefthand column, and the vowels in the top horizontal row (we are going to see one for the Maya later on in this book). Like syllabaries elsewhere – the Japanese *kana* comes to mind – there will be five or so signs for the vowels, and Ventris was able to hazard a guess which of these was most likely to begin a word.

He had two obstacles: the language was unknown, and he had no bilingual key. But previous work done by others had shown that the language had to be inflecting (like Latin or Greek); the logograms gave him the meanings of some of the sign sequences in the syllabary as well as the masculine and feminine endings for some words; and a few signs probably had the same values as similar ones in the much later Cypriote syllabary, a Greek script in use many centuries later on the island of Cyprus.

An enlightened guess led Ventris to the solution: that ancient Cretan place-names would appear on Linear B tablets from the Palace of Minos at Knossos, including that of Knossos itself. Applying this to his experimental grid, he found the entire script to be in Greek.

The question might now be asked, how does one know the type of script with which one is dealing? The answer to this lies in the number of individual characters or signs in the script. Look at these figures for deciphered or already known writing systems:[39]

Writing System	No. of Signs
Logographic	
Sumerian	600 (+)
Egyptian	2,500
Hittite Hieroglyphic	497
Chinese	5,000 (+)
"Pure" Syllabic	
Persian	40
Linear B	87
Cypriote	56
Cherokee	85
Alphabetic or Consonantal	
English	26
Anglo-Saxon	31
Sanskrit	35
Etruscan	20
Russian	36
Hebrew	22
Arabic	28

So, if an unknown script has a sign-list totalling between 20 and 35 signs, it is probably a system like an alphabet; if between 40 and 90 signs, the likelihood is that we are dealing with a "pure" syllabary; and if above a few hundred, the system is surely logographic. The number of phonetic signs in logographic writing systems is of interest, too: Sumerian has between 100 and 150, and Egyptian about 100, but since Hittite Hieroglyphic uses a syllabary for its phoneticism, the phonetic signs number only 60, within the usual range for "pure" syllabaries. And although, if DeFrancis is right, the number of phonetic signs standing for syllables in Chinese is huge, in China only 62 characters are exploited for their CV sound values to write foreign names in newspapers and the like, again in the range of "pure" syllabaries.

The fundamental pillars on which all successful decipherments have rested are five in number:

(1) The *database* must be large enough, with many texts of adequate length. (2) The *language* must be known, or at least a reconstructed, ancestral version, in vocabulary, grammar, and syntax; at the very minimum, the linguistic family to which the language of the script belongs should be known. (3) There should be a *bilingual* inscription of some sort, one member of which is in a known writing system. (4) The *cultural context* of the script should be known, above all traditions and histories giving place-names, royal names and titles, and so forth. (5) For logographic scripts, there should be *pictorial references*, either pictures to accompany the text, or pictorially-derived logographic signs.

In a few cases, one or two of these criteria may be dispensed with – Ventris, for example, managed very well without a bilingual inscription (but Linear B was largely phonetic) – and others not. No script has ever been broken, that is, actually translated, unless the language itself is known and understood. A case in point is Etruscan, the script of the original inhabitants of central Italy before the rise of the Roman state. There are over 10,000 Etruscan inscriptions, all written in an alphabet very similar to that of the early Greeks; thus, the pronunciation of every single word in them is well established. The problem is that no one is very sure about what these texts say: almost all of them are brief, and apparently pertain to funerary rites and beliefs, but the language which they record is utterly unrelated to any other on earth, and has not been spoken since the dawn of the Christian era. Etruscan can be *read*, but it has never been *translated*.

Bright youngsters who aspire to be second Ventrises and Champollions may be pleased to know that there are still about a half dozen early scripts still undeciphered. But I remain a pessimist: unless new information on them is forthcoming, they will stay that way for a long time to come. Take as an example the famous stamp-seals of the Indus or Harappan civilization of Bronze Age India.[40] There are several thousand of these seals, each with a lovely depiction of a bull or elephant or some such, accompanied by a very short inscription. As the sign-list reaches several hundred in magnitude, it must be a logographic script; but because no text is of any length, no bilingual inscription (say one in cuneiform and Harappan) has yet shown up, and the language is unknown (it has been hazarded to be an early form of the Dravidian tongues still spoken by millions in southern India, but this is disputed), the Indus writing system has *not* been deciphered – all claims to the contrary notwithstanding. Britons, Indians, Finns, Russians, and Americans, not to mention computers, have all worked on the problem, but "all the King's horses and all the King's men" have been unable to put together this particular Humpty-Dumpty.

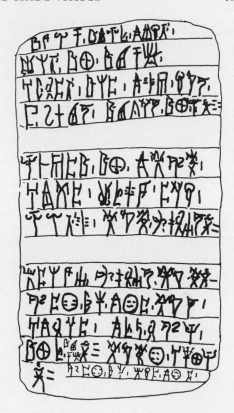

11 Linear B tablet from Pylos concerning the coastguard.

"Who shall read them?" Stephens' question was a good one: to him, the writings on the crumbling monuments and cities which he and his artist, Frederick Catherwood, had discovered in 1839–40 cried out for a Champollion to decipher them. As we shall see, a kind of bilingual text was unearthed in a Spanish library, and was published in 1864, twelve years after Stephens' death. In 1880, a facsimile of the greatest pre-Columbian Maya book had appeared and by the end of the last century, a very large body of Maya stone inscriptions was available to the scholarly world, in highly accurate photographs and drawings. In the early years of the twentieth century, Maya specialists certainly knew as much about "their" civilization as Champollion had known about ancient Egypt. And there was hardly a lack of pictures to interpret the Maya texts.

So why did it take so long to decipher the Maya glyphs? Why were there so many false starts and wrong turns? Why did would-be Maya decipherers pay no attention to what had been done along these lines in the Old World? And who, indeed, did answer Stephens' plea and finally read the script of the ancient Maya?

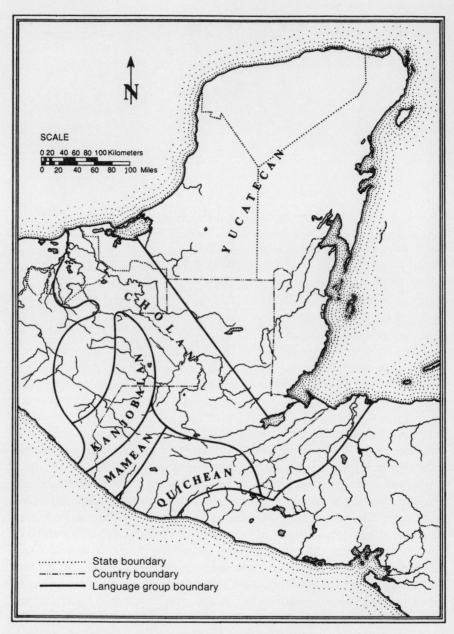

SCALE

0 20 40 60 80 100 Kilometers

0 20 40 60 80 100 Miles

Y U C A T E C A N

C H O L A N

K A N J O B A L A N

M A M E A N

Q U I C H E A N

.... State boundary

—·—·— Country boundary

——— Language group boundary

12 *Map of Mayan language groups.*

2 Lords of the Forest

Having been systematically undercounted by modern governments, no one precisely knows how many Maya Indians there are, but there are at least four million in southeastern Mexico, Guatemala, Belize, and Honduras. Ever since the Spanish Conquest of the early sixteenth century, the Maya have been subjected to the physical and cultural onslaught of the European and Europeanized population of these countries, to which they have responded in various ways – sometimes, like the "primitive" Lacandon Indians of Chiapas, Mexico, by flight into the dense forests. But even the forests themselves are being hacked down by the forces of progress at a dizzying rate, and bulldozers, modern roads, hotels, condominiums, and the like are transforming ancient Maya ways of life at a pace that could not have been predicted a half century ago. Meanwhile, in the Guatemalan highlands, an even worse tragedy is being acted out, as the indigenous populations are being uprooted and demoralized by a systematic program of extermination carried out by a succession of military regimes.

Creators of one of the most spectacular civilizations the world has ever known, the Maya today have been reduced to what anthropologists condescend to call a "folk culture," with little or no voice in their own destinies. How many vacationing tourists who visit the glorious ruins of Yucatán are aware that Mexican law forbids the teaching in schools of the Yucatec Maya tongue – the tongue of the people who built these pyramids? The modern world has been transfixed by the new demands of oppressed nationalities for their place in the sun, but little or nothing is heard from the millions upon millions of indigenous, "Fourth World" people in Latin America. How many heads of state in those countries have any "Indian" blood to speak of? And when has any Native American language been heard in the halls of the United Nations? The answer is "none" and "never." No imperial conquest has ever been so total, or a great people so shattered.

But it has not always been this way.

47

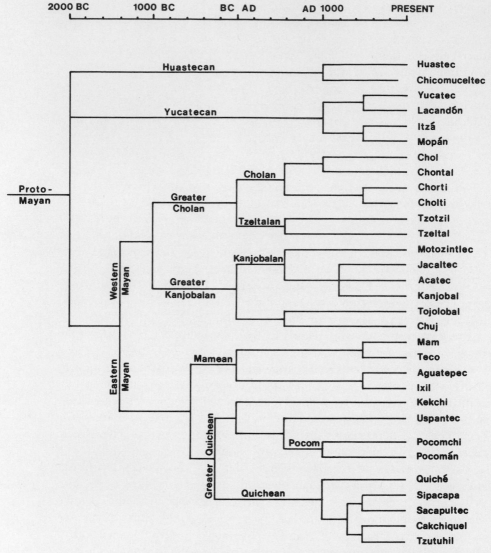

2000 BC   1000 BC   BC AD   AD 1000   PRESENT

Proto-Mayan

Huastecan
Huastec
Chicomuceltec

Yucatecan
Yucatec
Lacandón
Itzá
Mopán

Western Mayan

Greater Cholan
Cholan
Chol
Chontal
Chorti
Cholti
Tzeltalan
Tzotzil
Tzeltal

Greater Kanjobalan
Kanjobalan
Motozintlec
Jacaltec
Acatec
Kanjobal
Tojolobal
Chuj

Eastern Mayan

Mamean
Mam
Teco
Aguatepec
Ixil

Greater Quichean

Quichean
Kekchi
Uspantec
Pocom
Pocomchi
Pocomán
Quiché
Sipacapa
Sacapultec
Cakchiquel
Tzutuhil

13 Classification and time depth of the Mayan languages.

When Charlemagne was crowned Emperor by the Pope in St. Peter's in Rome, on Christmas Day in the year 800, Maya civilization was at its height: scattered throughout the jungle-covered lowlands of the Yucatán Peninsula were more than a dozen brilliant city-states, with huge populations, towering temple-pyramids and sophisticated royal courts. The arts, scientific learning, and, above all, writing flourished under royal patronage. Maya mathematicians and astronomers scanned the heavens, and tracked the planets as they moved across the background of the stars in the tropical night. Royal scribes – devotees of the twin Monkey-Man Gods – wrote all this down in their bark-paper books, and inscribed the deeds of their kings, queens, and princes on stone monuments and walls of their temples and palaces.

Even the mightiest empires have their day and finally crumble, awaiting resurrection by the archaeologist's spade. It was not long after 800 that things began to fall apart for the ancient Maya, who had enjoyed six centuries of prosperity during Europe's Dark Age, and city after city was abandoned to the encroaching forest. Then there was a final brief renaissance of lowland culture in northern Yucatán, to be followed by the final cataclysm brought about at the hands of the white foreigners from across the sea.

There are some thirty Mayan languages spoken today, some as closely related to each other as say, Dutch is to English, and some as far apart from each other as English is from French.[1] Just as languages scattered from Europe to Persia and India can be traced back to a common Proto-Indo-European ancestor, so can linguists reach back into the shadowy past to look for a common parent. Reconstructed as Proto-Mayan, this was spoken as far back as four thousand years ago, perhaps in the mountains of northwestern Guatemala, but no one is certain about exactly where. As time went on, dialects within the ur-language diverged to become separate languages. One of these was the ancestral form of Yucatec, still the mother tongue of hundreds of thousands in the Yucatán Peninsula. Another group included the ancestor of Tzeltal and Tzotzil (languages which one can yet hear in the markets and plazas of large Maya towns in the Chiapas highlands of southeastern Mexico), and of Cholan.

We now know that Cholan is to the inscribed texts of the Classic Maya cities what Coptic was to the hieroglyphic inscriptions of ancient Egypt. The three surviving Cholan languages today – Chol, Chontal, and Chorti – are still spoken around the ruins of Classic Maya cities (Chol at Palenque in the west, and Chorti near Copán in the east), a fact which led the late Sir Eric Thompson to propose some years ago that the Classic texts were in a form of Cholan.[2] Time has proved him right on this very important point.

But Yucatec must not be overlooked. Among the great Maya cities of the Peninsula to the north of the Cholans, probably everyone from lowly peasant farmers to great princes spoke Yucatec, and three of the four surviving hieroglyphic books are in that tongue (notwithstanding the fact that Cholan influence can be detected in the book preserved in the State Library of Dresden, eastern Germany). As we know from the complex ethnic situation in Europe, linguistic boundaries are not exactly impervious; in fact, they leak like sieves, and loan words pass back and forth. Suffice it to say at this point that there is plenty of evidence for such interchange of vocabulary going on between Yucatec and Cholan Maya for at least a millennium before the Spanish Conquest – evidence coming from the advanced state of the Maya decipherment.[3]

It should be borne in mind that all the various Mayan languages spoken today are the modern end products of linguistic evolution, and have been subject to various degrees of "linguistic imperialism" by the hispanic culture that has been dominant since the Conquest. In Yucatán, to give just one sad example, very few Maya can now count in their own native language beyond the number five – a people who could once count into the millions in Maya have been reduced to using mostly Spanish numbers.

We know far more about the Mayan languages than Champollion, say, could ever have known about Egyptian/Coptic. Indeed, very sophisticated techniques allow linguists to reconstruct with some confidence the vocabulary, grammar, and syntax of the Proto-Cholan language that was spoken at cities like Tikal, Palenque, and Yaxchilán, a great help to decipherers.[4]

Only a born optimist might tell you that the Mayan languages are easy to learn; they may be so for a Maya toddler, but for those of us who were brought up with the languages of Europe (including even Russian), these are *tough* for foreigners. One has only to listen to the marketwomen of Mérida, capital of Yucatán, or of a town under the volcanoes of Guatemala, to know that Mayan is very different from what we learned in school.

In the first place, these languages sound like nothing we have heard before. They make a very important distinction between *glottalized* and *unglottalized* consonants. The latter are pronounced "normally" as we do, but when the stop is glottalized, the throat is constricted and the sound released like a small explosion. We say that glottalization is phonemic, because it produces changes in the meaning of words. Compare, for example, the following pairs of words in Yucatec Maya:

Unglottalized	**Glottalized**
pop, "mat"	*p'op'*, "to shell squash seeds"
cutz, "turkey"	*kutz*, "tobacco"
tzul, "to put in order"	*dzul*, "foreigner"
muc, "to bury"	*muk*, "to permit"

Something else which seems unfamiliar to us is the glottal stop, phonemically significant in Mayan although usually ignored in texts of the Colonial period (I suppose because the natives knew when to use it, and the Spaniards didn't care). This is just a constriction of the throat or glottis, which English speakers use at the beginning of a word like *apple*, or in the exclamation *uh-oh!* Linguists write it with an apostrophe or a dotless question mark. Consider this sentence in Yucatec: *b'ey tu hadzahile'exo'ob'o'*, "thus they hit you [pl.]" – the *x* is pronounced like our *sh* – and you will get some idea of the sound of a language which must have taxed the ability of the early Spanish friars to understand and speak.

As if the phonology weren't difficult enough, there is the grammar, which bears not the slightest resemblance to anything we contended with when we learned ancient Latin, Greek, or any of the modern European languages. We are in another world altogether, with a different mindset.[5]

With the Mayan languages, roots are overwhelmingly monosyllabic, with the CVC (consonant-vowel-consonant) pattern dominant, but these are highly inflected, and there are special particles added to them. Words therefore tend to be *polysynthetic*, often expressing in one word what it would take a whole English sentence to do.

The Mayan languages, along with such utterly unrelated and scattered tongues as Basque, Eskimo, Tibetan, and Georgian, are *ergative*, a specialized linguistic term meaning that the *subject* of an intransitive verb (one that has no object; "to sleep" is intransitive) and the *object* of a transitive verb (such as "to hit") have the same case, or in dealing with pronouns, are the same. In Mayan, there are two sets of pronouns, which we will call Set A and Set B. In Yucatec Maya these are.

	Set A		Set B	
	Sing.	**Plural**	**Sing.**	**Plural**
1st	*in-*	*c-*	*-en*	*-o'on*
2nd	*a-*	*a-.....-e'ex*	*-ech*	*-e'ex*
3rd	*u-*	*u-.....-o'ob*	*-Ø*	*-o'ob*

Ø, by the way, means "nothing."

Transitive verbs take Set A affixes as subjects and Set B ones as objects. For intransitive verbs like "to sleep," a Set B pronoun is used for the subject. And, just to confuse things for the neophyte learner, Set A pronouns are used for the possessors of things. I would use the same 3rd person singular *u-* for "he" in "he hit him," and for "his" in "his book"; we are going to see this later in the Maya glyphs.

If, however, the action described in the sentence hasn't yet been finished, a Set A pronoun appears as the subject! This raises the question of tenses: they really don't exist in Mayan languages like Yucatec, or at least there are no past, present, and future of the kind familiar to us. In their place are *aspect* words or particles, and inflections; these indicate whether an action has been completed or not, whether it is just beginning or ending, or has been in progress for a while. As adverbs, they stand in front of verbs, and govern them. To talk of events in the past, you must differentiate the remote past from the more recent past; and to deal with the future, the particular aspect word which you must use depends on how certain it is that something will happen – there are the indefinite "I will walk," the definite "I am going to walk," and the very certain statement "I *will* walk."

It is just not possible in Mayan to use an imperfective verb (referring to actions or events in the past, present, or future that have not been completed) without sticking a date or a temporal aspect adverb in front of it. The Maya are, and have always been, very, very particular about time, far more than we are, and we will see this in the elaborate chronological skeletons on which all their texts are strung, even those written down in Spanish letters during Colonial times.

Here are a few examples of some Yucatec sentences, to give an idea of how these principles are put into verbal action. To begin with, here is a sentence using a transitive verb:

> *t u hadz-ah-o'on-o'ob*, "they hit us" (in the past)
> *t*, completive aspect, transitive verb
> *u-...-o'ob*, "they" (Set A)
> *hadz*, "to hit" (note glottalized *dz*)
> *-ah*, perfective suffix
> *-o'on*, "us" (Set B)

And another:

> *taan in-hadz-ic-ech*, "I am hitting you"
> *taan*, durative aspect
> *in-*, "I" (Set A)
> *hadz*, "to hit"
> *-ic*, imperfective verb suffix
> *-ech*, "you" (object, Set B pronoun)

And finally, a sentence with an intransitive verb:

> *h ueen-en*, "I slept"
> *h*, completive aspect, intransitive verb
> *ueen*, "to sleep"
> *-en*, "I" (Set B)

Remember the possessive?

> *in hu'un*, "my book"
> *in*, "my" (Set A)
> *hu'un*, "book"

Not only does time play a critical role in Maya verb constructions, but there is a whole class of intransitives which describe an object's or person's position and shape in space; there are distinct terms, for instance, for "lying face down" and "lying face up." These "positionals," as they are called, have their own inflectional suffixes.

As English-speakers, we take it for granted that one can speak of, say "four birds" or "twenty-five books," but this kind of numerical construction is impossible in the Mayan languages – between the number and the thing counted there has to be a *numerical classifier*, describing the class to which the object, animal, plant, or thing belongs. We have a glimmering of this sort of construction when we talk of "two flocks of geese" or "a pride of lions," but this is pale stuff compared to the richness of Mayan classifiers. Colonial Yucatec dictionaries list dozens of these, but only a handful are still in use in today's Yucatán, yet even these have to be interposed even when the number itself might be in Spanish.[6] If I see three horses in a pasture, I would count them as *ox-tul tzimin* (*ox*, "three"; *-tul*, classifier for animate things; *tzimin*, "horse" or "tapir"). However, if there were three stones lying in the same pasture, I would have to say *ox-p'el tunich* (*ox*, "three"; *-p'el*, classifier for inanimate things; *tunich*, "stone").

Until this century, when so much of the ancient system was lost, the Maya counted *vigesimally* – by base twenty – instead of *decimally* – by base ten – as we do (although we retain a trace of this in such archaic expressions as "three score and ten" for "seventy"). But, after all, physiologically we have twenty digits, not just ten, so the human dimension is very much present in the Mayan system. By means of it, they could count very large numbers – into the millions, if need be.

Compared with the languages of the Indo-European family, Mayan is fairly gender-blind: there really are no masculine, feminine, or neuter constructions in most of the grammar. One and the same pronoun is used for "he," "she," and "it." Nonetheless, male and female personal names and occupational titles are often prefixed by special particles indicating sex. In Yucatec, these are *ah* for men, and *ix* for women. Thus, we have in our early Colonial sources *ah dzib*, "scribe" (= "he of the writing"), and *Ix Cheel*, the mother goddess (= "Lady Rainbow").

It is not just enough for a language to have a grammar, it must have a syntax, too, so that words may be strung into sentences. Every language in the world has its own characteristic word order. For the ancient Egyptians, the order of a sentence with a transitive verb would have been verb-subject-object, or VSO, so that to express a sentence which in English would be "The scribe knows the counsel," a denizen of the Nile would have had to say "knows the scribe the counsel." We would use the SVO construction for this. But the Mayan languages generally use the order verb-object-subject or VOS ("knows the counsel the scribe"); moreover, with intransitive verbs which take no object, such as "the lord is seated," the verb still precedes the subject.

Given the fact that there are grammars and dictionaries for all the thirty-odd Mayan languages (and for Yucatec, a half-dozen major dictionaries from all time periods since the Conquest), one would have expected early would-be decipherers of Maya hieroglyphic writing to make some effort, as Champollion did with Coptic/Egyptian, to immerse themselves in one or more of the Mayan tongues. I would like to say that this was so, but it's not what happened. Incredible as it may seem, up until about two decades ago the Maya script was the only decipherment for which a thorough grounding in the relevant language was not considered necessary – there are still a few "experts" on the subject, hidden away in the dusty recesses of anthropology departments, who have only the foggiest idea of Maya as a spoken language (and not much of Spanish, for that matter).

We shall see the consequences of this ignorance in due time.

Once memorably described as a "green thumb jutting up into the Gulf of Mexico," the Yucatán Peninsula is a low-lying limestone shelf which emerged in fairly recent geological time from the waters of the Caribbean. Its northern half is extraordinarily flat, the only topographic relief being provided by the Puuc range, low hills arranged in a sort of inverted V across the border between the Mexican states of Yucatán and Campeche. The peninsula is honeycombed by caves, and by sinkholes (called cenotes from the Maya dzonot) which once were almost the sole source of drinking water in the Northern Maya Area.

Further south, the land becomes more elevated and the relief more pronounced. This is the Central Maya Area (or southern Maya lowlands), at the heart of which lies the Petén district of northern Guatemala, the geographic and cultural heart of Classic Maya civilization. To the east of the Petén, in Belize, are the impressive Maya Mountains, source of the granite used by the ancient Maya of the Central Area for milling stones to grind corn. In contrast to the northern reaches of the peninsula, here there are many rivers, above all the mighty Usumacinta (and its tributaries like the Pasión), which flows past innumerable ruins of Maya cities on its way to the Gulf of Mexico; and the Belize and New Rivers, draining into the Caribbean.

A traveler heading south on foot from the Petén would eventually encounter the incredibly rough karst terrain of the Verapaz country, with huge caverns – one of which, near the town of Chamá, was believed to be the entrance to Xibalbá, the Maya Underworld. Beyond this region

14 *Map of the Maya area, with major sites.*

he would climb sharply up, into the highlands of Guatemala and
neighboring Chiapas: a breathtakingly lovely landscape of volcanic
peaks as perfectly conical as Fujiyama, each sacred to the gods of the
Quiché Maya nation who ruled here on the eve of the Spanish Conquest.
In these relatively cool uplands there are many broad valleys, especially
the one straddling the continental divide, which now contains the

modern capital of Guatemala, and the enormous volcanic caldera which holds the sapphire-blue waters of Lake Atitlán, its shores dotted with picturesque Maya villages.

To the south and southwest of the highlands is the Pacific coastal plain, an oven-hot region of winding rivers, rich, alluvial soils, and a lagoon-and-mangrove-fringed coastline. This zone (grouped with the highlands into the Southern Maya Area by archaeologists) was never very Maya: indeed, the languages once spoken there were largely non-Maya. But it contributed decisively to the development of nascent Maya civilization further north and northeast, above all in the genesis of the sacred calendar, and in religious and civil iconography.

One has only to deplane at the airport of Mérida, Yucatán's major city, to know that one is in the tropics – coming from the cold north, the first step outside sometimes feels like opening the door of a sauna. Because the Maya realm lies entirely to the south of the Tropic of Cancer, yet considerably to the north of the Equator, there are two strongly marked seasons (neither of them, of course, with snow!). The dry season lasts from the end of November until mid or late May, during which it very seldom rains, especially in the northern half of the peninsula and in the Southern Maya Area. Then, as the month of May nears its end, thunderclouds begin massing each afternoon, and torrential rains begin: the voice of the rain god Chac is heard all across the land. By midsummer, the downpours taper off somewhat, to begin again in earnest until they end in November.

It was during those wet six months of the year that all Maya life and Maya civilization itself was in the hands of the gods, for upon those rains the Maya corn farmer depended. The Maya people were as much in thrall to the mighty thunderclouds of summer as the Egyptians were to the annual rise and fall of the Nile.

A quarter of a century ago, before so much had been mindlessly leveled by lumbering and for cattle farming, a dense rainforest covered much of the southern part of the Maya lowlands, where annual rainfall is heavy. As one moves north over the Yucatán plain, conditions are drier, and the forest cover becomes low and scrubby, the trees usually dropping their leaves in the height of the dry season. In the midst of this tropical forest are extensive patches of grassy savannas, often burned deliberately by the Maya to encourage game like deer, which come to nibble on the young shoots pushing up in the ashes. For many centuries, Maya maize farmers, like farmers throughout the world's hot lands, have coped with the forest, paradoxically, by temporarily destroying it. The Maya peasant will select a forest plot during the dry season and fell it – using steel tools like the machete today, but in the past employing only axes of chipped and ground stone. In late April or May, when daytime temperatures are at their almost unbearable maximum, he (and they are invariably men) will fire the now desiccated fallen trees and brush; the sky turns a dusky yellow with the smoke from thousands of such fires, and the sun becomes a dull orange ball. Then, just before the rains come, he takes his digging stick and gourd seed container, and plants his maize, beans, and other cultigens in holes made through the ash layer. With luck and according to the benevolence of "Father Chac," the rains will come, and the seeds will sprout.

Our farmer can plant again using the same plot, or *milpa*, but in the space of only a few years the fertility of the soil begins to decline (maize is a hard taskmaster), and weeds crowd out the young corn plants. It is time to abandon this plot, and clear a new one. This kind of shifting cultivation, or "milpa agriculture," is dominant today wherever lowland farmers are found, and for over a century archaeologists have thought that this was the only kind of farming the Maya knew. If so, then lowland populations could never have been very large, for it requires a great deal of land to support a farming family.

But thanks to modern aerial reconnaissance and space-age remote sensing techniques, we now know of a far more intensive use of the land, practiced even before the beginning of the Christian era.[7] Called "raised field agriculture," it involved the cultivation of otherwise useless lowland swamps, by draining them with canals. Along and in back of the canals, rectangular raised plots were laid out, providing permanent gardens kept moist year-round by capillary action raising water to the surface from the adjacent canals. In those areas favorable to such techniques, crop yields were surely far higher than in the case of milpa agriculture, and settlement could be very stable as the same plots could be used indefinitely. All this changes the formula: ancient Maya population densities were probably not light at all, but very high.

What did they then grow and eat? All lines of evidence point to the overwhelming importance of maize, which according to fossil pollen evidence has been in the lowlands at least since 3000 BC, and from which the Maya on all social levels derived the bulk of their sustenance. This is what I was taught at Harvard in the 1950s, but about twenty years ago it became the fashion for bright graduate students to pooh-pooh corn as the Maya staple, making unsubstantiated claims that the ancient Maya relied more on breadnuts (eaten today only as a last resort in case of starvation) and on various root crops. I never accepted this, nor did some of my more conservative colleagues, and I am delighted that the very latest in chemical tests – the measurement of stable carbon isotope ratios in archaeological bones from the small Classic Maya city of Altún Ha, in Belize – show conclusively that the city's inhabitants ate mostly maize.[8]

Small wonder, then, that the youthful Maize God, along with Chac, is ubiquitous in Maya iconography, not only in the surviving books, but in the sculpture of great cities such as Copán and on funerary pottery. No one has yet come across a god of the breadnut tree, let alone a deity of root crops.

The Maya diet was rich in plant foods: maize taken in the form of tamales, and perhaps tortillas (although there is not much evidence for these from Classic times); beans, squashes and pumpkins; chili peppers; and tomatoes; along with a host of other cultigens and wild plants. Since the only domesticated animals were the dog (used for food as well as in hunting), the turkey, and the stingless bee, game such as deer, pacas, peccaries, wild birds, and fish played an important role in the cuisine.

Although often visually expressed in the most imaginative and even weird form, the world of nature in the Maya lowlands enters into almost every aspect of Maya religious and civil iconography. The jaguar, largest of the world's spotted cats, was literally "the king of the jungle," dangerous to humans, and yet, like us, at the top of its own particular food chain. Its pelt was the very symbol of royalty, and Maya dynasts were proud to claim affinity with that dread carnivore; at the same time, being a night hunter, the jaguar was intimately associated with Xibalbá, the Maya Underworld.

But a host of other life forms also permeated Maya culture: among them were the chattering spider monkeys and noisy howler monkeys, moving in black troops through the canopy layer of the forests; scarlet macaws in flashing red, blue, and yellow; and the quetzal, an inhabitant of the cloud forests to the south of the Petén, whose iridescent, green-gold tailfeathers were prized for royal headdresses and backracks. The reptile world was omnipresent, represented by crocodiles and caimans, denizens of the sluggish river systems; by iguanas; and by snakes like the boa constrictor and the venomous fer-de-lance.

Mayanists, in their enthusiasm for their subject, are apt to forget that the culture they are studying was part of a more widespread pattern or way of life that is called "Mesoamerican." Broadly defined, Mesoamerica comprises that part of Mexico and adjacent Central America which was civilized at the time of the Spanish Conquest. It includes most of central, southern, and southeastern Mexico (and encompasses the Yucatán Peninsula), Guatemala, Belize, and the westernmost portions of Honduras and El Salvador. Within its borders, many tongues were and are spoken, including of course languages of the Mayan family, and just about every kind of environment can be found: deserts, snow-capped volcanoes, temperate valleys, tropical lowlands, mangrove swamps, etc.

Yet within this babble of tongues and varied landscape, certain cultural traits are held in common. All of these people were farmers, cultivating corn, beans, squashes, and chili peppers; all lived in villages, towns, and cities, and traded in large and complex markets; all had books (although only the Zapotec of Oaxaca, the Maya, and perhaps the people of Veracruz had true writing). Perhaps most importantly, all had a pantheistic religion which, while not uniform everywhere, had significant elements in common, such as a sacred calendar based on a cycle of 260 days, and the belief that it was absolutely necessary to shed human blood – either one's own or that of captives – in honor of the gods and ancestors.

At one end of the Mesoamerican time-span stand the Aztec and their mighty empire, best known of all since their civilization was destroyed – and recorded – by the Spanish conquistadors. The language of their empire (which impinged upon, but never included the Maya) was Nahuatl, an agglutinating tongue blessedly free of the complexities which make the Mayan languages so difficult; this was the lingua franca of most of non-Maya Mesoamerica, used by traders and bureaucrats alike.

So what is at the other end, the earlier part, of the time-span? Archaeology has gone a long way to answer this question, but it is first necessary to show how this time-frame has been separated into manageable segments by archaeologists. Here is the generally accepted scheme (based in part on radiocarbon dating and in part on the Maya calendar):

Paleo-Indian Period, 20,000?–8000 BC
In this remote age (the Late Pleistocene or Ice Age), hunters and gatherers of Siberian origin colonized the New World and Mesoamerica. Large game animals such as mammoths and wild horses roamed the continent.

Archaic Period, 8000–2000 BC
Within Mesoamerica, small bands of Indians began to turn to the planting of plant seeds, rather than their mere collection. Cultural selection resulted in the domestication of almost all the food plants, above all maize; and this led to the establishment of the first permanent villages by the close of the Archaic, along with the arts of sedentary life such as pottery and loom weaving.

Pre-Classic (or Formative) Period, 2000 BC–AD *250*
At one time thought to be a kind of New World "Neolithic" with the spread everywhere of peasant villages and simple fertility cults based in female clay figurines, we now know that Mesoamerican

civilization first took root in this time-frame, initially with the Olmec, and later with the Zapotec and Maya.

Classic Period, A D 250–900
Supposedly the Golden Age of Mesoamerican culture, dominated by the great city of Teotihuacan in the central Mexican plateau, and by the Maya cities in the southeast. In fact, it can best be defined as that period during which the Maya were carving and erecting monuments dated in their Long Count system.

Post-Classic Period, A D 900–1521
A purportedly militaristic epoch which followed upon the downfall of Classic Maya civilization, marked by the overlordship of the Toltec until about 1200, and later by the Aztec Empire, which covered almost all of extra-Maya Mesoamerica. The Post-Classic cultures were, of course, extinguished by the Spaniards.

Exactly when the Maya highlands and lowlands were first occupied is as yet unknown, but small camp sites of early hunters have been found in the mountain valleys of Guatemala, and Archaic settlements are scattered across Belize (and probably would be discovered throughout the lowlands, if one knew what to look for).[9] Since chipped-stone tools don't talk, there is no way to be sure whether these people were Mayan-speakers or not, but they may have been. Certainly by 1000 B C, when burgeoning populations dwelling in sedentary villages and even towns were spread throughout, some form of *ur*-Mayan must have extended throughout the Maya area.

The origins of Classic Maya civilization must be sought in the Pre-Classic. Since the early part of this century, Maya archaeologists – a jingoistic lot – have taken a totally Mayacentric view of Mesoamerican culture history: it was "their" beloved Maya who first domesticated corn, who invented the Mesoamerican calendar, who gave the light of civilization to everyone else. One might compare this to the terracentric, pre-Copernican view of the Solar System. In this case, the iconoclastic role of Copernicus and Galileo was taken by the pioneers of Olmec archaeology, such as the Smithsonian Institution's Matthew Stirling, and the Mexican artist-archaeologist Miguel Covarrubias. In the 1930s and 1940s they found, buried in the coastal plain of Veracruz and Tabasco in Mexico, a far earlier civilization, capable of carving and moving multi-ton colossal heads (portraits of their rulers), of fashioning magnificent figurines, masks, and plaques of blue-green jade, and even, late in the Olmec development, of writing and the "Maya" calendar.[10]

When the very first reports of this venerable culture were published, the reaction of the Mayanist community varied from frosty to downright hostile. The attack on the claimed antiquity of Olmec culture was led by Eric Thompson, the formidable British-born "brains" of the Carnegie Institution of Washington's Maya program.[11] We will be hearing more about him later.

However, to the consternation of the "Maya buffs" (Matt Stirling's phrase), the radiocarbon dates on Olmec sites like La Venta showed that the Olmec were even older than Stirling and his colleagues had surmised: at really ancient centers like San Lorenzo, a huge site that I excavated in the 1960s, Olmec culture, complete with massive stone monuments and pyramid-building, was in full flower by 1200 BC, about a millennium before anything that could be called civilization had arisen in the tropical forests of the Maya lowlands.[12] Although the Maya buffs are still fighting a rearguard action, most Mesoamericanists have little doubt that the Olmec – with their strange art style, pantheistic religion focussing on were-jaguars and other composite creatures, and ceremonial building programs – were the first to put together what we know of as Mesoamerican culture.

The Olmec (a name, by the way, given them by archaeologists – we don't know what they called themselves) were not alone as culture-builders during the middle part of the Pre-Classic. By about 600 BC, in and near Monte Albán, a hilltop redoubt-city in the Valley of Oaxaca, Zapotec rulers began to erect monuments celebrating victories over rival chiefdoms; these not only showed their unfortunate captives after torture and sacrifice, but they recorded the name of the dead chief, the name of his polity, and the date on which the victory (or sacrifice) had occurred.[13] Thus, it was the Zapotec, and not the Maya or Olmec, who invented writing in Mesoamerica.

A word here about the dating system used at Monte Albán and subsequently throughout southeastern Mesoamerica. The basis of this calendar was the sacred count of 260 days, the result of the never-ending permutation of 13 numbers with a rigid sequence of 20 named days. Bars and dots are used for the numbers, a dot standing for "one" and a bar for "five" (thus, the number "six" would be a bar and a dot, "thirteen" two bars and three dots). There are many speculations about the origin of such a period (it approximates the nine months of human gestation, for instance[14]), but one can visit Maya villages today in the Guatemalan highlands where the calendar priests can still give one the correct day in the 260-day count – it has not slipped one day in over twenty-five centuries. Now, run this count against the 365 days of the solar year, and one will get the 52-year Calendar Round, the Mesoamerican equivalent of our century.

Somehow or other, the Calendar Round was diffused down from the Zapotec-speaking highlands to the late Olmec of the Gulf Coast and

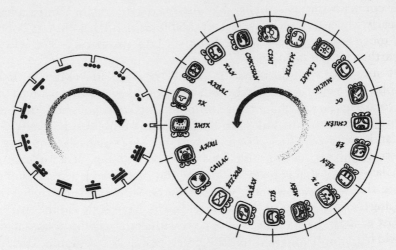

15 *The Maya 260-day count, in which 13 numbers intermesh with 20
named days.*

among peoples on the western and southwestern fringes of the Maya realm.[15] Within that broad arc, an even more extraordinary development took place in the last century before Christ, near the end of the Pre-Classic. This was the appearance of that most typical of all Maya traits, the Long Count calendar, among peoples for whom Maya was probably (at best) a foreign language. Unlike dates in the Calendar Round, which are fixed only within a never-ending cycle of 52 years and thus recur once every 52 years, Long Count dates are given in a day-to-day count, which began in the year 3114 BC, and which will end (perhaps with a bang!) in AD 2012.

In the wake of the Olmec civilization, which had declined to the point of unrecognizability after the fifth century BC, a host of chiefdoms sprang up on the Pacific coastal plain of Chiapas and Guatemala, and in the area to the west of Guatemala City, all of which were honoring their rulers and gods by erecting flat stone monuments (which archaeologists call stelae) fronted by round or animal-shaped "altars." The complicated, narrative art style which appears on these stones is called "Izapan," after the huge site of Izapa, lying near the Chiapas-Guatemala border. What is important is that some of these chiefdoms had a form of writing (largely unreadable), and some were eventually fixing important events not only with Calendar Round dates, but with the Long Count.

Eventually, according to our still sketchy archaeological information, the lowland Maya of the Petén and Yucatán forests adopted this highly non-egalitarian way of life, so that by the time of Christ there were towns and even cities ruled by royal dynasties all over the region. In contrast to their contemporaries in the highlands and on the Pacific coastal plain, the early Maya architects had an inexhaustible supply of limestone and lime mortar to work with, so that stone architecture was the rule: instead of earthen mounds topped by perishable, thatched superstructures, great masonry temple-pyramids rose to the sky, supporting upper temples of limestone containing narrow rooms built on the principle of the corbel arch.

The full extent of these Late Pre-Classic building programs in the lowlands will never be known, since in any particular Maya site early constructions are usually covered over with towering constructions of the Classic period. Archaeologists have been lucky in finding a few sites where there is little or no Classic occupation, and luckiest of all in locating the vast city of El Mirador, in the northernmost Petén, which is almost entirely Late Pre-Classic.[16] This behemoth of the ancient New World has temple-pyramids which reach a height of over seventy meters above the jungle floor, with massive architectural groups connected by causeways. All of these constructions were coated with white plaster and painted, usually a deep red; and here, as at other Late Pre-Classic sites, gigantic stucco masks of great Maya gods (above all, the malevolent bird-deity known to the later Quiché Maya as Vucub Caquix) flank the stairways that reach the summits of the pyramids.[17]

In effect, the more we learn about the Late Pre-Classic in the Maya lowlands, the more "Classic" it seems. When, then, does the Classic begin? Completely arbitrarily, we begin it with the very first Maya monument bearing a contemporary (not a retrospective) Long Count date. This is a broken limestone stela found by the University of Pennsylvania project at Tikal, in the heart of the Petén. On one side is a richly bedecked Maya ruler, literally festooned with jade ornaments, while on the other is a Long Count date corresponding to a day in the year AD 292.[18] Twenty-two years later, a subsequent Tikal dynast appears on the Leyden Plate, a jade plaque found in a Late Post-Classic context in a mound near the Caribbean coast. We now know that this records the ruler's accession to the throne, and quite typically he is depicted trampling a sorry-looking captive – a theme that will be repeated over and over among the warlike Classic Maya.

Even if we round off the date for the opening of the Classic to AD 250, it now looks as if many of the elements that made up Classic Maya civilization are already present by then: cities of limestone masonry ruled over by an elite class, carved stone monuments celebrating the doings of the rulers, lavish royal tombs underneath temple substruc-tures, at least some elements of the calendar (especially the 52-year Calendar Round), extensive trade in luxury goods, and most important of all (from our point of view), writing.

Let us jump ahead and assume (rightly) that most Classic Maya inscriptions can now be read; how this came about will be the subject of future chapters. I suppose this is once again putting the cart before the horse, but it enables us to make sense out of what decades of intensive and extensive archaeological research in the Maya lowlands have produced.

Classic Maya civilization flourished for about six centuries, in Old World terms roughly from the reign of the Roman emperor Diocletian, that formidable producer of Christian martyrs, to King Alfred of Wessex, defeater of Danes. The Prophet Mohammed was contemporary with the transition from the Maya Early to Late Classic; when he fled from Mecca to Medina, marking the start of the Islamic Era, the great Maya ruler of Palenque, Pacal or "Shield," had been on the throne for eight years.

Unlike the empires of the Old World, there never was any imperial organization or overall hegemony of one city over the rest among the Classic Maya. Rather, the lowlands were organized into a series of small city-states – at least twenty-five of them in the eighth century, during the Classic apogee. The distance from any particular capital to its frontier with another state would seldom be more than a day's walk. Some cities were bigger than others, and certainly had more influence over the development of Maya culture: certainly Tikal, a giant among Maya centers, Copán in the east, Palenque in the west, and Calakmul to the north of the Petén were in this category; and so probably were the very late cities of Uxmal and Chichén Itzá in the northern Yucatán Peninsula.

Accurate censuses are a product of the modern Western world and the Ottoman Empire; we certainly have none for the Classic Maya. It is for that reason that we must take all population estimates for their cities with a large grain of salt. Very conveniently for today's archaeologists, the Classic Maya built their thatched-roof houses on low mounds of earth and masonry, and these can be mapped and counted; having accomplished that, you have to decide how many people might have lived in such a house, and how many of them were occupied at any one time in a given city. "Guesstimates" of how many people lived in Tikal thus vary wildly, all the way from eleven thousand to forty thousand – probably the latter is closest to the mark, given the current evidence for intensification of agriculture in some parts of the Maya area as seen in raised fields.[19]

As for the total Maya population in the lowlands, that cannot even be guessed at. Certainly there were many millions, but it should be kept in mind that there were extensive areas with no good arable land, such as high mountains (in southern Belize) and grassy savannas; the deep, rich, black soils favored by the Maya in the Petén just are not found everywhere, and in the northernmost part of the peninsula soils are so thin and rocky, and the vegetation so scrubby, that the economy there must have depended not upon farming but upon activities like salt-making, bee-keeping and trade.

Classic capital cities can be recognized not only by their sheer size, but also because only these seemed to have almost exclusive rights to publicly displayed, monumental inscriptions, such as carved stelae, so-called "altars" (in fact, probably thrones), and lintels. These were usually associated with specific buildings within the cities, and often (as at Piedras Negras on the Usumacinta River), the stelae were lined up in a single row before a temple-pyramid. As among the pharaohs of Egypt, the hereditary rulers and their families and ancestors were celebrated in these inscriptions and in the relief pictures described by the associated texts. These were no primitive democracies or nascent chiefdoms: the royal family and the nobility were the aristocratic patrons of artists, scribes, and architects alike, whose only goal was to glorify the gods and the ruling house.

Reflecting their highly stratified society, there was a whole hierarchy of cities, towns, and villages among the Classic Maya. Biggest of all were the giants like Tikal, Naranjo, Seibal, Palenque, Yaxchilán, Copán, Uxmal, and Cobá. Somewhat lower down were smaller centers like Dos Pilas, Uaxactún, Caracol, and Quiriguá, which still, according to what their monuments say, maintained a more-or-less independent political life – although Uaxactún was beaten in war by its neighbor to the south, Tikal. But lesser centers sometimes bested larger ones: little Dos Pilas clobbered Seibal at one point, and Caracol overwhelmed Naranjo and even Tikal.[20]

Notwithstanding the pious claims of a past generation of archaeologists, blood and gore were the rule not the exception among the city-states of the lowlands.[21] The stelae and lintels of many sites record the victories of great kings and their companions-in-arms. One of the favorite themes of Classic Maya reliefs is the stripping, binding, and trampling of important captives, for whom sacrifice by decapitation (probably after lengthy torture) was the sure outcome. The marvelous late eighth-century murals of Bonampak, a site in the Usumacinta drainage discovered by a pair of American adventurers in 1946, show an actual Maya battle in progress: it was fought in the jungle between spear-wielding warriors, with the victorious king in jaguar-skin battle-jacket taking his noble prisoner.[22] It must have been a very noisy affair, indeed, as the long, wooden war trumpets sounded above the usual whistling and shouting which we know from Spanish accounts were typical of Maya hostilities. In other rooms at Bonampak, the unlucky prisoners are tortured under the direction of the king, an heir-apparent to the throne is presented, and, finally, the king and his nobles in their great quetzal-feathered headdresses and backracks whirl in a victorious sacrificial dance.

Among the Classic cities, Tikal is probably the best known and most completely studied.[23] Founded well before the beginning of the Christian era, this enormous center was always conservative and even stodgy among its more innovating contemporaries, rather more like Philadelphia or Boston than New York or Chicago. Residential units (three or four house mounds centered on a little plaza) are scattered over an area of some sixty square kilometers (thirty-two square miles); nowhere in the city can streets or avenues be detected, or anything resembling a grid pattern. As one gets closer to the "ceremonial center" of Tikal, these residences become grander, and some must have served as palaces for nobility and royal retainers.

So high are the six temple-pyramids of Tikal that they now project far above the tall forest canopy. Each rises in a series of terraces, and is fronted by a stairway of vertiginous steepness. At the top is a masonry temple topped by a roof comb, a soaring, non-functional construction meant to emphasize the heaven-reaching properties of the temple. The rooms within are narrow indeed, mere corbel-vaulted slots, but the doorways of the outer rooms have fine, sapodilla-wood lintels carved with enthroned or standing Maya rulers.

I have read in many books that the Maya pyramids were nothing like the Egyptian ones in that they weren't used for royal tombs. That this is sheer, unfounded nonsense has been shown again and again, most of all by the clandestine tomb robbers who have been supplying the pre-Columbian art market with fine Classic vases and jades for many years now. Archaeologists are slow learners! At any rate, during the University of Pennsylvania excavations at Tikal back in the early 1960s, the most splendid royal tomb was found at ground level inside Temple I, which dominates the Great Plaza of Tikal, and it can be proved that this temple, and probably most others like it in the Maya lowlands, were built to house the remains of dynastic leaders. Cheops would have felt right at home.[24]

Although some specialists think that the extensive architectural complexes called "palaces" were just that, some are not so sure. The Central Acropolis at Tikal has a number of such multi-roomed, range-like buildings, and speculations on their function have varied from royal residences, to lineage temples, to theological seminaries.[25] They may even have been all of these.

Few Maya cities in the southern lowlands lacked ball courts. Rubber – the cured sap of the Castilloa elastica tree – was a Mesoamerican invention, one of the many gifts of the New World to the Old, and was used mainly for rubber balls (these astonished the conquistadors when they saw them bouncing around Aztec courts – in fact, Cortés was so impressed that he took a troop of ballplayers to Spain to show them off to Charles V). The game was played throughout Mesoamerica in masonry courts, the main playing surface being confined between two parallel walls with sloping batters. The rules, which are not well understood, were strict about what part of the body could be used to propel the ball; hips were favored, but the flat of the hand was *verboten*.[26]

The more we learn about the Classic Maya ball game, the more sinister it becomes. In Tikal as elsewhere in the Maya realm, major captives were forced to play a no-win game against the ruler and his team, with eventual loss and preordained human sacrifice as the outcome.

Situated far from the rivers or streams, Tikal like other cities of the northern Petén had a perpetual water problem, and the rulers were forced to build enormous reservoirs; there are ten of these in the central part of the city, and these tided the population over the long dry season. Seasoned explorers will tell you that it is entirely possible to die of thirst in the jungle.

Since it is now possible to read most of the public inscriptions of Tikal, it is also possible to get some idea of the major ceremonial events witnessed by thousands upon thousands of Maya spectators. But we can never reconstruct, even in our imaginations, the full sweep of ancient pageantry: the sounds of the wooden and conch-shell trumpets, the drums and rattles, the massed choruses, the clouds of incense, the gorgeous multi-colored costumes and masks of the participants and the sweeping quetzal plumes in their shining blue-green and gold colors. The major transition points in a royal life were marked by the pomp and ceremony accompanying rites of passage – his birth, his presentation as heir-apparent, his accession to the throne, his marriage, and his death (I say "his," as almost all known Maya rulers were men). Every victory called for an elaborate ceremony, followed sooner or later by the protracted and elaborate sacrifice of the defeated, usually by beheading.

Much of this was calendrically and astrologically controlled, and the astronomers and scribes played a major role in setting the dates for at least some of these events. The completion of certain cycles in the Long Count called for major celebrations and the ritual shedding of their own blood by the ruler and his wives, and so did important anniversaries or jubilees of important red-letter dates such as the taking on of the rulership (again, I am reminded of an analagous practice among the ancient Egyptians). At Tikal, the major temple-pyramid complexes are linked by broad causeways, and one can conjure up brilliant processions over them of royalty, nobles, courtiers, and musicians headed towards these mausoleums sacred to the memory of past rulers.

Death and ancestor-worship were deeply ingrained into the culture of the Maya elite who ran city-states like Tikal. The deceased ruler was buried with enormous pomp on a special litter, and a great pyramid erected to house his funeral chamber.[27] Accompanying him were offerings of food and drink contained in pottery vessels painted or carved with Underworld scenes of the most macabre nature, jade and marine-shell jewelry, and prized animals like jaguars and crocodiles. For reasons that will become clear in later chapters, we conclude that the Maya believed that their noble dead were really immortal, to be resurrected as gods and worshipped in perpetuity by their royal descendants. Death for the elite was tantamount to a recycling of the royal essence.

I have taken Tikal as my typical Classic Maya city, but each one was as different in its own way as Sparta was different from Athens in Classical Greece. What is important to remember is that all this civilization was created with a technology which really was on a Stone Age level. Metal tools were unknown in any part of Mesoamerica until copper and gold metallurgy was introduced from northwestern South America shortly before AD 900, by which time the Classic was over. Our own technology, of which we are so proud, has done little more for the Maya area than destroy it; without any of the scientific wonders of the modern world, the Maya fashioned a sophisticated and learned civilization in the midst of a jungle.

Maya civilization, which reached its peak of achievement in the eighth century, must have contained the seeds of its own downfall. While speculations about the *why* of the Classic Maya collapse are plentiful, there are pitifully few facts.[28] As early as the final decade of the eighth century, a few cities no longer put up carved monuments with Long Count dates, and may well have been at least partially abandoned. In the ninth century, however, failures of this kind began to multiply, and regime after regime crumbled almost like modern business firms going into bankruptcy after a stock market crash. The little heir-apparent whose rites are celebrated in the Bonampak murals, painted around AD 790, may never have acceded to the throne, as the political life of the city was shortly to disappear. Palenque, Yaxchilán, and Piedras Negras were finished as great centers about the same time as Bonampak, as was Quiriguá in the southeast.

The record speaks for itself. Here are some dates for the last known dynastic monuments:

Copán	820	Caracol	859	Uaxactún	889
Naranjo	849	Tikal	879		

Writing books and articles on the supposed causes of the collapse is a growth industry among Mayanists. All sorts of hypotheses have been proposed, many of them postulating some kind of agricultural debacle – past scholars have thought this resulted from soil depletion through overuse of the land, or from climatic deterioration, and so forth. Granting that the topic is a good one for term papers, in the almost total absence of data there is little agreement on what might have caused this immense and certainly tragic demise of one of the world's few tropical forest civilizations.

We all know about the barbarians at the gates of Rome as that great empire crumbled. Not surprisingly, there is evidence for this kind of thing among the Maya. In AD 889, at the enormous city of Seibal on the Pasión River, four stelae were put up around a very non-Maya four-sided temple.[29] Three of these stelae show powerful leaders with foreign-looking visage adorned with moustaches, a rare trait among the Classic Maya elite. At the same time, Seibal was being inundated with a kind of orange pottery known to have been manufactured in the lower reaches of the Usumacinta, on the hot, swampy plain of the Gulf Coast. That was the realm of the Putún Maya, a Chontal-speaking people who in Post-Classic times were the great seagoing traders of Mesoamerica, with a hybrid Mexican-Maya culture.[30]

Perhaps the Putún presence at Seibal – in fact, their invasion of the southern lowlands – was the result, rather than the cause, of the Maya collapse, as they took over trade routes abandoned by the *anciens régimes* of the Classic cities. The Putún may have had a great deal to do with the flourishing of the northern cities of the Peninsula both during and after the collapse. The magnificent "Puuc-style" architecture of such centers as Uxmal, Kabah, and Chichén Itzá in Yucatán persisted through the tenth century, as did hieroglyphic writing on public monuments.

Be that as it may, all of the southern lowland cities had ceased to function in any meaningful way after AD 900, and while peasant squatters continued to occupy some of them, much of this vast area reverted to the jungle. The cultural cataclysm was as profound as the physical. When the Maya elite who had ruled these centers disappeared, so did most of their knowledge and traditions. These had been in the hands of the scribes, who as scions of the royal houses may well have been slaughtered along with their patrons. Yes, I (like Eric Thompson before me) believe that revolutions swept the region, although I will admit that hard evidence for this is difficult to find. "The Revolution has no use for scientists" said the tribunal which consigned Lavoisier, founder of modern chemistry, to the guillotine in 1794. I can imagine equally unwanted scribes and astronomers being killed, and thousands of books being destroyed. We know that they *had* books, since they are often shown in Classic art, and traces of them have been found in Maya tombs, but not one Classic book has come down to us today through those twin cataclysms: the Classic collapse and the Spanish Conquest. Dealing with the period between the collapse and the arrival of the Spaniards is frustrating – on the one hand, there are rich historical sources on these centuries which come to us from post-Conquest Spanish and native writers, but on the other, these are often extremely equivocal and difficult to make sense of. The greatest source of confusion, at least for the Maya lowlands, is that dates for events are no longer given in the day-to-day Long Count, but in a truncated and repetitive version known as the Short Count. This is rather as if in a thousand years from now a historian knew only that the American Revolution had begun in '76, without knowing exactly which century was being talked about. Scholars can play ducks and drakes with data expressed in such a chronological framework, and so they have.

Notwithstanding the fact that all four known Maya codices come from this period, I don't intend to spend much time on the Post-Classic, as Maya inscriptions are virtually unknown for this time-span. The Post-Classic Maya world is a very different place, indeed.

The first part of the Post-Classic story begins with Chichén Itzá in north-central Yucatán, a city founded in the Late Classic. The name means "Mouth of the Well of the Itzá," so-called from its famous Well of Sacrifice, a huge, circular cenote or limestone sinkhole into which many captives were hurled on the eve of the Conquest. Mayanists are still fighting about the dating, and even the direction of culture flow, but my own admittedly conservative opinion is that strong influence from the highlands of central Mexico arrived there as a result of a foreign invasion in the latter part of the tenth century. At this point, Chichén Itzá became the capital of the entire Peninsula, with a substantial part of the native Maya population concentrated within sight of its Castillo, the great four-sided pyramid that dominates the Post-Classic city.

Who were the invaders, and whence did they come? According to Aztec historians, the mighty Aztecs themselves had been preceded in central Mexico by a great people of immense culture whom they knew as the Toltec, ruling from their capital Tollan ("Place of the Reeds"), or, as the Spaniards called it, Tula. Thanks to a succession of Mexican and American archaeological expeditions, the Toltec city has been found and excavated.[31] Located some seventy kilometers (forty-two miles) northwest of Mexico City, it is not very prepossessing; dominated by a pyramid with a temple roof held up by huge, stone figures of grim-looking Toltec warriors, its style of art and architecture can also be detected at Chichén Itzá. There, in far-off Yucatán, specifically Toltec traits derived from Tula can be detected, such as the reclining figures called "chacmools" by archaeologists, and reliefs of prowling jaguars and eagles eating hearts.

Our Aztec sources tell us that Tula was ruled by a god-man calling himself Quetzalcoatl, or "Feathered Serpent," and our Maya sources speak of the arrival from over the water of a warrior-king called Kukulcán – also meaning "Feathered Serpent." Some revisionist Maya scholars want to see Tula as derived from Chichén, rather than the other way around, but I find this difficult to swallow. No one can deny that Toltec Chichén was splendid, with its Temple of the Warriors, Great Ball Court (the largest in Mesoamerica), and Castillo, in comparison to the somewhat shoddy Tula; but keep in mind that Mongol Beijing was far more magnificent than the felt yurts from which Genghiz Khan's hordes had started out, and Fatih Mehmet's Ottoman towns were no match in opulence for the Constantinople which he conquered in 1453.

A truly thorny problem is that of the Itzá. They show up in the annals of Yucatán – the quasi-historical and semi-prophetic Books of Chilam Balam – as distrusted, somewhat lewd foreigners who had wandered like a band of troubadours all over the Peninsula. It is reasonable to suppose that they also were Putún Maya, with a good overlay of Mexican culture. Some place them at Chichén in the early thirteenth century, and they at least gave their name to this venerable city, perhaps undeservedly; at any rate, it is fairly well documented that in the latter part of the century, the Itzá founded Mayapán, a walled town in the scrubby jungle southeast of Mérida, from which they dominated most of the northern lowlands for almost two centuries.[32]

Mayapán itself is a wretchedly built little capital, dominated by a runty, four-sided pyramid imitating the Castillo of Chichén Itzá. According to the histories, it was ruled by the Cocom family; to guarantee a steady flow of tribute, these warlords held the leading families of the rest of Yucatán as hostages within Mayapán's walls. This was the so-called "League of Mayapán" which once gripped historian Oswald Spengler, of all people, author of *The Decline of the West*. But the Cocom themselves were eventually overthrown, and Mayapán reverted to tick-infested scrub.

When the first Spanish explorers touched upon the coast of Yucatán in 1517, the Peninsula was divided into sixteen "city-states," each striving to establish its boundaries at the expense of neighbors and thus often in a state of war with each other. Not so long ago, this was thought to be an example of sociopolitical degeneration from what old-time archaeologists like Sylvanus Morley had thought of as the "Old Empire" of Classic times. But we now know that this pattern was in reality typical of the Maya throughout their long history. There never was an "Old Empire," or a "New" one either, for that matter. The overall hegemony which had been attained first by Chichén Itzá and then by Mayapán was a total anomaly.

Each of these "city-states" at the time of the Conquest was headed by a ruler called the *halach uinic* or "true man," an office passed down in the male line. He resided in the capital town, and ruled the provincial towns through nobles called *batabo'ob* (singular *batab*), heads of noble patrilineages related to that of the *halach uinic*. The *halach uinic* was the war leader, and under him was an elite group of braves called the *holcano'ob*, whom the invading Spaniards had every reason to fear. The priesthood was enormously influential, as much of the lives of these Maya was ruled by religion and the exigencies of the calendar; especially important was the chief priest, the *Ah Kin* ("He of the Sun"). Among the duties of the priests were to keep the books and the calendar, regulate the festivals and the New Year celebrations, conduct baptisms, and officiate at sacrifices (both human and animal).

The Spanish sources, including Bishop Landa who has given us the fullest account of Maya life on the eve of the Conquest, describe Yucatán as a prosperous land. The people were divided between nobility, the freemen of the soil, who did all the farming, hunting, bee-keeping, and the like, and the slaves. The last group seem to have had little economic importance, and slavery in the Greco-Roman or antebellum plantation sense was unknown in pre-Spanish Mesoamerica.

I have said little in this chapter about the Maya highlands of Chiapas and Guatemala, because they play little part in our story except during the late Pre-Classic, when for the only time in their history the highland Maya dynasties produced inscribed stone monuments. In the fifth century AD they fell under the sway of the great city of Teotihuacan, that enormous metropolis to the northeast of Mexico City which seems to have had most of the Maya area under its control for almost a century and a half. At some time in the Post-Classic, Putún Maya swashbucklers, whose depredations in the lowlands are becoming better known as research continues, intruded into the highlands, replacing native Cakchiquel and Quiché Maya ruling lineages with their own dynasties. Other similar kingdoms were found among the Mam and Pokomam.[33]

The Quiché was the most powerful of these states, until smashed by that most horrible of all the conquistadors, the brutal Pedro de Alvarado. Perhaps the lasting glory of the Quiché is that they managed to preserve well into the colonial era (when it was written down using Spanish letters) the supreme Maya epic, known as the *Popol Vuh* or "Book of Counsel" – by any reckoning the greatest achievement of known native New World literature.[34] As we shall see, this has proved to be the key to some of the deepest and most esoteric secrets of Classic Maya culture.

3 A Jungle Civilization Rediscovered

The rediscovery of the Maya cities, buried for almost a millennium underneath the tropical forest canopy, was the product of Bourbon acuity and Bourbon stupidity. Charles III, who ruled Spain and its overseas dominions from 1759 until his death in 1788, is usually described both as an "enlightened despot" and as the greatest of the Bourbon kings. It was due to his sagacity and to his talent for administrative reform that the inexorable decline of Spain as a colonial power was at least temporarily reversed, although he had few successes on the international scene.

Other than hunting, his great passion was learning and science, and for the first time since the Conquest, the royal palace began to express a scientific interest in the peoples and natural setting of Spain's New World possessions. Charles is best remembered today for rendering the Inquisition ineffective and expelling the Jesuits from Spanish territory; but he definitely furthered knowledge in the best tradition of the eighteenth-century enlightenment. Unfortunately, he was followed by far more obdurate rulers, the kind of Bourbons for whom the saying was coined, "they learned nothing and they forgot nothing." The consequence of their policies was that Spain lost almost all of its Latin American colonies in the various independence movements that began around 1810 and culminated in 1821.

As the Spanish hold on countries like Mexico and Peru disappeared, scientific exploration by foreigners, hitherto excluded from Spanish possessions, became a reality, and a considerable amount of new information from men such as the German polymath Alexander von Humboldt was published in Europe and the young United States. The Bourbon loss was surely the world's gain.

But to return to Charles III's domains, and Central America as it was in the late eighteenth century. Until it was ceded to Mexico in 1824, Chiapas was part of Guatemala, which had been a Spanish province ever since its brutal conquest by Pedro de Alvarado. Rumors of the existence of a large, ruined city near the village of Palenque in Chiapas had been reaching the ears of Josef Estachería, President of Guatemala's Royal Audiencia, and in the year 1784 he ordered a report on it by a local official.[1] This failed to satisfy Estachería, so the next year he dispatched the royal architect in Guatemala City to conduct an investigation. This man had the temerity to return with an amateurish report and very poor drawings of what he had seen.

Finally, the exasperated Estachería selected a bright Spanish captain of dragoons, Antonio del Río, and a fairly competent artist named Ricardo Almendáriz, and ordered them to proceed to Palenque. It was not until 3 May 1787 that they reached the ruins, nestled in the foothills of the Sierra Madre de Chiapas just above the Gulf Coast plain, and covered by dense, high jungle. After rounding up a large contingent of local Chol Maya to clear the bush with axe and machete, del Río, at the end of their labors, stated "... there remained neither a window nor doorway blocked up," a claim which luckily for posterity was not entirely the case.

Acting under orders from Juan Bautista Muñoz (Charles III's royal historiographer) to Estachería, del Río made a collection of artifacts, including a magnificent relief-carved figure holding a waterlily plant which we now know was a leg of a throne in the Palace at Palenque. These were duly shipped from Guatemala to the *Gabinete Real de la Historia Natural* (Royal Collection of Natural History) in Madrid, not far from the Royal Palace.

In June 1787 del Río submitted his report on Palenque, along with the drawings by Almendáriz, to Estachería, who forwarded them to Madrid. Various copies were made of the drawings, and sets were deposited in suitable archives, but, as with many reports delivered to bureaucrats, that was the apparent end of the matter.[2]

The story then jumps to George IV's England of 1822, the year that Shelley died; on 2 November, in London, there appeared a volume entitled *Description of the Ruins of an Ancient City*.[3] This was none other than an English translation of del Río's report, accompanied by a long-winded, thoroughly amateurish essay by the deservedly forgotten Dr. Paul Felix Cabrera. Of lasting importance are its seventeen plates taken from one of the sets of Almendáriz drawings. At the bottom edge of nine of the drawings appear the initials of the engraver, "JFW," known to be the incredible, flamboyant Jean Frédéric Waldeck, to whom we shall return. As Maya scholar George Stuart says, these plates constitute "the very first published depictions of Maya writing carved on stone,"[4] and had a profound influence on both sides of the Atlantic, as did del Río's matter-of-fact and remarkably accurate prose account.

On the other edge of the southern Maya lowlands is the great, Classic city of Copán, in the western part of what is now Honduras. Knowledge

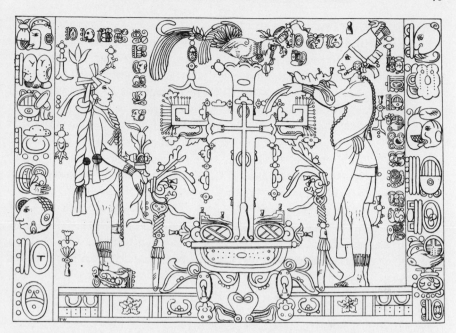

16 *Tablet of the Temple of the Cross, Palenque. Drawing by Almendáriz, engraved by Waldeck, in del Río, Description of an Ancient City.*

of its ruins had probably been preserved throughout the Colonial era, since there had always been Chortí Maya settlements in the rich Copán valley. Be that as it may, in 1834 the Liberal government of Guatemala sent the colorful Juan Galindo on an exploratory expedition to Copán.[5] Born in 1802 in Dublin, the son of an English actor and an Anglo-Irish mother, Galindo turned up in Central America in 1827, then two years later joined the invading Liberal army of General Morazán, creator of the Central American Confederation.

Appointed governor of the Petén, our adventurer took advantage of his situation by exploring Palenque in 1831, from which he concluded first of all that the local native Indians were descended from the people who had actually built Palenque, and secondly that Maya civilization had been superior to all others in the world. Published short notices by him on the subject completely ignored del Río's pioneering 1822 report.

Galindo went to Copán three years later. He drew up a report which was published in 1836 by the American Antiquarian Society (located in Worcester, Massachusetts, this was to be the only institution backing Maya research until the end of the century). Galindo's account of Copán is surprisingly good, but unhappily lacks illustrations. In it, he described the wonderful stelae and other monuments, including the four-sided stone that is now known as Altar Q – only recently recognized as a portrait gallery of the Copán royal lineage. In some respects, Galindo was ahead of his time: he believed that the writing on the monuments expressed the phonetics of the language, he decided that human sacrifices took place at certain temples (a remarkably modern viewpoint), and he gave detailed, accurate information on a tomb excavated by him, which had been exposed in the great section of the Acropolis cut away by the Copán River. And, most important to our story, he suggested, in spite of differences, the general similarity of Palenque and Copán – in architecture, sculpture, and even writing, which took the form of "square blocks containing faces and hands and other identical characters."

After these triumphs, it was downhill all the way for Galindo, as the Liberal regime in Central America collapsed and suffered defeat. He himself was murdered in 1840 by a group of Hondurans.

It would take a small encyclopedia, or perhaps a five-hour celluloid Hollywood epic, to do ample justice to the life and career of "Count" Jean Frédéric Maximilien Waldeck, the self-styled "first Americanist."[6] Even the feats of the beloved Baron Munchausen sometimes pale by comparison with Waldeck's. In his cutting Boston manner, the historian William H. Prescott once confided to Mme. Fanny Calderón de la Barca that Waldeck was a person who "talks so big and so dogmatically . . . that I have a soupçon that he is a good deal of a charlatan."[7]

Even Waldeck's exact place and date of birth are in doubt. He variously gave his birthplace as Paris, Prague, and Vienna, and while he was apparently a naturalized French citizen, at one time he carried a British passport. He claimed to have been born on 16 March 1766, which would have made him 109 years old on the date of his death, 29 April 1875 (the late Howard Cline, who produced a fascinating article on Waldeck, described this latter event as "apparently one of the few unequivocal facts about his career"[8]). Waldeck at one time attributed his longevity to an "annual dosage of horse-radish and lemon that he took in liberal quantities every spring"; it must have worked well, since it is said that at age eighty-four he fell in love with an English girl, married her, and fathered a son.

Like his fabled predecessor Munchausen, Waldeck was a name-dropper of stupendous proportions. He told his admirers that he had been on cordial terms with Marie Antoinette, Robespierre, George III, Beau Brummel, and Byron, and that he had studied art in Paris under David (his neoclassical style did, in fact, resemble David's). According to the Count (a noble rank impossible to document), he had been a soldier on Napoleon's Egyptian expedition of 1798, which fired his interest in archaeology.

What is for sure is that he prepared some of the plates for the 1822 del

Río report on Palenque, for the London publisher Henry Berthoud. Three years later, he was on his way to Mexico as a mining engineer, at which he was a failure. Stranded in that alien land, he turned his hand to a variety of trades to make ends meet, but became increasingly interested in the pre-Conquest past of Mexico.

Armed with what seemed like ample funds (these eventually gave out), Waldeck lived among the ruins of Palenque from May 1832 to July 1833, clearing the site and preparing drawings. The Count was miserable in his surroundings, for he could not abide the heat, humidity, and insects, of which there are an abundance at Palenque. He also clearly loathed Mexico and the Mexicans, from the President down to local campesinos; nor did he harbor tender feelings towards fellow archaeologists and explorers. Eventually he found new financial support from that eccentric Irishman, Lord Kingsborough, and went to Uxmal in Yucatán in 1834, producing further drawings and architectural reconstructions, some of them fanciful in the extreme.

By this time, the choleric Count was persona non grata in Mexico, and he found it expedient to remove himself to England and Paris, where he spent the rest of his long life (it has been claimed that he died from a stroke when he turned his head to look at a pretty girl passing by him at a sidewalk cafe, but this is also said to be apocryphal). As soon as he arrived in Paris, he got to work turning his drawings into lithographs, which were printed in 1838 in a luxurious folio volume entitled *Voyage pittoresque et archéologique dans ... Yucatán ... 1834 et 1836.*[9]

Unhappily, all of Waldeck's published work on the Maya is as untrustworthy as the tall stories he told. He had his own theory of Maya origins, one which he maintained until the end of his life, namely, that Maya civilization had been derived from the Chaldeans, Phoenicians, and especially the "Hindoos," and he felt it necessary to include elephants in his neoclassical renderings of the Palenque reliefs, not only in the subject matter but in the hieroglyphs as well. But both George Stuart and Claude Baudez, who have seen the original Waldeck working drawings in the Ayer Collection of the Newberry Library, Chicago, assure me that they are of high quality. In spite of that, one can put no credence in his finished lithographs, which have always been treated with disdain by Mayanists, and rightly so.

In July 1519, two years before the final assault on the Aztec capital of Mexico-Tenochtitlan, Hernan Cortés and his hard-bitten conquistadors gathered at a newly-founded town on the Veracruz coast to divide up their spoils.[10] These were considerable, for they included not only loot gathered by them from the coastal Maya and from the Totonac of the

Gulf Coast, but also some precious objects sent to them as a kind of bribe by the far-off Motecuhzoma the Younger, emperor of the Aztec. One-fifth of this booty – the Royal Fifth – was destined for Charles V in Spain, who had just been elected Holy Roman Emperor.

According to Francisco López de Gómara, Cortés' private secretary, the Royal Fifth included some books, folded like cloth, which contained "figures, which the Mexicans use for letters"; these were of little value in the eyes of the soldiers, he tells us, "as they did not understand them, they did not appreciate them."[11]

The Royal Fifth reached Spain safely, accompanied by a small contingent of native men and women who had been rescued from captivity and gory sacrifice at Cempoallan, capital of the Totonac. Traveling first to Seville, then to the royal court at Valladolid, and eventually to Brussels (where the metalwork was greatly admired by that former goldsmith Albrecht Dürer), the strange people and objects aroused the kind of interest that a landing of extraterrestrial aliens would today. In a letter to a friend in his native Italy, Giovanni Ruffo da Forlí, Papal Nuncio at the Spanish court, described the books in these terms:

I had forgotten to say that there were some paintings of less than a hand-span all together, that were folded and joined in the form of a book, [that being] unfolded, stretched out. In these little paintings there were figures and signs in the form of Arabic or Egyptian letters ... The Indians [these were the Totonac captives] could give no account of what they were.[12]

An even more observant eyewitness of the exotic items that had arrived at Valladolid was Ruffo's close friend, the Italian humanist Peter Martyr d'Anghiera, whose *The Decades of the New World* was the first great account of the lands newly discovered by the Spaniards, and of its inhabitants. Peter Martyr tells us that the books were made of the inner bark of a tree, that their pages were coated with plaster or something similar, that they could be folded up, and that the outer covers were wooden boards. Here is what he says about what was written on them:

The characters are very different from ours: dice, hooks, loops, strips, and other figures, written in a line as we do: they greatly resemble Egyptian forms. Between the lines are marked out figures of men and animals, principally of kings and magnates, by which one can believe that there are there written the deeds of each king's ancestors.[13]

Other topics written in the books, according to Peter Martyr, were "the laws, sacrifices, ceremonies, rites, astronomical annotations, and certain computations, and manners and times of planting."

There can now be no doubt that these books were Maya, for no other people of Mesoamerica had a writing system which looked anything like this or could record such things – the mathematical computations alone would be a sure clue that we were dealing with the Maya. Furthermore, the non-Maya scribes of Mexico generally wrote on screenfold books made out of deer hide rather than the bark-paper favored by the Maya.

I reconstruct the presence of these codices in Valladolid as follows. When Cortés left Cuba in February 1519, he crossed over the stormy Yucatán Channel from Cuba, and made landfall on the offshore island of Cozumel, where the frightened Maya took flight into the bush. Ransacking the houses deserted by the natives, the Spaniards came across "innumerable" books, among which must have been the items sent back in the Royal Fifth. Now, among the passengers arriving in Valladolid with the booty was Cortés' close ally Francisco de Montejo – the future conqueror of Yucatán – who had already learned a great deal about Maya life from his debriefing of one Gerónimo de Aguilar; this Aguilar had been a shipwrecked captive of a Yucatec Maya lord for eight years until his escape, and surely knew all about Maya writing. Finally, we know that Montejo was closely questioned while in Valladolid by the ever-curious Peter Martyr on all kinds of things.

What happened to these precious Maya books? One of them, at any rate, might just have ended up in Dresden. In 1739, Johann Christian Goetze, director of the Royal Library at the court of Saxony, in Dresden, purchased a strange book from a private collection in Vienna.[14] Cataloged by him in 1744, little notice was taken of it until 1796, when an odd but distinctly charming five-volume work appeared in Leipzig. This was the *Darstellung und Geschichte des Geschmacks der verzüglichsten Volker*, "Depiction and History of the Taste of Superior Peoples" by one Joseph Friedrich, Baron von Racknitz.[15] The baron worked in Dresden as a kind of polymath stage manager for whatever theatrical performance or other public event the Elector of Saxony wished to have put on, and even invented a chess-playing machine for his royal patron. His *Darstellung* is basically a cross-cultural work on interior decoration, with hand-colored depictions of rooms in all sorts of styles, from Pompeiian to "O-Tahitian."

When my late friend Philip Hofer showed me this curiosity in Harvard's Houghton Library in the early 1960s, I was immediately attracted to a plate showing a room in "the Mexican taste," for on its walls and ceiling were motifs taken directly from what we now know of as the Dresden Codex, the greatest of the four surviving Maya books: animal-headed gods and bar-and-dot numbers, and Maya serpents greet the spectator. I only wonder whether anyone two centuries ago had the temerity to build such a room!

While the eccentric von Racknitz has provided us with the first pictorial reference to the Dresden, his flight of fancy had no repercussions whatsoever in the scholarly world. That was not the case with the explorer Alexander von Humboldt, whose beautiful atlas, *Vues des Cordillères, et monuments des peuples indigènes de l'Amérique* appeared in 1810.[16] Among its sixty-nine magnificent plates was one showing, in absolutely exact detail, five pages from the Dresden Codex. This was not only the first publication, even in truncated form, of a Maya codex, but it marked the very first time that *any* Maya hieroglyphic text had been accurately presented. Admittedly, the pages are somewhat out of order (three of the five pages of the Venus tables are shown, but page 49, which should follow 48, is omitted), but at least here was something into which a scholar could get his teeth. It would still be another seventy years before anybody would make real sense out of the entire seventy-four-page manuscript.

During the first half of the nineteenth century, Americanist research was replete with eccentrics: the dead hand of the academy had yet to stifle the unbridled enthusiasms of a small band of amateurs in Europe and America. Among these was Edward King, Viscount Kingsborough, an Irish nobleman obsessed with the notion that the ancient Hebrews had populated the New World. To prove his point, he published his massive folio series, *The Antiquities of Mexico*.[17] Now these are not just "folio," but "elephant folio" – George Stuart says that each volume weighs between 20 and 40 pounds. Altogether there are nine of these, the last two issued in 1848. But by then Kingsborough had been dead eleven years: bankrupted by a long ride on his costly hobbyhorse, he expired in a debtor's prison.

To illustrate the first four of his blockbusters, Kingsborough hired the Cremona-born artist Agostino Aglio, whose task it was to make watercolor copies of all pre-Conquest codices known to be in the libraries of Europe. Aglio was a very good choice: he was well known in England for his decoration and frescoes in churches, country houses, and theaters (he did the decorations for the Drury Lane Theater), and was considered a very competent watercolorist. In 1829 and 1830 the first seven volumes were issued, one of which contained the complete Dresden Codex in faithful reproduction.

Then why didn't some bright Champollion settle down and begin work on the Maya script then and there? Probably in part because sets of *The Antiquities of Mexico* were extremely rare (as they are today). For instance, in 1843, the American explorer and newspaperman B.H. Norman claimed that there was but one set in the entire United States.[18] And, it must be remembered, Landa's account of the Maya days and months, so vital to the workings of the Dresden, was not to turn up until 1863.

*   *   *

Athanasius Kircher (1602–80), the Jesuit priest whose ideas about the nature of Egyptian writing held up its decipherment for more than a century.

Jean-François Champollion (1790–1832), the Frenchman who finally deciphered Egyptian hieroglyphic writing.

Michael Ventris (1922–56). This young architect broke the Linear B code of the Mycenaean Greeks.

4 One of the fine lintel carvings from Yaxchilán, Mexico. The text now reveals this to be a depiction of the ruler's wife, Lady Xoc, crouching before the "Vision Serpent" in the year AD 681 (cf. p. 258).

5 Detail of the remarkable Late Classic murals at Bonampak, Mexico, c. AD 790. The ruler Chan Muan and his subordinates stand in judgment over captives.

6 Air view of the center of Tikal, Guatemala, the largest of the Classic Maya cities.

7 Detail of Stela 11, Seibal, Guatemala; the non-Maya features of this leader suggest that he might have been a Putún invader.

Opposite

8 Jean Frédéric Waldeck (1766?–1875), eccentric French artist and adventurer, and an early explorer of the Maya city of Palenque.

9 Constantine Samuel Rafinesque (1783–1840), polymath Franco-American naturalist who discovered Maya bar-and-dot numeration.

10 John Lloyd Stephens (1805–1852), the American lawyer whose explorations brought the Maya civilization to world attention.

Above

11, 12 The side and back of Stela A, Copán, Honduras, engravings from drawings made by Frederick Catherwood, artist on Stephens' expeditions.

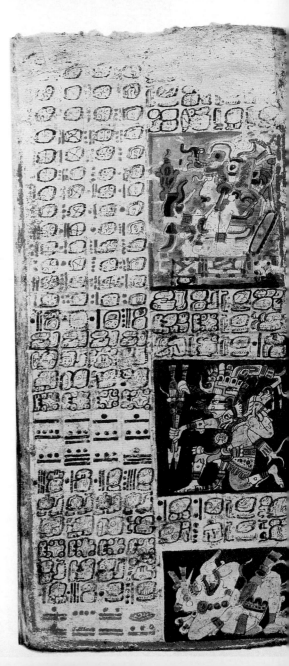

13 Charles Étienne Brasseur de Bourbourg (1814–1874), French abbé who brought to light Landa's *Relación* and other important manuscripts which illuminated ancient Maya culture.

14 Ernst Förstemann (1822–1906). In his studies of the Dresden Codex, this German librarian worked out many of the details of Maya calendrics and astronomy.

15 Page 49 from the Venus Tables of the Dresden Codex, as published by Förstemann in 1880.

18 Léon de Rosny (1837–1914),
French Orientalist and
decipherer of the Maya glyphs
for the world-directions.

19 Eduard Seler (1849–1922),
German scholar and leading
Mesoamericanist of his
generation; he was a formidable
foe of the phonetic school
represented by Cyrus Thomas.

20 Cyrus Thomas (1825–1910),
pioneer American
anthropologist and main
proponent of the phonetic
approach to the glyphs in the
late nineteenth century.

Constantine Samuel Rafinesque-Smaltz (1783–1840) is one of those people on whom there never was, is not now, and never will be, agreement.[19] Not even those who knew him well could agree on what he looked like, whether he was tall or short, bald or had a full head of hair, whether he was corpulent or thin, and so on. The only reasonably accurate portrait of him appears in the engraved frontispiece of his *Analyse de la Nature*, brought out in Palermo, Sicily, in 1815; there he is a sideburned little man with dark hair brushed down over his forehead in the fashion of the times.

Born to a French father and a German mother in Galata, Turkey, just across the Bosphorus from Constantinople, Rafinesque showed early aptitude as a naturalist, and arrived in the United States on this pursuit in 1802. Returning to Europe in 1805, he spent the next ten years in Sicily, where he made lasting contributions to the study of Mediterranean fishes and mollusks. Then, back he went to the United States, where he passed the rest of his life. Sadly, he died a pauper in Philadelphia, so indebted to his creditors that his landlord tried to sell his cadaver to a medical school to settle his rent.

With the kind of naive enthusiasm that seems to have been endemic in the young republic, Rafinesque tried his hand at everything. Here is his own assessment of himself:

Versatility of talents and of professions, is not uncommon in America; but those which I have exhibited ... may appear to exceed belief: and yet it is a positive fact that in knowledge I have been a Botanist, Naturalist, Geologist, Geographer, Historian, Poet, Philosopher, Philologist, Economist, Philanthropist ... By profession a Traveller, Merchant, Manufacturer, Collector, Improver, Professor, Teacher, Surveyor, Draftsman, Architect, Engineer, Pulmist [sic], Author, Editor, Bookseller, Librarian, Secretary ... and I hardly know myself what I may become as yet ...

A fraud? This is what some of my anthropological colleagues think, who refuse to accept as authentic Rafinesque's *Walum Olum*,[20] the creation and migration story of the Delaware Indians, which he claimed to have copied from the tribe's original bark records. But this is definitely *not* what those who know his zoological and botanical work say – Rafinesque established countless species of living organisms still considered as valid, and came up with a Darwinesque theory of evolution long before Darwin's *Origin of Species*. And this is *not* what Mayanists now say.

It is to George Stuart of the *National Geographic* that we owe the rediscovery of Rafinesque's pioneering efforts in the decipherment of the Maya script. In contrast to Waldeck's Munchausenesque pipe-dreams, Rafinesque's work rates serious consideration. One has first to consider what was available to him in the years from 1827, when he submitted a letter to the *Saturday Evening Post* on the subject, and 1832, the period in which he was deeply interested in the subject.

The only half-way reliable publication of Maya monumental inscriptions which had yet been published were the Almendáriz drawings (reworked by Waldeck) in the del Río report of 1822. If one takes a close look at the Almendáriz version of the tablet of the Temple of the Cross at Palenque, and compares it with a modern rendering of the same subject, one can see how truly bad it is. In the first place, the glyphs in the vertical columns on either side of the scene have been selected at random, in no particular order, from the much larger text. Even worse, they have been so childishly and sloppily drawn that even today it takes a good deal of intuition to guess what the originals might have looked like. From this kind of publication a genius could not have made much progress in decipherment, not even Champollion, Rafinesque's contemporary.

By contrast with this sorry situation, let us look at what was available to Champollion by 1822, when he wrote his famous letter to M. Dacier, and later. From 1809 on, the French scientific team which had accompanied Napoleon in Egypt began publishing the great *Description de l'Égypte*, with its superb and accurate plates – indispensable to the young decipherer; nothing on this scale was to appear in the Maya field until the end of the century. Even Kircher's engravings of the obelisks in Rome were superior to the sorry stuff on the Maya then available to Rafinesque.

With the Dresden Codex, things were on a slightly better footing. Rafinesque had seen the plate illustrating five of its pages in Humboldt's atlas, and this gave him some ideas, but he probably never did see the complete Kingsborough publication of the manuscript.

A pioneer in the field of "vanity publishing," Rafinesque had his own periodical, the *Atlantic Journal and Friend of Knowledge*, which he filled up with articles of his own composing, on every subject on earth. His *First Letter to Mr. Champollion*, giving his ideas about Maya writing, appeared in 1832 in the very first issue, and in the next issue readers could find his *Second Letter*; he had intended to write a third, but the news of Champollion's death precluded this.[21] The mere fact that he knew about and approved of the great Egyptological advances that had been made on the other side of the Atlantic, even though these were far from universally accepted at the time by the scholarly world, shows that very little moss grew on Rafinesque.

It is what he said in his *Second Letter* that modern Mayanists find so astonishing. He first of all characterized the Otulum (Palenque) hieroglyphs pictured in del Río as an entirely new kind of script, profoundly different from that known in Mexican (i.e., non-Maya) manuscripts, and proceeded to these points:

Besides this monumental alphabet, the same nation that built Otulum, had a Demotic alphabet belonging to my 8th series; which was found in Guatimala [sic] and Yucatan at the Spanish conquest. A specimen of it has been given by Humboldt in his American Researches, plate 45, from the Dresden Library, and has been ascertained to be Guatimalan instead of Mexican, being totally unlike the Mexican pictorial manuscripts. This page of Demotic has letters and numbers, these represented by strokes meaning 5 and dots meaning unities, as the dots never exceed 4. This is nearly similar to the monumental numbers.

The words are much less handsome than the monumental glyphs; they are also uncouth glyphs in rows formed by irregular or flexuous heavy strokes, inclosing within in small strokes, nearly the same letters as in the monuments. It might not be impossible to decypher some of these manuscripts written on metl paper: since they are written in languages yet spoken, and the writing was understood in Central America, as late as 200 years ago. If this is done it will be the best clue to the monumental inscriptions.[22]

I will have to take my hat off to Rafinesque. Here is what he has accomplished, using the sketchiest and most unpromising material:

(1)   He has seen that the inscriptions of Palenque and the writing of the Dresden Codex represent one and the same script.

(2)   He was the very first to realize the values of the bars and dots in the Maya number system, anticipating Brasseur de Bourbourg by over three decades.

0   1   4   6   19

17 Maya bar-and-dot numeration.

(3)   He has suggested that the language represented by this script is still spoken by the Maya of Central America, and knowing this, it will be possible to decipher manuscripts like the Dresden.

(4)   Once the manuscripts can be read, so can the monumental inscriptions.

The example of Champollion was ever before him: "In Egypt, the Coptic has been found to be such a close dialect of the Egyptian, that it has enabled you to read the oldest hieroglyphs. We find among the ancient dialects of Chiapa, Yucatan and Guatimala, the branches of the ancient speech of Otulum."

And who could disagree with Rafinesque's prophetic words: "Inscriptions are monuments also, and of the highest value, even when we cannot read them. Some of these will be hereafter, since those of Egypt so long deemed inexplicable, have at last found interpreters. So it will be at a future day, with those of America."[23]

"Being intrusted by the President with a Special Confidential Mission to Central America, on Wednesday, the third of October, 1839, I embarked on board the British brig Mary Ann, Hampton, master, for the Bay of Honduras."[24] And so began the voyage, just over one hundred and fifty years ago, that was to bring to light the full glory of Maya civilization. The names of Stephens and Catherwood are as inextricably joined in this great enterprise as names like Johnson and Boswell, or Gilbert and Sullivan, or Holmes and Watson: one just cannot think of one without the other.[25]

John Lloyd Stephens was thirty-four years old when he set off with his artist, Frederick Catherwood, on the sea trip to Belize and beyond. Stephens was a lawyer *manqué*, a stalwart of the Democratic Party in New York, and already a highly successful travel writer – his *Travels in Egypt, Arabia Petraea, and the Holy Land* (1837) had been highly praised by Edgar Allan Poe and had brought him a small fortune in royalties. After a New York bookseller had apparently drawn his attention to the newly discovered ruined cities of Central America, he absorbed what he could find in the books of del Río, Galindo, Humboldt, and Dupaix (an Austro-French officer in the Spanish army who had made a considerable archaeological survey of Mexico at the beginning of the century).

The Englishman Frederick Catherwood was forty, and a respected topographical artist with extensive archaeological experience in the Mediterranean and Middle East. He had accompanied Robert Hay's Nile expedition, where he prepared highly detailed drawings and inscriptions using the *camera lucida*, a "portable apparatus with a prism that enabled the artist to see and draw images of scenes or objects projected onto paper."[26] He was to use this device to good effect with the Maya monuments.

The two had met four years before in London, and become friends; thus, it was no surprise that when Catherwood settled in New York to practice architecture, Stephens persuaded him to accompany him to Central America. Out of this collaboration came the landmark 1841 publication, in two volumes, *Incidents of Travel in Central America, Chiapas, and Yucatán*; and, following a second trip to explore Yucatán, the *Incidents of Travel in Yucatán* of 1843.[27] Every Mayanist, myself included, keeps these often reprinted masterpieces on his bookshelf in a place of honor, since they mark the very genesis of serious Maya research. I never get tired of rereading my own copies – there is always something fresh to find in Stephens' delightful, unpretentious prose, and inspiration in Catherwood's crisp engravings.

Their story has been told many times, even in children's books, and there is no need to repeat it here. But it might be worth examining just what they did contribute to Maya research, and to look at some of

Stephens' almost prophetic insights, drawn in part from his familiarity with the civilizations of the Old World.

Setting aside their exploration of the Guatemalan highlands (where there are no Classic period inscriptions at all), they surveyed, described, and drew the major buildings and monuments of Copán, Quiriguá, and Palenque in the southern lowlands, and Uxmal, Kabah, Sayil, and Chichén Itzá in the north – along with several sites in the Puuc area that have since received little or no archaeological attention. Stephens and Catherwood were the first since the days of the Spanish Conquest to visit the clifftop ruins of Tulum on the east coast of the Peninsula. Needless to say, all this was done under the most trying conditions, long before the age of bug repellents, antibiotics, and anti-malarial pills; our travelers clearly suffered, but never complained, and Stephens' prose retains its equanimity throughout (unlike that of Waldeck and other more choleric explorers).

Stephens' "President" was Martin van Buren, and the delicate mission with which he had been entrusted was to find who was then in power in Central America, and to deal with him on behalf of the United States. Luckily for us, his duties as special agent took up very little of his time. Although Stephens typically minimized the threat, he and Catherwood were in very dangerous territory, at considerable risk to life and limb.

Their explorations were carried out methodically and meticulously. Here Catherwood's Egyptian experience stood him in good stead. On arrival at Copán, that stupendous Classic city in westernmost Honduras, Catherwood went immediately to work: "Mr. Catherwood made the outline of all the drawings with the camera lucida, and divided his paper into sections, so as to preserve the utmost economy of proportion."[28] This kind of exactitude in dealing with the baroque Maya sculptural style and with the complexities of the inscriptions had never been used before among the Maya cities – certainly not by the somewhat inept Almendáriz and the over-imaginative Waldeck. Later on, for their London publisher John Murray, the drawings were reduced and engraved on steel.

The quality of the illustrations in the 1841 and 1843 publications was a quantum jump away from anything that had been heretofore published on the antiquities of the New World. One has only to compare Catherwood's rendering of the great tablet of the Temple of the Cross at Palenque with the garbled version in the del Río 1822 report to see the difference. The same holds true with Catherwood's more purely architectural drawings: many years ago (when I was still an undergraduate at Harvard), I was at Uxmal, armed with a copy of Stephens and Catherwood. Catherwood's superb plate of the facade of the Governor's

Palace at Uxmal is folded into the volume. Standing in front of the same Palace, I directly compared the original with the copy: setting aside the reconstructions that had been carried out by the Mexican government in this century, they were virtually identical. Stephens and Catherwood could have lied and exaggerated like Waldeck about the Uxmal ruins – who among their readers in 1843 would have known the difference? – but they did not.

Both Stephens and Catherwood would have known a great deal about the recent history of the Egyptian decipherment, and about Champollion's brilliant successes. Stephens was convinced that the monuments of cities like Copán contained the record of the dynasties that had ruled them, a highly reasonable point of view derived from their knowledge of the ancient civilizations of the Old World, but one which was to be pooh-poohed by later generations of Mayanists. Here is his statement about Copán: "One thing I believe, that its history is graven on its monuments. No Champollion has yet brought to them the energies of his inquiring mind. Who shall read them?"[29]

On contemplating the richly carved hieroglyphs on the back of Copán's Stela F, Stephens comments: "... we considered that in its medallion tablets the people who reared it had published a record of themselves, through which we might one day hold conference with a perished race, and unveil the mystery that hangs over the city."[30]

On the subject of the age of the Maya ruins, and the identification of the language spoken by those who had carved its inscriptions, Stephens' views were remarkably similar to those advanced a few years earlier by Rafinesque. Did he arrive at these ideas independently? According to the late Victor von Hagen, a biographer of Stephens whose citations are often not entirely trustworthy, shortly before his death in penury, the "Constantinopolitan" (as one of Rafinesque's enemies called him) wrote to Stephens claiming priority in the interpretation of the hieroglyphs, and this was subsequently acknowledged by Stephens.[31] This is a forgotten corner of intellectual history that may never see much light.

Unlike Kingsborough, Waldeck, and the like, Stephens was sure that the ruins were *not* many thousands of years old, and that they had *not* been left by colonizers from distant lands.

I am inclined to think that there are not sufficient grounds for the belief in the great antiquity that has been ascribed to these ruins; that they are not the works of people who have passed away, and whose history has become unknown; but opposed as is my idea to all previous speculations, that they were constructed by the races who occupied the country at the time of the invasion by the Spaniards, or of some not very distant progenitors.[32]

Conclusion 1: the ruined cities were constructed by the ancestors of the modern Maya.

Here is another coolly reasoned paragraph from the pen of Stephens:

There is one important fact to be noticed. The hieroglyphics [of Palenque] are the same as were found at Copán and Quiriguá. The intermediate country is now occupied by races of Indians speaking many different languages, and entirely unintelligible to each other; but there is room for the belief that the whole of this country was once occupied by the same race, speaking the same language, or, at least, having the same written characters.[33]

Conclusion 2: the writing system of Palenque in the west and Copán and Quiriguá in the east is one and the same.
Conclusion 3: there was once a single language and script distributed across the southern lowlands.

Then what about the codex in Dresden, Germany, that had been partly illustrated by Humboldt? Near the end of the 1841 volumes, Stephens showed side-by-side (*fig. 18*, overleaf) the top of Altar Q at Copán and a section from the Venus tables taken from Humboldt, and called attention to the strong similarity between the two scripts.
Conclusion 4: the monumental inscriptions and the Dresden Codex represent a single system of writing.

Prompted by his discoveries, yet fully aware that much was still to be done, Stephens had three suggestions for the future. The first task would be to search in local convents for manuscripts relating to the native inhabitants which might determine the history of one of these ruined cities. In this respect, Stephens practiced what he preached. During their return visit to Yucatán in 1841 and 1842, the two explorers made a firm friend in the Yucatecan scholar Juan Pío Pérez, then *jefe político* of the town of Peto in the very center of the Peninsula. Pío Pérez was the compiler of one of the great dictionaries of Yucatec Maya, and an indefatigable copier of native histories, which were plentiful in the villages and towns of Yucatán.

Appended to the first volume of the 1843 *Incidents of Travel*, readers could find Pío Pérez's contribution, *Ancient Chronology of Yucatán*, giving for the first time a remarkably detailed account of the workings of the Maya calendar, in which the native names for the months and days were given (but not, of course, the corresponding glyphs – these would only be known with the later discovery of the Landa *Relación*). And in Volume II they could read the original Maya and an English translation of an important chronicle from the town of Maní, in which such ancient cities as Chichén Itzá, and Mayapán played a part. For the very first time, then, scholars were applying Maya documents from the Colonial period to the understanding of the pre-Conquest past.

Number Two on Stephens' list of suggestions was nothing less than the decipherment of the hieroglyphic texts. But could even someone as brilliant as Champollion have cracked this script with the materials at hand in the early 1840s? I doubt it. Catherwood's plates, even the magnificent lithographs which he brought out in his portfolio *Views of Ancient Monuments* (London, 1844) are indeed stunning, but they are simply not up to the standard set by the *Description de l'Egypte*. On a scale of accuracy, they are somewhere between Almendáriz and the monumental corpus produced by Maudslay at the end of the century, which really is comparable to what Napoleon's *savants* had done for Egypt. Even if the plates in *Incidents of Travel* had been up to those standards, there were too few of them, and these represented only a handful of Maya sites (really Copán, Palenque, and Chichén Itzá). With a script this complex, that is just not sufficient for a decipherment.

Both Stephens and Rafinesque had correctly grasped that the Mayan languages were involved in the script, just as Champollion (and Kircher before him) had tumbled to the fact that Coptic was a survival of Egyptian; but no European or American scholar had yet thought it worthwhile to learn a Mayan tongue, with one possible and very curious exception. This was one B.M. Norman, an American journalist who had been in Yucatán at the same time as Stephens and Catherwood, from December 1841 until the following April, and who jumped on the Stephens bandwagon by bringing out his own book of travels, *Rambles in Yucatán* (New York, 1843).[34] The book is on the whole worthless, since Norman had little grasp of history or much else; to him the ruins were immeasurably ancient: "The pyramids and temples of Yucatan seem to have been old in the days of Pharaoh," and "Their age is not to be measured by hundreds, but by thousands of years." The plates in the book are also of no value, artistic or otherwise.

Be that as it may, Norman scored one hit among many misses: the Yucatec Maya language. He owned a copy of the very rare Yucatec grammar published in 1746 by the Franciscan Father Pedro Beltrán, from which he prepared an English summary, for inclusion in his *Rambles*. From this, any interested scholar could get a pretty good idea of how the Maya pronoun system worked, as well as verbs and conjugations. Norman obviously was serious about this, for he added an appendix of over 500 Maya words, apparently elicited by himself from native informants, along with the names for the numbers up to 100. I have no idea of what he intended to do with this, but would-be Champollions, if any existed then (they didn't) could have profited from it.

Stephens' third suggestion for future research is the most intriguing of all, even if it belongs more to the realm of fiction than fact. This would be the search for a true "lost city," one that would still have living Maya Indians, carrying on their civilization intact. Perhaps it lay in "that vast and unknown region, untraversed by a single road, wherein fancy

18 Altar Q, Copán (top) compared with a detail from the Venus pages of the Dresden Codex: as published by Stephens, 1841.

pictures that mysterious city seen from the topmost range of the Cordilleras, of unconquered, unvisited, and unsought aboriginal inhabitants."[35] This was the yawning expanse of the forest-covered Petén, which Stephens and Catherwood had only skirted on their travels, lying between British Honduras (or Belize) and the lower Usumacinta.

The great "lost cities" of the Petén – Tikal, Uaxactún, Naranjo, Nakum, Holmul, Yaxchilán, and the like – were only discovered long after these pioneer explorers had passed from the scene, and of course had been in ruins for a millennium. But Stephens' notion lived on in H. Rider Haggard's great adventure story *Heart of the World*;[36] I count this among my most treasured books, and have read it many times (the late A.V. Kidder stated that this is what got the youthful Sylvanus Morley hooked on the Maya[37]).

Stephens and Catherwood never returned to the scene of their triumph. Having contracted a deadly case of malaria while involved in the construction of a railway across Panama, Stephens died in New York City in October 1852. Catherwood did not long survive him. In 1854, he went down on the steamship *Arctic*, after it had collided with another vessel during an Atlantic crossing.

No, they didn't decipher the lost script of the ancient Maya. But these two will live forever in the hearts of Mayanists, for they founded and defined an entirely new field of study. We are still building on that foundation.

4 Forefathers:
The Dawn of Decipherment

It is a fact of scientific life – at least, a fact of archaeological research – that the truly great discoverers have occasionally been extraordinarily sloppy. This was certainly the case with the Abbé Charles Étienne Brasseur de Bourbourg, the man who brought to light the great manuscripts on which so much of our knowledge about the ancient Maya rests.[1]

It must have been wonderful to have been an *abbé* in nineteenth-century Europe, for you had the best of two worlds: on the one hand you were steeped in a kind of sanctity, and on the other you could move freely in the living world of the flesh, with all its earthly pleasures, both intellectual and otherwise. One has only to think of the Abbé Franz Liszt, with his mistresses and illegitimate offspring. Now no longer in use, the title had originally applied only to governors of monastic abbeys, but in France it had been extended to anyone who wore an ecclesiastical dress. Brasseur, like Liszt, wore his very lightly.

Born in 1814 in northern France, Brasseur had early on supported himself as a hack novelist, but after entering the minor orders of the church embarked upon a life of travels and discovery which took him often to Canada, the United States, and Mesoamerica. He acquired an abiding interest in Mesoamerican languages and history. In 1855, he had the very good fortune to be assigned by friendly Church authorities in Guatemala City as parish priest in Rabinal, a Quiché Maya town in the Guatemala highlands, where he began his studies of the Quiché language; the result of this stay was the *Rabinal Achi*, an authentic and unique pre-Conquest drama which was delivered to him orally by a native informant who had committed it to memory.

It was about the same time that he stumbled on the manuscript of an amazing work called the *Popol Vuh*, then in the hands of a bibliophile friend in the Guatemalan capital. This was nothing less than the sacred book of the Quiché Maya nation that had ruled much of the country on the eve of the Conquest. The *Popol Vuh* is now generally considered to be the greatest single work of native American literature. Fully aware of what he had in his hands, Brasseur began to translate it into French while in Rabinal, and published it together with the Quiché text (which had been written down with Spanish letters) in 1861, on his return to France. Unfortunately, he had been "scooped" by the German explorer Carl Scherzer, who four years prior to this had brought out a Spanish translation made in early Colonial times.[2] Regardless of who had priority, the repercussions caused by the reappearance of the Popol Vuh – a majestic epic that begins with the Creation of the universe – continue to reverberate down to our times.

Only eight years after Catherwood's ship had gone down, our abbé made the discovery that was to revolutionize the study of the ancient Maya. In the year 1862, while ferreting out materials relating to the Americas in the library of the Royal Academy of History in Madrid (in a collection that was then totally uncataloged in the modern sense), Brasseur came across the manuscript of Bishop Diego de Landa's Relación de las Cosas de Yucatán ("Account of the Affairs of Yucatán"). He published this two years later,[3] and the world of Maya scholarship was changed forever.

What Brasseur had uncovered was not the original of Landa's Relación, written in Spain around 1566, but an anonymous copy work of several hands, apparently dating to 1661: it is clearly an abridgment of a much larger treatise which, alas, has never come to light. Nonetheless, it is not only a gold mine of informed information on all aspects of Maya life as it was in Yucatán on the eve of the Conquest, but also, in spite of the denial by generations of epigraphers, the true Rosetta Stone for the decipherment of Maya hieroglyphic writing.

We know Landa's visage from a late portrait copy in the convent of his great Franciscan church in Izamal, Yucatán, itself built on top of an enormous pyramidal mound complex, probably of the Late Formative period. From his ascetic face with downcast eyes, it would be impossible even to guess at the inner conflicts and motivations which would have led him to be so hated by his fellow Spaniards in the peninsula, and so loved and at the same time feared by the Maya whose souls he was trying to save. Landa was born on 12 November 1524 in Cifuentes, a town near Guadalajara in the Spanish province of New Castile.[4] In 1547 he went to Yucatán with five other Franciscan priests, and in 1549 was named assistant to the guardian of Izamal – curiously enough, a town which prior to the Conquest had venerated the supreme Maya god Itzamná, inventor of writing.

Landa has had a very bad press, and in part deservedly so. He was a fanatic as far as native idolatry was concerned, and in 1562 started his infamous, and perhaps illegal, proceedings against that practice, often exercising enormous and quite unFranciscan cruelties on his victims.[5]

We have already seen that almost all the surviving books of the lowland Maya perished in his terrible *auto da fé* in Maní at that time. Not being then a Franciscan bishop, who alone had the right to conduct an inquisition of this sort, he was accused by his enemies (there were many) of having exceeded his authority, and in 1563 was recalled to Spain to defend himself. It was in those black years for Landa that he wrote his great *Relación*, surely from notes and other materials which he had brought with him on the long voyage from Yucatán.

Landa was exonerated, and returned in 1572 to Yucatán, this time as Bishop, dying seven years later among his beloved Maya. It was to be another century and a half before his bones were returned to Cifuentes, his birthplace, but even these were destroyed in the bitter Spanish Civil War of the 1930s.[6] It seems that this troubled and turbulent man was never to find peace.

Brasseur was an enthusiastic man, and I can imagine his enormous excitement at seeing what Landa had put down about the Maya calendar, for this was the very first time that the names of the days in the 260-day calendar and the names of the months in the approximate solar year of 365 days appeared with their appropriate hieroglyphs. Remember that Brasseur already had the complete Dresden Codex at hand in the Kingsborough edition. In 1859, the French orientalist Léon de Rosny, later to become a perceptive student of Maya writing, had found another Maya codex in a dusty corner of the National Library in Paris, which he published in facsimile the same year that Brasseur brought out his Landa edition. Based on what Landa gave, the energetic abbé was able to identify the day and month signs in both the Dresden and Paris codices, and from that piece of information worked out the bar-and-dot numerical system (in fact, reinventing the wheel, for Rafinesque had already discovered how the numbers functioned).

In short, from the *Relación* any decipherer, including Brasseur, could have been able to interpret any Maya hieroglyphic date expressed in terms of the 52-year Calendar Round (*figs. 19, 20* overleaf). That must have been excitement enough as Brasseur turned the pages of the manuscript in Madrid. But more lay ahead: this was none other than Landa's explanation of how the Maya writing system actually worked – language made visible. I have said that Brasseur was a sloppy scholar, and nowhere is this laxity more evident than in his translation of this part of the *Relación*,[7] which has brought down on him the opprobrium, often unfair, of a century of Mayanists. It is worthwhile to put down what the great Franciscan actually said, not what Brasseur wanted him to say, for this is the heart of my book.

*   *   *

1. Imix

2. Ik

3. Akbal

4. Kan

5. Chicchan

6. Cimi

7. Manik

8. Lamat

9. Muluc

10. Oc

11. Chuen

12. Eb

13. Ben

14. Ix

15. Men

16. Cib

17. Caban

18. Edznab

19. Cauac

20. Ahau

19 *The twenty Maya day signs, in Landa, the Madrid Codex, and the inscriptions.*

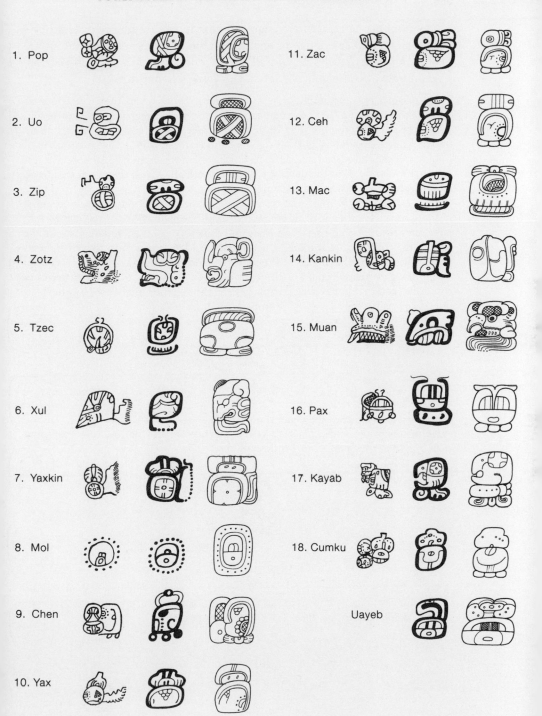

1. Pop

2. Uo

3. Zip

4. Zotz

5. Tzec

6. Xul

7. Yaxkin

8. Mol

9. Chen

10. Yax

11. Zac

12. Ceh

13. Mac

14. Kankin

15. Muan

16. Pax

17. Kayab

18. Cumku

Uayeb

20 The eighteen Maya month signs, in Landa, the Dresden Codex, and the inscriptions.

It is not easy to read or translate the text in the Academy of History's manuscript; in places it seems slightly garbled, for remember that we are dealing with a sort of "Reader's Digest" condensation made by scribal bureaucrats about a century later. But here is what it says:[8]

These people also used certain characters or letters with which they wrote in their books their ancient affairs and their sciences, and with these and with figures and some signs in the figures, they understood their affairs and they made others understand them and taught them. We found among them a large number of books in these their letters, and because they had nothing in which there was not superstition and lies of the devil, we burned them all, which they regretted to an amazing degree and which caused them sorrow.

Of their letters I will give here an A,B,C, since their ponderousness permits nothing more, for they use one character for all the aspirations of the letters and, later, they unite with it part of another and thus it goes on *ad infinitum*, as will be seen in the following example. *Le* means *noose* and *to hunt with it*; to write *le* with their characters (we having made them understand that these are two letters), they wrote it with three, placing for the aspiration of *l* the vowel *e*, which it carries in front of it, and in this way they do not err even though they might use [another] *e* if, out of curiosity, they so wish. Example:

e   l   e   lé

Afterwards, at the end, they affix the part which is joined.

Ha means water, and because the *h* has *a* before it, they put it at the beginning with *a*, and at the end in this fashion:

a   ha

They also wrote in parts, but in one way or another that I shall not give here nor will I deal with it except by giving a full account of this people's affairs. *Ma in kati* means *I don't want to* and they write it in parts in this fashion:

ma   i   n   ka   ti

There follows their A,B,C:

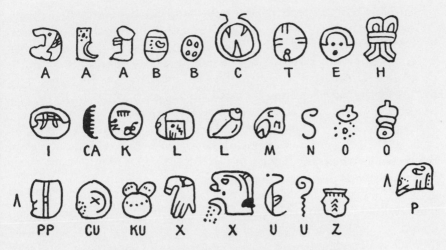

21 *The Landa "alphabet" and examples given by Landa.*

Of the letters which are missing, this language lacks them and has others added from our own for other things of which it has need, and already they do not use these their characters at all, especially the young people who have learned ours.

Here, then, was the long-sought key to the Maya hieroglyphs, the Rosetta Stone that had been a dream of Mayanists since the days of Rafinesque, Stephens, and Catherwood. The ancient Maya had written with an alphabet, and all that remained for someone like Brasseur was to apply it to the surviving books; he would then have in his hands the voice of the Maya scribe speaking to us from the mist-shrouded past. An easy task for the great abbé, with his immense command of the Mayan languages.

But, wait a minute! Just take a look at Landa's "A,B,C": why are there three signs for *a*, two for *b*, and so forth? And why do some of his "letters" stand for a consonant followed by a vowel (*cu, ku* in the "A,B,C," for example)? There is definitely something odd about this abecedary, this primer of Landa. Even the ebullient Rafinesque, if he had still been around, would have cautioned Brasseur to slow down. And a comparative knowledge of scripts in other parts of the world might have helped, for by 1864 Egyptian decipherment was at an advanced stage, the syllabic cuneiform script of the Persians had been cracked, and so had the more complex cuneiform script of the Babylonians and Assyrians.

Nothing, however, could hold Brasseur back, least of all when he uncovered yet another Maya codex in 1866. A friend in Madrid, Don Juan de Tro y Ortolano, a descendant of Cortés, had shown this family heirloom to Brasseur, and he published it in Paris three years later with the support of Napoleon III himself.[9] Brasseur had christened it the "Troano" in honor of its owner; but in 1875 another fragment turned up in Madrid, the so-called "Cortesiano," which was soon recognized by Léon de Rosny as part of one and the same codex. Both are now joined in the Museo de América in Madrid, and the entire screenfold manuscript (with fifty-six leaves painted on both sides, the longest known for the Maya) is known to the scholarly world as the Madrid Codex.[10]

Brasseur's commentary accompanying the Troano facsimile is a case study in the fallacy of misplaced concreteness. Without the least idea of the order in which the Troano glyphs were to be read (he got them backwards), he began applying Landa's "A,B,C," *as an alphabet*, to each glyph. The results were disastrous: his readings were nonsensical and patently false, although he remained oblivious to criticism. His incredible carelessness even led him to invent a letter for the Landa "alphabet" which is nowhere to be found in the original. As a result, any kind of phonetic approach to Maya hieroglyphic writing was thrown into an opprobrium from which it took almost a century to recover.

Brasseur went off the deep end, and not just in his ill-founded application of the data from Landa. As historian Robert Brunhouse has told us, ". . . as book after book appeared, his ideas grew more strange and his explanations more attenuated, so that serious readers who had respected him increasingly lost confidence in his utterances. Why his fertile imagination got the better of him is not clear."[11]

Diffusionist obsessions seem to have been the trap of many otherwise sane Americanists, who just could not bring themselves to believe that New World civilizations were autochthonous. Remember the Lost Tribes of Israel hobbyhorse that bankrupted Kingsborough? Well, in Brasseur's case his hobbyhorse was the myth of Atlantis, the continent that had supposedly sunk beneath the waves in ancient times, from which cataclysm refugees bearing the arts of civilized life had supposedly reached Yucatán and Central America.[12]

In his old age, not long before his death, alone in Nice in 1874, this engaging cleric took up residence in a hotel (now a Holiday Inn) on the Piazza Minerva in Rome. I wonder whether he ever thought about the obelisk placed on the back of its charming little elephant in the piazza – the Minervan Obelisk – and the utterly absurd attempt at its decipherment made two centuries before by the Jesuit Athanasius Kircher. Kircher, though, has survived only as an eccentric but instructive footnote to intellectual history; Brasseur's name will always be bright among Mayanists, if only for his truly great archival discoveries. On the subject of phoneticism and the utility of the Landa "A,B,C," he was right for all the wrong reasons; the right reasons would only appear in the next century.

There have always been two intertwined threads in the long cord of Maya decipherment: the phonetic-linguistic thread of the kind abortively pioneered by Brasseur, and the calendrical-astronomical one. It is the latter that was to triumph as the nineteenth century wore on, and it was mainly to be associated with Germany (as phonetic interpretations tended to be the preserve of Frenchmen and Americans). Among these Germans, the great – some would say almost superhuman – figure was Ernst Förstemann, Royal Librarian of the Electorate of Saxony in what is now eastern Germany.

Förstemann certainly does not sound like a superman: his life was the prosaic one of dusty shelves and library index cards.[13] But Förstemann's real adventures took place in the mind, and there is no doubt that he had a genius for solving complex problems. I would compare him not to Sherlock Holmes, but to his brother Mycroft, unraveling mysteries while never moving from his armchair in the mythical Diogenes Club.

Born in Danzig in 1822, the son of a teacher of mathematics in the Danziger Gymnasium, Förstemann studied linguistics and grammar under scholars like Jakob Grimm (of the famous brothers Grimm), doing research on German place-names, and received the Ph.D. degree in 1844. Then he entered the prosaic life of librarian in Wernigrode, Saxony. Finally, in 1867 Förstemann was attached to the Dresden Library. One can only guess how long he had been puttering there before he became intrigued with the strange codex that his predecessor Goetze had brought back from Vienna in the previous century, and how long before he thought of doing something about it.

According to his admirer and intellectual follower Eric Thompson (who of course never knew him), Förstemann was fifty-eight when he began his studies on the Dresden Codex, and continued publishing on Maya subjects until the year of his death (1906, when he was eighty-four).[14] It is impossible to think about this man – in many ways the exact opposite of Brasseur, the French romantic – without thinking of the Dresden. From this document, as Thompson has rightly said, "The whole framework of the Maya calendar was elucidated by him."

Förstemann's first task was to bring out an incredibly accurate facsimile of the Dresden, using the new technique of chromophotography.[15] I count myself very lucky to have bought this great edition at a book auction in New York, for only sixty sets were issued. Given the severe damage that the original suffered in World War II (it was under water for a while during the bombing of the city), the 1880 publication is a unique record for epigraphers. In that same year Förstemann began publication of his great studies on the codex.

Aided by Landa's days and months, and with a strong mathematical bent acquired in his childhood, by 1887 he had discovered:

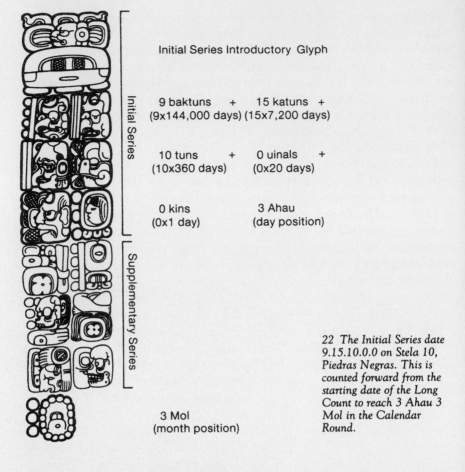

Initial Series Introductory Glyph

Initial Series

9 baktuns   +   15 katuns   +
(9x144,000 days) (15x7,200 days)

10 tuns   +   0 uinals   +
(10x360 days)   (0x20 days)

0 kins   3 Ahau
(0x1 day)   (day position)

Supplementary Series

3 Mol
(month position)

*22 The Initial Series date
9.15.10.0.0 on Stela 10,
Piedras Negras. This is
counted forward from the
starting date of the Long
Count to reach 3 Ahau 3
Mol in the Calendar
Round.*

(1)   the Long Count, a day-to-day count of consecutive days, unbroken since its inception at the Calendar Round day 4 Ahau 8 Cumku, thousands of years in the past.

(2)   that the Maya used a vigesimal (base twenty) system of calculation, instead of decimal (base ten) like ours.

(3)   how the 260-day (*tzolkin*) almanacs work in the Dresden.

(4)   the Venus tables in the Dresden – how the Maya calculated and prognosticated for the 584-day apparent cycle of the planet Venus as seen from Earth.

As if this weren't enough for one man, in 1893 (by which time he was seventy-one) he announced his recognition of the lunar tables in the Dresden, now known to be a table warning of possible eclipses (considered to be a calamity by the Maya).

So far, so good. But what about all those inscribed monuments lying mouldering in the stillness of the tropical forest? "Who shall read them?" Stephens had asked. The problem here lay in the almost total absence of a monumental corpus: the detailed, accurate illustration of the stone and stucco inscriptions of the Classic Maya, on the scale of the *Description de l'Égypte*. There was really little excuse for this other than the generally retarded nature of Maya research as compared with the rest of the world. After all, photography had been around for a long time: by 1839, daguerreotypes of Egyptian monuments were being brought back to Paris (Catherwood, in fact, had used the method sporadically while with Stephens in Central America), and the negative-positive technique of modern photography had been invented the next year by Fox Talbot in England. The French explorer Désiré Charnay[16] and the thoroughly eccentric Augustus le Plongeon and his wife[17] had used photography sporadically in the Maya lowlands, but none of their results could have aided the process of decipherment very much.

23 *Désiré Charnay (1828–1915) on the trail in Chiapas, Mexico.*

By 1879, the situation began to improve. In that year, one Charles Rau of the Smithsonian Institution published part of the tablet from the Temple of the Cross at Palenque in a form that any epigrapher could have used since it appeared in a microscopically accurate photographic plate.[18] It was through a close study of Rau's publication, and through his knowledge of the codices, that the American scholar Cyrus Thomas established in 1882 that the reading order of Maya writing was from left to right, and top to bottom, in paired columns[19] (if Brasseur had known this, he might not have committed such imbecilities with the Troano).

Then came Maudslay, one of the very few figures in Maya research about whom everybody seems to agree. Like his predecessors Stephens and Catherwood, only superlatives seem adequately to describe this great but modest and self-effacing man – a fitting antidote to some of the colossal egos that have taken up the Maya stage in the last century or so.

Alfred Percival Maudslay[20] was born in 1850, and received the classical education of an English gentleman at Harrow and Cambridge. He began his career as private secretary to the Governor of Queensland in Australia, then went to Fiji with Sir Arthur Gordon, becoming British Consul in Samoa in 1878 and, finally, Consul General in Tonga. After this colonial stint in the South Seas (charmingly recalled in his 1930 memoirs, *Life in the Pacific Fifty Years Ago*), he was called to the New World on business – overseeing a gold mine in Mexico and fruit property in California, where he met the young American who was to be his wife and companion on his Central American explorations.

Maudslay had read Stephens, and was drawn to the Maya ruins. In 1881 he made the first of seven undertakings in Central America, all entirely at his own expense. Maudslay had set himself the task of providing as complete and accurate a record possible of the architecture, art, and inscriptions of the major known Maya cities, in particular Quiriguá, Copán, Chichén Itzá, Palenque, and the recently discovered Yaxchilán, which lay on a U-shaped bend along the Usumacinta River. To make this record, he used an immense wet-plate camera; the plates had to be developed on the spot. To make casts, he had to bring in all the materials necessary (plaster, papier mâché, etc.). All of this work, plus the difficulty of setting up camps and supplying them with food, had to be done in the rain and the heat, in regions bereft of all but the most rudimentary trails.

Compared with the grim competitiveness of today's typical Maya field archaeologist, Maudslay seems almost a saint. The best-known example of his unmatched generosity of spirit concerns an unexpected meeting at Yaxchilán with the French explorer Charnay, who had believed that he (Charnay) had been the first at the ruins, and who had intended naming them "Lorillard City" for his patron the tobacco baron Pierre Lorillard. Here is Charnay's account of the meeting:[21]

We shook hands, he knew my name, he told me his: Alfred Maudslay, Esq., from London; and as my looks betrayed the inward annoyance I felt: "It's all right," he said, "there is no reason why you should look so distressed. My having the start of you was a mere chance, as it would have been mere chance had it been the other way. You need have no fear on my account, for I am only an amateur, traveling for pleasure. With you the case of course is different. But I do not intend to publish anything. Come, I have had a place got ready for you; and as for the ruins I make them over to you. You can name the town, claim to have discovered it, in fact do what you please. I shall not interfere with you in any way, and you may even dispense mentioning my name if you please." I was deeply touched with his kind manner and only too charmed to share with him the glory of having explored this city. We lived and worked together like two brothers, and we parted the best friends in the world.

Making a record of this sort may have been harrowing, but getting the results of his great research safely back to London, casts and all, must have been equally daunting. At any rate, they did get there, and Maudslay employed an artist, Miss Annie Hunter, to draw, from the casts and photographs with which he furnished her, accurate lithographic plates of every monument and inscription. For Maudslay had found his publisher in the persons of his friends the biologists Frederick Du Cane Godman and Osbert Salvin. Beginning in 1889, when the first fascicle came out, Maudslay's monumental *Archaeology* was to appear as an appendix to the multivolume work *Biologia Centrali-Americana*; the whole of his *Archaeology* reached its final form as one volume of text and four of plates.[22]

It is impossible to exaggerate the importance to Maya research of Maudslay's published work. For the very first time, Maya epigraphers had large-scale, incredibly accurate illustrations of complete Classic texts, not just the amateurish sketches of Almendáriz or even worse, the absurdities of Waldeck. With all of this available by 1902, and with good facsimiles of all the codices at hand, then why didn't some latter-day Champollion come along and *really* crack the Maya code? It seems strange in hindsight, but the odds were against it happening, for no one then engaged in Maya research had the kind of linguistic training and clarity of vision that enabled Champollion to make his great breakthrough.

I have spoken of Maudslay's extraordinary generosity. This certainly came into play with the American editor Joseph T. Goodman, whose work on the hieroglyphs had reached his attention in 1892, and which he offered to publish as an "appendix to an appendix," at the end of his monumental opus.[23] Maudslay, rather surprisingly, had made no direct attempt at decipherment, but Goodman had, and Maudslay was impressed with his findings on the monumental inscriptions.

Goodman, born in 1838, was a journalist, and he had begun his career early. Before he was twenty-three, he had become owner and editor of the *Territorial Enterprise* of Virginia City, in what was then Nevada Territory. This had been the site of the fabulous gold strike of 1859 known as the Comstock Lode, and Virginia City was a Wild West town par excellence: it had a hundred saloons in 1870, in a population of thirty thousand! Among students of American literature, Goodman has a certain claim to fame as the person who gave a young man named Samuel Clemens his first writing job in 1861, as a reporter on the *Enterprise*; in fact, Clemens first signed his name as "Mark Twain" on a humorous contribution to Goodman's paper. Goodman became rich on his Comstock Lode investments, and moved to California, where he founded the *San Franciscan* (Twain was a contributor to the first number). He then bought a large raisin orchard in Fresno, California, and in the 1880s began his Maya studies.

The rather vainglorious announcement of his results, which appeared in 1897 in Maudslay's *Biologia*, has rankled with Mayanists ever since. According to Goodman, he had been working on the monumental inscriptions since 1883 – but Maudslay's publications on them did not start appearing until 1889, and it is improbable that Goodman could have had a great deal at hand in California before then that would have allowed much serious research. Twain's "Joe" Goodman claimed that, entirely independently of Förstemann, he had unraveled the secret of the Long Count and the 4 Ahau 8 Cumku starting date, but Eric Thompson came up with enough internal evidence to make a good case against him: there can be little doubt that Goodman was quite aware of what Förstemann had already published on the Dresden.

It would be easy to put Goodman down as a frontier-type boaster from the world of "The Jumping Frog of Calaveras County," but he had made some truly lasting contributions. For one thing, the calendrical tables which he published with Maudslay are still in use among scholars working out Maya dates. Secondly, he deserves credit for discovering the "head variants" which can substitute for bar-and-dot numbers in Long Count dates (*fig. 24*). But far more significant than these was an article blandly entitled "Maya dates" which appeared in 1905 in the *American Anthropologist*,[24] which proposed a correlation between the Maya Long Count calendar and our own, backed by solid evidence from Landa and other colonial sources, and from the codices. This was an amazing achievement, not so much for the decipherment as for Maya culture history in general, for until then Maya Long Count dates on Classic Maya monuments had been "floating": the scholarly world did

0, mi   5, ho   10, lahun   15, holahun

1, hun   6, uac   11, buluc   16, uaclahun

2, ca   7, uuc   12, lahca'   17, uuclahun

3, ox   8, uaxac   13, oxlahun   18, uaxaclahun

4, can   9, bolon   14, canlahun   19, bolonlahun

24 Head variants for the Maya numbers, with equivalents in spoken Yucatec.

not really know exactly which centuries were included in Copán's span, for example, or when the last Long Count date marking the end of the Classic had occurred. Like many great discoveries (such as Mendel's law of heredity), Goodman's discovery lay forgotten or scorned for many years, until the Yucatecan scholar Juan Martínez Hernández revived it in 1926, giving further proof of its correctness; Eric Thompson later emended it by three days.[25] In spite of oceans of ink that have been spilled on the subject, there now is not the slightest chance that these three scholars (conflated to GMT when talking about the correlation) were not right; and that when we say, for instance, that Yax Pac, King of Copán, died on 10 February 822 in the Julian Calendar, he did just that. Goodman lives.

In his autobiography dictated in 1906, Mark Twain had these characteristically lighthearted words to say about Goodman, his onetime employer:

He was here a year ago and I saw him. He lives in the garden of California – in Alameda. Before this Eastern visit he had been putting in twelve years of time in the most unpromising and difficult and stubborn study that anybody has undertaken since Champollion's time; for he undertook to find out what those sculptures mean that they find down there in the forests of Central America. And he did find out and published a great book, the result of his twelve years of study. In this book he furnishes the meanings of these hieroglyphs, and his position as a successful expert in that complex study is recognized by the scientists in that line in London and Berlin and elsewhere. But *he* is no better known than he was before – he is only known to those people.[26]

But Goodman had the last word. When Twain died in April 1910, Goodman told Albert Bigelow Paine, the great writer's first biographer, "I am grieved – and yet glad that Mark made so good an ending. God knows how mortally afraid I was that somebody would land him in a dime museum before the finish."[27]

The turn of the century, between the nineteenth and twentieth, marks the great age of the recorders, and in this Maudslay certainly takes first place: work on the Maya inscriptions necessarily begins with him. But not far behind was the cantankerous, German-born Austrian, Teobert Maler.[28] Like Maudslay a superb photographer, using a large-format camera with wet plates instead of the wholly unsatisfactory 35mm substitutes of later generations of Mayanists, Maler recorded in enormous detail the stelae and lintels of a whole range of sites not even dreamed of by earlier explorers. By the 1890s, Americans had begun to chew gum in earnest, and chicle – the basic ingredient – had to be extracted by experienced chicle-hunters from trees in the forests of the southern Maya lowlands. The *chicleros*, an improvident but courageous group of rascals on the whole (I used to know some), cut hundreds of trails through the Petén, uncovering dozens of heretofore unknown Maya cities. This was a world undiscovered by Stephens, Catherwood, Waldeck, and even Maudslay, and Maler was its pioneer. Charles Pickering Bowditch, the very proper Bostonian who was the financial sponsor for the Central American research at Harvard's Peabody Museum, hired the cranky and impossible Maler to explore and survey such sites as Yaxchilán, Piedras Negras, Seibal, Tikal, and Naranjo. Beginning in 1901 and continuing until 1911 (some time after the exasperated Bowditch had cut off Maler's funds), Maler's great photographs of monuments appeared in the plates of volume after volume of the Peabody's Memoirs.[29] Although, unlike Maudslay's Biologia, the plates are not accompanied by drawings, perhaps this is just as well since Maler was a terrible draftsman and had really little idea of what Maya glyphs should look like: I doubt if he even knew what a Long Count date was. But this great series exactly complements Maudslay's; both constitute a true corpus and along with the published codices constitute the base on which the true decipherments of the present century have rested.

According to the dictionary, a Pyrrhic victory is one gained at too great cost.

This was the outcome of a battle that raged in the late nineteenth and early twentieth centuries between two rival camps. On one side were those in France and the United States who took Landa's "A,B,C" seriously, and who viewed the Maya script as largely phonetic in nature. On the other side were the rejectionists: those who pooh-poohed the Landa "alphabet" and who adopted a basically Kircherian view of the glyphs – as "picture-writing" or "ideographs" (whatever those might be). The rejectionists, largely German, won the day, but the cost was a half-century delay in the decipherment.

The first salvo in the war was, of course, fired by the indefatigable Brasseur de Bourbourg, whose abortive effort at reading the Troano using Landa's "A,B,C" as an alphabet has already been discussed. Brasseur had fallen into the same trap as the Swedish diplomat Åkerblad had done sixty years before, in trying to read the demotic script on the Rosetta Stone: because the few words that Åkerblad had deciphered in the demotic text had been alphabetically written, he came to believe that the entire system was exclusively alphabetic.[30] Brilliant though he was, Åkerblad got nowhere, for the script is logographic.

Brasseur's compatriot de Rosny had a much firmer grasp of the problems involved in Maya writing. Léon Louis Lucien Prunol de Rosny (1837–1914) was a distinguished orientalist, with a bibliography encompassing works on Chinese, Japanese, Korean, Thai, and Vietnamese, as well as more general works on language and writing systems.[31] He was the first since Rafinesque to try placing the strange writing of Central America (which he called *calculiforme*, "pebble-shaped," really not a bad description) in a larger framework, in a study which appeared in 1870. This unusual man, probably the best-prepared would-be Maya decipherer of the last century, was, like Brasseur, a mighty discoverer – he found the Paris Codex in 1859, and recognized the Cortesiano as part of the Madrid Codex in 1883. But it is de Rosny's 1876 *Essai sur le Déchiffrement de l'Écriture Hiératique de l'Amérique Centrale* ("Essay on the Decipherment of the Hieratic Writing of Central America") on which his fame rests. In it, he correctly identified the glyphs for the world-directions (*fig. 25*) and was the first to pick up phonetic elements in the day and month signs given by Landa and the codices.

De Rosny, and his Spanish translator and supporter Juan Rada y Delgado, were convinced that Abbé Brasseur and his followers had failed so miserably because they had not really read and understood what Landa had told us: that the Maya did not use *just* the "certain characters and letters" which he gave us in his "A,B,C," but also "figures" and "some signs in the figures." In other words, the Maya script was a mixture of phonetic signs and logograms. It is a tragedy that the clarity of vision shown by these two men was to be obscured in the smoke of the polemical battle which was about to begin.

After Brasseur, the figure most closely identified with the phonetic approach was the pioneer American anthropologist Cyrus Thomas.[32] Born to immigrant German parents in 1825, in eastern Tennessee, Thomas had received the frontier education of the times, such as it might be. He early practiced law in Illinois, and briefly entered the Lutheran ministry, but it was the life of science which claimed him. Thomas became an entomologist and agronomist (his bibliography includes such endearing titles as "Further from the Army Worm," and "Spiders – are they poisonous?"), but the last twenty-eight years of his long life (he died in 1910) were spent with the great U.S. Bureau of American Ethnology. Thomas was a stubborn and argumentative man, and he fought the good fight for scientific truth: the most lasting of his victories was his demolition of the racist idea that the prehistoric earthworks of the eastern United States were the handiwork of some non-Indian race of Moundbuilders.

Thomas began publishing on Maya writing in 1881, just about the same time that Förstemann was embarking on his work on the Dresden, and it is clear that Thomas from the beginning had a very different outlook from that of the German school. In 1882 he brought out his own study of the Troano part of the Madrid Codex, identifying in it for the

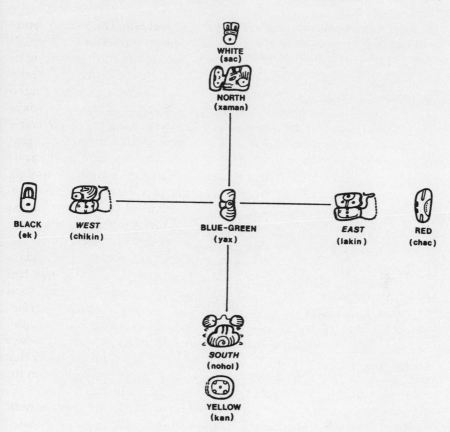

25 *The world-directions as discovered by de Rosny, and the associated colors later
discovered by Eduard Seler.*

first time the New Year ceremonies which take up four of its pages.[33]
Landa describes these rituals, which occurred at the end of each year in
late pre-Conquest Yucatán, in enormous detail, and Thomas' keen mind
saw the connection with what he was seeing in the Troano: the first time
that an ethnohistoric account had been used in decipherment. Simultaneously, his scientific training showed in the rigor with which he
established once and for all the true order of reading of the Maya glyphs.

By the late 1880s, Thomas had become convinced that much of the
Maya system was phonetic, or at least, as he put it in an 1893 article in the
American Anthropologist,[34] "in a transition stage from the purely
ideographic to the phonetic." Thomas had been struck by a statement
made by the Franciscan commissary-general Fray Alonso Ponce, who
had been in Yucatán in 1588. Ponce described the Maya folding-screen
books, and the writing in them, as follows:

The natives of Yucatán are, among all the inhabitants of New Spain, especially deserving of praise for three things: First, that before the Spaniards came they made use of characters and letters, with which they wrote out their histories, their ceremonies, and the order of sacrifices to their idols, and their calendars, in books made of bark of a certain tree. These were on very long strips, a quarter or a third (of a yard) in width, doubled and folded, so that they resembled a bound book in quarto, a little larger or smaller. These letters and characters were understood only by the priests of the idols (who in that language are called Ahkins) and a few principal natives. *Afterwards some of our friars learned to understand and read them, and even wrote them* [my italics].[35]

Thomas could not believe that the missionaries would have bothered learning a script which consisted merely of symbolic characters.

A fellow American, the distinguished linguist and ethnologist Daniel Garrison Brinton of Philadelphia, who knew his languages and sources very well indeed, was of the opinion that the Maya glyphs were "ikonomatic"; by this abstruse word, he meant that they were based mainly on the rebus, the "puzzle-writing" principle so important to all early known scripts.[36] This was the method used by the Aztec and possibly other people in non-Maya Mexico to write their place-names. An example cited by Brinton comes from the Aztec tribute list, the sign for a place called *Mapachtepec*, meaning "at Raccoon Hill." Instead of showing a raccoon, the scribe drew a hand, or *ma-itl*, grasping a bunch of Spanish moss, *pach-tli* in Nahuatl (the Aztec language). For *tepec*, "at the hill," the scribe drew a conventionalized mountain.

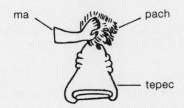

26 *Aztec rebus writing:* Mapachtepec.

Now Thomas not only believed that Maya scribes had progressed beyond this supposed evolutionary stage, but that like Egyptian, the Maya system probably included phonetic-syllabic signs, "ideographic" signs (today we would call these "logograms"), and possibly even semantic determinatives. Even more astonishing is Thomas' suggestion that "it is probable that the same character may be found in one place as phonetic and in another as retaining its symbolic significance" – in short, he was suggesting polyvalence! Small wonder that David Kelley has recently asserted: "I believe that he had a clearer view of the nature of the script than any other man of his period."[37]

There is a kind of pathos in Thomas' work that almost makes one weep. As Kelley has said, both Thomas and de Rosny went far beyond their evidence, and opened themselves to justified attack. But both of them scored some real hits in deciphering the codices, and a few of their readings are still valid. We shall see these two scholars championed in our own time by none other than Yuri Knorosov, who has always regarded them as pioneers.

The attack on the phoneticists began in earnest in 1880, when the American Antiquarian Society in Worcester, Massachusetts published a pamphlet called "The Landa Alphabet; a Spanish Fabrication," by one Philipp J.J. Valentini, Ph.D.[38] I have no idea who Valentini was, but he sounds like an extremely acerbic fellow, a sharp-tongued schoolmaster lecturing to a group of dim-witted pupils. Although the pamphlet is little more than a now-forgotten curiosity, it is worth looking into, for Valentini's approach and methodology were to be used as a club over the phoneticists well into our own century.

One part of Valentini's argument comes from the early Colonial period in non-Maya Mexico, particularly from those regions in which Nahuatl (Aztec) was the spoken language. The natives were required to learn by heart the Pater Noster, the Ave Maria, and the Credo. As Valentini so nicely puts it, "It was a difficult task for the teachers [the friars] to force the foreign long Latin text into the stolid or rather illiterate heads of the poor Indians." So what did the friars do? In a part of the world where only picture-writing had been known, they drew pictures of objects, the Nahuatl names of which began with sounds similar to those which began the appropriate words in Nahuatl. Thus, for *Pater noster*, they drew a banner (*pantli*) and a prickly-pear cactus (*nochtli*); and so it went.

Since Valentini could not bring himself to believe that *any* "Central American hieroglyphics" could have been anything but picture-writing, he thought that Landa must have been up to the same tricks with his Maya. So he reconstructed the following scenario, complete with his "poor Indians":

Let us fancy our learned Bishop Landa sitting in the refectory of his convent in Mérida. A group of barefooted Indians stand waiting at the door and their elected speaker is beckoned by Landa to approach the table. In response to his question what object he would think of and draw when hearing the sound of *a*, the man, with somewhat doubtful hand begins to trace before him, this little picture ...

Let *us*, in turn, temporarily set aside the fact that Landa's principal informants were Juan Nachi Cocom and Gaspar Antonio Chi, both noble princes and hardly likely to have been the barefoot hayseeds imagined by Valentini; these were scions of the royal Yucatecan houses, and were probably trained scribes themselves. Landa, then, according to

Valentini, must have gone through the Spanish alphabet in so far as it was applicable to the Maya language, pronouncing the letters one by one and letting his native stooges select an appropriate picture of something in the real world for each sound in turn. To pull this particular rabbit out of the hat, Valentini had at hand a copy of the Pío Pérez dictionary of Yucatec Maya.[39] But Valentini was as slipshod in this exercise as the principal target of his attack, Brasseur. For instance, he explained Landa's sign *ca* as a picture of a comb, selected by the illiterate Maya "because the Maya word *caa* means to pull a man's hair out"; today this is generally accepted as a representation of a fish fin ("fish" is *cay* in Yucatec).

Nonetheless Valentini, for all his knuckleheadedness, had hit on something real: the signs given by Landa's informants truly *did* represent sounds made by Landa as he pronounced for his Maya friends the *names* of the Spanish letters. Yet picture-symbols of the sort envisioned by Valentini they were not.

But Cyrus Thomas was a far more credible scholar than Brasseur, and his papers called up a more formidable array of opponents, this time in Germany.

This was the Germany of Bismarck, with its newly found unity and with an empire, fresh from the crushing defeat which it had recently inflicted upon the French. In culture, learning, and science it had few equals in those days, and certainly in the field of Americanist research there was simply no one quite of the stature of the Prussian scholar Eduard Seler, the intellectual giant whom Eric Thompson once called "the Nestor of Middle American Studies."[40] Born in 1849 to poor parents, Seler had married a very rich and cultivated woman, and never had to worry about financial matters throughout his long life. He also had the good fortune to attract the patronage of the Duc de Loubat, who not only bankrolled his Mesoamerican trips, but also published Seler's lengthy and detailed studies of the Mexican codices, complete with color facsimiles of the manuscripts. Incredibly well prepared for his research (he knew most of the major languages of Mesoamerica and gave classes in Maya and Nahuatl), blessed with an encyclopedic mind, and an exceptionally good visual memory, Seler was the founder of Mesoamerican iconographic research: he was the first to demonstrate from pre-Conquest art and books that there was a fundamental unity to Mexican and Maya thought and religion. His output was stupendous: his collected essays alone fill five very thick volumes, and all of them are still worth reading.

He must have been a wonderful man, with his long white beard, seated in his great scholarly library and poring over manuscripts and books, the very picture of the Old World professor. In an affectionate reminiscence, Seler's niece Lotte Höpfner (who was raised by her aunt and uncle), recalls the old man:

In wintertime, in a small greenhouse next to the library, worked my uncle, standing on foot, using a large writing-desk. On warm summer nights, this desk was placed in a projection and lit by a light protected from the wind. How many times, on returning from dances late at night, going up to the Fichteberg hill, did I see that light shine through the thick foliage of the garden and emphasize the silhouette of the old scholar of lengthened skull and long beard! His seer's gaze wandered off in the distance: surely Seler received his scientific revelations in the deep silence of the night.[41]

The last years of Eduard and Caecilie Seler were sad, indeed. They suffered greatly during and after World War I, and in November 1922 the dean of Americanist research, by then sick and aged beyond his years, died in his Berlin home. His ashes were placed in an Aztec-style urn in his wife's family mausoleum in Steglitz, Caecilie's eventually joining his. But his spacious house and the unique library were utterly destroyed in the siege of Berlin at the close of World War II.

Seler was the center and focal point of a brilliant German circle of Americanists, in a tradition that had begun with Förstemann. Among these was Paul Schellhas, close associate of Förstemann, who brought out in 1897 a classification of the deities in the Maya manuscripts which is still in universal use as the basis for dealing with each god or god-complex, along with the glyphs associated with each deity.[42] Schellhas wisely decided to indicate each god only with a capital letter from our alphabet, and we still refer to God A, God B, God K, God N, and so on even though in some cases we can now read their names as they were known to the ancient Maya.

One would have thought that Seler himself, with his formidable command of languages, ethnohistory, archaeology, and every known Mesoamerican codex, would have been just the person to make a Champollionesque decipherment of the Maya script, but in actuality his devotion to detail and his suspicion of intuitive thought effectively blocked any such breakthroughs. In fact, the only Maya decipherment for which he can claim credit is the identification of the glyphs for the major world-colors (colors associated with the four directions of the world in the Maya codices: fig. 25).[43]

Now to return to Cyrus Thomas: how could a Tennessee frontiersman stand up in debate with a walking encyclopedia like Seler? The answer is, he didn't.

The battle royal between Thomas and Seler appeared in the pages of the American journal Science in the years 1892 and 1893.[44] Thomas had made the mistake of presenting his phonetic readings from the codices as a "key" to the hieroglyphs, and Seler took up the challenge. It did not

take long for the Prussian scholar to demolish most of Thomas' readings
on the basis of faulty identification of both the objects depicted and of
individual glyphs. Seler was certainly right in rejecting this as a "key,"
but it is not too clear what Seler thought about Maya writing as a system,
if he thought about it at all. And occasionally Seler, like all of the
German school a believer in the semasiographic nature of Maya
hieroglyphs, seems to have accepted some sort of phonetic reading, but
always with a proviso.

The proviso was that while Landa's letter symbols "without doubt
possessed a certain phonetic value," and while the Maya probably wrote
in the manner indicated by Landa in early Colonial times, originally they
could not write texts in this way but adopted the "Landa method" on the
instigation of the missionaries. Shades of Valentini. And shades of
Kircher, too, for Seler throws at Thomas his contention that "without
doubt, great part of the Maya hieroglyphs were conventional symbols,
built up on the ideographic principle."

In the face of this onslaught, Thomas gave up abjectly. In 1903, the
seventy-eight-year-old Thomas published a general article called
"Central American Hieroglyphic Writing" in the Annual Report of the
Smithsonian Institution.[45] Here is what he now said: "the glyphs, so far
as determined, are to a large extent symbols (not phonetic characters),
used to denote numbers, days, months, etc." Not only is the "inference
of phoneticism doubtful," but because about half of the inscriptions
consist of "numeral symbols, calendar symbols, etc.," one can only
conclude "that they contain little, if anything, relating to the history of
the tribes by whom they were made." A people with writing, but without
written history! This is hardly what Stephens had predicted, standing in
the ruins of Copán so many years before.

But this was the general consensus of Maya scholarship in those days.
Maya numbers and Maya dates had conquered all, and the phoneticists
had fallen on the field of battle. Some years later, the young Alfred
Marston Tozzer met the aged Goodman only a year before the latter's
death.[46] He describes the encounter thus:

It was at a lunch at the Faculty Club, Berkeley, in September 1916; and the writer,
because of his studies along the same line, had the honor of sitting next to Mr.
Goodman, then just seventy-eight. It was a personal moment long anticipated and
never to be forgotten.

The veteran scholar discussed the Maya texts for upwards of an hour, always
emphasizing more and more the importance of the numerical elements, and finally
in conclusion stating as his belief that it was not history of which they treated, but
of arithmetic and the science of numbers; and that the only promising method of
approach to the meaning of the yet undeciphered characters – the method by
which he had made all his great advances, he added – was the mathematical, and
not the phonetic, indeed he rejected the latter with some show of impatience.

5 The Age of Thompson

Until his death in 1975, only a few months after being knighted by Queen Elizabeth II, John Eric Sydney Thompson dominated modern Maya studies by sheer force of intellect and personality.[1] Thompson never held a university post and never had any students; he never wielded power as a member of a grant-giving committee, or as an editor of a national journal; and within the organization that he served for so many years, the Carnegie Institution of Washington, he made no executive decisions. Yet on either side of the Atlantic, it was a brave or foolhardy Mayanist who dared go against his opinion.

I don't find it easy to write about Eric Thompson dispassionately even at this late date: I am torn between admiration for him as a scholar and a liking for him as a person, and an intense distaste for certain aspects of his work and for the way he treated some of his opponents. Unlike some who met with his disapproval, Eric (as I feel bound to call him) usually tolerated me as a kind of "loyal opposition," although he occasionally directed some sarcastic barbs in my direction. We had a mutual friend in the Americanist archaeologist Geoffrey Bushnell of Downing College, Cambridge University. After reading a series of somewhat heretical articles and reviews by myself, Eric told Geoffrey that "Mike Coe is another Joe the Fat Boy: he likes to make people shiver" – a sardonic reference to one of the characters in *The Pickwick Papers*. From then on, I signed my letters to him as "Joe the Fat Boy," and he signed his as "Mr. Pickwick."

I suppose that it was his prose style that first tempered my enthusiasm for some of Eric's publications. He did not wear his learning lightly, and his articles and books usually carried a heavy freight of literary and mythological references; I find most annoying the irrelevant quotations from English poets and prose writers that head chapters of his magnum opus, *Maya Hieroglyphic Writing*.[2] The sheer pretentiousness of all this appalled me, but it had great appeal among archaeologists, I'm sorry to say. This was especially true in Latin America. The Mexican archaeologist Alberto Ruz, a very close friend of Thompson's, had this to say in an obituary:

For the presentation of his research and conclusions, Thompson possessed magnificent gifts as a writer. His concepts, perfectly organized, flow with clarity, borne by a language at once simple, precise, and rich, discreetly adorned with literary and historic allusions in which his broad humanistic erudition flowers.[3]

I once conveyed my feelings about Eric's style to a very cultured Mexican scholar, explaining to him that to be really effective, English prose has to be written in the simplest way possible – basically that a writer in our language should try to be more like Hemingway, and less like Thompson. I am afraid that my message did not get across.

There is a distinct tendency today among the younger generation and among the victims of his acerbic attacks to dismiss Thompson altogether: he was very, very wrong about the nature of Maya hieroglyphic writing, so he must have been wrong about everything else. I do not feel this way. Thompson made some tremendous discoveries and should be given credit for them. Nevertheless, his role in cracking the Maya script was an entirely negative one, as stultifying and wrong as had been Athanasius Kircher's in holding back decipherment of ancient Egyptian for almost two centuries.

Eric Thompson was a product of the Edwardian era, raised as a member of that upper middle class that gave pre-World War I England its doctors, military officers, lawyers, clergymen, and sometimes its literary men – the well-off professionals of a very comfortable and well-educated society. He was born in 1898 on New Year's Eve, the younger son of a London doctor. In 1912 he left the house at 80 Harley Street to enter public school, the ancient Winchester College; in later life, he was to dedicate one of his books to its medieval founder, William of Wykeham, who had "cast his bread upon the waters."

When the Great War came, Eric was caught up in it while yet a boy. Lying about his age, he joined the London Scottish Regiment and served in the horrifying world of the trenches, where he was severely wounded. Sent back to England to recuperate, he ended his army career as an officer in the Coldstream Guards. With the Armistice, rather than immediately entering one of the Oxbridge universities as a more typical member of his class might have done, Eric went off to Argentina. The Thompsons were actually an Anglo-Argentinian family, and his father had been born in that country. Eric made his way to the Thompson *estancia* at Arenaza, 331 kilometers west of Buenos Aires, which they had owned since the 1820s, and he spent the next four years happily working cattle as a gaucho, becoming completely fluent in Spanish – he was, in my experience, one of the very few non-Latin Mayanists to be at home in that language (most of them are near monolingual).

Argentina in those days was a deeply divided society, with a great deal of labor unrest and class conflict. The large influx of foreign workers and peasants which had previously fueled the Argentine economy had led to a radicalized underclass as this economy worsened, and there were xenophobic, anti-"Bolshevik" massacres in 1919, the year after Eric reached the country. The Thompsons surely would have been among the great land-owning elite challenged by this leftist movement, and it may have been this milieu which formed Eric's tenacious attitudes about the Communist menace.[4] Speculation perhaps, but there can be no doubt that his uncompromisingly conservative political stance in later years colored his reaction to a more intellectual threat from "Bolshevik" Russia.

Returning to England in 1922, Eric entered Cambridge, where he read for a certificate in anthropology under A. C. Haddon. I have no idea why he chose anthropology, for in my experience, Eric really had little use either for the subject, or for the people who practiced it. There is little or no reference in any of his published work to the past greats of the field, or to any of their findings or theories. For instance, Eric wrote much about Maya religion, but one would be hard pressed to discover any awareness of such powerful thinkers on the general subject as Durkheim, Fraser, or Malinowski. It is as though one were pursuing a career in evolutionary biology, and decided to ignore Darwin.

One might perhaps excuse this, but it definitely affected his future work on the Maya glyphs. What is probably anthropology's greatest strength is its comparative approach to human and cultural variation, across time and space. Thompson's mentor Haddon was a pioneer practitioner of comparative studies. Basically, anthropologists long ago discovered that peoples around the world on similar levels of cultural complexity have come up with extraordinarily similar institutional responses when faced with similar problems – for example, the invention of hieroglyphic writing systems as an answer to the needs of nascent political states. Thompson never once acknowledged that what we know about early civilizations in the rest of the world – in China, Egypt, Mesopotamia, or the Mediterranean – might throw light on his beloved Maya. They were unique.

Be that as it may, Eric's interest in the Maya began in Cambridge. During his stay, he saw Alfred Maudslay receive an honorary degree, and, using S.G. Morley's *An Introduction to the Study of the Maya Hieroglyphs*,[5] published in 1915, he taught himself Maya calendrics. One fateful day in 1925, Eric wrote to Morley, then running the Carnegie Institution's project at Chichén Itzá, asking him for a job. His selling point, as he tells us in his autobiography,[6] was that he knew how to compute Maya dates, a particular passion with Morley. The response was positive, and after he had been interviewed in London by the American archaeologist Oliver Ricketson and his wife Edith (both of whom had been digging at Uaxactún), he was hired by Carnegie.

Sylvanus Morley must have been a wonderful man to know – all who did are unanimous in praise of him as a human being (but not necessarily as a scientist). His long-time colleague A.V. Kidder once described him as "that small, nearsighted, dynamic bundle of energy."[7] Born in 1883, until the close of his life in 1948 he was the ancient Maya's spokesman to the outside world, a popularizer in the best sense of the word, through his books, lectures, and magazine articles. I know of more than one archaeologist who was drawn to the field as a boy by reading one of Morley's *National Geographic* contributions, vividly illustrated with a color rendition of a purported virgin in filmy *huipil* being hurled into the Sacred Cenote at Chichén Itzá.

Morley took his A.B. at Harvard in 1907 and an A.M. in 1908. His early interest had been Egyptology, but he was steered to the Maya field by F.W. Putnam, then Director of Harvard's Peabody Museum, and by the young Alfred Tozzer, a neophyte teacher in the Anthropology Department who was to be mentor of most of the outstanding Mayanists of the last generation and the great editor of Landa's *Relación*.

Harvard was the pioneer institution in Maya research, and in 1892 had fielded the first real archaeological expedition to the Maya jungles – in this case, to the ruins of Copán.[8] In those days of gunboat diplomacy and pliant banana republics, under a generous contract the Peabody over the next several years was able to bring back (legally) a treasure trove of Classic Maya monuments from Copán, realizing, at least in part, Stephens' dream when he bought the site for fifty dollars. But for the first time a real excavation program was under way in a Maya city. Thus began the era of the great expeditions, which eventually was to see the entry of Carnegie, the University of Pennsylvania, Tulane University (under the colorful and bibulous Frans Blom), and Mexico's National Institute of Anthropology and History. This was a kind of golden age which lasted up until World War II.

Carnegie was always the leader in the field, with monetary and human resources which no university could match. The story of how it was drawn into this kind of activity has often been told.[9] In brief, three scholars were invited by the Carnegie Institution of Washington to submit competing plans for a large-scale program of anthropological research. In retrospect, the best was clearly that of the British ethnologist W.H.R. Rivers, for a huge research project among the fast-changing and threatened cultures of Melanesia; but Morley had presented a comprehensive plan for Maya research, and it was this that was accepted in July 1914, largely on the basis of the pint-sized epigrapher's boundless enthusiasm for his subject.

Off went Morley the next year to do fieldwork among the monuments of Copán, which he published in a huge volume in 1920. Morley knew that many ruined cities must lie undiscovered in the vast Petén region of northern Guatemala – where Stephens had once fantasized a still-inhabited great city – and longed to find them. Chicle (as we have seen, the raw material for chewing gum), was tapped by native *chicleros* from the chicozapote tree, and these often grew in profusion near Maya ruins (the ancients had used their wood for architectural lintels and beams), so Morley advertised a bounty of twenty-five dollars in gold to any *chiclero* who reported to him an unknown ruin with inscribed stones. Among other ruins, this largesse led to the discovery of Uaxactún, a day's walk north of Tikal, named by Morley from a stela bearing an 8th cycle date (Uaxactún = "8 Tuns").

Due to a misunderstanding on the part of trigger-happy Guatemalan troops, who thought they were revolutionaries, Morley's party was ambushed on the return journey from Uaxactún across the British Honduras border, and the expedition doctor lost his life. Morley barely escaped with his.

"Vay" Morley was a born leader of men, and beginning in 1924 he went about recruiting young archaeologists for a double-barreled investigation of the ancient Maya, centered at Uaxactún in the south under the direction of the Ricketsons, and at the far more accessible Chichén Itzá in the Yucatán Peninsula, where he set up his own headquarters in the old hacienda. It was not long before Chichén was a Mecca for foreign tourists visiting Yucatán, who were often entertained by the ebullient "Vay" himself. Morley had developed an idea about Maya civilization which he was to retain until his dying day:[10] that the cities in the south, such as Copán and the Petén centers, had been part of an "Old Empire," a united theocracy ruled over by enlightened priests for whom warfare was abhorrent. This peaceful Arcadia eventually disintegrated for unknown reasons, and the population fled north in two great migrations to found a "New Empire," with cities such as Uxmal, Labná, Kabah, and Chichén Itzá. Eventually these also succumbed, this time to nasty, idol-worshipping militarists from central Mexico.

In these days when the dead hand of professionalism reigns supreme in archaeology, it is pleasant to look back on the kinds of people whom Morley brought into Carnegie, and the life that they led. Few of them had that union card of modern times, the Ph.D. (although he was called "Dr. Morley" by everybody, even Morley had never earned the degree). It is said that the Smith brothers, Bob and Ledyard, were recruited for the Uaxactún dig by Oliver Ricketson at the bar of Harvard's very social Fly Club. Gus Strömsvik, later to direct the Carnegie project at Copán, was a rough-hewn Norwegian sailor who had jumped ship in Progreso, Yucatán, and who began work at Chichén repairing the expedition's trucks. Ed Shook entered his career as a Carnegie draftsman, and Tatiana Proskouriakoff as a staff artist. All turned out to be very, very fine archaeologists.

No Carnegie archaeologist ever had to time his digging with an academic schedule, for they never taught; nor did they have to spend endless hours preparing proposals for uncertain funding, for the Carnegie cornucopia was eternal; and none of them, with the exception of the boss himself, had to devote enormous time and energy to negotiating excavation permits with foreign governments, for Carnegie had long-term agreements with Mexico, Guatemala, and Honduras. Staff artists were available both in the field and back at home base in Carnegie's Cambridge headquarters (next to the Peabody), and they were guaranteed prompt publication. Paradise! No wonder envious colleagues called Carnegie "The Club."

In hindsight, Morley's failings as a leader of a large-scale scientific project became clearer as time went on. However much he might command the devotion of his staff and the admiration of his superiors in Washington, it is a sad fact that in spite of seventeen years of research at Chichén Itzá by Carnegie, this world-famous city yet remains an archaeological enigma: specialists are still arguing about its nature, its chronology, and even the reality of the Toltec "invasion" believed by traditionalists like myself to have resulted in some of its most famous buildings, such as the Castillo. Most of the archaeologists employed by Morley spent their time putting fallen buildings back together for the edification of the tourists, and very little in reconstructing a cultural picture of ancient Chichén anchored in a firm chronology. The young Thompson wasted his considerable talents in this kind of work, directing the reconstruction of the frieze on the Temple of the Warriors, and did not relish the task:

I labored for weeks in the incandescent sun of Yucatán fitting the stones together, moving them sometimes nearly forty yards to see if I could make a fit. Part of the time I had a Maya assistant to do the carrying, but in my memory it seems that I personally shifted every blessed stone.[10]

In contrast, the Uaxactún project under Oliver Ricketson, and later the Smith brothers, was a resounding success, giving the first full picture of the life and death of a Classic city that is still valid and useful today. The handwriting was on the wall regarding Morley, and in 1929 the Carnegie archaeological program in the Maya area was reorganized and placed under the direction of Alfred Vincent Kidder, an old friend and associate of Morley who had become the pioneer digger and synthesizer of Southwestern Pueblo prehistory.[11] Kidder *was* a Ph.D., a truly professional, anthropologically-oriented archaeologist, and just the man to lead "The Club" over the next few decades. Morley spent the rest of his life laboring in the epigraphic vineyard that had been his first love, anyway.

Well, what about Morley as an epigrapher? He liked to say that his main job was to "bring back the epigraphic bacon"; but what kind of bacon was this? Let us look into his two major works on the subject. The *Inscriptions of Copán* of 1920[12] is a huge tome, with 643 pages, 33 plates, and 91 illustrations; but the real blockbuster, the "Fat Boy" of Maya epigraphy, was issued in 1937–38, *The Inscriptions of Petén*[13] in five volumes containing a total of 2,065 pages, 187 plates, and 39 maps. Now, assuming that you have before you Maudslay's *Biologia Centrali-Americana*, compare his work with Morley's, and you will see what has gone wrong. In place of Maudslay's magnificent photographs, all made with his elephantine, large-format, wet-plate camera, Morley's are terrible. Even worse are the black-and-white renderings in *Copán* and *Petén*: crude and lacking in essential details, they are no match for the magnificent lithographic plates prepared for Maudslay by his artist Annie Hunter.

But the real problem lies even deeper than this. Morley's "epigraphic bacon" consisted of almost nothing but dates, and lots of them. Morley had an undoubted genius for wresting Long Count and Calendar Round positions from the most unpromising material – eroded and broken stelae lying in the jungle, often covered with lichens and moss. Given the prevailing view of the nature and content of the Classic Maya inscriptions then held by Morley and just about every other specialist during the heyday of Carnegie, it is little wonder that these vast tomes – unlike Maudslay's – virtually ignored all parts of the text that were not explicitly calendrical or astronomical. All those little inscriptions so beautifully carved and incised beside the figures of what were then supposed to be Maya priest-rulers were simply left out. Morley, then, never did produce from his years of work at Copán and in the Petén a real corpus of Maya inscriptions, nor did any of the other Carnegie people, including Thompson. Unlike Maudslay, they apparently never thought it worthwhile.

It was probably just as well that Thompson left Carnegie and Chichén Itzá at the close of the 1926 season, for his intellect was too powerful to be squandered on architectural reconstruction. He was offered, and accepted, a post at Chicago's Field Museum of Natural History, which allowed more scope to his far-ranging interests. Eric was a fine dirt archaeologist, and he conducted digs at various sites in British Honduras (in a way, it is a pity that it was not he but Morley who had run the Chichén project, for we would certainly now be in a much better position to talk about it). But even more important to his future thinking about the ancient Maya, he took time off from digging to study the living Maya themselves – the Kekchi and Mopán in the south of the colony, and the Itzá Maya of Socotz in the west.

Among his workmen and ethnological informants was a young Socotz Maya named Jacinto Cunil, who was to become Eric's lifelong friend and *compadre* (co-godparent). The influence of this man on Thompson cannot be overestimated: the last chapter of the 1963 *Rise and Fall of Maya Civilization*[14] (note the Gibbonian cadence), which summarizes his views on the Maya, is essentially a paean to Jacinto as an exemplar of those virtues and traits which he ascribed to Cunil's distant ancestors: moderation in all things, honesty, humility, and a profound religious devoutness. That may have been the case, but there was another side to Cunil – whom I got to know quite well during the summer of 1949 – a mental world of which Eric must have been aware, but which he managed to edit out in his books. Moderate though Jacinto usually was, in my experience he could be quite an uncanny person, almost a fanatical mystic. To use the Classical terminology so favored by Eric, he was far more Dionysian than Apollonian in his outlook and personality. And from what we now know of the ancient Maya, based on the testimony of the glyphs and the iconography, it was this mysterious, truly weird aspect of Cunil's *persona* that had prevailed among the elite rulers of the Classic lowland cities.

In short, the ancient calendar priests according to Thompson were basically High Church Anglicans like himself, and he felt a deep affinity with those ancient wise men and astronomers. It is no surprise that his main contribution to decipherment was restricted to the calendar and to the influence of the ancient gods over Maya life. Taking up where Förstemann and Goodman had left off, he began to concentrate on calendrical problems during his days at Chicago, and even more when he was hired as a staff researcher by Carnegie in 1936 (a position which he was to keep until the dissolution of Carnegie's Maya research program in 1958).

A close associate in this enterprise was a New York based chemical engineer named John E. Teeple, who had been encouraged by Morley to study Maya calendrical problems as a hobby. In a brilliant series of articles that began in 1925, Teeple solved the mystery of what epigraphers had been calling the "Supplementary Series," and which

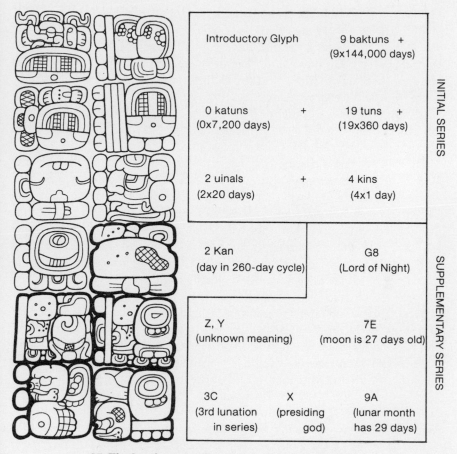

Introductory Glyph	9 baktuns + (9x144,000 days)	
0 katuns + (0x7,200 days)	19 tuns + (19x360 days)	INITIAL SERIES
2 uinals + (2x20 days)	4 kins (4x1 day)	
2 Kan (day in 260-day cycle)	G8 (Lord of Night)	
Z, Y (unknown meaning)	7E (moon is 27 days old)	SUPPLEMENTARY SERIES
3C (3rd lunation in series) X (presiding god)	9A (lunar month has 29 days)	

27 *The Supplementary Series, on Lintel 21, Yaxchilán.*

had stumped Goodman, Morley, and Charles Bowditch of Harvard's Peabody Museum.[15] It will be remembered that the texts on most Classic monuments begin with the Initial Series, a Long Count date which reaches a day and a month in the 52-year Calendar Round. Now, between the day and month glyphs there usually appears a cluster of other glyphs, some with numbers attached, comprising the "Supplementary Series."

Teeple proved that most of these glyphs, which had been given non-committal letter designations, presented lunar data for the particular day (or night) of the Initial Series: the number of days since the last New Moon, the position of that particular lunation in a cycle of six moons or lunar months, and whether that lunar month contained 29 or 30 days (the Maya eschewed fractions or decimals). Even more astonishing was

Teeple's finding that the astronomers of Copán had calculated with a formula that held 149 moons to be equal to 4,400 days; that would work out in our terms to 29.53020 days for an average lunation, only 33 seconds off its known value! Teeple went on to show the relation between these calculations and the Eclipse tables that had been pinned down in the Dresden Codex by the American astronomer Robert Willson in the early decades of this century. All this added credibility to the almost universally held notion that the Maya inscriptions dealt exclusively with calendrics and astronomy.

Thompson had a distinct gift for this kind of work: like his friend Teeple, he would have made an excellent Maya calendar priest. The first big question he tackled was that of the correlation between the Maya and Christian calendars. We have seen that Goodman had come up with a proposed correlation, but this was generally rejected in 1910 when Morley published his own,[16] later to be espoused by the young archaeologist/art historian Herbert Joseph Spinden; instead of fixing the Classic period to about AD 300–900, as indicated by Goodman's scheme, this would have pushed it back by some 260 years.

When Juan Martínez Hernández resurrected the Goodman correlation in 1926, Thompson joined suit. He defended his position until the end of his days, even when most "informed" opinion and even the new radiocarbon technique seemed to go against him. In this case, time has proved Goodman, Martinéz, and Thompson exactly right.

Now let us go back to the so-called "Supplementary" (or better, "Lunar") Series on the monuments. At the head of the line, immediately following the day glyph, is a sign which was given the designation "G"; Glyph G is actually a succession of alternative glyphs. Thompson showed that there are nine of them, forming a cycle of nine different glyphs in series, over and over and over.[17] This can have nothing to do with the moon. Eric was a lifelong admirer of Eduard Seler, who had died while Thompson was still punching cattle in the Argentine pampas. Seler's great strength – and it was to become Thompson's as well – was his remarkable knowledge of both the central Mexican and the Maya data. The learned Prussian was as much at home with Mexican codices like the Borgia as he was with the Maya manuscripts, and it led him to great insights into the nature of the Venus and New Year pages in the Dresden.

Eric knew that the Colonial period sources on the Aztec, and the codices themselves, tell us that there were Nine Lords of the Night, a succession of nine deities ruling over the hours of darkness, each with his or her own augury (good, bad, or indifferent), and he showed that functionally and structurally, at any rate, the Maya and Mexican sequences must be related. This was quite an achievement, and once

G1　　　　G4　　　　G7

G2　　　　G5　　　　G8

G3　　　　G6　　　　G9

28 Glyph G: the Nine Lords of the Night.

again demonstrated the fundamental unity of Mesoamerican systems of thought – even though it must be admitted that even now we cannot read the names of the Maya gods of Glyph G, or provide a one-to-one correlation with the Mexican series.

Having demonstrated that a cycle of nine was running concurrently with all those other cycles in the incredibly complex permutation calendar of the Maya, Thompson went on to unearth yet another cycle in the grand scheme of the ancient calendar: this measured 819 days, the product of the magic numbers 7 (the number of the earth), 9 (the heavens), and 13 (the underworld).[18] To this day no one knows exactly what it means, but the cycle was important among the Classic elite for ceremonies associated with the world-directions, world colors, and with the enigmatic God K or Kauil, patron god of the royal house. Perhaps the great causeways found at lowland cities like Tikal saw huge processions over these "royal roads" on days beginning 819-day cycles.

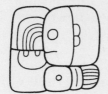

a.

29 *Direction-count glyphs:*
a. Posterior Date ("count
forward") Indicator. b. Anterior
Date ("count backward")
Indicator.

b.

Ever since Goodman's times, students of the subject had known that there were other dates on the Classic monuments in addition to the Initial Series date, and they confusingly called these the "Secondary Series"; these were given as positions in the Calendar Round, reached by "Distance Numbers" counted either forward into the future or backwards into the past. Such "extra dates" could be anywhere from a few days to millions of years from the Initial Series date, and for a very long time nobody knew why most of them were there. Some clearly fell on anniversaries of the opening date – say, at 5-tun (5 × 360 days), 10-tun, or 15-tun intervals, while others marked the endings of great periods in the steady march of the Long Count (as 1 January 2000 will certainly be marked in our own calendar). Thompson contributed significantly to the study of these calculations, by recognizing the so-called "count forward" and "count back" indicator glyphs, and the glyph for the 15-tun period.[19]

That still did not answer the nagging question of what all those dates really meant. Was it true that the Maya worshipped time itself? If there was no history in the inscriptions, then maybe that is what those old calendar priests were up to. Thompson thought that the answer to at least part of this question had been provided by the ever-resourceful Teeple, who used to while away the time spent on long train journeys in this kind of exercise. In 1930, Teeple came up with his Determinant Theory,[20] an extraordinarily involved and complex way of proving the existence of something which we now can say never existed in the first place. In its way, it reminds me of all those beautiful experiments undertaken by physicists in the last century to probe the nature of the "aether" which was then supposed to suffuse the empty spaces of the universe.

Briefly, Teeple claimed that at least some of the "odd" dates in the records – those that did not fall on period endings – were attempts by the Maya to bring their Calendar Round, which did not take into account leap days or leap years, into adjustment with the true length of the solar year (about 365¼ days). The determinants were supposed to express the error that had accumulated since the mythical beginning of the Long Count calendar in the fourth millennium before Christ. A little over thirty years were to elapse before the Determinant Theory went the way of the inter-galactic aether, and disappeared forever: Teeple had wasted his time.

Benjamin Lee Whorf is one of the most intriguing and sympathetic characters in all of Maya research. While his impact on the science of linguistics has been enormous (arguments still rage over his theories), his efforts to decipher the non-calendrical part of the Maya hieroglyphs have fallen on barren ground, and are now regarded as little more than intellectual curiosities. And yet these efforts were worth making in the first place, and in my view kept open an avenue of investigation that otherwise would have been hermetically shut by the powers that be – especially by Thompson.

There are curious contradictions about Whorf. While he looked rather like the old-time Hollywood star Robert Taylor, there he was pursuing a fairly prosaic life in the Hartford insurance business. He was at the same time mystic and scientist, theoretically rigorous and often factually slipshod.

Whorf was born in Winthrop, Massachusetts, in 1897, the son of a commercial artist.[21] Graduating from the Massachusetts Institute of Technology in chemical engineering, he went to work in fire engineering protection for the Hartford (Connecticut) Fire Insurance Company. Like two other gifted Yankees in the same line of business (the composer Charles Ives and the poet Wallace Stevens), his professional work in Hartford Insurance allowed him plenty of opportunity to follow his particular hobbyhorse. In Whorf's case, it was the study of language. In 1928, his studies took him to the Nahuatl (Aztec) language, and his lifelong research in the larger language family (Uto-Aztecan) to which Nahuatl belonged.

Eventually, he became a really good linguist, largely under the influence of Edward Sapir whom he met in 1928. When Sapir came to

Yale's newly founded Department of Anthropology three years later, Whorf enrolled in his first class as a special student, and worked on the Hopi language of Arizona, another member of the Uto-Aztecan group. This was his lasting contribution to knowledge. Whorf's research led him to believe, as his literary executor John Carroll has said, that "the strange grammar of Hopi might betoken a different mode of perceiving and conceiving things on the part of a native speaker of Hopi,"[22] a hypothesis that became enormously influential in intellectual circles through a series of popular articles that he wrote for the MIT *Technology Review*. If Whorf (and his mentor Sapir) were right, then perhaps all of us have been conditioned in our view of the world and reality by the particular grammar in which we think and speak.

At about the same time that he first encountered Sapir, Whorf became obsessed with the Maya glyphs, and was encouraged in this pursuit by Herbert Spinden, then at the Brooklyn Museum, and by Alfred Marston Tozzer at Harvard. Tozzer, born in 1877, was a pivotal figure in the Mayanist world, at once the trainer of most of the significant figures in the field, and a gadfly and iconoclast. He never got on particularly well with the Carnegie establishment; I remember well my first meeting with Tozzer – a dapper little man with a toothbrush moustache – in the halls of the Peabody Museum, when I was still an undergraduate, and his indignant, high-pitched denunciation of Morley's *The Ancient Maya*,[23] which had just appeared and which I had only just finished reading with wonder and admiration.

In 1933, Whorf published his "The Phonetic Value of Certain Characters in Maya Writing" in the *Papers* of the Peabody Museum.[24] Tozzer's introduction seems designed to annoy his stick-in-the-mud colleagues: "It is with no little satisfaction that the Peabody Museum publishes his paper on a subject which most Maya students have long felt was practically closed. With great acumen and courage Whorf dares to reopen the phonetic question."

Amazingly, Teeple had also encouraged Whorf to publish, and even defrayed the cost of some of the illustrations – this in the face of the fact that he (Teeple) had written only three years before: "I can foresee the clear possibility that when the Maya inscriptions and codices are deciphered, we may find absolutely nothing but numbers and astronomy, with an inter-mixture of mythology or religion."[25] Perhaps his generosity reflects the sympathy of one chemical engineer for another.

Right from the beginning, Whorf insisted that a writing system must record spoken language, and thus its study should be in the domain of linguistics. Past attempts to decipher the glyphs using the Landa "alphabet" were "hastily constructed by people who were not scientific linguists," which was certainly the case. "Landa's list of characters has certain earmarks of being genuine and also of being the reflex of a phonetic system." It was genuine because: (1) the *u* sign is the 3rd person subject when prefixed to a verb, or the 3rd person possessive, or the construct of a following genitive when before a noun (in today's parlance, this would be an ergative construction); (2) the "double writing" of various sounds (two signs each for *a*, *b*, *l*, *u*, and *x*) is the natural reflex of a system that had several ways of representing such simple sounds – we would now call this polyvalence; and (3) when Landa's sources gave him the signs for the syllables *ca* and *ku*, this was the "natural reflex of a syllabic system."

Naturally enough, Whorf occupied himself exclusively with the codices, since the texts are usually accompanied by pictures which might give clues as to the reading, and he showed by examples in the Dresden that the block of glyphs over each picture has a linguistic structure: with verb first, then the object, and the subject (usually a god) last, closely reflecting the usual VOS order of Yucatec Maya – recall "knows the counsel the scribe?"

Sadly, when it came time to apply these highly valid generalizations to the nitty-gritty of deciphering glyphs, Whorf seemed to go to pieces, and made errors as egregious as any in Brasseur and Thomas. Whorf was an atomist, both in this paper and in another that he brought out in 1942: as the young epigrapher Steve Houston has recently put it,[26] "Whorf argued that signs could be reduced to even smaller parts, a hook indicating one sound, doubled lines another" – a very odd position to take by someone who knew how other early writing systems in the Old World worked. This sloppiness left him open to attack from the Mayanist establishment.

Whorf did, however, score a few hits. He correctly identified the sign for the verb "to drill" in the codices, and gave it the yet-unproven reading *hax* (Thompson later adopted this without giving Whorf credit), and used Landa's *ma* and *ca* signs to decipher the month sign of Mac (*ma + ca*), a harbinger of the great breakthrough which was to be made ten years later in the Soviet Union. And he was surely right in his reading of the name-sign for God D in the codices as *Itzamná*, the Maya supreme deity in late pre-Conquest Yucatán.

Whorf did not have to wait very long for the attacks to begin. In the January 1935 issue of *Maya Research* the Irish solicitor Richard C.E. Long, a close friend of Thompson, brought out an article entitled "Maya and Mexican writing"[27] which pretty much expressed the received opinion of Whorf's opponents, who were many. I will omit mention of the details of Long's refutation of Whorf's individual readings, for there can be no doubt that Long was right and Whorf was wrong. I will turn instead to Long's major points, for here the case was the reverse.

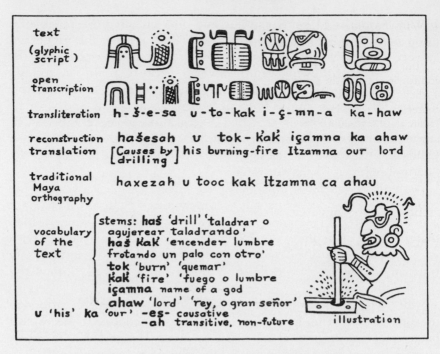

30 Whorf's attempt at deciphering page 38b of the Madrid Codex: an example of his atomistic approach to the glyphs.

To Long, only "true" or "complete" writing can express every word of the language; in contrast, "embryo" writing cannot, even though it may still transmit some information. The Maya script is "embryo" writing: "I do not think that in any instance there is a real grammatical sentence," Long tells us. He doesn't even accept Whorf's verbs *as* verbs. There simply isn't room to say much, once one sets aside the known numerical and calendrical material. Grudgingly accepting that a small amount of phoneticism might exist in certain non-calendrical glyphs, he claims that these are comparable to the rebus or puzzle-writing of the Aztec, and, like that other "embryo" script, are probably confined to the writing of personal and place-names.

But Long's real, underlying agenda is his unwillingness to grant the brown-skinned Maya a culture as complex as that of Europe, China, or the Near East. Here are a pair of telling quotes: "E. B. Tylor said long ago that writing marked the difference between civilization and barbarism...." "... the fact remains that no native race in America possessed a complete writing and therefore none had attained civilization according to Tylor's definition." The same quasi-racism was to color Ignace Gelb's *Study of Writing* of 1952, and I am afraid other works of this century.

Whorf answered Long in the October 1935 issue of *Maya Research*,[28] using eerily prophetic language:

... this position of Long's is methodological in implication. It might be a comforting one, in the sense that it would absolve archaeologists of responsibility if they fail to take up the problem of deciphering those combinations of characters. For if Mr. Long is right we may have the soothing assurance that these "hieroglyphics" cannot make definite, positive statements; statements that might require us to revise archaeological theories about the Maya or about general cultural history. Therefore we may proceed almost as though they did not exist.

Here Whorf proved himself about fifty years ahead of his time, and he did so again with his prediction that "it will eventually be possible to reconstruct the languages of the Old Empire [i.e., Classic] cities just as our scholars have reconstructed Hittite."

Whorf died on 26 July 1941, after a "long and lingering" illness, at age forty-four. Thompson chose not to criticize Whorf's work while he was still alive, apparently content with the drubbing that it had received at the hands of Long. But nine years after Whorf's death, Eric rose (or fell) to the occasion, in an appendix to his *Maya Hieroglyphic Writing*.[29] This he headed with a barbed quotation from John Buchan: "It is an old trait of human nature when in the mist to be very sure about its road." The opening line of the first paragraph gives a telling example of Eric's brand of invective when he was on the offensive – or defensive:

It had been my intention to ignore Whorf's attempts to read the Maya hieroglyphic writing, supposing that all students of the subject would by now have consigned them to that limbo which already holds the discredited interpretations of Brasseur de Bourbourg, de Rosny, Charency, Le Plongeon, Cresson, and Cyrus Thomas.

Thompson then went for the jugular, taking three of Whorf's weakest cases, and worrying them to death, while at the same time deliberately skirting the truly important part of the Whorfian message, his general statements about the probable nature of the script. On the unwary or unwise, this methodology makes a great impression – you attack your opponent on a host of details, and avoid the larger issues. Eric did this with Matthew Stirling in 1941 when he "proved" to his own satisfaction and that of most of his colleagues that the Olmec civilization was later than the Classic Maya;[30] in the 1950s when he "proved" his Russian opponent, Knorosov, to be wrong; and again in a posthumous article which "proved" that the Grolier Codex was a fake.

There is almost no way to defend Whorf's readings – they are almost all wrong. But his real message – that Maya writing must phonetically record one or another Mayan language – lives. Whorf's Maya research was a tragedy with an ultimately happy ending.

I have very mixed feelings about what some consider not only Thompson's greatest work but the alpha and omega of all Mayanist research: his *Maya Hieroglyphic Writing* of 1950.[31] In the face of my dislike of many aspects of this huge work, I still use it as a textbook in my course on the subject, and virtually force my students to buy it. For anyone wanting to know how the Maya calendar and astronomy actually worked, this book is a must. Eric was a superb iconographer, and came up with very astute and generally correct insights about Maya religion and mythology – here Jacinto Cunil was a positive influence. Setting aside the heavy overlay of artsy-literary allusions there is much still to be learned from the book. I view it not as a kind of Summa Hieroglyphicae of the Maya script, as many do, but as a sort of gigantic, complex logjam which held back the decipherment among a whole generation of Western scholars, held in thrall by its sheer size and detail, and probably also by Thompson's sharp tongue.

First, though, the good news. Eric did present some new readings in his 1950 work, and these have generally held up in the light of the great decipherment of our time. He established that one sign, very common in the codices where it appears affixed to main signs, can be read as *te* or *che*, "tree" or "wood," and as a numerical classifier in counts of periods of time, such as years, months, or days. In Yucatec, you cannot for instance say *ox haab* for "three years," but must say *ox-te haab*, "three-*te* years." In modern dictionaries *te* also means "tree," and this other meaning for the sign was confirmed when Thompson found it in compounds accompanying pictures of trees in the Dresden Codex. He also hit upon the reading of *tu* for another affix appearing before counts of days; this is the 3rd person possessive which changes cardinal numbers like "three" into ordinals ("third"). This was indeed an advance, since it made it possible for him to read the peculiar system of dates used on lintels in Yucatecan sites like Chichén Itzá.[32]

31 Readings of glyphs by Thompson. *a.* te, "tree," "wood"; numerical classifier. *b.* ti, "at," "on," "with." *c.* tu, "at his/hers/its."

a.   b.   c.

As might be expected, Thompson's views on the Landa "alphabet" were distinctly ambivalent, but he was the first to see that Landa's *ti* sign which ends his sample sentence *ma in kati* ("I don't want to") functions as the Yucatec locative preposition *ti'*, "at," "on"; that it could also have functioned as a purely phonetic-syllabic sign, as the bishop implied, was something that Eric simply could not allow.

Here were three glyphs, then, that the leading anti-phoneticist of his day was reading in the Yucatec Maya tongue. That begins to sound subversive! Even further, back in 1944[33] he had shown that the pair of fish fins, or at times a pair of fishes, which flanked the Month-patron head in the great glyph which always introduces an Initial Series date on a Classic monument, is a rebus sign: the fish is a shark, xoc in Maya (Tom Jones has recently proved that xoc is the origin of the English word "shark"). And xoc also means "to count" in Maya.

These decipherments were all major advances, but Thompson failed to follow them up. Why? The answer is that Thompson was a captive of that same mindset that had led in the first century before Christ to the absurd interpretations of Egyptian hieroglyphs by Diodorus Siculus, to the equally absurd fourth-century AD Neoplatonist nonsense of Horapollon, and to the sixteenth-century fantasies of Athanasius Kircher. Eric had ignored the lesson of Champollion.

In a chapter entitled "Glances Backward and a Look Ahead," Thompson sums up his views on Maya hieroglyphic writing. "The glyphs are anagogical," he says. Now Webster defines anagogy as the "interpretation of a word, passage, or text (as of Scripture or poetry) that finds beyond the literal, allegorical, and moral senses a fourth and ultimate spiritual and mystical sense." The glyphs are not expressing something as mundane and down-to-earth as language, but something much deeper, according to Thompson:

Without a full understanding of the text one can not, for instance, tell whether the presence of a glyph of a dog refers to that animal's role as bringer of fire to mankind or to his duty of leading the dead to the underworld. That such mystical meanings are imbedded in the glyphs is beyond doubt, but as yet we can only guess as to the association the Maya author had in mind. Clearly, our duty is to seek more of those mythological allusions.[34]

The epigrapher's task, then, is to find these mythological associations for every sign – this will bring us to "the solution of the glyphic problem," which "leads us, key in hand, to the threshold of the inner keep of the Maya soul, and bids us enter." Athanasius Kircher would have recognized all this.

If Thompson had little use for anthropologists, he had even less for linguists, a viewpoint which received ample confirmation when a review of Thompson's book by the linguist Archibald Hill of the University of Virginia appeared in a linguistics journal.[35] In it, Hill had the gall to suggest that given the fact that the language of the glyphs is known, and given the presence of clues to the content of the writing in the codices in the accompanying illustrations, then perhaps the failure of a real decipherment "invites the suspicion that there have been shortcomings in the method by which the problem has been attacked." "The present book reveals what many of these shortcomings are. Thompson is unaware that his problem is essentially a linguistic one. . . ." Worst of all, "Thompson assumes, as have all Maya scholars with the exception of Whorf, that many of the glyphs represent, not Maya words or constructions, but universal ideas." "A glance through this or any of the other publications in Maya hieroglyphs will amply confirm the statement that the intimate dependence of the inscriptions on Maya language is unfortunately minimized." Hill's review must have been a bitter one for Eric, for it not only extols Whorf, another linguist, but pillories the style of the book as "discursive, interlarded with quotations from literature and the arts."

Thompson's reply[36] was swift and characteristic: "In writing a review one should know something about the subject under discussion and should have read the book with some care. Dr. Hill . . . fails in both respects." "Dr. Hill feels that he is more at home when faced with Whorf's ideas on decipherment. When a colleague read my manuscript, he remarked of the discussion of Whorf's methods 'Why flog that dead horse? There can't be a person who takes seriously Whorf's fantastic work.'" The linguistic approach was useless: "One cannot translate all glyphs into modern Yucatec because many of them are ideographic and in many cases the corresponding archaic term is now lost."

32 *Glyph for* chikin, *"west."*

An example invoked by Thompson to defend what Hill had castigated as the "semi-romantic approach" – that is, a partial dependence on ethnology and mythology for translation – is the glyph identified in the last century as the sign for the direction which is *chikin*, meaning "sunset" (and, by extension, "west"), in Yucatec. Eric claimed that the hand which appears over the sun glyph is "completion," and that the whole combination means "completion of sun"; it would thus be entirely logographic. This in retrospect was an unfortunate choice of his, for we now know that the hand is the glyph for the sound *chi*, and that when placed above the logogram *kin* the combination does indeed read *chikin*. But typical of Thompson, he ignored Hill's main point while zeroing in on subsidiary details. Hill was relegated to the limbo into which Whorf had been hurled.

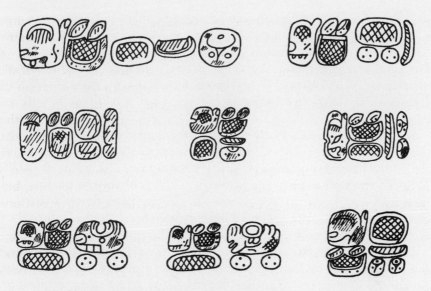

33 Clauses isolated by Beyer at Chichén Itzá. These ones are now all
read as Kakupacal (see pp. 159–160).

A far more formidable enemy, however, than any of these despised
linguists was waiting just over the horizon.

Although few admitted it, by mid-century the decipherment of the non-
calendrical part of the inscriptions and codices was really no further
advanced than it had been fifty years earlier. In an appraisal published in
1940, Morley probably spoke for most of his colleagues when he said
that "time in its various manifestations, the accurate record of its
principal phenomena, constitutes the major content of Maya writing...."[37] Thus far, not one name for any of the ancient Maya centers
had been identified, "much less that for any of the different rulers of its
many city states," and Morley could state that "the writer strongly
doubts that any place name will ever be found in the Maya stone
inscriptions." "One may hazard the guess that the remaining undeciphered glyphs deal with ceremonial matters."

Apart from the almost plaintive stabs at decipherment by linguists –
speedily quashed by Thompson – the only shaft of light to penetrate the
epigraphic gloom was an analysis of the inscriptions of Chichén Itzá
carried out in the 1930s by Hermann Beyer,[38] a short-tempered German
employed by Tulane's Middle American Research Institute in New
Orleans. What he did was to identify recurring sequences of glyphs –
which we now recognize to be clauses (fig. 33); and while he made no

pretense of actually being able to read or translate these sequences, it was a structural approach which was to prove extremely fruitful in later decades when the great decipherment actually took off. Beyer was a very fine scholar, even though he often drove colleagues like Morley to distraction. When World War II came, the poor man, already suffering from cancer, was taken off to a concentration camp in Oklahoma, where he died in 1942.

But another German, Paul Schellhas – the same one who had classified the gods in the codices – was completely pessimistic. "The character of the Maya hieroglyphs is principally ideographic," he wrote in 1936. Whorf's attempts at phonetic readings would probably be the last, and he agreed with Long that the glyphs "are by no means a real writing in our sense, and no counterpart to the Egyptian hieroglyphs," since they are not able to reproduce the language.[39]

In 1945, at the war's end, when Schellhas was a very old man of eighty-five, he published his last paper in the Swedish journal Ethnos.[40] The title posed the question: "The decipherment of Maya hieroglyphs: an unsolvable problem?" Schellhas' despondent conclusion was that it was, in fact, unsolvable.

If so, seldom in the history of science had so many brilliant minds labored so long with so little to show for their effort. Who would read the glyphs? No one, apparently.

6 A New Wind from the East

The Union of Soviet Socialist Republics in the autumn of 1952 was a most unlikely place and time for a great breakthrough in Maya decipherment. Only seven years before, the Soviet Union had emerged from a war that had cost it twenty million lives and untold suffering. With its people held in the iron grip of the world's most ruthless dictator, terrorized by Stalin's political police and the Gulag system, the nation's only aim seemed to be the glorification of the pockmarked "leader, teacher, friend," whose days were numbered. Stalin in fact died the very next year, but the hold of the Party, the bureaucracy, and the KGB was to remain strong for the next few decades.

In those fear-ridden days, intellectual innovation was nearly an impossibility. From 1946 until his demise in 1948, Stalin's henchman Andrei Zhdanov instituted a program of xenophobic repression in the arts and sciences that virtually put a halt to creative work in and out of the universities. And in 1948, Comrade Trofim Lysenko triumphed in his struggle to replace genetics with his own brand of hare-brained pseudo-science – he had the dictator's ear, and his enemies did not. The price of dissent was the Gulag or worse.

It was thus improbable that under such dreadful circumstances anything new or exciting would emerge in the world of Soviet scholarship, least of all in Leningrad: in 1949, the paranoid Stalin ordered almost the entire leadership of the city to be arrested on trumped-up charges and "shortened by a head," as Stalin liked to put it, and Zhdanovism reigned in Leningrad University and in the various institutes under the mantle of the Academy of Sciences of the U.S.S.R. But in October 1952, a new number of the anthropological journal *Sovietskaya Etnografiya* (a publication largely given over to "scientific" Marxism-Leninism and replete with praise for the great Stalin) contained an article entitled *"Drevniaia Pis'mennost' Tsentral'noi Ameriki"* ("Ancient Writing of Central America").[1] The author was a thirty-year-old investigator in Leningrad's Institute of Ethnology, and his article would eventually lead to the cracking of the Maya script and enable those distant Lords of the Forest to speak to us in their own voice. A Russian, a citizen of Stalin's vast domains, effectively isolated from the rest of the intellectual world, had accomplished what generations of more fortunate Mayanists in the outside world had failed to do.

The article's then-unknown author, Yuri Valentinovich Knorosov, was born to ethnic Russian parents on 19 November 1922 (12.15.8.10.13 13 Ben 6 Zac in the Maya system), in the Ukrainian city of Kharkov.[2] Entering Moscow University at the age of seventeen, he was eventually swept up in World War II and joined the Red Army in 1943.

That Knorosov survived the terrible carnage of that conflict is a miracle. Serving as an artillery spotter in the 58th Heavy Artillery, his unit reached Berlin at the beginning of May 1945, during the death throes of the Third Reich; the Soviet Flag flew at last over the Reichstag. The young artilleryman found the National Library on fire. Out of the thousands of books being consumed, he managed to snatch one from the flames. Incredibly, it was the one-volume edition of the Dresden, Madrid, and Paris codices published in 1933 by the Guatemalan scholars Antonio and Carlos Villacorta. Knorosov brought this old trophy back home with him, along with his four battle medals.

Demobilized, Knorosov returned that year to Moscow University, where he concentrated in Egyptology; but Japanese literature, the Arabic language, and the writing systems of China and ancient India also claimed his attention. Some of his mentors at the university, believing him to be a born Egyptologist, tried to persuade him to abandon Chinese and to preoccupy himself less with archaeology and ethnology. But comparative studies were Knorosov's real *forte*, and his enquiring mind could not be confined to Egypt.

The spark that had been implanted in the ruins of Berlin by the finding of the Villacorta book was nourished by his professor, Sergei Aleksandrovich Tokarev, a specialist on the peoples of Siberia, eastern Europe, Oceania, and the Americas (Marxism had at least the merit of encouraging a comparative approach), who had read Paul Schellhas' pessimistic article on the impossibility of ever reading the Maya glyphs. In 1947, Tokarev posed his brilliant pupil a question:

If you believe that any writing system produced by humans can be read by humans, why don't you try to crack the Maya system?

Many thought Knorosov too young, too imprudent for such a difficult task, but Tokarev's reply was, "Youth is the time to undertake bold enterprises." Knorosov's response was to learn Spanish and to commence a translation of – and commentary on – Bishop Landa's *Relación*; this became his doctoral dissertation and the foundation of his pioneering work on the decipherment.[3] He completed his studies in Moscow and took up a research post in Leningrad's Institute of Ethnology; there he has been ever since, in his first-floor office in Peter the Great's old Kunstkammer above the banks of the Neva.

Knorosov's great achievement indicates that even in those days, considerable advances could be made by Soviet scientists and scholars, as long as they stayed clear of tabooed subjects like Mendelian biology, Freudian psychology, and Western social theory; the rapid development of the Soviet nuclear weapons and space programs is ample evidence for this. But bearing in mind the Zhdanovian atmosphere which prevailed in the research institutions and journals, it is hardly surprising that the nineteen pages of the *Sovietskaya Etnografiya* article were preceded by a brief comment by the editor, S.P. Tolstov (author of a Stalinist diatribe entitled "Anglo-American Anthropology in the Service of Imperialism"), in which he extolled the Marxist-Leninist approach which had enabled the young Knorosov to triumph where bourgeois scholars had failed. Tolstov thus provided ammunition for the unrelenting attacks of the man who was to be Knorosov's most bitter foe: Eric Thompson.

After the semi-mystical and pseudo-literary ramblings by Thompson, the Knorosov paper seems like a model of logical presentation. Incidentally, neither here nor anywhere else in his published writings does Knorosov *ever* invoke the sacred names of Marx, Engels, or Stalin, contrary to what many of his Western detractors, and even supporters, have claimed.

After a description of Landa's opus, and Landa's exposition of the script, Knorosov explores the history of attempts to decipher the noncalendrical Maya glyphs, and the ups and downs of the Landa "alphabet," taking his account up to the gloomy Schellhas paper of 1945. What he says next sets the stage for his own unique contribution. It will be remembered from Chapter 1 that Sylvanus Morley, following a scheme that dates back to the Victorian anthropologist E.B. Tylor, proposed that writing systems had progressed from pictographic, through ideographic (with Chinese given as an ideographic system *par excellence*, since according to Morley each sign stands for an idea), to phonetic. Roundly denouncing this scheme for its hyper-evolutionism, Knorosov demonstrates that these supposed stages coexist in all early scripts, including Egyptian, Mesopotamian, and Chinese, and he gives examples proving it. These kinds of scripts he calls *hieroglyphic*, and places Maya writing squarely with them.

Hieroglyphic writing, in this sense, is typical of state societies, in which they are maintained as a monopoly by a class of priestly scribes. In such systems one finds "ideograms" (now known as logograms), which have both conceptual and phonetic value; phonetic signs (like the monoconsonantal signs of Egypt); and "key signs" or determinatives, classificatory signs with conceptual but not phonetic value.

Here is what Knorosov says about the Landa "alphabet," flying in the face of received opinion:

Signs given by D. de Landa, in spite of a century of attack upon them, have exactly the phonetic meaning that he attributed to them. This does not mean, of course, either that these signs cannot have other meanings, or that they exhaust the phonetic signs of the Maya hieroglyphs.

Knorosov accepted what both Valentini and Thompson had accepted before, that the signs Landa's informants produced were a response to each letter of the Spanish alphabet as he (Landa) then pronounced them in the Spanish of that day. Thus, *b* would have sounded like English *bay*, *l* something like *el-lay*, and *s* like *essay*; for *h*, the cleric would have said something like *ah-chay*. According to Valentini, the bewildered natives would have matched these sounds with pictures of "ideograms" of things, the names of which sounded vaguely like what they were hearing from the cleric's mouth; in no way could these signs be interpreted as phonetic.

Knorosov takes another tack, based on his broad knowledge of scripts in other parts of the world. To him, most of the signs given by Landa were not alphabetic, but *syllabic*: except for the pure vowels, each sign stands for a consonant-vowel (CV) combination (as in Japanese *kana* writing). The principles under which Maya scribes operated are similar to those of other hieroglyphic systems: (1) signs can have more than one function, that is, a single glyph might sometimes be phonetic, at other times stand for a morpheme (the smallest unit of meaning); (2) the writing order might be inverted for calligraphic purposes, a principle known to Egyptologists since Champollion's day; and (3) phonetic signs might sometimes be added to morphemic ones to lessen ambiguity in the reading (remember that phonetic-morphemic combinations constitute most of the characters in Chinese script).

Next, Knorosov closely compares some of the texts in the codices with the pictures that accompany them, especially in the Dresden. Apart from its remarkable astronomical content (Venus tables and tables giving warning of solar or lunar eclipses), most of the Dresden Codex contains innumerable 260-day counts of *tzolkins* divided up in different ways; each division of the *tzolkin* describes an action of a specific deity on that particular day; above the god or goddess concerned is a text usually containing four glyphs; at least one of these glyphs, as Seler, Schellhas, and other early scholars had recognized, has to refer to the deity, followed by an epithet or augury. It was the much-maligned Whorf who saw that the first of the signs, in the upper left, ought to be the verb or something like it, and the second, in the upper right, the object of the sentence.

In his article, Knorosov calls attention to the passage at the bottom of page 16 in the Dresden. Here the same goddess – almost surely the young lunar deity – is seated facing left. In the text above her, her glyph appears in the lower left. Just in back of her head in each picture is a specific bird. In the first case, this is a mythical horned owl long recognized to be the Muan Bird associated not only with the Maya Underworld but also with the topmost, thirteenth heaven. The head of this same creature can be found in the first position in the text, preceded by the bar-and-dot number "thirteen." Logically, then, the rest of the signs in the initial position above our Moon Goddess should name the other birds associated with her, but it will be seen that unlike the case of the Muan Bird, they have no pictorial content. Seler and his followers, ignoring the Landa "alphabet," would have labeled them "ideographs" or something similar. We shall see what our young Russian does with them.

The logic of his procedures goes thus (fig. 34, overleaf):

(1)   Let us begin with the sign for "west," first identified by Léon de Rosny in 1875. As we saw in the last chapter, this is read in Yucatec Maya as chikin, and consists of a sign like a grasping hand (phonetic chi), followed by the logographic sign for "sun," kin.

(2)   Landa's ku plus chi appear above the picture of the Vulture God in Madrid 40a and elsewhere. The combination is thus to be read as ku-ch(i), "vulture" in Colonial and modern Maya dictionaries, the final vowel of CV-CV combinations remaining silent in syllabic writing.

(3)   cu (also in Landa) plus an unknown sign, over the picture of a turkey, must be the word read in Colonial and modern Maya as cu-tz(u), "turkey." (Here Knorosov hints at the Principle of Synharmony, which he elaborates further in later papers: that in CV-C(V) writing of CVC words, the vowel of the second syllable is usually (but not always) the same as the vowel of the first.) The unknown sign must therefore be tzu.

(4)   cu plus an unknown sign, over a picture of the Moon Goddess carrying a burden (Dresden 16b and elsewhere) must be cu-ch(u), "burden." The unknown sign is thus chu.

(5)   chu plus ca (Landa) plus ah or ha (Landa), over a picture of a captive god must be chu-c(a)-ah, "captured." We shall see that this reading will play a crucial role in the decipherment of the monumental inscriptions of the Classic cities.

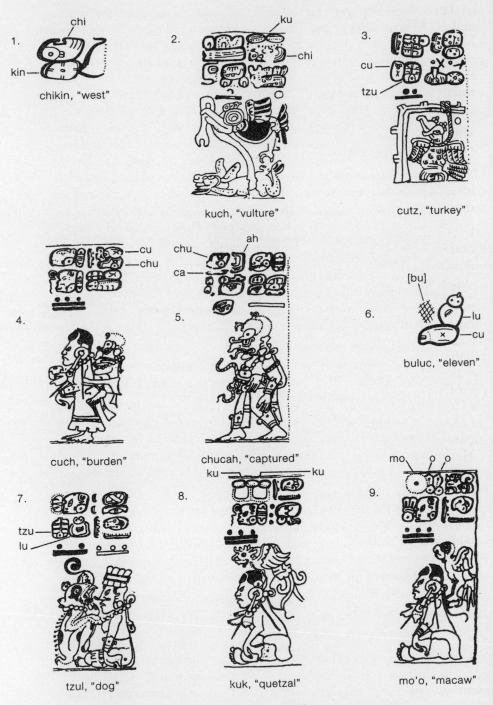

1. chikin, "west"

kin — chi

2. kuch, "vulture"

ku — chi

3. cutz, "turkey"

cu — tzu

4. cuch, "burden"

cu — chu

5. chucah, "captured"

chu — ah — ca

6. buluc, "eleven"

[bu] — lu — cu

7. tzul, "dog"

tzu — lu

8. kuk, "quetzal"

ku — ku

9. mo'o, "macaw"

mo — o — o

34 Knorosov's methodology. For key to numbers 1–9, see main text.

(6) In Dresden 19a, in a position which should contain the bar-and-dot number "eleven" above a column of day-signs, there are three glyphs. The first of these is defaced, but the second is one of Landa's *l*'s – presumably *l* followed by an unknown vowel – and the third is *cu*. Since "eleven" is *buluc* in Yucatec Maya, the missing sign must be *bu* and Landa's second *l* must be *lu*.

(7) *tzu* plus *lu* over a picture of the Dog God in Dresden 21b and elsewhere must be *tzu-l(u)*, "dog" in one of our earliest Maya dictionaries, the Motul.

(8) Returning to our Moon Goddess with birds, where she is pictured with a quetzal, the relevant glyph is clearly Landa's *ku* reduplicated. This must then be *ku-k(u)*, "quetzal" in all Mayan languages.

(9) An unknown sign plus reduplicated *o* (in Landa), over the goddess pictured with a macaw must be *mo-o-o* (or *mo'o*), "macaw." The unknown glyph is thus *mo*.

What about the glyph which follows the name of each bird? Knorosov notes a phonetic substitution for the usual, logographic sign for the month of Muan (usually expressed by the head of the Muan Bird), in which the first sign is a cartouche with a curl in it; he thus reads it as the syllable *mu*. This also precedes Landa's *ti* in the glyphic combination mentioned above, and it, in turn, is preceded by Landa's *u*, the 3rd person possessive. We must therefore here decipher it as *u mu-t(i)*, "her bird (or omen)." An entire glyph block in this famous passage ought to be parsed as "[bird-name], her bird (or omen), the Moon Goddess, augury or epithet."

He even finds a good example of phonetic reinforcement, with the logographic sign for "sky, heaven," *caan*, followed by an affix which he interprets as *na*.

Freely admitting that some of his decipherments were first made by Cyrus Thomas (whom he admires), Knorosov points out that the words deciphered are ordinary, well-known ones registered in all the Yucatec vocabularies, and are not hypothetical. His epoch-making article concludes, "The system of Maya writing is typically hieroglyphic and in its principles of writing does not differ from known hieroglyphic systems." If he was right, then Landa's "alphabet" was truly the Rosetta Stone (although he never calls it that) to the cracking of the script, and Knorosov's methodology would lead the way to the full decipherment.

The Soviet media were not slow to pick up on a story which cast glory upon the scientific prowess of the U.S.S.R., and Knorosov's achievement was broadcast throughout the world, even appearing in the pages of the *New York Times*. A gauntlet had been cast down to Western epigraphers, particularly to Thompson, who was hardly one to avoid a challenge like this.

Thompson chose to fire the first cannonade in his one-sided war with Knorosov in the 1953 issue of the Mexican journal *Yan*,[4] a short-lived anthropological publication edited by Carmen Cook de Leonard, a good friend of Eric's who was perpetually at odds with Mexico's Institute of Anthropology and History. Eric's opening paragraph gives the reader a hint of what is to follow:

During recent years, claims of "first things in the world" which have emanated from Moscow have gone from the invention of the submarine to the invention of baseball. A little-known claim of this sort pertains to the discovery of the principles which are the key to the decipherment of the hieroglyphic writing of the Maya of Central America....

After quoting at length Tolstov's tendentious introduction extolling Marxist-Leninist methodology, Thompson claims (wrongly, in fact) that Knorosov repeats such cant; what the young Soviet *actually* did in his first section was to accuse Thompson and Morley of taking a mystical approach to the glyphs through their notion of a cult of time – a fairly just charge!

It will be recalled that Thompson dealt posthumously with Whorf by paying no attention whatsoever to Whorf's larger points, and devoting much ink to the latter's minor mistakes (and mistakes they were), like a terrier worrying a rat. He did exactly the same with this new menace from behind the Iron Curtain. After wholeheartedly accepting the old Valentini explanation of the Landa "alphabet," Thompson chides the Russian for the fact that five of his fifteen decipherments had already been made by Thomas (as Knorosov makes clear in his article); and Thomas, he was quick to point out, "worked in a horizon previous to Lenin." Next, Thompson eagerly pounced on a clear-cut bloomer: Yuri Valentinovich had identified an animal on Dresden 13c as a jaguar, when it is surely a doe. Gleefully, Eric illustrates this creature side-by-side with an indubitable jaguar also from the Dresden, "so that readers may reflect on the Marxist jaguar." As Knorosov had rather slipshoddily read the glyphic combination accompanying this picture as *chacmool* ("great claw"), a known epithet for the jaguar, the whole epigrammatic edifice thrown up by the Russian collapses like a house of cards, in Thompson's jaundiced view.

At the close of his contemptuous review, Thompson poses a question: does Knorosov have any "scientific honor"? The answer is clearly "no." In conclusion:

... this could be an authentic example of the effects of strict Party cooperation by a small group who work in research in Russia. For the good of the Free World, it is hoped that it is so, as far as military research is concerned.

The great Mayanist had spoken: Knorosov's methodology was not even worth a sentence, and his so-called "decipherment" was a Marxist hoax and propaganda ploy.

During Thompson's lifetime, it was a rare Maya scholar who dared to contradict the field's Grand Panjandrum on this or most other questions – certainly not in print. But, in 1955, the Swedish linguist and Sinologist Tor Ulving published a remarkable appreciation of the 1952 article in the Swedish journal *Ethnos*.[5] Following a summary of the Soviet's approach and findings, here is his evaluation of what Knorosov had accomplished:

It will be the task of the experts in Maya hieroglyphics to give the final verdict on the value of the new decipherment here briefly outlined. But even now it can safely be said that its importance in the history of Maya glyph deciphering cannot be questioned [he presumably had not read Thompson's diatribe]. The troublesome fact that it is presented in a language inaccessible to most scholars of the Western world must be no excuse for them not to familiarize themselves thoroughly with it. For the first time the writing system has been shown to be built up according to principles prevailing in other primitive writings. This is already a strong indication that the new decipherment is laid on a sound basis. It is further hard to believe that so consistent a system of syllabic signs, with phonetic values that seem to fit all combinations where they occur, could have been worked out if it were not essentially correct.

Sweden may have been open to such a new avenue of research, but Germany (the home of Förstemann, Seler, and Schellhas) was certainly not. The next year, in 1956, the young German epigrapher Thomas Barthel – who had been a cryptographer with the Wehrmacht during the war – took up where Thompson had left off (but minus the Cold War polemics), at a meeting in Copenhagen of the International Congress of Americanists.[6] This was a meeting also attended by Knorosov, who had managed to sneak into the large entourage of the great expert on Siberian archaeology, Academician Okladnikov, and he delivered a paper (in English) at the same session. By this time, there was considerably more for an enemy of Knorosovian methodology to get his teeth into, for Knorosov in 1955 had brought out a more ambitious work in Spanish translation; his new readings included a great many of mainly morphemic references, and I must with some sorrow say that even those most sympathetic to his approach from the very beginning have felt that with many of these, Yuri Valentinovich has strayed off the mark – or at least did not provide the justifications that are so strong with his phonetic work based upon Landa.

Be that as it may, Barthel stressed that the Cambridge (i.e., Thompson) and the Hamburg schools (he then taught there) saw eye-to-eye on the Knorosov problem.

Barthel's career is a curious one. Like some sort of *doppelgänger*, his career in decipherment parallels that of Knorosov's in many ways, yet unlike the Soviet's, has left few intellectual offspring. Both have devoted their lives to epigraphy, both have tried to crack the Maya script, and both have put their minds to the Rongo-rongo script of remote Easter Island. To my mind, where Barthel went wrong was in his unswerving loyalty to the anti-phonetic tradition of his German predecessors (he noted that his Copenhagen paper was given on the fiftieth anniversary of Förstemann's death), but perhaps even more in his unwillingness to see the Maya script as a true writing system like those of the Old World civilizations – a view matched by Thompson and his friend Richard Long. Knorosov's background in comparative studies, whether Marxist or not, gave him the strength that they lacked.

Some thirty-five years ago, Mérida was Mexico's quietest backwater, a gleaming white city of largely one-story houses, with many bronzed Maya women clad in dazzling white *huipils* in the streets and markets; Yucatec Maya could still be heard throughout, and it had a deserved reputation as being a safe, spotlessly clean provincial capital. I had married the daughter of the noted geneticist and Russian exile Theodosius Dobzhansky in March of 1955; Sophie was an undergraduate major in anthropology at Radcliffe, I was a beginning graduate student at Harvard (we actually met over a lab table, filling human skulls with mustard seed to measure cranial capacity). I proposed taking her to the Maya area, which she had never seen, over the next Christmas holiday, and in late December and early January of 1955–56,[7] we found ourselves in Mérida, as a base for excursions to sites like Uxmal and Chichén Itzá.

Our hotel in Mérida was the Montejo, a thoroughly old-fashioned hostelry in Colonial style. We were delighted and somewhat awed to find that a fellow guest was the famous Carnegie artist-archaeologist Tatiana Proskouriakoff, a slim, nervous, brown-haired lady then in her mid-forties. I had gotten to know many of the Carnegie people, including Eric Thompson, because their Cambridge headquarters at 10 Frisbie Place was cheek-by-jowl with the Peabody Museum, where the Anthropology Department was based, so "Tania" was an old acquaintance, so to speak.

Tania was definitely interested in Maya writing, but she always deferred to Eric's opinions (as did the rest of the Carnegie crowd); her epoch-making findings about the subject-matter of the inscriptions were not to see the light of day for another five years. But even though she pretty much toed Eric's particular line, Tania was a gloriously contrary person. In fact, she was legendary in this regard: if you said, "Tania, isn't this a nice day?," Tania would deny it, but a few minutes later comment on how good the weather was. Given this, and given her (often denied) interest in things Russian – like my parents-in-law, she, too, was an exile – it is hardly surprising that she would have expressed a curiosity about the work of Yuri Knorosov.

One of my manias is the collecting of books on Mesoamerica, a disease that began in my student days, and one that I have never once regretted. Prowling through Mérida's scattering of bookstores, all badly stocked, we did come across one of the last copies for sale of the great, early Colonial, Yucatec Maya dictionary edited by Martínez Hernández, along with a grubbily-produced little pamphlet[8] turned out by the "Biblioteca Obrera," apparently a front organization of the then-illegal Communist Party of Mexico. While the other titles in the series included J.V. Stalin's "Economic Problems of Socialism in the U.S.S.R." and "How to be a Good Communist" by Liu Shao-chi, this one was an unauthorized Spanish translation of most of Knorosov's 1952 Sovietskaya Etnografiya bombshell.

I read this through several times. It made incredibly good sense to me, in fact seemed to be the first sensible treatment I had read of the non-calendrical portion of the script. In the light of what I knew of Oriental scripts (I had just spent two years in Taiwan, and was currently studying Japanese at Harvard with Edwin O. Reischauer), it made even more sense. Since Sophie was bilingual in English and Russian, we reached the conclusion that Knorosov's work ought to reach a wider audience in the United States and elsewhere through translation.

Tania had bought the same pamphlet, and when she finished it, we could see that she was deeply interested, but I believe that until Eric's death she was torn between a conviction that Knorosov might just be right, and her fear of Eric's disapproval. She never did reconcile these two attitudes. "Maybe he's got something, but I just don't know" was her usual reaction.

I felt considerably fewer qualms about opposing Thompson, even though I was but a young neophyte in the Maya field, and Thompson had been at it for decades. Years of strict education and discipline in New England boarding schools had made me reluctant to accept authority without question, and I had long agreed with Thomas Jefferson that "a little rebellion now and then is a good thing." Much as I respected Eric Thompson for his vast erudition, I sensed that, in certain areas, that particular emperor had no clothes. One of these was his absolute unwillingness to grant the Olmec of Veracruz and Tabasco, the carvers of great stone heads, any priority in the development of civilization over the Classic Maya; Eric had marshaled vast quantities of facts to crush the Olmec and their enthusiasts, but I had the gall to publish a refutation when I was yet a graduate student, thereby alienating various Thompsonians, young and old alike.

My other act of subversion was to write directly to Knorosov, expressing my interest in his work and support for his ideas about early writing systems. In my letter of 20 August, 1957, I said in one paragraph:

> If I correctly understand your viewpoint, the Maya script would be very much like modern Japanese writing. As you know, the Japanese have a large number of Chinese ideograms (*kanji*) to express the roots of their words; for an essentially non-affixing language like Chinese this would suffice, but not for grammatically complex Japanese. Consequently, Japanese affixes are expressed by syllabic signs (*kana*) ultimately derived from the ideograms. However, any Japanese sentence can be expressed entirely by *kana*. It appears that it is this dual nature of Maya writing which has led Thompson, on the one hand, and Whorf, on the other, astray. You have conclusively demonstrated syllabic affixing in the Maya script and that Thompson's so-called "decipherments" are no more than guesses at the meaning of some ideograms.

I was wrong about affixing: syllabic writing has turned out to be pervasive throughout the Maya script. I was also wrong about "ideograms." This was part of a correspondence that extended over the years; I get a degree of satisfaction thinking about the puzzlement of all the spooks who opened and read this mail, for this was the period when the CIA was scanning all correspondence with the Soviet Union, and their KGB counterparts were doing a like job, on *their* side.

Knorosov's doctoral thesis on Landa was published in 1955, and he sent us a copy. Sophie and I wrote a laudatory review in *American Antiquity*, calling attention to his work on decipherment. This must have displeased Thompson, but what really must have galled the great Mayanist was when we called attention to the Soviet's telling comparison of Thompson with Athanasius Kircher! And matters were made even worse when Sophie's translation of a new paper by Knorosov outlining his methods and decipherments appeared in the same journal in 1958,[9] ensuring a wide audience among Mayanists and linguists for those subversive views from behind the Iron Curtain.

Dave Kelley – David Humiston Kelley, to give him his full name – must surely be unique in the annals of Maya studies.[10] A lively mixture of Irish puckishness and New England Yankee sobriety, Dave's large frame, bald head, and leprechaun smile are familiar features at professional meetings, where he can always be expected to present a paper that may be unusual and even outrageous, according to one's lights, but is usually grounded in the most impeccable scholarship.

I have known Dave since the days when we were fellow undergraduates at Harvard, and I have always been struck by his immense knowledge of whatever is strange, outlandish, and out-of-the-way anywhere in the world. UFOs, the genealogy of Irish and Armenian kings, trans-Pacific diffusion, and lost continents have all claimed his attention at various stages of his career. He is a born non-conformist, and it is small wonder that he has pursued his own untrammeled path in Maya decipherment, to the disgust of Eric Thompson.

East Jaffrey is a delightful, old-fashioned New Hampshire village in the shadow of Mt. Monadnock, and it was there that Dave spent much of his youth, in a Victorian frame house with two aunts. I will never forget the day that he invited me up there with other student friends. There were the two aged maiden aunts in rockers. Up on the third floor was Dave's own room, which one entered through a horrific wall mural depicting the destruction-of-the-world page from the Dresden Codex, painted by his younger brother. The shelves were lined with archaeology books, sci-fi pulp magazines of the most outré sort, and UFO literature. This was clearly not your average Harvard student.

Dave was born in Albany to an Irish Catholic father and a Yankee mother, and passed his early years at school in upstate New York. His career as an archaeologist was set at age fifteen. His Aunt Alice Humiston (one of the two old ladies I met in East Jaffrey) was then Chief Cataloguer for the University of California in Los Angeles Library, and a friend of Miss Margaret Morley, Sylvanus' niece. Miss Morley recommended *Digging in Yucatan* by Ann Axtell Morris (wife of a Carnegie archaeologist) as something a boy might be interested in.[11] So, Aunt Alice sent him a copy. Two of the plates in the book fascinated him: one, near the beginning, showed a tremendous mound of dirt at Chichén Itzá, with people standing on it, while in the second one, near the end, that same mound had turned into the resplendent Temple of the Thousand Columns. As Dave puts it, "I thought, hey, that's something I'd like doing."

A few years later, Dave wrote to A.M. Tozzer about getting into Harvard, and Tozzer replied encouragingly. Following a three-year stint in the Army, Kelley entered Harvard as a freshman in 1946, where he became one of Tozzer's two last student advisees (William Sanders, who was to specialize in central Mexico, was the other). Tozzer was an exacting teacher: he covered the blackboard in the seminar room with bibliography in a minute hand, and one was expected to read everything, including even those sources that did not support your point of view.

"This included people like Eric," Dave told me, "of whom he was not overly fond, and whose opinions he didn't always respect." Dave and myself were both lucky in that Carnegie's Division of Historical Research, which was responsible for the study of the Maya, occupied an old frame building right next to the Peabody Museum, and Dave saw a great deal of both Eric Thompson and Tania Proskouriakoff.

Dave Kelley recognizes that his relationship with Thompson was never particularly close; Eric obviously disliked Dave's non-conformist views on the historical nature of the Classic monuments and inscriptions (in which he anticipated a revolution that was to follow), his non-acceptance of the Thompson (or GMT) correlation (about which in fact Thompson proved to be right), his theories about the trans-Pacific diffusion of the Mesoamerican calendar from west to east (Dave made this the subject of his Ph.D. dissertation), and his interest in phoneticism.

It was chance that brought Kelley and Knorosov together, an event that turned Dave into the Russian's most effective spokesman in the West. During the summer of 1956, Dave was in Scotland and Ireland, characteristically researching Woodrow Wilson's genealogy for a friend who was writing the President's biography; he took advantage of his stay in Europe to cross over to Copenhagen for the International Conference of Americanists.[12] There he was transfixed by the presentation of Knorosov (of whom he had previously never heard), and after meeting him, chatted with him in Spanish, their only *lingua franca* (both spoke it badly, according to Dave).

Returning to Harvard that fall, he found a conspiracy in progress. For several years running, those students who were interested in Mesoamerica had joined together in an informal seminar which we called the "Mesa Cuadrada" ("Square Table") in emulation of the Mesa Redonda ("Round Table") which had existed for many years in Mexico. The speakers we managed to bring in, and our student talks, were a lot more interesting than the more official seminar series sponsored by the Anthropology faculty, and we had a larger attendance than they did, to the annoyance of the authorities. During the academic year 1956–57, it was my turn to be Mesa Cuadrada president, and with Tania's surreptitious help I organized an evening session entirely devoted to the implications of Knorosov's work. It was quite a session. In line with Knorosov's comparative approach to early writing systems, we had presentations on the Egyptian script from William Stevenson Smith of Boston's Museum of Fine Arts, and on the Chinese script by a Chinese scholar from Harvard's Yenching Institute (his name now escapes me). For historical perspective on past attempts at phonetic decipherment, linguist John Carroll, Whorf's literary executor, talked on that much-maligned innovator, and for Knorosov's own theories and decipherments, we had Dave Kelley himself. I still have Tania Proskouriakoff's proposed outline for the session (see Appendix A), and it shows that she had an entirely modern approach to this controversial subject: she was, in retrospect, years ahead of her time.

I thought that it was only fair to invite Eric Thompson to present his point of view, but he turned us down on the probably spurious excuse that his blood pressure wouldn't stand it. It just wasn't Eric's style to defend his position on the glyphs in a public forum, especially among lowly graduate students.

Dave went on to a teaching post at Texas Technological College in Lubbock Texas, and there prepared what was to be his most influential paper – and one that was studiously ignored by Thompson for the rest of his life. Entitled (in translation) "Phoneticism in the Maya Script," it appeared in 1962 in the respected Mexican journal *Estudios de Cultura Maya*, and was a long and thoughtful defense of Knorosov's phonetic-syllabic readings, and a refutation of Thompson's attacks, which were increasing in frequency and stridency.[13] But Kelley took Knorosovian methodology into an entirely new area for the very first time: into the monumental inscriptions.[14] As Classic Maya civilization was disintegrating in the southern lowlands, the great city of Chichén Itzá in the center of the northern Yucatán Peninsula entered a period of vigorous growth; within the space of a few decades in the ninth century a number of stone lintels were carved with long glyphic texts (some first published by John Lloyd Stephens in the last century). It was from these inscriptions that Hermann Beyer had isolated repeating glyph combinations and clauses back in the 1930s, and Kelley's eye was caught by one of these.

35 *Glyph for* lakin, *"east."*

In this particular cluster, Dave recognized Landa's (and Knorosov's) syllabic *ka*, *ku*, and *ca*, as well as the upside-down Ahau sign that Knorosov had identified as *la* in the sign for "east," *lakin*. Preceding *la* was a crosshatched glyph that Dave concluded was an allograph (or variant) of the "open" sign read by the Russian as *pa*. Put together, all of

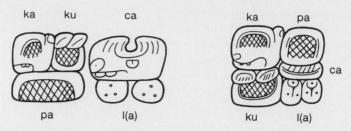

36 *Kelley's reading of* Kakupacal *at Chichén Itzá. These are*
variant spellings based upon the Maya phonetic syllabary.

the glyphs spelled out *ka-ku-pa-ca-l(a)*, or Kakupacal ("Fiery Shield"),
mentioned in the post-Conquest chronicles as a valiant Itzá captain. This
was a tremendous achievement: a personal name was found to have been
written in a stone inscription by scribes operating under the rules
discovered by Knorosov; it was an achievement which presaged the
present generation of decipherers. And it brought us closer to one of
John Lloyd Stephens' dreams, that histories recorded in the Colonial
documents might be linked in some way to events in the ancient Maya
cities.

Notwithstanding Thompson's disapproval of somebody he liked to
believe was on the lunatic fringe, Kelley persisted in his determination to
put phoneticism on a firm basis: underneath all of that Irish mischie-
vousness there is a rockbed of good sense. When Dave's massive
Deciphering the Maya Script appeared in 1976,[15] a year after Thompson's
death, even the most loyal Thompsonians were faced with irrefutable
evidence that Knorosov had been right and Eric very, very wrong.

Let us return to 1957. With the demise of the Carnegie program in Maya
archaeology, Thompson had left the United States for his new home in
Essex, where he was immersed in preparing his long-planned *Catalog of
Maya Hieroglyphs*, a prodigious task that was finally published five years
later.[16] He and I continued to correspond, I on my part trying to explain
to him why I thought that Knorosov and Kelley had something. I imagine
that he was quite peeved at our review of Knorosov's Landa, and
considerably nettled by the reference to Athanasius Kircher. On the
27th of October he sat down to type this letter to me:

Dear Mike

> You can't believe – oh, surely not
> When the centuries of the world are so high –
> You'll not believe what, in their innocence,
> These old credulous children in the street
> Imagine

And these children? Not Christopher Fry's but the Witches coven which rides wild at midnight in the skies at Yuri's command. Dave Kelly [sic], who chases Quetzalcoatl, Xipe, Tonatiuh, and Xolotl[17] as lightly across the atolls of the Pacific as I once chased Marble Whites and Red Admirals with my butterfly net into the limestone quarries of an England which vanished in 1914, and Burland[18] and those fugitive nuns of the Abbey Art Center in holy New Barnet, who dance with lightsome toe on cups of steaming cocoa, and, fluttering on the outskirts, poor sex-starved Tania seeking in the oracle of once Holy Russia a droshky which can carry her to a Chekhov bliss ...

Well, the old bull ought to be at bay, but he isn't; he's just quietly chewing the cud out at pasture. I seem to remember two years ago everyone was saying its all up with old J.E.S.T.; C-14 has blown his correlation sky high, and he's the only one that doesn't know it ... Well, looks to me now that with the new C-14 readings the old 11.16.0.0.0 correlation is right back on top, where it obviously had to be for historical, astronomical, archaeological and every other reason.

I can watch with equanimity the Burlands and Dave Kelly's [sic] running after Yuri, for I know that exactly the same thing will happen to Yuri as has happened to all the other guys who tried to read glyphs in that way from Cyrus Thomas to Benjy Whorf. Now that I have found that there are at least 300 affixes in the Maya glyph writing (I have 296 to date and haven't finished yet), I am more than ever certain that there never was any system such as Yuri propounds.

That's why I didn't have to have the old blood pressure checked before I read the latest Yuri outburst.[19] With my Constable view of mellowed red brick and white house across the Valley and with a fairly successful return (provided one can be conveniently blind at times) to the 18th century, I can take matters quietly as I proceed with my catalogue of Maya glyphs which, I know, will be a rich mine in years to come for Yuri and others of his kidney who will prove to their own satisfaction that the glyphs on the last prisoner of P.N. 12[20] say Epstein me fecit. That's why I don't have high blood pressure, and stayed away from your Mesa Cuadrada, for as the poet has it:

> May I govern my passions with absolute sway
> Grow wiser and better as strength wears away,
> Without stone or gout to a gentle decay.

Well, Mike, you're going to see the year A.D. 2000. Paste this in the flyleaf of Maya Hieroglyphic Writing; Introduction, and see whether I'm all wet then. Yours

In gentle decay
Eric T.

Eric was indeed right in one respect: the *Catalog* has become an indispensable tool for all Maya epigraphers (everybody uses the Thompson or "T" numbers in referring to glyphs), and the followers of Yuri certainly do mine it. The irony is that all modern glyph specialists are of Knorosov's "kidney."

It was in vain that I answered Eric's letter by suggesting that he hadn't really addressed the general theory of Maya writing which his antagonist had advanced, but concentrated only on details. It was not long before another missive came from his pen, saying in part:

Thank you for your good letter. I think that we are arguing at cross-purposes. I don't claim that there is no phonetic element in Maya writing, especially by the time the present edition of the Dresden was written. What I object to is the K. approach, which I consider completely untrained. If he has hit the nail once or twice, fine, but I would put into his mouth (although fool is not correct in his case) 3 lines of Cowper:

> I am not surely always in the wrong;
> Tis hard if all is false that I advance,
> A fool must now and then be right by chance.

New fuel was added to the fire when my wife's translation of Knorosov's 1958 article came out in *American Antiquity*,[21] for in it Knorosov twitted Thompson in these terms: "Some authors consider as decipherment any plausible interpretation of unknown signs." He went on to say:

In contrast to the determination of the meaning of separate hieroglyphs by indirect clues, decipherment is the beginning of an exact phonetic reading of words written in hieroglyphic form. As a result of decipherment, the study of texts becomes a branch of philology [linguistics].

In other words, Knorosov was denying Thompson any merits as a decipherer. As an example of Thompsonian "method," Knorosov pointed a finger at Eric's interpretation of the accepted hieroglyphic combination for "dog" (already read as *tzul* by Knorosov). It consists, as we have seen, of two signs, one of which appears to be the ribs and backbone of an animal. Thompson says that this is a metaphorical sign for "dog" because in Mesoamerican mythology the dog accompanies the shades of the dead to the world beyond the grave – hardly a case of "decipherment" in Knorosov's definition of the word (incidentally, the glyph in question provides an excellent example of the rebus origin of phonetic signs, for in Yucatec Maya, *tzul* means both "dog" and "backbone," the syllabic sign *tzu* being the end result).

Thompson's increasing annoyance and bitterness are tellingly revealed in a comment he published in the same year:[22]

A review [the one in *Yan*] expressed at some length my unfavorable impression of the first paper by the Russian Knorosov, who, treading in the footsteps of so many discredited enthusiasts, claims to have discovered (nestling in the bosom of Marxist philosophy) the key to the decipherment of the Maya glyphs. His second and much fuller publication, containing large numbers of purported decipherments, has recently appeared. My enthusiasm is still in deep freeze.

In spite of his assertions as to the worthlessness of Knorosov's publications, Thompson spent a great deal of time refuting them – which is something he never bothered to do with dozens of lunatic and semi-lunatic fringe efforts to crack the glyphs which have appeared in every decade for the last seventy-five years. What made Knorosov even more dangerous was that his work had appeared in English in a journal which was – and still is – the "house organ" for all U.S. archaeologists, whether Mayanist or not. It is therefore no surprise that Eric's major counterblast appeared in the same journal in 1959.[23] With the title "Systems of hieroglyphic writing in Middle America and methods of deciphering them," it reveals all of Thompson's faults and none of his strengths. Repeating once again the Valentini arguments about the Landa "alphabet," he then moves to missionary writing systems used by the Spaniards in sixteenth-century Mexico, such as Testerian, with which the friars tried to inculcate phoneticism among the natives, and implies that the Landa abecedary was one of these.

Thompson then describes past attempts at using the Landa "alphabet" as "making silk purses out of sows' ears"; these are all "thoroughly discredited" (one of his favorite words). He spends the remainder of the article on certain details of his opponent's claimed decipherments, and pounces on the fact that there are sometimes reversals of the usual left-to-right order in the glyphs – ignoring the fact that change of order due to aesthetic or scribal considerations was among Knorosov's hieroglyphic principles. But our friend Athanasius Kircher would have been proud of one of Eric's summary paragraphs:

No fire-faced prophet brought me word which way behoved me to go, as Housman put it. I can claim neither to have deciphered the Maya glyphs nor to know of any system to replace the one I have attacked, for I suspect that Maya writing, like Topsy, just grew. Rebus writing is surely an important factor and rebus pictures also. Clearly glyphic elements represent both words and syllables (often homonyms). There are ideographs, glyphs with roots in mythology [his so-called "metaphorograms"], and bits and pieces of half a dozen other attempts to write [my emphasis].

In his 1962 Catalog he presents the same messy picture of the script:[24] "In short, we are confounded by an unsystematic hodgepodge of slow growth. Hodgepodges, of course, lack either keys or locks to fit them." But how any scribe could communicate with such a hodgepodge, or how such communications could ever be read, in any sense of the word, was a question left as unanswered by Thompson as it had been by Kircher some three centuries earlier.

One of Eric's very last diatribes against the Red Menace came in 1971, in his preface to the third edition of Maya Hieroglyphic Writing.[25] As usual, Eric misstates Knorosov's position by claiming that the latter views Maya script as entirely phonetic, then takes up his Cold War cudgel:

A point of some importance, I feel, is that with a phonetic system, as with breaking a code, the rate of decipherment accelerates with each newly established reading. It is now nineteen years since it was announced with such fanfare of tabarded heralds of the U.S.S.R. that after nearly a century of abortive bourgeois effort, the problem had been solved by this Marxist-Leninist approach. I would gladly make a pilgrimage to Marx's grave in Highgate Cemetery to give thanks, were that really so. Alas! The first flow of alleged decipherments has not swollen to a river, as it should with successful solving of a phonetic system; it has long since dried up.

He took one final kick at Knorosov in his *Maya Hieroglyphs Without Tears*,[26] a British Museum pamphlet of 1972 which now has little other than curiosity value in spite of its elegant appearance (Kircher's publications were very handsomely published, too – the coffee-table books of their time).

We know in retrospect that Thompson was completely off the mark, and Knorosov right on it. You might well ask, why did it take so long after Knorosov's 1952 article for the flow of decipherments to swell into a river? Why did the Maya decipherment take so very long as compared to, say, Egyptian or the cuneiform scripts or Hieroglyphic Hittite? I am sorry to say that the major reason was that almost the entire Mayanist field was in willing thrall to one very dominant scholar, Eric Thompson, who by the force of his personality, his access to the resources of the Carnegie Institution of Washington, his vast learning, and his acerbic – even cruel – wit, was able to stem the Russian tide until his demise in 1975. Most Mayanists had (and have) little grounding in linguistics or epigraphy; by default, they left the field to Eric, who, by bombarding them with endless references to dead poets and Greek gods, effectively robbed them of their critical faculties.

Even Knorosov's major publication on the subject, the massive and minutely documented *Pis'mennost Indeitsev Maiia* ("The Writing of the Maya Indians"),[27] which appeared in 1963, made little impression on Thompson's constituency, even when my wife brought out a translation of selected chapters from it, with a typically cautious introduction by Tania. I stuck my neck out in 1966, when my book *The Maya*[28] was the first popular work on Maya civilization to praise the Knorosov approach; the reviews which I received from the experts were characteristically negative on this subject. As late as 1976, Arthur Demarest, then a student at Tulane University, was able to publish a contentious and ill-advised attack on Knorosov's decipherment in a respected series,[29] including the lofty statement: "It is hardly necessary to conclude that Knorosov's system is invalid ... He is not the first scholar to create an erroneous decipherment, and he will probably not be the last."

Dissenters like Dave Kelley and myself found ourselves on the outside, as far as our views on the Maya script went, but beyond the confines of archaeology we discovered an important group of allies: the linguists. These had not forgotten the rough treatment meted out by Thompson oñ their colleagues Benjamin Whorf and Archibald Hill. Some of the specialists on the Mayan languages, such as the much-respected Floyd Lounsbury at Yale (who was subsequently to play a major role in the decipherment), thought very highly of Knorosov, and knew a great deal more than Eric did about writing systems in general. And I had heard a rumor that one very distinguished linguist had flatly claimed that, once Thompson had been gathered to his ancestors, *he* would crack Maya writing!

Arrogant or not, there was a certain accuracy in what the anonymous linguist predicted, for the take-off period of the great decipherment came only after Thompson died in 1975, and the linguistic contribution to this extraordinary intellectual feat was a powerful one.

In the final year of his life, the Queen conferred a knighthood on Thompson in recognition of his many contributions to Maya studies. I have no idea why I had a premonition, but when I saw the New Year Honours list published in the *New York Times*, I knew I would see Eric's name on it, and there it was, along with Charlie Chaplin's. I immediately wrote him my congratulations; his letter of thanks expressed his chagrin that Alfred P. Maudslay had never received such an honor. Wrong, and perhaps wrongheaded, on some important matters, Thompson was certainly not wrong on everything, and he made many very real contributions to the subject. I cherish my copy of *Maya Hieroglyphic Writing*, complete with pasted-in letter, as he had stipulated.

Why was Thompson so bitterly opposed to Knorosov and everything he did or published? One reason might have been his deep religiosity, which led him to prefer "metaphorograms," almost mystical Kircherian explanations for the glyphs. Another might have been his detestation of Communism and Soviet Russia. But his obsession with Knorosov, to the point where he felt it necessary to pound away at him year after year, with every means fair or foul, suggests to me something else: he feared Knorosov's theories because, at bottom, he knew they were correct.

My suspicions that this was so stem from a consideration of the figures illustrating glyphs for the Maya months in *Maya Hieroglyphic Writing*.[30] For each month, Thompson had his artist draw a series of glyphs, from the earliest to the latest forms; naturally, the last in each series is the glyph as it appears in Landa's *Relación*. Now, the names of the months as they were known in late pre-Conquest Yucatán mostly bore little relation to these glyphs as they were read and pronounced in Classic times. Accordingly, as we now understand, Landa's informant prefixed some of them with helpful phonetic-syllabic signs defining their "modern," Yucatecan sound. For example, to the left of Landa's Pop (the first month) is a reduplicated sign which reads, as Floyd Lounsbury discovered, *po-p(o)*. Eric had all such signs stripped off for his *Maya Hieroglyphic Writing* of 1950.

How, I ask, and why, should he have done this unless he had recognized and censored out phonetic writing – or what Knorosov would have called phonetic reinforcement? This evidence suggests that he must have been entertaining such phonetic ideas at least two years before Knorosov burst on the scene, and then suppressed them as they didn't fit in with his "hodgepodge" notions about the script, or with his "metaphorograms." The savagery of the salvos that he sent Knorosov's way demonstrates to me, at least, that he knew he was wrong, and very much in the wrong. Once having made his declaration of war in the *Yan* review, he couldn't rescind it.

So Thompson, like Seler before him in his dispute with Cyrus Thomas, had a victory of a sort. But it was very short-lived: in less than four years, as many as a hundred-and-thirty-five participants were to attend the Albany conference on phoneticism in Maya hieroglyphic writing. The sun had set on the Thompson era.

7 The Age of Proskouriakoff: The Maya Enter History

It was Tsar Peter the Great who exiled the Proskouriakoffs to Siberia. In June 1698 (one year after the last independent Maya kingdom at Tayasal had surrendered), the Streltsy musketeers had risen up against the young despot – a revolt immortalized in Moussorgsky's opera *Khovanshchina*. But the Streltsy failed and suffered the most terrible punishments; the lucky ones were banished, including the ancestor of the woman whose brilliant research was to bring the ancient Maya civilization into history.[1]

Tatiana Proskouriakoff was born in 1909 in Tomsk, then the largest city in Siberia.[2] Tomsk lies on the headwaters of the Ob River, on a rail spur leading north from the Trans-Siberian Railway. Notwithstanding its remoteness from St. Petersburg and Moscow, it was hardly a frontier town in the early part of this century: it boasted a university, various museums, libraries, and scientific societies. Tania's family belonged to that great and unsung class of intelligentsia – scientists, writers, teachers, and so forth – that had given pre-Revolutionary Russia its considerable distinction in the arts and sciences.

Avenir Proskouriakoff, her father, was a chemist and engineer, and her paternal grandfather had taught natural science, while her mother Alla Nekrassova (daughter of a general) was a physician. In 1915, Avenir was commissioned by the Tsar to go to the United States to inspect munitions and other equipment destined for the Russian war effort. Tania, her older sister Ksenia, and her parents set sail that autumn from Archangel on the White Sea but the ship became locked in the ice; simultaneously, the two girls came down with scarlet fever and diptheria (Ksenia also contracted measles!). They had to be carried back across the ice, but finally left Russia by the following summer.

Their destination was Philadelphia. Following the Russian Revolution of 1917, this became their permanent home. Yet it was not so foreign to them, for the Proskouriakoffs found themselves among a group of intellectual White Russians, the very milieu in which they had lived back in Tomsk. Tania and her sister entered grade school; among her schoolmates and by her sister, Tania became known as "Duchess," not because of any false pride on her part, but because her young contemporaries had recognized that here was someone who outshone them all. If Tania ever had a Russian accent in those early days, she soon lost it, for when I knew her she spoke unaccented, East Coast American English; but she always retained the ability to speak the language, and could write Russian in a fine, pre-Soviet hand.

When Tania graduated from Pennsylvania State University with a degree in architecture in 1930, the country had just entered the Great Depression, and jobs in her new profession were almost non-existent. She worked for a while in a Philadelphia department store, then out of boredom she began making drawings for one of the curators in the University Museum, at very low pay.

Tania's drawings of artifacts attracted the attention of Linton Satterthwaite, Jr., a lanky, pipe-smoking archaeologist who had become director of the museum's massive excavation program at Piedras Negras, a ruined Maya city of the Classic period on the right bank of the Usumacinta River in Guatemala. Satterthwaite was looking for an artist to do architectural reconstruction drawings of buildings uncovered at the site, and Tania landed the job – all travel and expenses paid, but no salary (these were lean times for museums, too). Tania's life as a Mayanist had begun.

That irascible Austrian, Teobert Maler, had explored Piedras Negras at the close of the nineteenth century, and had produced for the Peabody at Harvard a magnificent photographic record of its splendid stone monuments – stelae and lintels. But the site was, and still is, in a very dilapidated state.[3] "Penn" had been digging at "P.N." since 1931, and Tania worked there under Satterthwaite's direction from 1934 to 1938. Archaeological camps run the gamut from Spartan – even sordid – conditions at one end of the comfort scale, to luxurious at the upper end, and there was no question as to which category the Piedras Negras dig belonged. It is said that a uniformed houseboy served cocktails every evening (Satterthwaite liked his dry martinis); whether true or not, Tania was lucky to work for a highly competent archaeologist with a dry sense of humor and real competence in the glyphs.

Tania's task was to produce an architectural restoration of Structure P-7, and a perspective drawing of the Acropolis as it might have looked during the Late Classic. Her watercolor rendering shows the pyramid-temples and range structures covered with gleaming white plaster, with the Usumacinta winding through jungle-covered hills in the background. Apart from the almost deserted appearance of the complex (in line with the then-current notion that Classic cities were near-empty "ceremonial centers"), what is striking are the rows of stelae standing in groups before two of the pyramids flanking the broad stairway. Our young artist was to file these P.N. stela groups in a recess of her mind, and they would be remembered with notable results many years later, in her Cambridge apartment.

Satterthwaite was one of those scholars who take most of their learning with them to the grave. He published very little; what did reach print was often couched in prose so elliptical and obscure that even the experts had difficulty following his arguments. Somewhat mischievously, Thompson once told me that he had never been able to finish Satterthwaite's "Concepts and Structures of Maya Calendrical Arithmetic"[4] through to the end. Yet by all accounts he was an excellent teacher and a sympathetic colleague who kept an open mind to every point of view, and he certainly did not take everything that Thompson said as gospel truth. Although he never actually deciphered a single Maya hieroglyph, he was a figure to be reckoned with in the Maya field.

Tania's reconstructed Acropolis perspective immediately kindled the enthusiasm of the Carnegie Institution's ebullient Sylvanus Morley. He dreamed up the idea that Tania should do a whole series of reconstructions of the most significant Maya sites, and in 1939 he sent her to Copán for that purpose. Tania became a full-fledged Carnegie employee, with a real salary for the first time in her life; this was a post she would occupy for the rest of her life.

Copán in the late 1930s must have been quite a place. Carnegie's excavation and restoration program was directed by the colorful Norwegian Gustav Strömsvik, whose picaresque career was noteworthy even by Mayanist standards. In the late 1920s Gus and a fellow crewman had "jumped ship" from their merchantman while it was anchored off Progreso, on the north coast of Yucatán; days later, two battered dead bodies washed ashore, and it was assumed that they were the two deserters. It is said that once a year, Gus used to travel to the Progreso cemetery to grieve over his own gravestone. Subsequently, Gus made his way to Chichén Itzá, where he had heard of a "gringo" archaeological project, and Morley gave him a job repairing the expedition's trucks, for Gus was not only a fine sailor but a very good mechanic and engineer.

It was not long before Strömsvik was helping to dig and reconstruct buildings at Chichén. His talents in this line led Morley and Kidder to select him for the Copán project, where he turned out to be one of the finest field archaeologists on the Carnegie staff. Ian Graham describes the scene at Copán:

Proskouriakoff traveled alone to Copán, and once there, found life at the staff camp distinctly wild. Having been brought up in a very proper European household, she was surprised considerably by the battery of bottles displayed on a table in the camp *sala*, and more so on finding out how much the consumption of their contents enlivened the nightly games of poker, especially on Saturdays. One Sunday morning, annoyed with the men for sleeping so late, she opened the door of Gustav Strömsvik's room and let his parrot in. Soon there was a duet of squawking, the parrot having gotten Strömsvik by the mustache.[5]

A home movie, made by John Longyear when he was a Harvard graduate student preparing a thesis on the ceramics of Copán, shows a young and very good-looking Tania swigging beer from a bottle at the same camp, so she must have adapted at least somewhat to the regime.

After Copán, Tania journeyed to Chichén Itzá and the sites of the Puuc region in Yucatán, making measured drawings in preparation for her reconstructions, all of which appeared in her *Album of Maya Architecture* in 1946.[6] It being increasingly clear to "Doc" Kidder that this woman was considerably more than an artist, he appointed her in 1943 as a full-time staff archaeologist.

From her school days on, everyone who knew Tania seems to have been in agreement that hers was an extraordinary, unusual mind. One facet of it certainly leaned towards the artistic: she was a highly competent draftswoman, and a fine artist with a perceptive and appreciative eye for the visual arts. But she also had a strong scientific bent and a gift for logical analysis. Being raised in a family of scientists certainly helped hone her scholarly talents. When she applied herself to a problem – and she was a "loner," usually working by herself in self-imposed isolation – her mind operated like the proverbial steel trap.

Unlike so many Russian exiles, Tania was a convinced rationalist and atheist. She greatly enjoyed an argument, and perhaps she had deliberately taken an extreme position on this subject, but I remember her trying to convince me that one should not even listen to Bach's B-Minor Mass because it was religious! Be that as it may, such a mindset predisposed her to seek rational explanations in everything, even Maya art and writing, and it steered her well away from the kinds of semi-mystical mumbo-jumbo that so entranced Eric Thompson. On the down side, though, she had absolutely no interest in the iconography of Maya art, and went so far as to deny that there were any gods at all among the Classic Maya. Here is where Eric was surely on the right track, and Tania not.

Tania's penchant for rigorous formal analysis was applied to a body of about four hundred Maya monuments from the Classic, resulting in a method of dating each one stylistically within a span of twenty to thirty years. Her 1950 monograph, *A Study of Classic Maya Sculpture*,[7] allowed specialists to compare stylistic dates against Maya dates; but Tania went further, and provided an evolutionary picture of how Maya relief sculpture changed from earliest times through the Maya collapse. The book, which placed her in the forefront of Maya research, gave her an unparalleled view of the whole corpus of Maya art on stone, and led her inexorably to ask questions which, when finally answered, turned the whole Mayanist world upside down.

My Harvard undergraduate education concluded in 1950, but I skipped my graduation, thus inadvertently missing George Marshall's speech to the senior class, in which he announced what was to become the Marshall Plan for a Europe in ruins. With a guilty conscience, I decided that I had better be present to receive my Ph.D. degree from Harvard, which was awarded in June 1959. With spare time on my hands, I wandered over to the Peabody to see Tania. I found her in her usual spot: seated at a table in the museum's basement smoking room, for Tania was a chain smoker and had been so ever since she was sixteen.

I could see that Tania, always somewhat of a nervous person, was unusually excited over something, and she told me what it was: she had discovered a "peculiar pattern of dates," as she put it, at her old site of Piedras Negras. Before her was a chart on which she had graphed all of the dates on P.N.'s many stelae. Referring to the chart, Tania explained to me what this pattern meant; the subject-matter of the texts on the monuments was *history*, plain and simple, and not astronomy, religion, prophecy, and the like. The figures on the stelae and lintels of the ruined Maya cities were mortal men and women, and not gods, or even priests, for that matter.

I was truly thunderstruck. In one brilliant stroke, this extraordinary woman had cut the Gordian knot of Maya epigraphy, and opened up a world of dynastic rivalry, royal marriages, taking of captives, and all the other elite doings which have held the attention of kingdoms around the world since the remotest antiquity. The Maya had become real human beings.

Tania told me that she had submitted a detailed paper on her findings to *American Antiquity*; when it appeared next year under the title "Historical Implication of a Pattern of Dates at Piedras Negras, Guatemala,"[8] the entire field of Maya research was revolutionized. We had entered the Age of Proskouriakoff.

A window on how her mind worked is provided by an article she published next year, 1961, in the University Museum's journal

Expedition,[9] at the invitation of her old friend and early supporter Satterthwaite. Written for a popular audience, it is a remarkable example of logical exposition, explaining the sequence of events that led to her momentous discovery.

It all began in 1943, Tania said, when Thompson changed the date of Piedras Negras Stela 14 from A D 800, which was the date Morley had assigned it, to A D 761. Eric described it as one of a group of stelae showing "gods seated in niches formed by the bodies of celestial dragons," and remarked that this correction made Stela 14 the first to be erected in its particular row in front of Temple O-13.

Several years later, Tania noticed not only that P.N. Stela 33 had a similar scene (although no niche), but that *all* monuments of this type were the first to be set up in a given location (i.e. in a row in front of a particular pyramid). Subsequently, at every *hotun* (a five-tun interval, something less than five years), a monument with another motif was erected in the same row until another similar row was started near another temple. In short, there were distinct *sets* of monuments, each beginning with a niche stela.

At that time, Tania thought that such "niche" stelae represented the dedication of a new temple (a rather Thompsonian point of view): the ladder which was depicted marked with footsteps leading up to the niche must have symbolized the rise to the sky of the sacrificial victim, whose body was sometimes shown at the foot of the ladder. She then searched for a glyphic expression peculiar to these stelae which might indicate human sacrifice.

"What I found instead started an entirely new train of thought and led to surprising conclusions." And this is what she found:

(1)   There was a date just prior to the erection-date (always a hotun-ending) on each "niche" stela; this earlier date was always immediately followed by a sign which Thompson had nicknamed the "Toothache Glyph" since it consists of a head with its jaws bound up (or a moon-sign so tied up).

(2)   Anniversaries of this event, whatever it was, were often subsequently recorded, but only on monuments of the same group.

(3)   The only dates two groups of stelae had in common were some marking the ends of conventional time-periods (in the Long Count), thus proving that each set of monuments presents an independent set of records.

(4)   It is not the date associated with the "Toothache Glyph" that is earliest in each set, but another which is anywhere from 12 to 31 years earlier; this "Initial Date" is always immediately followed by a sign that

appeared to Thompson like a frog's head looking upward, hence the nickname "Upended Frog Glyph." Teeple, parenthetically, thought that this sign stood for a new moon day or for the same moon age. This Initial Date could not have had much public importance since it is noted only retrospectively after the "Toothache Glyph" event had taken place, and it is only then that it begins to be noted by anniversaries.

37 Dynastic event glyphs identified by Proskouriakoff. a. Birth ("upended frog"). b. Accession ("toothache").

a.   b.

Tania then framed three hypotheses to account for her findings:
—The "Upended Frog Glyph" date is the birth date of the person in the niche.
—The "Toothache Glyph" date is the accession date of the person in the niche.
—The entire set of records represents the lifetime of a ruler.
Taking only those sets whose full span was known, she calculated the length of time covered by each set: it came out to 60, 64 and 56 years, certainly what one would expect the normal lifetime of a ruler to be.

Her next step took her even deeper into the long-vanished world of these lords of the forest: this was the search for their personal names and titles. These glyphs should differ in each set, she reasoned, while the event glyphs would remain constant. Tania found what she was looking for – nominal phrases of three or four glyphs – but she had yet to prove that these in truth were related to the sculptured figures. Here she turned to Stelae 1 and 2 from Piedras Negras; the front side of each shows a male figure, but it is extremely eroded. On the back of each stela is a hefty, robed figure. Perversely, but probably in line with the dogma that the Classic Maya lived in a kind of theocracy, the long-held notion about such figures was that they were male priests, but Tania's work knocked this delusion into a cocked hat: the robed figures are *women*, as a far earlier generation of Mayanists had thought all along.[10] To return to our stelae, the birth dates on both are the same, and they are followed by the same pair of name glyphs, each prefixed with a profile, female human head. Tania identified the latter as the proclitic classifier for women (now read as *na*, the Classic form of the later Yucatec *ix*, "Lady——"). The

38 The prefix (na) for female names and titles.

woman on Stela 3 stands alone, but on Stela 3 seated next to her is a very small, robed individual with another birth date 33 years later than the first, and with her own name and female proclitic. There can be only one possible conclusion: that the portraits on the two stelae are of a single woman (surely the wife of the man on the obverse), and the little figure is her daughter. Ergo, the monuments show real people and their lives, along with their names and titles.

Like many great discoveries, Tania's was of such simplicity and of such downright obviousness, that it is a wonder that epigraphers like Morley and Thompson – who had all the data at their fingertips over a long period of time – did not hit upon it long ago. Tania was right when she said, "In retrospect, the idea that Maya texts record history, naming the rulers or lords of the towns, seems so natural that it is strange it has not been thoroughly explored before."[11]

In truth, there had been a few criers in the wilderness, but their voices were generally ignored. Remember that Stephens had said of Copán, as far back as 1841, "One thing I believe, that its history is graven on its monuments." In his day, little or nothing of the dates on the stones of the Classic cities could be read or understood. But in 1901, Charles Bowditch, a wealthy, aristocratic Bostonian who was the "angel" for the Peabody Museum's expeditions to Central America, was already an authority on Maya chronology. Here is what he had to say in commenting on Teobert Maler's report on Piedras Negras and its monuments: "Let us suppose the first date of Stela 3 to denote the birth; the second the initiation at the age of 12 years 140 days, or the age of puberty in those warm climates; the third, the choice as chieftain at the age of 33 years 265 days; the fourth his death at the age of 37 years 60 days."[12] After a parallel interpretation of Stela 1, he asks, "Could the two men represented on these stelae have been twins having the same birthday?"

David Kelley has justly commented on this passage: "If Bowditch or some contemporary scholar had gone on to check the glyphic context of this acute idea, scholars studying the Mayan writing might have been saved some sixty years of dubious astronomical interpretations."[13]

And back in 1910, Herbert J. Spinden, who had pioneered the study of Maya art and in this respect was a forerunner of Proskouriakoff, took a sharp look at the subject-matter of Maya reliefs.[14] "Judging by the graven pictures," he wrote, "many monuments of the southern Maya are memorials of conquest," with depictions of both victors and vanquished. "Now it is obvious that the presence of vassals and overlords on the monuments increases the probability that actual historical events are being commemorated and that actual historical personages are being portrayed."

Spinden then called attention to Piedras Negras Stela 12, which shows a war chief above bound captives, guarded by what Spinden thought were two soldiers (they are actually *sahalo'ob*, subsidiary war leaders); on or near the bodies of both victors and victims are groups of glyphs, and "it seems reasonable to suppose that names of both persons and places are recorded." Amazingly, as David Stuart has pointed out to me, in this same article he indicated a bat-glyph compound on this and on many other monuments both at P.N. and elsewhere which "may have some general meaning as 'here follows a name'"; almost eighty years later, David was indeed to identify this compound as introducing the name of the carver.

Spinden was truly a precursor of much that we take for granted today, and it is a tragedy that so many of his insights about Mesoamerican civilization were pushed aside and ignored during the Age of Thompson as a consequence of his lifelong espousal of a Maya–Christian correlation which proved to be untenable. I met him in his very old age, when he was admittedly senile, but he was once a truly original thinker.

Although we have come to think of the later Sylvanus Morley as a leader of the anti-historical, worship-of-time school, the early Morley had been of different mind. Impressed by the numerous Spanish accounts that the late pre-Conquest Maya kept detailed histories in their folding-screen books, Morley wrote in 1915:[15] "For this latter reason the writer believes that the practice of recording history in the hieroglyphic writing had its origin, along with many another custom, in the southern area, and consequently that the inscriptions on the monuments of the southern cities are probably, in part at least, of an historical nature."

The way Thompson and an older, but not necessarily wiser, Morley had it, the Classic Maya were unlike any other civilized people who ever lived, and they were unlike even Mesoamerican neighbors such as the Mixtec, whose passion for their own history is expressed in a number of late codices. Again, Thompson could talk himself (and his colleagues such as Morley) into any position if it coincided with his own preconceptions and predilections. In 1950 he was still able to state, in his *Maya Hieroglyphic Writing*:[16]

I do not believe that historical events are recorded on the monuments. The almost complete absence of dates, other than period endings, common to two cities ... is, I believe, due to the almost limitless choice of dates in gathering information on the katun endings. A priest in one city, gauging the aspects of a katun ending, might put more emphasis on lunar influences, and be governed accordingly in his choice of dates; priests in other cities may have regarded solar influences as paramount, and chosen dates with that in mind.

Teeple's cleverly devised but totally erroneous Determinant Theory – explaining dates other than "round" ones as solar year corrections to the calendar – held Thompson captive. He simply could not conceive of Jacinto Cunil's priestly ancestors as writers of mundane history. To Eric, even the scenes showing captives may have been religious at bottom, the unfortunate ones being destined for sacrifice in some important ceremony (which they were!), and not celebrating conquest. Like the Marxists that were so much on his mind, Eric was always finding what he knew was there in the first place.

Thompson's reaction to Tania's 1960 heresy was uncharacteristically mild, notwithstanding the demolition of one of the pillars supporting his general views about the Maya. Peter Mathews was once told by Tania that she had felt badly for not letting Eric know about her discoveries in time for him to correct the foreword to the 1960 edition of *Maya Hieroglyphic Writing* and save himself from retrospective embarrassment. When she *did* give him her still-to-be-published paper, Eric's immediate reaction was "That can't possibly be right!" But after he had taken it home and read it that night, by the following morning he had made an about-face: "Of course you're right!"[17] Russian she may have been, but Tania was no Red Menace.

The reader will have noted that Proskouriakoff's great breakthrough had very little to do with the Maya language: the texts might as well have been written in Swedish or Swahili for her immediate purpose, for her approach was purely *structural*. She was not the only epigrapher who worked largely in this mode, which was really concerned with meaning and interpretations rather than readings in one or another Mayan language. Because of her interest in Knorosov, I do know that Tania was concerned with linguistic decipherment, but it played little part in her own research, and progressively less so as she moved from middle into old age.

The same could be said of her friend Heinrich Berlin, a German-born grocery wholesaler in Mexico City who had escaped Hitler's persecutions in the 1930s. As an avocation, Berlin had for many years been structurally analyzing the inscriptions of Palenque, a task made lighter than usual by the high quality of Alfred Maudslay's epigraphic record, and by the new inscriptions and other discoveries made during the 1940s and 1950s by Alberto Ruz and other Mexican archaeologists.

Ruz's most spectacular find – a discovery of stellar magnitude – had been the crypt and sarcophagus in Palenque's largest pyramid, the Temple of the Inscriptions; this is to play a role in the next stage of the story, in Chapter 8. Suffice it to say here that the sides of the sarcophagus are carved with human figures accompanied by glyphs, and in 1959, one year before Tania's *American Antiquity* article, Berlin suggested that those glyphs were the names of the ancestors of the individual buried in this spectacular Late Classic tomb.[18] In other words, the inscription must have been historical.

Back in 1940, Morley could state "... indeed, the writer strongly doubts that any place names will ever be found in the Maya inscriptions."[19] But in 1958, a short paper by Berlin appeared in the French *Journal de le Société des Américanistes*, announcing the discovery

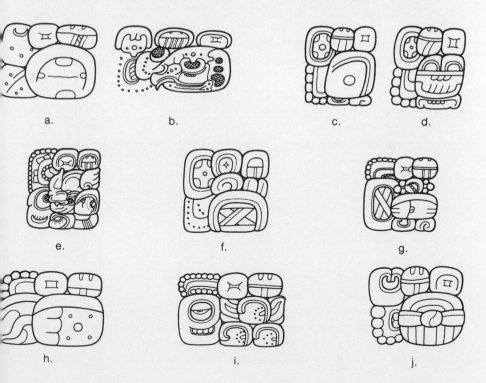

39 *Berlin's great discovery, Emblem Glyphs. a, b. Palenque. c, d. Yaxchilán. e. Copán. f. Naranjo. g. Machaquilá. h. Piedras Negras. i. Seibal. j. Tikal.*

of what he called "Emblem Glyphs," for want of a better term.[20] An Emblem Glyph consists of three parts: (1) a so-called Ben-Ich superfix, the meaning and reading of which were only to be established some years later; (2) a special prefix to which Thompson (wrongly it turns out) assigned a water association; and (3) a main sign which Berlin realized varies with the city with which it is linked. This was a truly important discovery with far-reaching consequences for the future of Maya research, but the question remained (and it is still being debated) whether Emblem Glyphs represent place-names, or the names of tutelary divinities of the cities, or the dynasties that ran them.

Be that as it may, Berlin succeeded in isolating Emblem Glyphs for Tikal, Naranjo, Yaxchilán, Piedras Negras, Palenque, Copán, Quiriguá, and Seibal (fig. 39); many more are now known. Occasionally a city will have more than one Emblem: Yaxchilán, for instance, has two, and Palenque as many as three. He was quick to point out that from time to time, Emblem Glyphs of one city will appear in the inscriptions of another, indicating some sort of relationship, and hinted that a study of Emblem Glyph distributions might enable the analysis of Maya political geography to be made.

Like Hermann Beyer before him, Berlin was interested in the structure of texts, and the isolation of recurring clauses: he saw that Emblem Glyphs sometimes were associated with what he called "useless" katuns – katun glyphs with Ben-Ich superfixes and with number prefixes – but he had no explanation for these. It would be left to Tania to find out the meaning of Ben-Ich Katuns and to find the personal names that appeared with them and with Emblem Glyphs.

Berlin went on to publish further studies in Palenque texts – one of his outstanding successes was his detection of the "Palenque Triad" of gods,[21] which we shall see enter so importantly into the mythological history of the site, and much of his work formed the substructure for Floyd Lounsbury's brilliant research of the next few decades. I have asked people who knew him (he died in 1987) why Berlin had no interest in phonetic analysis of the sort pioneered by Knorosov, and why he paid no real attention to the problems of linguistic decipherment. Linda Schele tells me that she once asked him this, and his reply was that "he was too old for such things."

But this cannot be the full answer. In 1969, he published in *American Antiquity* a short and decidedly sour review of my book *The Maya*, which he clearly did not like (he seems not to have approved of any of my work, for that matter; I never knew him, so this could not have been personal).[22] Here is his parting shot:

Coe briefly treats the topic of Maya hieroglyphic writing, and he reveals himself as an ardent follower of the phonetic-syllabic readings launched by Yuri Knorosov.

Unfortunately, Coe does not mention Eric Thompson's severe criticism of the Knorosov approach and thus the reader is led to believe that the latter is an undisputed positive achievement in the decipherment of Maya hieroglyphics, which this reviewer feels it is not.

In his hostility to this approach, Berlin was at least consistent. His valedictory work in epigraphy appeared in 1977 under the title "Signs and Meanings in the Maya Inscriptions";[23] one would look in vain in it for any mention of Knorosov's publications or anything else in the same vein. I suspect that for Berlin the possibility that the ancient Maya actually spoke a Mayan language was of no consequence.

As it winds northeastward on its journey to the Gulf Coast plain, the Usumacinta makes a small loop; within this loop, on what is now the Mexican side of the Mexico-Guatemalan border, lies the Classic city of Yaxchilán, explored by Maler and Maudslay in the last century. The city is laid out in the typical loose Maya fashion on a series of natural terraces and steep hills rising above the river bank, and has long been famous for the beauty of its relief sculptures, the best of which were removed by Maudslay to the British Museum. Apart from its stelae and hieroglyphic stairways, most of the carvings at Yaxchilán are found on the undersides and front edges of a number of flat, limestone lintels which span the doorways of its most important temples.

Aided by the splendid graphic record and photographic record left by Maudslay and Maler, Tania Proskouriakoff turned her attention away from Piedras Negras to the Yaxchilán reliefs, which she briefly touched upon in her 1960 article but analyzed more fully in 1963 and 1964, during that decade when she was at the height of her scholarly powers.[24] Here again she worked out a dynastic history for a Maya city, but she limited this to the short span of slightly more than a century when most of the site's sculpture was carved and its visible buildings erected. This cultural effervescence was largely the doing of two aggressive, warlike leaders of the eighth century, both of whom had the head of a jaguar in their name glyphs. The earliest of the pair she nicknamed "Shield-Jaguar," since the head was prefixed by something resembling a shield; "Shield-Jaguar" had a very long life, dying in his nineties, and was succeeded by his son, whom she called "Bird-Jaguar," whose nominal glyph is preceded by some kind of bird.

40 *Rulers of Yaxchilán.*
a. Shield-Jaguar. b. Bird-Jaguar.

a.   b.

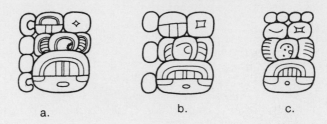

41 "Ben-Ich Katuns." a. 2nd "Ben-Ich Katun." b. 3rd "Ben-Ich Katun." c. 4th "Ben-Ich Katun."

In this line of research, Tania accomplished three things. First, she showed how the personal names of rulers were generally followed by the Emblem Glyph of that particular city. Second, she solved the problem of the Ben-Ich Katuns: these inform the onlooker in which katun of his life the ruler then was when such-and-such an event took place, counted from his birth (for example, I am in my 4th Ben-Ich Katun as I write these words, for I am now sixty-two). Third, she established that war events involving capture – and these are frequent in the Yaxchilán records – are always represented by a glyphic combination for which she cites Knorosov's reading *chucah*, the past tense of *chuc*, "to capture." And fourth, Tania recognized that the lintels sometimes celebrated important bloodletting rites, such as on the famous Lintel 24, which depicts a wife of Shield-Jaguar pulling a rope set with thorns through her tongue on her husband's birth anniversary, and isolating the event glyph to go along with this gruesome but important rite.

As a result, it becomes almost ludicrously simple for all but the most illiterate Mayanists to scan the text and interpret the scene on Yaxchilán Lintel 8, a relief celebrating a battlefield event of 9 May 755. On it, Bird-Jaguar and a companion (now known to be Kan-Toc, one of his war leaders or *sahalo'ob*[25]) are taking captives; the richly garbed Bird-Jaguar seizes his captive by the wrist, while the less sumptuously clad assistant has *his* by the hair. The unfortunate captives are identified by the names carved on their thighs, as Spinden had surmised. The text begins at the top left with the Calendar Round date 10 Imix 14 Tzec, followed by *chucah*, "he captured." After this verb is the name of Bird-Jaguar's captive. At the top of the right-hand column is a glyph compound which we now read (phonetically) *u ba-c(i)*, "his captive," the sentence ending with Bird-Jaguar and the Yaxchilán Emblem Glyph. A shorter text in the middle of the lintel names the battle-companion and *his* captive.

If the reader turns back to Chapter 2, it will be seen that the Mayan languages "prefer" the transitive sentence order verb-object-subject, or VOS, as opposed to our SVO. This is exactly how the hieroglyphic

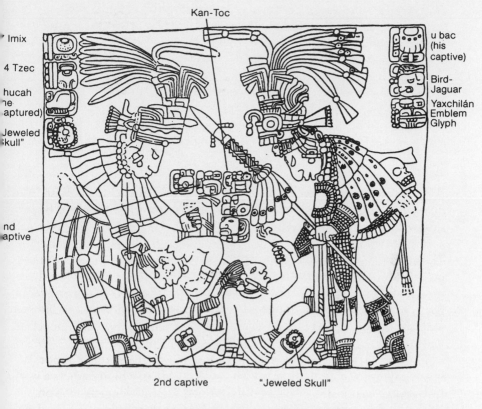

Kan-Toc

Imix

4 Tzec

hucah
he
:aptured)

Jeweled
;kull"

nd
aptive

u bac
(his
captive)

Bird-
Jaguar

Yaxchilán
Emblem
Glyph

2nd captive   "Jeweled Skull"

42 Lintel 8, Yaxchilán, a war record of Bird-Jaguar.

sentence on Lintel 8 behaves, and so do most texts in the inscriptions which involve transitive actions. Quite naturally, the Mayan linguists in various universities soon began to prick up their ears at what was going on in the epigraphic world; they had held their peace after their colleagues had been so forcefully put down by Thompson. At last, the Classic inscriptions were being shown to reflect Mayan speech, as the linguists Whorf and Hill had surmised.

The stage had been set for a concerted attack on the Classic Maya inscriptions throughout the lowland cities. But let us pause to consider what epigraphers were faced with in the decade of the 1960s. Given the almost half century that Carnegie had been in the Maya field, one would have expected them to have produced a mighty corpus of all known Maya monumental texts on the order of, say, the wonderful record produced for Egypt by Napoleon's scholarly team in only a few years.

One would have assumed that Carnegie would have followed in the footsteps of Maudslay, and employed a staff of first-rate photographers and artists whose only task would have been to publish every known inscription which had not already appeared in Maudslay's *Biologia Centrali-Americana.*

Yet neither Morley nor Thompson, Carnegie's two leading epigraphers, felt any obligation or necessity to get such a program under way. As I have said earlier, Morley's *Inscriptions of the Petén* is a sad comedown from the high plateau reached by *Biologia.* Maler's fine photographs, published by Peabody at the beginning of the century, proved to be of great use to Proskouriakoff when she worked on Piedras Negras and Yaxchilán, but there really is no substitute for a graphic presentation that includes a detailed, accurate drawing of a relief inscription side-by-side with a photo at the same scale.

If one were ungenerous, it could be surmised that the Morley/Thompson failure in this line was linked to their continuing inability to make much headway with decipherment; in dog-in-the-manger style, they may have felt that if *they* couldn't crack the script, they were not going to make it easy for anybody else to do so. Certainly Thompson would not have relished the thought of present or future Kelleys or Knorosovs with ready access to the entire written record of *his* Maya.

The phone rang at my New Haven home one summer evening in 1969. It was my old friend Stanton Catlin calling from New York's Center for Inter-American Relations. Stanton had been Assistant Director of the Yale Art Gallery when I first came to New Haven in 1960, with a strong interest in the art of Latin America. His message was that the Stella and Charles Guttman Foundation was interested in a major financial commitment to the decipherment of the Maya hieroglyphics, and in particular felt that high-speed computers were the answer. What did I think about this, and did I have any suggestions?

It did not take me long to react: "Going into computers now would be money down the drain. It was tried in the Soviet Union and it doesn't work, as Knorosov made clear. Anyway, it's putting the cart before the horse, because the one thing now holding up progress is the lack of a real Corpus of Maya Inscriptions. Why don't you set up and finance a program which will put into usable form all those inscriptions which are yet to be properly recorded?"

Stanton went back to the Guttman people, and it was agreed that an advisory committee would be set up, which would meet in New York. At my suggestion, this included Tania Proskouriakoff (naturally), Yale's Floyd Lounsbury, and Gordon Ekholm, curator at the American Museum of Natural History. We met, and there was no disagreement as to who (to repeat Morley's phrase) would "bring back the epigraphic bacon": Ian Graham, a British explorer and aficionado of all things Maya. Graham's credentials were excellent, since he had discovered and published a host of new sites and monuments as a result of a number of exploratory journeys he had made by foot and muleback through little-known regions of the Petén. Most importantly, the quality of the record he had brought back, which reached the standards set by his countryman Alfred Maudslay, clearly pointed to him as the person to undertake the Corpus.[26]

Graham submitted a proposal to the Foundation that September and it was accepted. The Corpus was on its way. Given that Graham lived in Cambridge and had space to work in the Peabody, and moreover was closely associated with Tania, it seemed to the committee that the Peabody should be the headquarters of the project; and it was there that Carnegie had deposited its vast archives of photographs and notes after its bureaucrats in Washington decided to fold up all archaeological operations in 1958. What with the excellent visual record being prepared by the University of Pennsylvania's massive program at Tikal, and with the magnificent drawings of the Palenque reliefs that would soon begin appearing, Mayanists were at last beginning to have a body of material for analysis comparable to the *Description de l'Egypte* which had made possible so many of Champollion's decipherments.

There is a Chinese curse which goes, "May you live in interesting times." For an American academic like myself, the 1960s and early 1970s were certainly just that. They were marked by a more-or-less continuous turmoil as students demonstrated for civil rights for blacks in America, and against our involvement in Vietnam. Even at a campus like Yale, which was relatively untouched by the violence which gripped other universities, it was not easy to concentrate on ivory-tower pursuits such as the study of a people who had lived in the Central American forests over a thousand years ago.

At one time, I was in the eye of the storm, since the leader of the student strike which paralyzed Yale in May 1970 was a student in the Anthropology Department, and I was its chairman, with direct responsibility for three highly inflammable buildings. On May Day, thousands of demonstrators poured into New Haven, some of them threatening to burn the whole place to the ground, and the National Guard took up positions around the campus.

And yet for me, as for many other colleagues, this was in some ways the most intellectually stimulating period I had ever experienced, harrowing though it often was. Those long-haired students could be obstreperous, indeed, but they had truly inquiring minds.

Through the latter part of the 1960s, I was immersed in the pre-Maya Olmec, and had a major archaeological dig on my hands at the site of San Lorenzo Tenochtitlán, on the Gulf Coast of Mexico. But I didn't entirely lose touch with the Maya field, and it was clear to me that exciting things were going on. Through my students, particularly an undergraduate named David Joralemon, I was drawn deeply into iconography, both Olmec and Maya, and it seemed to me that this study, like that of Maya epigraphy, was about to take off.

In other words, the time was ripe, not for the political revolution that so many of our more idealistic students were confidently predicting (they got Watergate instead), but in my own narrow intellectual world, for a revolution in the understanding of the hemisphere's most advanced pre-European culture: the Classic Maya. With Thompson's influence waning and Knorosov's star rising, particularly among the linguists, with linguistics and art history about to join hands with epigraphy, with the endless possibilities opened up by the discovery of the historical nature of the inscriptions, something was bound to happen.

And happen it did, just before Christmas 1973, in the most beautiful of all Maya cities: Palenque.

Left, Sylvanus G. Morley (1883–1948) and his
wife Frances; right, J. Eric S. Thompson (1898–
1975) and his wife Florence. Taken at Chichén Itzá
in 1930 during the Thompsons' honeymoon.

(right) Sylvanus Morley beside Stela F at
Quiriguá, Guatemala, about 1912. Morley's
publication of the inscriptions fell below the
standards established by Maudslay and Maler.

Benjamin Lee Whorf (1897–1941),
brilliant American linguist whose attempt at
phonetic decipherment met with failure.

24 Yuri Valentinovich Knorosov in Leningrad, about 1960.

25 Sir Eric Thompson in his English garden, 1974. Until his death the next year, Thompson remained a bitter enemy of the Knorosov approach.

26 David H. Kelley in 1991, the principal American champion of Knorosov's work on the Maya hieroglyphs during the fifties and sixties.

Tatiana Proskouriakoff's reconstruction of the
[Acr]opolis at Piedras Negras, Guatemala. She proved that
[the] Maya stelae lined up before pyramids were dynastic
[rec]ords.

(right) Stela 14 from Piedras Negras. In her 1960 paper,
[Pro]skouriakoff showed this to be an accession monument.

[T]atiana Proskouriakoff (1909–1985), from a group
[pict]ure of the Carnegie staff at Mayapán, Mexico, 1952.
[Eigh]t years later she published the paper which
[revo]lutionized Maya research.

[H]einrich Berlin (1915–1987), at Mayapán in 1954. This
[Germ]an-born grocery wholesaler and part-time epigrapher
[disc]overed Emblem Glyphs.

31 The Temple of the Cross sanctuary at Palenque, reconstruction watercolor by Proskouriakoff. At the back of the sanctuary is a tablet showing Pacal and Chan-Bahlum worshiping a world tree.

Opposite

32 Crypt and sarcophagus in the Temple of the Inscriptions, Palenque, the burial chamber of the great ruler Pacal (AD 603–683).

33 Merle Greene Robertson at Palenque; artist-photographer and organizer of Palenque Mesas Redondas.

34 Linda Schele at work in Washington, D.C., 1985. Artist, epigrapher, and teacher, she has been one of the chief architects of the new vision of the Maya based on decipherment.

35 Floyd G. Lounsbury at Copán, 1988. Yale anthropologist and linguist, he was the theoretician of the modern decipherment.

36 Late Classic Maya polychrome vase from the Chamá area, Guatemala. Shown here is one of a pair of twin lords, probably the Maize God and his brother.

37 Pages from the Grolier Codex, a Toltec-Maya book dealing with the planet Venus.

38 David Stuart aged eight, drawing a monument at Cobá, Mexico.

39 David Stuart at home in Washington, D.C., 1986. The following year he was to bring out his path-breaking *Ten Phonetic Glyphs*.

40 Inscription in Naj Tunich cave, Guatemala, eighth century AD.

41 Y.V. Knorosov in Leningrad, 1989.

42 The last page of the Dresden Codex, depicting the destruction of the universe. The sky dragon (Itzamná) and the old creator goddess release floods, while the war god (God L) hurls darts.

43 The Monkey-man Scribe from the Scribe's Palace at Copán, Honduras.

8 Pacal's People

Palenque, the most enigmatically moving of all Maya sites, has held its secrets for over twelve hundred years. The location is imbued with a quality that reaches out and draws one irresistibly. Enigmatic though it might be, its architecture sings out to us with a Mozartian sort of richness and classical elegance – not mute like the heavier, more richly conservative architecture of most other Classic Maya sites. Originality and harmony shine out of the mellow Palenque limestone. The presence of its builders is felt across the centuries by those who give themselves completely to the Palenque experience.[1]

Princeton's Gillett Griffin, who wrote this emotional description, is an emotional person, but it is no exaggeration. For over two centuries the incomparable beauty of this Classic city, located on the western edge of the lowland Maya realm, has continued to inspire this kind of prose in its visitors.

Set in the lower foothills of the Sierra de Chiapas, and surrounded by high, tropical forest, the city occupies a commanding position looking north over the great Usumacinta plain. By some time early in the seventh century, its architects had learned how to span large, airy rooms with lightly built vaults and mansard roofs, giving the city's structures a spaciousness that is missing in the massively-constructed palaces and temples of other Maya sites. And under the aegis of its two greatest kings, Palenque artists reached heights of elegance in carved relief and molded stucco seldom achieved elsewhere in the land of the Maya.

It was these reliefs with their sophisticated scenes and long glyphic texts that so entranced Antonio del Río and his artist Almendáriz; the romantically eccentric Waldeck; Stephens and Catherwood, those founding fathers of Maya archaeology; and Alfred Maudslay. Remember that long before Maudslay's magnificent record was compiled towards the end of the last century, Constantine Rafinesque had linked the inscribed texts of Palenque (then called "Otulum" after the stream that runs through the site) with the writing in the Dresden Codex – a kind of writing that he suggested would one day be translated since the Mayan language which it recorded was still spoken in the "Otulum" area. Prophetic words.

While no map of the entire city has ever been published, we know that it is large, although the center of the site, which is what today's tourist hordes see, is relatively compact. Set among a conglomeration of buildings is the Palace, a vast labyrinth of range-type structures enclosing interior courtyards, built over a period of time by successive rulers; it was the richly stuccoed pilasters of these buildings that so gripped Stephens and other early travelers. Rising above it is Palenque's strange tower, from the top of which one can have a stunning view of the site and the surrounding countryside.

To the southeast of the Palace is the Cross Group, dominated by the Temple of the Cross, so named because of the cruciform world-tree found at the center of the relief in its temple-top sanctuary. The Maya, both ancient and modern, have had many curses laid upon them, and fantastic theorizing by the lunatic and near-lunatic fringe is one of them. The Temple of the Cross relief has been a frequent target of crackpot notions; back in 1956, my wife and I sat in a Mérida cafe next to an American who first identified himself as an Apostle of the Church of Jesus Christ of Latter-Day Saints (Reorganized), and then assured us that Jesus had returned to Earth after the Crucifixion and preached to the multitudes from the Temple of the Cross.

Fantasy and science fiction aside, the three temples of the Cross Group have a common pattern: each has an inner, mansard-roofed sanctuary with a large, limestone relief at the back, on which two costumed figures (always the identical ones, one tall and one short) face in towards a cult object. The accompanying glyphic texts are very long and complex, with lots of dates. Who are these personages, and what do the texts say? Generations of epigraphers had failed to provide an explanation.

To my way of thinking, the two greatest archaeological discoveries ever made in the Maya area were the murals of Bonampak (brought to light by Giles Healey in 1946) and the tomb inside the basal pyramid of Palenque's Temple of the Inscriptions.[2] No really large-scale excavations had been undertaken at Palenque before 1949, when the Mexican archaeologist Alberto Ruz Lhuillier was chosen to lead an intensive digging program by the Instituto Nacional de Antropología e Historia (INAH). This was financially backed by Nelson Rockefeller in line with his interest in cultural interchange between the United States and Latin America. In those days, Ruz was among the brightest of the younger generation of Mexican anthropologists, not at all the crusty, xenophobic autocrat that he later became; whatever I or anyone else eventually came to think about him, that he was a great discoverer in a class with King Tut's Howard Carter cannot be denied.

The great moment in Ruz's life took place on Sunday, 15 June 1952.

On that day, after several seasons spent clearing the fill blocking a secret, corbel-roofed tunnel reaching from the floor of the upper temple to ground level of the Temple of the Inscriptions, Ruz and his workers gazed into an underground crypt surpassing an archaeologist's wildest dreams: in the midst of the chamber was a mighty limestone sarcophagus covered by an enormous carved slab, while around the walls of the crypt were nine stuccoed reliefs of lords or gods in archaic costume. On raising the massive slab with jacks, Ruz encountered the remains of a great ruler lying in a fish-shaped cavity. Over the face had been placed a mosaic mask of jade, the fingers had been covered with jade rings, and in fact almost the entire body had been festooned with jade, the most precious substance the Maya knew.

It was clear to Ruz that this great personage (whom Ruz came to call "8 Ahau" from the supposed birth date carved on the edge of the sarcophagus lid) had ordered the construction of this sepulcher and the huge pyramid which covered it in his own lifetime, much in the manner of those pharaohs of ancient Egypt. But it was not left to Ruz to discover who this man really was, and what he meant to Palenque's history.

A new dawn for Maya studies, and a leap forward for the decipherment, began in the small town of Palenque (not far from the ruins) on a hot August afternoon in 1973, on the back porch of a comfortable, thatched-roof house owned by a wiry, white-haired artist and her husband.

Merle Greene Robertson, the owner-artist, was born and raised in Montana,[3] and speaks both English and Spanish with a strong Western twang (with Merle, "Palenque" comes out as "plenky"). Merle has been painting since childhood – her parents encouraged her talents by allowing her to embellish the blank walls of her room. She majored in art at the University of Washington, but finished her college education at the University of California in Berkeley. After a stint of teaching art and architecture at a military academy in the Bay area, where her husband Bob was headmaster, Merle and Bob Robertson moved to the Robert Louis Stevenson School in Pebble Beach, California.

By the early 1960s, Merle was taking students on tours of Mexico, where she became smitten with Mexican culture and archaeology. Before long, she was applying her artistic talents to recording Maya monuments in the lowland jungles, and exploring previously unknown (or little-known) ancient cities in the headwaters of the Usumacinta. Merle proved to be an incredibly resilient jungle traveler, accomplishing long journeys by foot, mule, and jeep in search of stelae to photograph or take rubbings from. As David Joralemon remarks, "When Merle is off in the jungle, she can survive on leaves and a thimble of water."

So entranced was Merle by Palenque, that she and Bob built their second home in the town, and this became an obligatory stopping point for countless foreign archaeologists and aficionados of Maya culture, and above all a Mecca for "Palencophiles." From 1964, Palenque became Merle's obsession – to record it all before its delicate stucco and limestone reliefs, under attack from air pollution caused by Mexico's petrochemical industry, crumbled into oblivion. Merle applied for, and got, INAH's permission to record the sculpture of Palenque; hanging from rickety scaffolding, or spending long, hot hours in the steamy, stygian interior of the Inscriptions tomb, Merle came up with a documentation in photographs, drawings, and rubbings that surpassed Maudslay's in detail and accuracy.

On that day in August 1973, a small group of friends sat on Merle's porch and chatted about Palenque. Present at that moment of creation were fellow artist Gillett Griffin, Curator of Pre-Columbian Art at Princeton's Art Museum; Linda Schele, whose story we will shortly come to, and her husband David; David Joralemon from Yale; and Bob Robertson. Gillett suggested that a "round table" on Palenque might be a good idea, bringing together all those interested in the art, archaeology, and epigraphy of the city. Opinion was unanimous: let's do it as soon as possible, and let's call it (as David Joralemon had suggested) a *Mesa Redonda*.

Merle is a born organizer, an incurable optimist, and a warm human being liked by almost everybody in the field – a rarity in a study currently so rife with interpersonal nastiness. The invitations went out. This would prove to be the most important Maya conference ever held.

The Primera Mesa Redonda de Palenque opened on 14 December of that year, and closed eight days later.[4] We held a working session each morning, usually under the thatched roof of a spacious salon or *champa* owned by Moises Morales, a short, intense man who looks rather like Peruvian novelist Vargas Llosa. Moises had come with his family to Palenque from northern Mexico, after a stint in the Mexican air force. For many years the chief guide to the ruins, Moises is fluent in at least four languages, and is intimately acquainted with the Lacandons and with the rain forest that they inhabit (although most of it has now been cut down, courtesy of the Mexican government). Through him the people of the village, many of them Chol Maya, learned what we were up to, and it was not long before we were holding special afternoon sessions for them, at times with as many as fifty local residents present.

For the very first time epigraphers were brought together with art historians, astronomers, dirt archaeologists, and just plain enthusiasts. There was a Yale flavor to the meeting, with not only three faculty members in attendance but also three of our most brilliant students: Jeff

Miller (whose promising career was soon to be cut short by his death a few years later), Larry Bardawil, and David Joralemon. In particular, David's paper on Maya blood sacrifice and blood symbolism revealed a whole world of elite behavior and paraphernalia that had been overlooked: the Classic rulers of cities like Yaxchilán and Palenque, assisted by their wives, regularly perforated their penises with horrific, deified bloodletters fashioned from stingray spines.

During the afternoons we could go right to the ruins to test many of the exciting ideas that had been raised in the course of the morning presentations and discussions – we could go directly to the tablet of the Temple of the Foliated Cross, for instance, and see that in fact one of the figures was brandishing Joralemon's ornate, deified penis-perforator. Led by Linda Schele, we made long exploratory hikes to parts of the city that few of us had seen; I can remember that we were sometimes accompanied by a balding American tourist whom we had dubbed "Daddy Warbucks" from his striking resemblance to a comic-strip character, plus his large, mongrel dog which kept trying to trip everyone up on the often-slippery trails.

There is some mystic chemistry that produces those rare conferences that generate true intellectual excitement, that prove to be turning points in the understanding of a major body of knowledge. The Primera Redonda de Palenque was one such, but most of the chemistry seems to have been concentrated in the meeting of three persons who had never even heard of each other before they met in Moises' *champa*: Floyd Lounsbury, Linda Schele, and Peter Mathews.

Floyd Lounsbury's interest in languages began early, for, as he says, "coming off a farm in Wisconsin, in an atmosphere that really belonged to a century ago, I had the notion that you weren't really educated unless you could read both Greek and Latin."[5] He *did* take Latin in high school; and studied Greek, too, once he had reached the University of Wisconsin in 1932. Floyd's family was dirt poor, having lost their farm at the start of the Depression; he had borrowed fifty dollars from his high school English teacher to go to the university, and he had hitchhiked all the way to Madison.

Floyd's major in college was mathematics, and his dream was to go on to a higher degree in the subject in Göttingen, in Germany (few in Wisconsin at that time had really heard of Hitler). But he began to take philological courses as well – High German, Norse, and other Indo-European languages – and even a phonetics course. It was the brilliant linguist Maurice Swadesh who interested Floyd in Amerindian languages, and Swadesh landed the financially strapped student a WPA job

with the Oneida Indians at Green Bay, Wisconsin, which began Floyd's
lifelong involvement with the complex Iroquoian languages of North
America. As his colleagues and students know, Floyd is not only a
linguist but also a polyglot; there are probably no tongues more difficult
than Oneida and its relatives, but Floyd mastered them.

When he was drafted after Pearl Harbor, his mathematical back-
ground got him placed in meteorology. During his four years in the
Army Air Force, he was a weather forecaster in the Territory of Amapá,
Brazil. One day, a letter arrived in Brazil, offering him a Rockefeller
Foundation fellowship; he took it with him in 1946 when he went on to
graduate work at Yale in anthropology and linguistics.

Initially, like most other linguists at the time, Floyd had no interest
whatsoever in writing systems; to him, all real intellectual excitement for
a linguist was to be found only in spoken language, not in scripts, and he
wrote his dissertation on Oneida verbs. He read a bit about Mesoamerica, and took a superficial glance at the Maya script, "but it just didn't
interest me at all, because everything I read seemed to me like a morass. I
thought, if you'd ever step into that field, it would be like one of those
pools of quicksand – you'd just step in, and down you'd go, and that
would be the end of you!" About the only work that tickled his curiosity
was Whorf's 1942 Smithsonian article – understandable enough for a
fellow linguist.

Yet the seed had been sown on fertile ground, and when he was hired
by Yale as an instructor in the Anthropology Department, Floyd took
up the study of Sumerian cuneiform; and he had always been intrigued
by Chinese characters. Then he received a letter from Dick Woodbury,
editor of *American Antiquity*, asking him to review two translated articles
by a young Russian who had made some claims about deciphering the
Maya hieroglyphs. These turned out to be Knorosov's papers in the
1952 and 1954 volumes of *Sovietskaya Etnografiya*, and they so fired his
interest that he got the Villacorta edition of the codices out of the
library. "This was the first thing that made any sense," Floyd has told
me.

At first, Floyd took up the glyphs as a hobby: "What really got me
hooked was not the decipherment, but the mathematical puzzles of the
Dresden Codex."

After a few years of studying the Dresden, Floyd thought that he might
venture teaching a graduate course on it. At first, he gave this in alternate
years, but it finally blossomed into a full-year course. On coming to Yale
as a young faculty member, I sat in on this course not once, but twice. It
was an extraordinary experience. It was like being in the presence of a
thinking machine: on being asked a difficult question, Floyd would
pause with a slight smile on his face, while the computer in his brain

worked out the puzzle, and its answer. It is small wonder that both faculty and students held Floyd in a mixture of awe and affection.

Back in the Age of Thompson, it wasn't considered necessary to know *any* Mayan language to be a glyph expert. Thompson, for example, could neither speak nor read Yucatec or any other member of the Mayan language family; he relied on Ralph Roys, Carnegie's authority on Yucatec, when he thought he needed some linguistic expertise, which given his conviction that the glyphs had little or nothing to do with spoken Maya, was seldom indeed. Even today there are Maya epigraphers (none of them exactly in the forefront of decipherment) who haven't mastered the language, or at least picked up a working knowledge of it. Contrast this with those who work on Old World scripts – it would be unthinkable for a cuneiform specialist not to know Akkadian or some other early Semitic tongue, or for a Sinologist not to speak Chinese. But Maya studies have been a world apart for over a century.

Convinced, like his linguist colleague Arch Hill, that the glyphs *did* reproduce speech, Floyd took advantage of his course to bring native speakers of Yucatec and Chorti Maya to New Haven to act as informants for his students in field linguistics, and from them he absorbed a fairly complete grasp of the lowland languages – Yucatec and Cholan – in which the ancient scribes had worked. It is by no means easy to learn any Mayan language, but the difficulties pale when compared with the task of mastering Oneida.

In 1971, Elizabeth Benson – then Curator of Pre-Columbian Art at Dumbarton Oaks – and I put together a conference on Mesoamerican writing systems at "D.O." in Washington.[6] It was a curious conference. We had asked Floyd, then a Fellow at D.O., to chair it and give a paper; and Tania Proskouriakoff presented important new findings on glyphs for bloodletting rituals on the Yaxchilán lintels, but characteristically denied that much progress was being made on the decipherment! Yale's art historian George Kubler argued that the glyphs were mere *aides-mémoires*, and approved Thompson's claim that they had nothing much to do with the spoken word. But Floyd's presentation was what made the whole conference worthwhile: it provided the methodology for most of the progress of the next twenty years.

Floyd's paper was about the so-called "Ben-Ich" affix.[7] Although Tania had shown that in combination with a number coefficient (never more than "five") this expressed the current katun of a ruler's life, beginning with his birth, this said nothing about the *reading* of "Ben-Ich." The compound's first component is the day-sign Ben (as it is read in Yucatec), while the second seemed to earlier researchers to look like an eye, on very shaky grounds, and therefore got the label *ich*, "eye" or

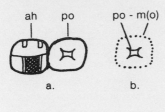
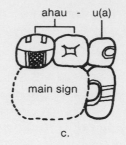

43 *Lounsbury's reading of the "Ben-Ich" affix. a. The ah po reading. b. pom, "incense." c. ahau, "ruler," "king."*

"face" in Yucatec. In his methodical way, Floyd examined these and other possible hypotheses, and noted three things:

(1)   "Ben-Ich" usually functions as some kind of title for both men and gods (Thompson had once suggested the male proclitic *ah* as a reading).

(2)   The day-sign Ben is actually *Ah* in several highland Mayan languages.

(3)   The supposed "*ich*" sign was used by Landa, in reduplicated form, as an apparent phonetic reinforcer for his glyph for Pop, the first month. Following Knorosov's Theory of Synharmony, this combination would have to be read *po-p(o)*, and therefore "Ich" must be *po*.

(4)   Copal incense is *pom* in all Mayan languages. The glyph accompanying pictures of incense balls in the codices is a combination of the inner device of the *po* sign with the dotted-line surround of Knorosov's *mo*. This conflation of elements represents the word *po-m(o)*, confirming the *po* reading for "Ich."

(5)   *ah po* is a title recorded in a Cakchiquel Maya dictionary from the highlands, as well as in the Quiché epic, the *Popol Vuh*. In the lowlands, *ahpop* ("he of the mat") and *ahau* ("king") are also titles, and could have been lowland readings of the original *ah po*. In fact, it was Floyd himself, at a much later date, who provided the proof that "Ben-Ich" was read as *ahau* in many lowland cities, by proving that the reading for a frequent postfix in the compound was final *-u(a)*; this served as a phonetic complement to *ahau*.[8]

It was hard for anybody to refute Floyd's analysis, based as it was on the hard evidence of linguistics, epigraphy, ethnography, and iconography; it was also presented in the most logical, no-nonsense way. The lesson here was that Maya glyphs, as Knorosov had claimed, really *did* match the spoken word. At one point during that weekend, Tania visited Floyd's apartment near D.O. When Floyd expressed his conviction that Knorosov was on the right track, Tania said that she thought he was probably right, and urged Floyd to "keep going with it."

On the final day of the D.O. conference, Floyd gave a brilliant summary of everything that had been said, and gave an eloquent discourse on the early history of writing, showing that what Knorosov had found out about Maya script fitted perfectly with what was known about early scripts in the rest of the world.

It was David Joralemon who told Floyd about the upcoming Mesa Redonda planned for Palenque, and urged him to go. Floyd, one of the most modest and unassuming people of my acquaintance, demurred, saying that while he might know something about the codices, he had done little work with the inscriptions. He finally gave in to our persuasion, but he had no intention of presenting anything. But Don Robertson, pre-Columbian art historian at Tulane, whom Merle had gotten as program chairman, put pressure on him to give something, so Floyd began reading up on Palenque, and especially an article by Berlin on the inscription of the Temple of the Cross, with its discussion on dates and the intervals between dates. This appealed to his mathematical instincts, and he thought he might do something on that.

But what he ended up doing was not that at all.

The minute I met Linda Schele at the Palenque conference, I thought, "Here's somebody who would never have made the Carnegie 'Club' ": with shirttails hanging over her faded jeans, her then-chubby face wreathed in smiles, her salty Southern speech, her ribald sense of humor, she would have horrified Eric Thompson, Harry Pollock, and the rest of the Carnegie crowd.[9] I knew nothing about her, except that she was an artist who had drifted into Palenque with her architect husband David, and fallen in love with the place. Merle thought very highly of her and liked her, but then Merle likes everybody. Quite a few of us were wondering, who in blazes is this person?

Linda is a product of west Tennessee. She was born in Nashville in 1942 to a traveling salesman of food-processing machinery and his commercial artist wife; the family milieu was right-wing Republican and "essentially redneck," according to Linda. When she was a girl, she developed a crush on the preacher in their Methodist church and wanted to be a missionary, "but then I got smart." By the time she was of college age, Linda had let her parents know that she wanted to be an artist, but to them that could only mean commercial art, "for the main point in life was to be commercially successful."

The closest college offering commercial art courses was in Cincinnati, Ohio, and that is where Linda went in 1960. To her horror, she found herself having to share a bathroom with two black girls; "my parents were bigots, I was a bigot," but she soon got over all of that. For one year she stayed with commercial art, but the College of Design, Art, and Architecture had its own humanities faculty, and she was deeply influenced by a young English teacher; it was he who introduced her to the world of ideas and to English literature. Shaken, she switched over to Fine Arts in her second year, and graduated in that field in 1964.

The experience with her undergraduate mentor had been "a rare, unreproduceable, intellectual journey into magic." In contrast, her subsequent experience studying in literature in the graduate school of the University of Connecticut was "nitpicking bullshit." After six weeks of this, she decided that was not what she wanted to do, and retreated to Boston, where she spent "the worst year of her life" working as a piping draftsman in the Electric Boat Company, trying to correct the fault in the piping system which had just led to the tragic loss of the submarine U.S.S. Thresher. Then, back to the University of Cincinnati, where she eventually got a master's degree.

Meanwhile, Linda was painting, in a style that she calls "biomorphic surrealism," vaguely resembling the work of artists like Gorky, Miró, and Klee. Her working methodology came from her Cincinnati painting teacher, who inspired her with the "philosophy of the happy accident" – in place of having a preconceived plan, (1) know your craft very, very well; (2) get your first mark on paper or canvas; (3) go on from there, "keeping yourself in an alpha state, so that when a happy accident happens, you are prepared to follow it wherever it will lead you." "That's what I do when I do research," Linda says. "I just set out a very, very large sort of vacuum-cleaner, trying to pattern all of the data that I can, without any predisposition of what is going to come, and then let the damn stuff pattern on me, and I start following the patterns wherever they lead me." Not Floyd's – or Tania's – methodology by a long shot, but it has led to truly important results.

By this time, Linda had married, and in 1968 she and David Schele moved to the University of South Alabama in Mobile, where she took up a job teaching art. Although she had sworn she would never go back to the South, both liked Mobile right away.

The turning point in her life came in 1970, when they decided to spend Christmas vacation in Mexico. They drove down that December in a van, with three students aboard. On arrival in Villahermosa, the Tabasco capital along the lower reaches of the Grijalva River, they were told about a nearby Maya site called Palenque, and about an interesting person named Moises Morales. They got to Palenque, and stayed twelve days, camping in the van in the site's parking lot. She did meet Moises, and she met Merle, who was making a rubbing of the magnificent tablet which had been found in the ruins of the Palace. "I was just goggle-eyed – Palenque hit me in the gut." So much so, that after she had gone with the students to see the Yucatán sites, she came back with David and the students to spend another five days at Palenque. "They couldn't get me away. I just had to understand what those Palenque artists were doing."

The following summer saw her once again in Palenque, "walking through the architecture," as she puts it, trying to work out the sequence in which the Palace complex had been built. She saw much of Merle and encountered the ever-enthusiastic Gillett Griffin for the first time; Gillett had just rediscovered the extraordinary, towered ruins of Río Bec, a Maya site which had been lost to the outside world since its initial discovery in the early years of this century. And there Linda was again in the summer of 1973, this time as Merle's assistant for the lighting of Palenque's myriad stucco reliefs so that they could be photographed. As a result, she was able to spend four whole days in the dank burial vault of the ancient ruler responsible for the Temple of the Inscriptions, closely examining the figures and the glyphs carved on his sarcophagus and on the surrounding walls.[10]

Being on sabbatical leave in England, Dave Kelley could not make it to Merle's Mesa Redonda. In his stead he sent one of his undergraduate students at the University of Calgary, Peter Mathews. For a few of us, the quiet Australian who arrived the first day with heavy suitcase in hand was an odd sight: apart from his moustache and long, dark hair, the mark of the undergraduate in those days, Peter wore a tee shirt hand-stenciled with the sinister figure of God L taken from the pages of the Dresden. What he had in that suitcase would change the course of the conference: a blue notebook annotated in Peter's minuscule hand with every Palenque date, the associated glyphs, and what anybody had ever written about the meaning of those dates.

Peter was a "faculty brat," the son of an economics professor at Australian National University in Canberra.[11] In high school he had concentrated on geology, and actually spent two and a half years doing geological field work in Australia, but he had always been interested in archaeology. In those days, the only archaeology taught on a university level was Classical; when Peter went off to the University of Sydney to study ancient Greece and Rome, he found himself in an excruciatingly boring course taught by a fuddyduddy professor. After a month of this, he went back home to Canberra.

Unhappily for him (and a lot of other young men) the Vietnam War was then on, and he was called up by the draft. But happily, the medical examiner was a sympathetic, anti-war intern who certified that he was unfit "because his father had asthma." Just the same, it seemed safer to be in a Canadian university, and so he went to the University of Calgary, justly famed for its archaeology program. For a whole academic year, he never had the temerity to introduce himself to Dave Kelley, but at the end of the year he screwed up his courage enough to ask Dave whether he might take his course next semester. Characteristically, Dave straightaway asked him home to dinner that very night.

In the next year or so, Peter spent nearly every evening at the Kelleys, absorbing Maya hieroglyphic writing. To really learn the glyphs, Dave set Peter the task of going through all of the published Palenque texts, in Maudslay and elsewhere, and transcribing them into the Thompson catalog numbers. It was immensely tedious, but a wonderful way to learn the glyphs. Then he worked out all the dates, with their glyphs, in his notebook. That is what he brought with him to the Palenque Mesa Redonda the following year.

Linda and Peter met at Palenque as complete strangers, but they soon began to put their heads together. Linda had already prepared a paper on the iconography and texts of the Cross Group, and knew about Berlin's isolation in those texts of four individuals whom he could designate only as A, B, C, and D since he had no idea of their names.

I was moderator at one morning session in Moises' *champa*. At one point, Linda put up her hand to ask, "Can Peter and I see if we can find more rulers?" My answer was "Sure, why not? Linda, you know every stone in Palenque, and Peter knows every glyph – why don't the two of you see if you can put together a dynastic history of Palenque? No one has attempted that yet."

That afternoon, I flew off by light plane with my students for a brief visit to Bonampak (which has what must be the world's worst and scariest airstrip). Linda and Peter retreated to Merle's house, working on a kitchen table with Peter's notebook. Floyd joined them, bringing with him a little card that contained his own mathematical formulas for getting Long Count positions for dates in the Calendar Round (most Palenque dates are given only by Calendar Round). Floyd was later to commit these formulas to memory so he could dispense with the card!

The first thing they did was to find all occurrences of a certain glyphic prefix which the ever-observant Berlin had noted as introducing the names of protagonists in the Palenque texts, but which he made no attempt to read as he had no interest in this problem.[12] This prefix had Landa's *ma*, a *kin* "sun" sign, and flanking elements previously identified by Knorosov as syllabic *na*; a few years later, Floyd was able to pin this prefix down as a title of highland origin to be read as *makina* ("Great Sun," or similar).[13] The identification of the royal prefix enabled them to find many or most rulers' names in the Palenque inscriptions.

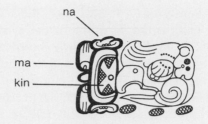

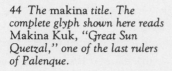

44 *The* makina *title. The complete glyph shown here reads* Makina Kuk, *"Great Sun Quetzal," one of the last rulers of Palenque.*

They worked with another hypothesis, drawing upon Floyd's knowledge of Mayan linguistics: that a time expression (date) would be followed by a verb, and that in turn by the subject of the sentence – a royal name plus titles which would most likely include the Palenque Emblem Glyph. Then they got involved in the name business – "What will we call these guys?" they asked of themselves.

"Two and a half hours later," Linda says, "we had it!"

That night, after dinner, the Linda and Peter show began, with Floyd acting as moderator and commentator. They held their audience in thrall as they presented their results, complete with big charts drawn by Linda. What they came up with was nothing less than the history of Palenque from the onset of the Late Classic period, at the beginning of the seventh century, through the city's demise – the span covering almost all of its architectural and artistic glories. History had been made before our very eyes. They had laid out the life stories of six successive Palenque kings, from birth to accession to death (an "event glyph," i.e. verb, identified by Floyd), the most complete king list for any Maya site.

What about their names? The first ruler on the list they had merely called "Shield," since that is what the logograph in his name depicted. To the rest they assigned Yucatec Maya names, depending largely on the nominal logographs; Shield's successor they decided should be called Can-Balam, or "Snake-Jaguar," since his sign combined the heads of these two beasts. When they had sat down, Moises immediately jumped to his feet: why should the names be in Yucatec, when the Palenque inscriptions were surely in Chol, the Mayan language still spoken in the area today? It was a sticky political moment, but reason prevailed. As Mayanists, the epigraphers realized that they had used Yucatec only out of habit, and that the language spoken by most of the Maya inhabitants of the southern lowlands was surely a form of Cholan.

Accordingly, we all adopted the Chol form of Can-Balam – Chan-Bahlum – and followed suit with the rest of the names. As a kind of ironic footnote to this decision, in recent years an inscription has turned up which indicates that Chan-Bahlum's name was, in reality, pronounced in Yucatec.[14] So the linguistic picture is a bit more complex than we had assumed back in 1973.

Makina "Shield," who headed Linda and Peter's list, was the great potentate buried in the spectacular tomb under the Temple of the Inscriptions. After 1960, Ruz came to call him "8 Ahau," since that seemed to be the ruler's birth date recorded on the sarcophagus lid, but what was his *real* name in Maya? That his name had to mean "shield" was not in doubt, for the logographic main sign was clearly the kind of small shield that Classic Maya warriors wore strapped to their wrists. But it was Dave Kelley in Calgary who had discovered that the Palenque scribes had alternative ways of spelling the great man's name: he found a purely phonetic-syllabic version consisting of a variant of Knorosov's *pa* sign, followed by *ca*, and terminated by the "inverted Ahau" or *la* sign of Knorosov. Hence, *pa-ca-l(a)*, or "Pacal."[15]

On my return to New Haven, I came across the same reading, without knowing that Dave had already hit on it. The next thing I did was to search for the word *pacal* in my extensive collection of Mayan-language dictionaries, and lo and behold, there it was on page 97 verso of the sixteenth-century Vienna dictionary (one of the earliest Yucatec dictionaries), glossed as *escudo*, "shield."

Looking at the different ways Pacal's name was written, one can see that the Palenque scribes liked to play around with their script, juggling logographic (semantic) with syllabic signs. *Pacal* could be written purely logographically, with a picture of a shield; purely syllabically; or logosyllabically, adding the "inverted Ahau" *la* sign as a phonetic complement to tell us that this shield-object ends in a final -*l*. All this was familiar to Floyd, with his first-hand knowledge of Old World cuneiform scripts, and would have been familiar to Egyptologists from Champollion on.

Who was Makina Pacal? His records are in several places, notably on the three great tablets which give their name to the Temple of the Inscriptions and which were set in the back wall of the upper structure. But the most obvious place to look for his history and forebears was on the edge of the sarcophagus lid, since it was already known that the text opened with his birth date on 9.8.9.13.0 8 Ahau 13 Pop (26 March 603), and there are other names and dates. After the Mesa Redonda, Floyd began working on the lid text, publishing his findings in the conference proceedings the next year.[16] One problem was that Pacal's predecessors were still unknown, since it had been only the later part of the dynasty that had been worked out that afternoon in Merle's kitchen. The other problem was that two of the names – Pacal and one other – appeared with an assortment of dates and what seemed to be "event glyphs" in what seemed to be a jumbled manner.

Floyd solved the whole business by showing that "event glyphs" that had a five-dotted quincunx as main sign went with "terminal dates," that

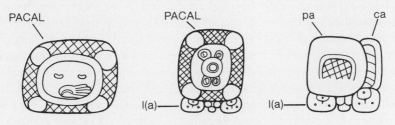

45 *Variant spellings of Pacal's name. Logograms in upper case, phonetic signs in lower case.*

is, they recorded the person's death. In one stroke, he resolved that dilemma: there were *two* Pacals, not one, as well as two other characters sharing the same name. So the other individuals named on the lid turned out to be Pacal's ancestors: his mother Lady Zac-Kuk ("White Quetzal"), his maternal grandfather, the first Pacal; and other forebears going back as far as AD 524.

Maya autocrats were as proud of their blue blood as any European king. To demonstrate his claim to legitimacy even in the afterlife, Makina Pacal had commissioned reliefs of some of his precursors to be placed around the outer surface of his stone coffin; each ancestor appears before a different species of tree or plant. Neither of his parents actually ruled the city-state of Palenque, notwithstanding the fact that Lady Zac-Kuk was the daughter of Pacal I, but they are found at either end of the sarcophagus.[17] The entire funerary chamber is the analog to the ancestral portrait galleries of England's stately homes.

Thanks to the careful architectural work of Merle and Linda, we know a good deal about the building programs of various rulers at Palenque, something that one still cannot say for other Maya cities. Pacal "the Great" began his career as a builder in AD 647, and went on to order the construction of most of the "houses" or range-type structures of the Palace, but his greatest achievement was his funerary monument, the Temple of the Inscriptions. The architectural works of Chan-Bahlum, his son and successor, are equally astonishing, above all the Cross Group, but his story comes later.

Every action has an equal and opposite reaction. The reaction to the Primera Mesa Redonda de Palenque began even before it opened. The storm signals were only too clear when Ruz failed to attend, even though he had been invited. Not only that, but there was not one INAH archaeologist there, and not one student from either the University or the huge School of Anthropology in Mexico City. Admittedly, Maya studies had never been a Mexican forte; almost all the great Mexican anthropologists of the past hundred years had concentrated on the Zapotec, Mixtec, and Aztec, and left the Maya to foreign investigators. But this kind of boycott was indeed unusual. There can be little doubt that it was organized by Ruz.

Alberto Ruz Lhuillier was originally not even a Mexican.[18] He was born in France of a French mother and a Cuban father (he was cousin to Fidel Castro Ruz, which may explain something of his political orientation). He arrived in Mexico in 1935, and eventually was naturalized. By the early 1940s, he had become the most promising Maya archaeologist among the younger Mexicans, and eventually organized the Seminario de Cultura Maya at the University; as editor of its publication Estudios de Cultura Maya, he brought out some of the best material ever written in the field, not the least of which was David Kelley's paper defending Knorosov's approach. There can be no question that he was for many years a positive force in the advancement of Maya studies, especially with his great excavations at Palenque.

That was an age of international scientific cooperation, as far as the Mexican anthropological establishment was concerned. Powerful, politically well-connected scholars like Alfonso Caso and Ignacio Bernal fostered a climate that made this possible.

But all that changed, beginning in 1970. On 1 December of that year, Luis Echeverría Álvarez was inaugurated as President of Mexico. For over six decades, Mexico has been a one-party state in which a President is something close to a god-king, and his policies carry down through every level of the political pyramid for six whole years. Widely held to be the architect of the terrible massacre of dissident students among the Aztec pyramids of Tlatelolco, just before the 1968 Olympics, Echeverría was nevertheless left-leaning and determinedly anti-American. I have been reliably told that one of his decrees ordered INAH to clear the gringo archaeologists out of Mexico.

While Echeverría, the "Supreme Leader," was no Communist, much of official cultural life in Mexico came under the direction of true believers in Marxism, the opiate of the intelligentsia throughout Latin America, and that included anthropology and archaeology. Stock Marxist phrases like "modes of production," "class conflict," and "inner contradictions" began to clog the Mexican archaeological literature, ironically at the same time that Soviets were beginning to free themselves from this particular intellectual straitjacket. As a result of Echeverría's anti-gringo edict, permits for Americans to dig in Mexico almost totally dried up during the next two decades, and scientific cooperation between the two neighboring countries became a thing of the past. Tourist ads boosting Mexico as the *amigo* country struck an ironic note among Yankee archaeologists.

Ruz was as orthodoxically Marxist as any of the rest, as a posthumous paper on the ancient Maya delivered in Merida shortly after his death in 1979 testifies.[19] Yet he and Eric Thompson remained close friends and scholarly allies, surely a contradiction in classic Marxist thinking. At any rate, he and INAH turned a cold shoulder on this and every subsequent Mesa Redonda de Palenque. The loss was theirs.

But Ruz obviously nurtured a deeper grievance against these upstart foreigners at Palenque. In that same year, 1973, his magnum opus on the Temple of the Inscriptions was issued by INAH, containing what he thought was the final, definitive study on the burial of his "8 Ahau" in the Inscriptions tomb.[20] When the two papers, the one by Floyd and the other by Linda and Peter, appeared in 1974 in the Mesa Redonda proceedings, Ruz exploded in a paroxysm of rage; as Linda puts it, "He saw his life's work going down the drain," for Ruz had contended that the sarcophagus lid text backed his assertion that the man inside, "8 Ahau" a.k.a. Pacal, was not more than fifty years old – but the three Mesa Redonda epigraphers had shown that he died at the age of eighty.

In spite of his close association with Thompson, Ruz had little knowledge of the glyphs, and his reading of the text on the edge of the lid was hopelessly wrong, conflating, for example, the dates and events in the two Pacals' lives, leading to wrong conclusions about the Long Count positions of the thirteen Calendar Round dates.

Ruz struck back as soon as he could, calling Linda, Peter, and Floyd *fantasistas*, "fantasists," in sarcastic articles published in 1975 and 1977.[21] He showed up at the Segunda Mesa Redonda de Palenque, the second round table, in December 1974. Linda tells the story: "He came to debunk us. He took old drawings of the Sarcophagus lid; he cut them up into individual glyphs, gave each researcher in the Centro de Estudios Mayas one glyph, and told them to find everything they could in the literature on it. He picked up the parts that he liked, and put them together to make his own reading – which is about what it sounded like."[22]

For Ruz, the "shield" glyph which the three had identified as Pacal's name was not that but a symbol of high status which had been given to his supposed "8 Ahau." In the discussion that followed, it turned out that Ruz was unable to sight-read glyphs, a necessity for this sort of work. Linda then stood up. "I tried to be as respectful as I could, I took Ruz step by step through our reading – date, verb, name, and Emblem Glyph."

Then Ruz, seconded by a young American student of Tania's, asked, "How do you know it's a verb?" Linda had no answer, and sat down – "I was utterly shot down. Right then and there I decided I was going to find out why it *had* to be a verb, and *nobody* was going to ask me that question again!" The happy outcome of this unpleasant confrontation was that Linda went on to graduate school at the University of Texas, learned Mayan linguistics, and wrote her ground-breaking Ph.D. dissertation on the verbs in Maya hieroglyphic writing. She finally answered the question.

As for Pacal's dates, Linda says, "his birth, accession, and death are attached to dates millions of years into the past and thousands of years into the future – if you want to move his dates around, you have to move *all* of those dates as a body."

When Betty Benson and I shared a taxi from the Villahermosa airport to that first Mesa Redonda in Palenque, we had already been working together for over ten years, she as the curator of the pre-Columbian section at Dumbarton Oaks, and I as an advisor to that part of D.O. Between us, we had put together the exhibit in Philip Johnson's stunningly beautiful wing at D.O., but more importantly, an intellectual program of fellowships, conferences, and publications that would unite art history and archaeology in one enterprise.

Betty is a lady, in the dictionary sense: "a woman of refinement and gentle manners." Her tact and unflappability made her the perfect person to bring together Latin Americans, Europeans, and Americans in the kind of international symposia and programs that D.O. specialized in. Having previously had charge of the great Bliss collection of ancient New World art when it was on display in Washington's National Gallery, she has a fine appreciation of the artistry of many cultures, but the Maya were and are her first love. I don't think that we disagreed on any important matter in all those years that we collaborated at D.O.

Betty was as euphoric as any of the rest of us with the success of Merle's Mesa Redonda. In the early spring of 1974, she realized that there was "money left over in the kitty" at D.O.[23] It struck her that it might be good to invite to D.O. all those people who had ever worked on the Palenque inscriptions for a conference. Heinrich Berlin sent his apologies, saying that he "was no longer involved with those things with which I used to toy of yore," but on one weekend in early April there was a gathering of Palenque specialists in the pre-Columbian seminar room in the basement of Johnson's wing at D.O.

The meeting began disastrously. I was present as an observer, and can testify that resentment and enmity hung in the atmosphere. The whole business got off to a bad start with George Kubler's bolt from the blue, "How do you know this is writing at all?" Tania, sitting there with Joyce Marcus, her student from Harvard, was being very Russian, i.e. very contrary. One obstacle was, as Floyd pointed out, that Tania "had her own theory about dynastic history, and ours were coming out a little different." But the main sticking point was that she just did not take to the somewhat rough-hewn and earthy Tennessean; to Linda's dismay, this one-sided antipathy was something that Tania never lost. So negative did Tania become about what the Palenque team had been doing that I began to think that Betty had made a ghastly mistake in ever convening such a group.

I couldn't take much of this, and left by Saturday noon for New Haven. By late the next afternoon, most of the participants, including Tania and Joyce, had also departed. Five die-hards stayed on, besides Betty: Linda, Peter, Floyd, Merle, and Dave Kelley. As Betty puts it, "at first they were in little two by two groups, engaged in desultory conversation. And suddenly there was a moment when Floyd and Linda and Dave and Peter were all down on the floor around a copy of Maudslay, and they'd got a new glyph. It was all because each of them knew something the others didn't. I thought, aha! – this is my group, and I will get them back together again."

What Linda had brought with her was what she had been working on since the Mesa Redonda. Back in Mobile, she had laid out and glued together all the Palenque texts published in Maudslay and elsewhere. She had then analyzed these not merely using dates alone, but whole sentences, finding patterns. Floyd had with him Merle's rubbings of the sarcophagus texts, Peter had his notebooks. They were "almost in a state of trance – from time to time Betty's arm would appear, delivering back-up reference material." In the three and a half hours that they had worked at Palenque in 1973, they had gotten the last two hundred years of its history; now, from 6:30 to 10 o'clock that night, they got the *first* two hundred years.

"All of the kings," exclaims Linda, "bam-bam, boom-boom, one after the other! And *nobody* who wasn't on the floor that night was ever invited back."

It was a true meeting of minds. Floyd said later that it was the only time he had ever worked *with* anybody – he had always worked by himself. Betty had piled up on one table all the Mayan-language dictionaries from D.O.'s excellent library, and they went back and forth to these. The meaning of a key glyph that looked like a leaf came up, in a context that suggested "lineage." Dave said that there ought to be a linguistic reference, and lo and behold! in the dictionaries there was the word *le* glossed as "leaf" *and* "lineage."

Betty did in fact have "her group," and she got them together for four more Mini-Conferences, three in Washington and one in Dave's home town of Jaffrey. They turned into more than just weekend meetings: the four epigraphers would arrive on a Wednesday, and not leave until the following Tuesday.

I asked Linda, who looks on them as the turning point in the modern history of decipherment, what the real contribution of Betty's Mini-Conferences had been. When they began, Linda explained, Knorosov's method of phonetic analysis was already in place; Proskouriakoff and Berlin's work had proved beyond any doubt that the inscriptions were historical. But even though the syntax of these texts was implied, everybody who had worked on the texts had examined only individual glyphs.

The Mini-Conference people went at particular inscriptions as whole texts. "Knowing that it reflected the real language, it had to have the syntactical structure of Mayan languages: there had to be verbs, there had to be adjectives, there had to be subjects. Even if you didn't know what the verb was, you knew *where* it was because of its position in the sentence." Floyd supplied the needed linguistics, but Linda was getting good at this, too. They used Distance Numbers – discovered years earlier by Thompson – to count forward to and back from dates to tell how verbs related to each other in time.

"We began dealing with full texts. We might translate a verb, say, as 'he did *something* on such-and-such a date.' We knew how old he was, and we knew what context it was being done in, so we could get – for the first time – eighty and ninety percent translation levels on texts."

When the Mini-Conferencers were not actually meeting, they were exchanging long letters with new findings and inferences, and publishing papers, often in Merle's Mesa Redonda series. Floyd had cracked the *makina* title by 1974, and went on to solve a mind-boggling mystery on the tablet on the back wall of the Temple of the Cross.

It will be remembered that like the tablets in the other two temples of the Cross Group, this one shows two figures facing in towards a cult object, in this case a cross-shaped tree surmounted by a fantastic bird. Exactly who these two characters were has puzzled Mayanists ever since del Río's explorations were published in London, but the Mini-Conferencers (or "Palencophiles" as they called themselves) quickly concluded that the bundled-up, smaller individual on the left was none other than Pacal himself, and the tall figure on the right was Chan-Bahlum, his son and heir, the ruler who had built all three temples in the Cross Group.[24] And the tree? That was surely a world-tree, probably the one that in both ancient and modern Maya thought stands in the center of the universe and sustains the heavens. It was to the very long text that flanks this scene that Floyd turned his attention.[25] If one calculates the

Long Count date which begins it at the upper left, this falls on 7 December 3121 BC, about six and a half years before the beginning of the present Maya era: clearly a mythological date. What transpired at that remote time was the birth of an ancestral goddess whom the epigraphers could only call "Lady Beastie" from the birdlike head which forms her name glyph. At the Methuselan age of 761 years she gave birth to a triad of gods who became the tutelary divinities of the Palenque dynasty. The inscription then travels down in time to describe the history of the Palenque kings through Pacal to his successor Chan-Bahlum.

What Floyd, always the mathematician, discovered was that the interval between "Lady Beastie"'s birth and that of Pacal – 1,359,540 days – is a multiple for no less than seven different time periods of importance to the Maya, and thus the birth of "Lady Beastie" is a totally *contrived* date, invented by the Palenque astronomer-scribes to give Chan-Bahlum and his distinguished father a divine ancestry. Now, one of the intervals in this magic number is the synodic period of Mars, thus confirming what Dave Kelley had been telling all of us since his student days, that many of the dates in the Classic inscriptions have an astronomical significance, above and beyond "real" history – an approach that has turned out to be established again and again in more recent research.

Floyd followed this up in 1980, when he showed that mythological birth expressions in the same Temple of the Cross text follow the rules of Mayan syntax, in which word order bears no resemblance to what we are used to in either English or Spanish.[26] He also identified a pattern of parallel couplets, a rhetorical device widespread in the indigenous cultures of the Americas, and in the Old World as well; the Psalms are filled with such literary devices, for example:

> He turneth the wilderness into a standing water,
> and dry ground into water-springs.

It is much used in modern spoken Maya, especially in ritual discourse, prayers, oratory, and other formal uses of language, but Floyd was a pioneer in matching it with Classic hieroglyphic texts. The lesson was that epigraphers had better start studying Mayan linguistics and Colonial-period literature – thumbing through dictionaries would not be enough.

Linda, smarting from Ruz's jibe at the Segunda Mesa Redonda, took this to heart, and her 1980 doctoral dissertation at the University of Texas not only established the meaning of specific "event glyphs" or verbs in dynastic statements – such as *chum*, "to be seated" (i.e., enthroned) for a picture of what Linda characteristically identifies as "an ass sitting down" – but she also showed how verbal affixes were used

46 *The "seating" glyph:* chumuan, *"he was seated."*

syllabically to write the grammatical endings to these verbs.[27] For
instance, in Mayan, *chum* belongs in a special category of verbs that
describe the position in space of the subject, and these have their own
inflectional endings. With Floyd's establishment of the true phonetic
readings for the syllabic signs T. 130 (*ua*) and T. 116 (*ni*), Linda was
eventually able to read the all-important "seating" glyph combination as
chumuan(i), "he was seated" – in perfectly grammatical Cholan, by now
generally accepted as the language of the Classic inscriptions.

By the latter part of the decade of the 1970s, progress was being made
on several fronts. A major breakthrough in figuring out dynastic history
was a paper that Christopher Jones of the University of Pennsylvania
published in *American Antiquity* in 1977.[28] Jones is the epigrapher for the
Tikal Project, and he had noted in various places on the Tikal
monuments that a ruler would be named, and then his name would be
followed by the name of a woman and that of a previous ruler. His
suggested explanation was that this was the ruler's mother and father.
When Linda read the article, she was inspired to make up a sheet of
similar examples from other sites, and she brought this to the final
Mini-Conference.

According to Linda, when Peter Mathews and Dave Kelley saw this
sheet, which included parentage statements for Yaxchilán, their reaction
was "My god. Do you know what this says? It says that Bird-Jaguar was
the son of Shield-Jaguar!" The result was that with these newly identified
parentage glyphs, which said, in effect, "X, child of Z," firm genealogies
could be worked out for every city where they occurred. In the next
decade, the exact phonetic reading of these glyphs would begin to come
in, with a new generation of epigraphers.

In those exciting days, discoveries came at the pace of a raging prairie
fire. Hardly a day or week seemed to pass without some amazing new fact
coming to light, or a new reading being made for a glyph, or someone
coming forth with a revolutionary new interpretation of older data. For
the first time in nearly one and a half centuries of Maya research, a band
of scholars had been able to associate temples, palaces, and monuments
with real people placed in a historical framework. They began to make

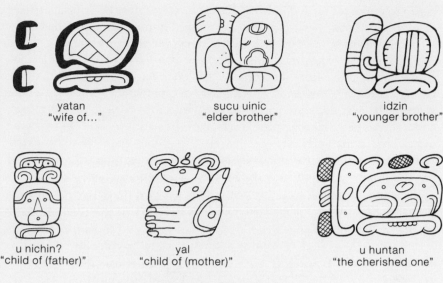

47 *Relationship glyphs.*

some kind of sense out of the often weird scenes pictured on the stelae and reliefs, so much of which seemed to involve lineage rites and the drawing of royal blood.

Now one could clear up mysteries that had intrigued scholars since the end of the eighteenth century. The oval tablet set in a wall of the Palenque Palace now turned out to be the back to a throne whose seat and legs had been removed by del Río and sent to his king, Charles III; and the scene on the tablet turned out to be Pacal the Great, seated on a Jaguar throne, receiving a royal headdress from his mother Lady Zac-Kuk on his accession. And it became evident that *this* was where all subsequent Palenque kings had been invested with power, until the end of the dynasty and Classic Maya civilization itself.[29]

Likewise, the Palace Tablet, a great slab discovered by Ruz, could be seen from its now-readable text to depict the accession of Makina Kan-Xul, the younger child of Pacal and Lady Ahpo-Hel (Pacal's principal wife), who succeeded to the rulership upon the death of his elder brother Chan-Bahlum; the royal parents had long since been dead, but they are shown handing to Kan-Xul the symbols of power which he was to don during the ceremony. Ill luck later struck the unfortunate Makina Kan-Xul, for he was captured by Toniná (as a captive monument at that site with his name and Emblem Glyph clearly indicate) and almost surely suffered death by beheading far from his native territory.[30]

All those iconographic details that had long eluded explanation now began to make sense, and in Mesa Redonda after Mesa Redonda, articles of clothing worn in rituals and ceremonially-manipulated objects all assumed meaning in the context of elite power and prestige.

The kinds of interpretations that were coming out of the Palenque conferences and Mini-Conferences spilled over to research in other parts of the Maya lowlands, particularly in Guatemala and Belize where xenophobia had not stifled ongoing excavations by foreign investigators, and where new hieroglyphic texts, tombs, and caches were being discovered constantly. It was at Tikal in Guatemala that the extra-ordinary Burial 116 was uncovered below the skyscraper-like Temple I on the main plaza of that huge city, and epigraphers could now understand that this was the tomb of a great king whose name was perhaps Ah Cacau, "He of the Chocolate," written with the Maya phonetic-syllabary.[31]

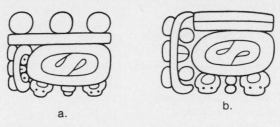

a.   b.

48 The "hel" or "change of office" glyph. a. the 8th in succession. b. the 10th in succession.

It was found that the Tikal kings, like those of Yaxchilán, employed a glyph (which Thompson, on not very secure grounds, read as hel, "change") to tell one which particular ruler in a numbered succession he was.[32] Regardless of how one reads hel – and there is little agreement even now on this point – the meaning of the numbered hel glyphs is well established, which makes the working out of dynastic lines a simpler task than it used to be.

During the latter part of the 1970s the word began to spread about what was going on at Palenque, and the annual Mesa Redonda began to grow beyond all expectations, like a snowball racing downhill. In 1973, only thirty-five of us had been gathered in Moises' champa, but only five years later, there were no fewer than a hundred-and-forty-two partici-pants from seven countries, and this figure continued to grow over the years. An even wider audience was eventually reached by the marvelous Maya Hieroglyph Workshops, which were begun in 1978 at the University of Texas in Austin, and have been held on an annual basis ever since.[33] These are basically one-woman performances by the charismatic Linda, a born showwoman if there ever was one, taking her rapt audience effortlessly through the most difficult material, from Knorosovian phoneticism to parentage statements. The ultimate tribute to her success has been the proliferation of similar workshops around the United States.

Naturally, there were (and are) those who did not take kindly to all of this, least of all the died-in-the-wool, true-blue, dirt archaeologists who began to feel that *their* kind of nuts-and-bolts research among the house mounds and cooking pots of the ancient Maya peasantry had been overshadowed by all this attention to the concerns of the Classic elite. With a few exceptions, they were notably absent at the Palenque Mesas Redondas and the glyph workshops, and continued to lecture and publish without giving any indication that the Classic Maya were a literate people. Their exasperation would begin to surface a decade later at (of all places) Dumbarton Oaks.

But no one could really deny that Sylvanus Morley, writing in 1940, had been totally wrong when he stated, "The ancient Maya indubitably recorded their history but not in the stone inscriptions";[34] or that "Pacal's people," that small, dedicated band of "Palencophiles," had brought us much closer to a complete reading of ancient Maya history and mental life.

9 Down into Xibalbá

It was 4 August 1968, and it was the feast day of Saint Dominic, patron of Santo Domingo Pueblo, southwest of Santa Fe. At one end of the hot, dusty plaza, a Dominican priest watched nervously as several hundred dancers arranged in two long rows pounded the earth with their moccasined feet as a mighty, collective prayer for rain, accompanied by the powerful baritone singing of a chorus and the beat of drums. As my family and I viewed this, the largest and in some ways the most impressive Native American public ceremony, a tiny cloud over the Jémez Mountains to the northwest got larger and larger, eventually filling up the sky; at last the storm broke, and the sky was crisscrossed by lightning, and the pueblo resounded with peals of rolling thunder.

On that memorable day, we came across Alfred Bush and Douglas Ewing, old friends of mine from the East. Both were officers of the Grolier Club of New York, a staid organization dedicated to the collection of rare old books and manuscripts. They had a proposal, which we discussed right then and there: would I be interested in organizing an exhibit at the Grolier on Maya hieroglyphic writing, using original documents?

I was, but cautioned that the European institutions would certainly be reluctant to loan the three known codices for a show in New York, and that on practical grounds alone, large stelae brought in from Mexico or Guatemala would be an unlikely proposition. We could always borrow a few smaller stone inscriptions – lintels or panels – from museums and private collections in the United States, but that would really not suffice if one wanted to say something about Maya writing and the "state of the art" regarding decipherment (remember we were in the post-Proskouriakoff-breakthrough but pre-Primera-Mesa-Redonda era).

But I had an idea. If we had to rely on U.S. sources only, then the majority of original Maya texts available to us were not on stone or paper, but on pottery. Sometimes these texts were remarkably long, as extensive as many monumental inscriptions. In the introduction to his 1962 *Catalog*,[1] Eric Thompson had pretty much dismissed ceramic texts as unworthy of study, concluding that they were mere decoration by basically illiterate artists choosing certain glyphs to put on their pots because they looked attractive – they reflected "the artist's wish to produce a well-balanced and aesthetically pleasing arrangement." And as a result this was naturally what the majority of Mayanists then believed.

I was led to question this untested assumption, since I had been among those who showed that Thompson had been wrong about the antiquity of Olmec civilization, and I was thoroughly satisfied that his views on the nature of the Maya script were untenable. I thought that if I could get enough Classic Maya pots and dishes with hieroglyphic writing on them under one roof, I would be able to see if Thompson was right or wrong.

Our plan for the exhibit got bogged down, as I was busy with my colleague Dick Diehl in getting our joint excavations at the huge Olmec site of San Lorenzo Tenochtitlán written up; we had been there for three field seasons, and like any other archaeological excavation, the actual digging was just the tip of the iceberg – it took years of analysis and writing to get it all into print.[2] But by early April 1971 I was ready to go to work on the Grolier show.

Before 1960, neither bona fide archaeology nor the antiquities trade had been able to come up with a sufficient number of elite Maya ceramics for anybody to make much sense of them. But after that date, changing political conditions in Guatemala had led to large-scale looting of lesser known – or still unknown – Classic sites in the Petén. Left-wing guerrillas, the right-wing army, local politicians, and a mass of landless, destitute peasants all got into the act. The more efficient, and therefore the more dangerous, of the despoilers had high-tech chainsaws at their disposal, and began slicing up Maya stelae for easy removal and sale.[3]

Apart from Guatemalan private collections, the major market for this material was New York, and, to a lesser extent, European capitals like Paris and Geneva – at least that is where the most reputable dealers were. Although it is easy to castigate these individuals as the primary culprits in the rape of the Petén, probably considerably more destruction was caused by a cabal of collectors, unscrupulous appraisers, and low-level dealers who imported planeloads of poor-quality material via Miami to donate to naive museums as tax write-offs. Be that as it may, there was an amazing number of Maya vases of the utmost beauty and scholarly interest available for study. Ironically, I found that these New York dealers, the target of much righteous indignation on the part of archaeologists, were a great deal more generous with material in their possession than those same archaeologists had been with *theirs*.

The public has the impression that it must take months or even years to install a major exhibit. I have learned that most shows are hurriedly mounted at the eleventh hour. In point of fact, I installed the Grolier show, entitled *The Maya Scribe and His World*,[4] on 17 April, the day on which it opened. Unpacking box after box of Maya ceramics, in the club's elegant halls, I began to note a very strange pattern emerging with the scenes painted on these vases: pairs of identical young men with very similar garb showed up again and again. The word "twins" flashed across my mind. That immediately triggered another neural linkage: "twins – *Popol Vuh*." I had read the *Popol Vuh*, the sacred book of the highland Quiché Maya, a number of times and twins are all-important to it.

The *Popol Vuh* was transcribed in Latin letters some time in the sixteenth century, most likely from a lost hieroglyphic original. Rediscovered by Brasseur de Bourbourg in the last century, and generally considered to be the greatest work of Native American literature, it has been translated many times.[5] The book begins with the creation of the world out of a primordial chaos, and ends with the Spanish Conquest. But it is the second part, immediately following the creation, that is of most interest to the student of Maya mythology and to the iconographer. Basically, it is a "harrowing of hell" involving two sets of divinely-born twins. The first pair, 1 Hunahpu and 7 Hunahpu (1 Ahau and 7 Ahau in the lowland Maya calendar), are handsome young men who enjoy playing ball on the surface of the Earth, but their noisy game outrages the lords of the Underworld or Xibalbá ("place of fright" in Quiché Maya), who summon them to their dread presence. After subjecting them to horrifying and disabling trials, they are forced to play a ball game with the sinister Xibalbans, which the twins lose and suffer death by beheading.

1 Hunahpu's head is hung in a calabash tree. One day, the daughter of a Xibalban lord passes by the tree and is spoken to by the head; when she holds up her hand to it, it spits in her hand and she is magically impregnated. Expelled to the surface of the world, she eventually gives birth to the second set of twins – the Hero Twins, Hunahpu and Xbalanque, "Hunter" and "Jaguar Sun." While they are yet boys, they perform various heroic acts – destroying monsters, and turning their obstreperous and jealous half-brothers into monkeys, an episode that led me later to an unforeseen discovery.

The boys shoot birds with their blowguns and otherwise divert themselves, but again their noisy ball-playing results in a summons to Xibalbá. Rather than suffering the fate of their father and uncle, Hunahpu and Xbalanque defeat the Xibalbans through trickery, and rise up to the sky to become the sun and the moon.

I soon came to see that many of these vases and plates, as I put them in

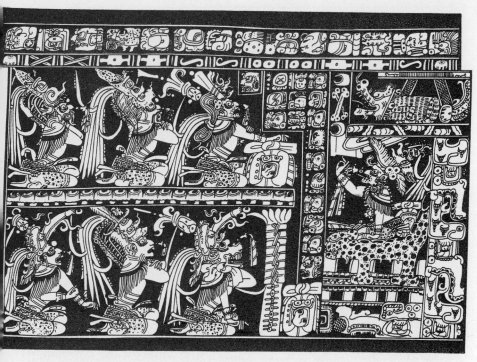

49 Rollout of a Late Classic vase. At the top is the Primary Standard Sequence and the owner/patron's name and titles. The scene below and the vertical text concern an assembly of the gods at the first moment of creation.

their exhibition cases, had remarkably specific pictorial references to the Xibalbá episodes in the *Popol Vuh*, and all further studies I have made of this sort of material have confirmed and even extended that interpretation. What does all this mean? Here we have to consider the *function* of these elite ceramics: although it is obviously impossible to be one hundred percent sure given the lack of records for most of these pots, the published archaeological evidence suggests that the ultimate destination of pictorial Maya ceramics, whether painted or carved, was to be placed – filled with food or drink – with the honored dead in a tomb or grave. When my artist Diane Peck rolled out these scenes for publication in the catalog of the show, I found that they were replete with Underworld, death imagery; they were peppered with the gruesome symbolism of death-skulls, crossed bones, disembodied eyes, vampire bats, and the like.

This by no means suggests that everything on the pots was taken lock-stock-and-barrel from the *Popol Vuh* – some of it was more historical – but it does imply that the Underworld section of the Quiché epic was shared by the Classic peoples of the lowlands, for use on pottery destined as funerary offerings. In fact, the *Popol Vuh* Hero Twins-Xibalbá story is only a surviving fraction of what apparently was once a huge Underworld mythology: there are dozens, perhaps hundreds, of weird, Xibalban deities on the vases and plates, in a complex scenography. But this crowded Underworld was an ordered place: as Edith Sitwell's Sir Joshua Jebb admonished his daughters,

> For Hell is just as properly proper
> As Greenwich, or as Bath, or Joppa!

I was able to see that there were two ruling gods in Xibalbá, usually depicted enthroned in their own palaces; these were Schellhas' Gods L (whom we have seen on the Temple of the Cross at Palenque) and N. In spite of the advanced years of these gods, they enjoyed the services of harems and evidently the attentions of the young Moon Goddess.

While Thompson considered God N – who functions as the deity of the end of the year in the Dresden Codex – as a Bacab,[6] a quadripartite deity who holds up the heavens, I saw that his glyphic name often contained Knorosov's *pa* sign over a logographic *tun*, and read it as "Pauahtun," an important god connected by Landa with end-of-the-year ceremonies. Only a few years ago, my former student Karl Taube has confirmed the reading by showing that the little "corn-curl" element that I had overlooked in the god's nominal glyph is the *uah* syllable – thus, *pa-uah-tun*. We shall find Pauahtun later at Copán.

One can be wrong for the right reasons (a specialty of Thompson's) but, conversely, right for the wrong ones. I saw twins on these pots, and jumped to the conclusion that these had stepped from the pages of the *Popol Vuh*. But the set of twins whom I identified with Hunahpu and Xbalanque, and whom I referred to as the "Young Lords," has turned out to be the sacrificed father and uncle of the Hero Twins. This again was the work of Taube, who has made the outstanding discovery that the father, 1 Hunahpu, is none other than the young Maize God of Maya iconography.[7] Just as every Maya farmer, in the act of planting, "sends" the maize seed to the Underworld, so was 1 Hunahpu – the Maize God – ordered to descend into Xibalbá; there he suffered death, and then resurrection by his offspring Hunahpu and Xbalanque.

Now, all of this may seem unconnected to the story of Maya decipherment, but painted and carved Maya ceramics from beyond the grave eventually came to play their role. And the new iconographic horizons that were opened up by the Grolier exhibit entered into that mix of art history and epigraphy that became the Mesa Redonda series at Palenque.

The real work on the Grolier exhibit began after it was over. This was the preparation of a catalog,[8] which as far as I was concerned should try to reach the same standards of accurate documentation as Maudslay had achieved with his *Biologia*. This meant rolling out all of the scenes – with glyphic texts – on those cylindrical vases. Years before, I had read in the *Illustrated London News* that the British Museum had invented a camera that would take continuous photographs of objects slowly rotated on a turntable, and asked Justin Kerr, the New York photographer engaged to work on the catalog, if he could devise a camera which would do this. Justin thought that it was possible, but it would take too long for him to create a prototype, so we settled for multiple shots of each vase. Justin's now-famous, "continuous rollout" camera materialized, but too late for the book.[9]

So it transpired that almost every vase was laboriously unrolled by my artist Diane Peck in black-and-white drawings, but this still gave me an accurate corpus on which to work. From this, and from dozens of published and unpublished Classic Maya vases, bowls, and plates, I put together a compendium of ceramic texts on 5 by 7 cards; I ended up with several hundred entries. That summer, I took all this material with me to our summer home in the Berkshire hills of Massachusetts, to work in peace and quiet.

With the distraction of five children, it was not always easy to get one's research done, or so I thought. Every warm day, they demanded to be taken to our swimming hole on the icy-cold Green River, near the Vermont border. They would bathe in the bone-chilling waters for hours, but twenty minutes was usually enough for me, so I would spend the rest of the time waiting for them to emerge while sitting with my 5 by 7 cards. Now, my mind is in many ways the reciprocal of Floyd Lounsbury's, and I suspect that each of us is under the control of a different cerebral hemisphere. While I have no ability to remember numbers and names, and certainly not much in the way of mathematical ability, I have almost total visual memory: once I see something, I never forget it, either in toto or in detail. Once stored into memory, these visual cues often sort themselves out into patterns. One such pattern began emerging as I sat listening with one ear to the gleeful shouts and splashes of my children.

It was already apparent to me that there were different kinds of texts on pictorial pottery, depending on their placement on the object. What I called "Primary" texts usually appeared in a horizontal band just below the rim of a vase, or in a vertical panel set off from the scene; while "Secondary" ones were actually within the scene, and connected to the actors in whatever drama was being portrayed. My guess, based on comparison with the way stone lintels worked, was that the Secondary texts contained the names and possibly the titles of the principal characters, often the unearthly denizens of Xibalbá. Later research has

50 *A Primary Standard Sequence text. a. Initial Sign. b. Step (substitutes for God N).
c. Wing-Quincunx. d. Serpent-segment. e. IL-Face. f. Muluc. g. Fish. h. Rodent-Bone.
i. Hand-Monkey. All these are nicknames, not decipherments.*

shown that this guess was correct, as it became apparent that specific
gods could be linked with specific name glyphs, and even with Emblem
Glyphs – the gods had their cities, too.

I began to notice a sameness about many of the Primary texts, that the
same glyphs, with minor variations, showed up over and over, and in the
same order. This aroused my curiosity, so back in our 1810 farmhouse I
cut these texts up into individual glyphs, and then lined up identical
glyphs in vertical columns. It turned out that I was dealing with some
sort of standard formula, which I christened the Primary Standard
Sequence (or PSS), and which almost always began with a glyphic
combination (a main sign and two affixes) to which I gave the name Initial
Sign. The order in which the twenty-one or so signs appeared was
absolutely fixed (I gave them all nicknames for mnemonic purposes, like
"Wing-Quincunx" and "Hand-Monkey"), but no one text ever
contained all of them. There might be only a few of the PSS glyphs on
some pots; in such abbreviated statements, the ones usually written
down were usually Initial Sign, God N, and Wing-Quincunx, in that
order.

And there were also interesting substitutions, which would make
possible a new interpretation of what at least part of the PSS was all
about. But the epigraphers who would open up these new vistas were still
in grade school when the PSS was discovered.

What was the meaning of this formula? I was sure that it had little or
nothing to do with the actions of individuals, sacred or secular,
portrayed on the vessels – that was the task of the Secondary texts. As
the PSS was often followed by what surely were names, Emblem Glyphs,
and the title *ba-ca-b(a)* (*bacab*, frequent on the monuments), I felt sure
that those terminal glyphs named the owner or patron, and his (or her)
city. Keeping in mind my Underworld interpretation of Maya funerary
ceramics, it is no surprise that I suggested that the PSS might be the
written form of a stock funerary incantation, perhaps like the Egyptian
Book of the Dead, meant to inform the soul of the defunct what he was to
encounter on his journey into Xibalbá. The whole Hero Twins tale was a

kind of Death and Transfiguration parable for the Maya elite, so why not a formulaic text or spell to assist the honored dead?

This was but a working hypothesis, and hypotheses can be altered or even demolished when other explanations become more plausible; during the 1980s, this is what happened, at least in part, to my "funerary chant" hypothesis about the PSS.

The Grolier was but the first of several exhibitions of Maya pictorial ceramics that I organized; a second was in Gillett Griffin's Princeton Art Gallery[10] and a third at the Israel Museum of Jerusalem.[11] By that time, Kerr's rollout camera was in full use. My feeling was then, and still is, that all of these materials, even though looted (like the majority of Greek pots or Chinese bronzes), ought to be put out in the public domain so that scholars could study them.

One whole class of vases was new to Maya studies; these were painted with calligraphic delicacy in black or brown on a cream or light tan background. They seemed to me to have been produced by the same artist-scribes who might have painted the Classic Maya codices, so I called them "codex-style vases." It was not long before the dirt archaeologists declared them all to be fake, since none of *them* had ever

51 *Gods of the scribes on Classic vases. a. Rabbit God writing a codex.*
b. the Monkey-man Scribes.

found such an object in their excavations. Since codex-style vase fragments have now been found on a bona fide dig at the site of Nakbé in the Petén, that particular canard can be laid to rest.[12]

I was impressed by the fact that a number of these vases showed pairs of individuals with monkey-like faces engaged in painting folding-screen codices which had jaguar-skin covers; these gleefully manic individuals, as well as other scribal gods, held brush pens in one hand and paintpots in the shape of halved conch shells in the other (fig. 51).[13] Again the *Popol Vuh* connection struck me with force. To go back to the story of the Hero Twins: when they were yet young boys perfecting their skills as blow-gunners and shooting birds out of the trees, their quite mean grandmother (the aged Creator Goddess of Maya cosmology) favored their spoiled half-brothers, 1 Batz and 1 Chuen ("One Monkey" and "One Artisan"). One day, the boys, always great tricksters, persuaded these two nasties to climb a tall tree to retrieve some birds that had become lodged in some high boughs, but the half-brothers became stuck up there. By magical means, the Twins gave their two adversaries long tails and pot bellies – in other words, turned them into monkeys – and they were unable to get down. The old woman laughed uproariously at the comic sight when they came back to the house. But, says the narrator of the *Popol Vuh*,

So they were prayed to by the flautists and singers among ancient people, and the writers and carvers prayed to them. In ancient times they turned into animals, they became monkeys, because they magnified themselves, they abused their younger brothers.

There is good evidence that the cult of monkey or monkey-man scribes was widespread over ancient Mesoamerica, and was found not only among the highland Maya but also in Yucatán at the time of the Spanish Conquest. Likewise, among the Aztec, the monkey was patron god of the artisans, musicians, and dancers. And why not? Our close relatives the monkeys were the most intelligent of the non-human animals encountered by people like the Maya, and so the Maya elevated them to a godlike status, just as the Egyptians took the baboon-god Thoth as patron of *their* scribes and the art of writing.

I will return to the Maya scribes and their gods in the next chapter.

The discovery of a new Maya codex is an exceedingly rare event. The Dresden, in all likelihood picked up by Cortés in Yucatán and shipped by him to Europe in 1519, only came to scholarly notice in the eighteenth century. The Madrid appeared in two sections at about the mid-point of the nineteenth century, and the Paris at about the same time. Dozens of claimants have reached collectors and museums since then, and all have proved to be fake. I keep a picture file on falsified codices, painted on both bark paper and, more usually, on untreated leather. They are truly inept and ugly – all of them, without exception. The modern "scribes" who turn out such spurious junk have not even a nodding acquaintance with the rudiments of the Maya calendar, let alone the iconography and the non-calendrical glyphs.

Just before the opening of the Grolier exhibit, I was told by a friend about a codex which might just be real. It was owned by the Mexican collector Dr. Josué Saenz, and I went to see it in his home in Mexico City. The purported codex was on bark paper coated with gesso (like the three real codices, but also like some phonies), but it looked real to me, with convincing calendrical signs and deity figures drawn in a kind of hybrid Toltec-Maya style, slightly similar to the reliefs of Chichén Itzá.

How had it reached the hands of Dr. Saenz? One day, it seems, a person had approached him with a proposition: they would fly him to an airstrip, and he would be shown a recently discovered group of pre-Columbian treasures. And so he went with them in a light plane to the secret landing spot; they had covered the compass with a cloth so he wouldn't know where he was, but Dr. Saenz is widely traveled and knew that he must be in the foothills of the Sierra de Chiapas, not far from the Gulf Coast plain. After landing, they brought him the pieces, which he was told had just been found in a dry cave in the area. They included a mosaic mask (certainly Late Post-Classic Maya); a small box carved with glyphs, including the Tortuguero Emblem Glyph (they were probably not far from this site, a satellite of Palenque); a flint sacrificial knife with a wooden grip in the form of a hand; and a codex. He was allowed to take these back with him to Mexico City "on approval," meaning that he would check their authenticity with his consultant, a person who makes a living doing this sort of thing for Mexican and foreign collectors, for a large fee.

The expert pronounced the mask[14] a fake (it ended up as one of the treasures of the Dumbarton Oaks collection). The verdict on the codex was also thumbs down, but Saenz was so intrigued by it that he bought it anyway, along with the little box (which I later published in the Mesa Redonda series[15]).

I returned to New Haven with a very good set of photographs which Dr. Saenz had given me. On showing them to Floyd Lounsbury, we both concluded that what we were looking at were ten pages of a twenty-page Venus Calendar; it was structurally similar to the Venus pages in the Dresden Codex, in that in its complete form it would have covered 65 cycles of the planet. There are many differences from the Dresden, though, the most important being that there are pictures of gods accompanying all *four* phases of Venus and not just its appearance as Morning Star. In Mesoamerican thought, Venus was an exceptionally malevolent heavenly body, and the Venus deities in the Grolier are shown hurling weapons and otherwise making themselves unpleasant, as in the Dresden. Unlike the Dresden, however, the intervals covered by each phase (reckoned as 236, 90, 250, and 8, totalling 584 days) were expressed by "ring numbers," that is, bar-and-dot coefficients tied up like bundles.

Floyd and I were convinced that Saenz indeed had the fourth known Maya codex. Even though its text was purely calendrical, I asked him to lend it to the show, which he did, suggesting it could temporarily be called the "Grolier codex." Shortly after I had installed it in its case, a *New York Times* reporter arrived with a photographer, and the next day "the Grolier Codex" was splashed across one section of the paper, with a somewhat blurry shot of three of its pages, taken at an angle.

Before long, I got a friendly letter from Linton Satterthwaite in Philadelphia, asking for more details on the codex. A little later, he sent me a copy of a letter he had received from Thompson, who had seen the *Times* article (but who never once looked at the original or asked me for photographs). Briefly, Thompson gleefully announced that I'd been "had" – the so-called "codex" was a clearcut fake.

By the time the catalog, which I called *The Maya Scribe and His World*, came out, I had a radiocarbon date on a fragment of bark paper from the codex: AD 1230 ± 130, just about perfect for the style and iconography, which is a kind of hybrid Maya-Toltec.[16]

Now, the very conservative Grolier Club had never handled anything like my catalog, and they were convinced it was not going to sell. So, at their insistence, Doug Ewing and I were obliged to sign a document accepting full financial responsibility for the volume (incidentally, I had paid for all of the line drawings out of my own pocket). When they asked me who should receive (free) review copies, my answer was "Nobody!": I saw no reason why free copies should be sent to orthodox Mayanists whose negative reactions I could predict with some accuracy, certainly not if Doug and I were going to foot the bill.

But, the Directors protested, we have always sent a copy to *The Book Collector* in England for review; so off went *The Maya Scribe* to end up in the hands of Eric Thompson, that most predictable of Mayanists. Eric's parting shot at me was let fly from beyond the grave. In 1975, after his knighthood, he had gone as guest lecturer on a tour of Bolivia, where he was severely affected by the altitude. By the time he returned to his Essex home he was a very sick person, and soon died.

His posthumous review in *The Book Collector*[17] paid no attention to the main theme of my book – that the scenes on pictorial Maya ceramics and the pottery texts were not mere decoration by a bunch of illiterate artists, but meaningful statements made by artists/scribes as conversant with the concerns of elite Maya culture as anyone else (it was only later that it was discovered that Maya scribes *were* elite). Nor was there any mention of the Primary Standard Sequence, something new to Maya epigraphy. Briefly, I got the same treatment that had earlier been meted out to Whorf and Knorosov: ignoring the main argument while concentrating on some detail where he thought the chances of a quick kill were best.

What Thompson went after was the Grolier Codex. I won't repeat all of his arguments, since they are only peripheral to the story of the decipherment, and each one of them can be refuted; but stacked up together, they made a pile which impressed his followers. Saenz' Mexican "expert," a friend of Thompson, contributed his bit which was an unsubstantiated rumor that the fakers had used some old bark paper which had been found somewhere in a cave; this would explain the radiocarbon date (I suppose they would have first dated the paper themselves so they would know in what style to paint the codex).

The dénouement of the Grolier Codex affair was that it is now considered authentic by almost all those Mayanists who are either epigraphers or iconographers, or both; that the archaeoastronomer John Carlson has shown that it contains concepts about the planet Venus which have come to light only *after* it was exhibited in New York;[18] and that it is probably the earliest of the four known codices, the Dresden having been shown by Karl Taube to have Aztec-influenced iconography.[19] Dr. Saenz has donated the manuscript to the Mexican government, but it presently languishes in a Mexico City vault.

The irony of the whole business is that if Brasseur de Bourbourg had come across the Grolier while rummaging around in archives during the mid-nineteenth century, it would be accepted by even the most rock-ribbed scholar as the genuine article.

I make no pretensions to be a great decipherer. Rather, I look at myself as more of an enabler, bringing advances in one area to the attention of people working in other areas. Occasionally, I am lucky enough to open some interesting vistas which had previously remained undetected. One of these vistas was into the macabre world of Classic Maya ceramics; here was an untouched area of iconography, with supernatural beings engaged in activities hitherto undreamed-of in Maya research. Who would have hitherto dared to suggest that Classic rulers – and gods – took hallucinogenic or inebriating enemas with special syringes? Yet such shocking behavior is recorded over and over again on the vases and bowls. Who would have thought of monkey-man scribes?

The pictorial ceramics revealed that Schellhas' simple picture, largely based on the codices, of a sparsely inhabited pantheon, falls far short of the mark: there are hundreds of Maya gods, most of them denizens of the Underworld. No alphabet in the world could ever provide enough letters to label them. A few of the Schellhas gods – D (Itzamná), L, and N (Pauahtun) – reign in Xibalbá, but there is a bewildering variety of animals, monsters, and men, often in composite form.[20] Art historians came to realize that most Maya iconography appeared in two places: on the costumes of royal personages as recorded on the stone monuments (these are virtual iconographic symphonies) and on the pottery.

For the decipherment, it became possible for the first time to take the texts on ceramics seriously. They *did* say something, even if the PSS resisted all attempts to crack it for more than a decade. Names and titles of actual personages *did* appear painted on pottery surfaces as well as carved in stone. And many of those outlandish supernaturals were named in the Secondary texts. For epigraphers, the universe of Mayanist research was definitely expanding.

But there was much muttering and grumbling from the wings. In reaction to the uncontrolled, and seemingly uncontrollable, looting that had produced all these pots, and in particular the sawn-up, mutilated stelae, there was a powerful lobby of Mayanists who were taking the position that one should not even *study* this material, as this would in effect be condoning the pillage. As most Europeans have come to realize, there is a powerfully puritanical streak in American culture which comes over our public life in waves. As an example, one field archaeologist has more than once been heard to express the hope that every Maya pot brought to light by non-archaeological hands be ground into fine dust. These are people who would have smashed up the Rosetta Stone because it had not been excavated by one of Napoleon's archaeologists.

I have no intention of getting mired in this problem, which is exceedingly complex and often awash with Pecksniffian hypocrisy. A further complication was that a definite rift began to open up between the epigraphers and iconographers, on one side, and the field archaeologists on the other, a split which was not merely over the looting issue, but much more profound: is the proper study of the Maya world the world of the elite rulers, or is it the everyday life of "ordinary Maya," whoever *they* might have been? By the end of the 1980s, this rift had begun to look like the Grand Canyon.

10 A New Dawn

Some decipherers begin young. It is said that the great Jean-François Champollion began his career at the age of nine, when he embarked on the study of eastern languages in Grenoble, and he was only seventeen when he published his first learned paper, a study of the Coptic etymology of Egyptian place-names recorded by the Greeks.[1]

But Champollion has nothing on David Stuart, the young Mayanist whose career must set a new record in epigraphic precocity.[2] In a way, David was preadapted to a life in Maya studies: his parents have co-authored a book on the Maya,[3] and his father George has long been the *National Geographic*'s expert on the subject and its archaeological editor. David was born in Washington in 1965. Most of his early schooling, though, was in Chapel Hill, North Carolina, where George was earning his doctorate in anthropology.

In 1968, at the tender age of three, David was taken on his initial trip to the archaeological wonders of Mexico and Guatemala. His very first memories are the ruins of great Mesoamerican cities like Monte Albán, Chichén Itzá, and Tikal, and he "cried his eyes out" when he was not allowed to climb to the top of Tikal's Temple I with his sister and older brothers.

The turning point in David's life came in the summer of 1974, when the entire Stuart family went to the Maya city of Cobá for five months. Cobá is unique among Maya sites: situated in the forests of Quintana Roo, in the eastern part of the Yucatán Peninsula, it is built among a cluster of waterlily-covered lakes, and its various suburb complexes are connected to the center by a network of *sacbe'ob*, or raised causeways. The eight-year-old boy found himself living in a thatched Maya hut among people who spoke largely Yucatec. The Stuarts were at Cobá for two summers, while George was engaged with a large-scale mapping project. As David was really not old enough to help with the cartography, he was left to his own devices. He had a lot of time, and would wander out on his own in the forest, coming across fallen sculptures from time to time.

During the 1975 season, two new stelae were found by the project, and George dropped everything to draw them; but David himself was always drawing when he was a child, so he did his own sketches of these reliefs and began wondering what all that writing meant. Luckily, at Cobá there was a small library which included Thompson's *Introduction*, and he began copying the drawings of glyphs in the back of the book, "just for the fun of it."

It was also a chance to experience the life of the present-day Maya. Although he didn't learn to speak the language, he managed to pick up an extensive Yucatec vocabulary while playing with the workers' children. The high point of the Cobá experience for the young David came in 1975, when there was a prolonged drought – not uncommon in the northern lowlands – and a *cha-chaac* ceremony was held in the ruined city's main plaza. A shaman or *h-men* ("he who does things") was brought in from the town of Chemax; under this man's supervision, an altar was built with four arches of green boughs tied at the top, and offerings were made to Chac, god of rain – offerings of *balche* (the native mead), cigarettes, and Coca-Cola. By this time, the boy was convinced that he should be a Mayanist.

It was during that summer of 1975 that Eric Thompson (by now Sir Eric) came to Yucatán for the state visit of the Queen, which included a tour of Uxmal. Afterwards, Thompson visited Cobá for the first time since 1930, when he and Florence Thompson had honeymooned in the ruins while Eric studied the site and its monuments. For the next week, the Stuarts drove the great man around Yucatán; for the young and impressionable David, "it was quite an experience to meet the man who had written the book."

David met Linda Schele in 1976 in Washington as a direct result of his parents' work on their *National Geographic* book *The Mysterious Maya* (the *Geographic* likes alliteration in its titles). Linda was a consultant for the project, and they invited her out to dinner at a Washington restaurant. The topic of conversation was the Maya script, and Linda was busily drawing glyphs on a pad. It was some time before she noted that the eleven-year-old boy at the table was looking over her shoulder; when he remarked, "Oh, that's a Fire glyph," she turned around in astonishment. Linda is a very lucky player of hunches: later on that same evening, she invited David to come down the following summer to Palenque, to spend several weeks helping her correct drawings of the Palenque inscriptions.

And so it came to pass. David did arrive at Palenque in the summer of 1976, along with his mother Gene. Linda tells me that David was "very self-contained, not wanting to be the center of attention, not wanting to bother anyone – quiet and withdrawn." They stayed in Merle's house, and, according to David, "I had a ball. Linda would give me a drawing of an inscription and say, 'OK, you go read this.' And I would go into Merle's library for an afternoon, and try to struggle with the dates, and figure out patterns, or anything that I could. And then I would come out and ask her a few questions. It was really drawing the glyphs rather than reading books that helped me the most. You just sort of brand the glyphs in your mind, even if you don't know what these things are."

What Linda handed the boy that first day was the tablet from Palenque's Temple of the Sun, in the Cross Group – one of Chan-Bahlum's great monuments. As she tells it, "In eight hours, with a little consultation, he had read the whole thing. In eight hours, he had gotten to the place it had taken us five years to get to!"

David's method was to take a legal-sized pad of paper and write down everything he could find out about every Palenque glyph, using books in Merle's superb library; each line would be a separate glyph block from a particular text. Sitting afterwards with Linda on the back porch (the birthplace of the Mesa Redonda series), he went over the texts with her. One of the things he noted was a particular compound glyph that often occurred on the Cross Group tablets with the names of gods and mortal rulers. His mentor Linda liked the idea and suggested that he write it up and give it at the next Mesa Redonda, to be held in June 1978.[4]

This he did, and the great ones of the field must have been amazed to hear a boy not yet turned thirteen hold forth with insight and accuracy on a very complex subject. It was an astonishing performance – even Champollion had attained the ripe age of seventeen before presenting his first paper at Grenoble!

It was not all glyphs, however, for the young epigrapher, for he was beginning junior high school back in Chapel Hill; but he was able to work on them whenever he had spare time.

All three Stuarts were in attendance at the great conference "Phoneticism in Mayan Hieroglyphic Writing," held in June 1979 at the State University of New York at Albany.[5] Like the first Palenque Mesa Redonda, this was a watershed in Maya studies and the decipherment of the script. The linguist Lyle Campbell set the tone when he stated at the outset: "No Mayan linguist who has seriously looked into the matter any longer doubts the phonetic hypothesis as originally framed by Knorosov and elaborated by David Kelley, Floyd Lounsbury, and others."[6] The Maya script was logographic – that is, a combination of logograms expressing the morphemes or meaning units of words, and phonetic-syllable signs. In other words, exactly what Knorosov had been telling us ever since 1952.

Yuri Valentinovich had been invited, and the State Department had notified the organizers that he was actually coming (my wife would have been interpreter), but this, as usual with the Soviets, proved to be a chimaera. Years later, Knorosov told us why he failed to appear. The problem, he told us, was not the Iron Curtain, but what he calls the "Golden Curtain": in the pre-Gorbachev era, the Party apparatchiks demanded exorbitant sums of money before any exit visa was granted, and Knorosov just didn't have it.

What made this meeting a "first" was the heavy participation of the linguists. Thompson's sharp tongue had consigned them to outer darkness, but things were different now. With Thompson gone, and with Knorosovian phoneticism now established, they saw new horizons ahead. On the one hand, the fact that for more than twelve centuries the Mayan languages had been written with a partially phonetic script gave them the opportunity for the first time to study an indigenous New World language family as it evolved over time. On the other, the linguists could contribute significantly to the decipherment, in several ways. One of these would be by reconstructing the vocabulary and grammar of the Cholan and Yucatec branches of Mayan as they were spoken in Classic times,[7] while another would be to bring their unparalleled knowledge of the structure of Mayan languages to bear on the analysis of hieroglyphic words and sentences.

Early on in the conference, Dave Kelley stood up and pinned a large chart to the wall. Essentially, this was a grid of all those syllabic signs that Knorosov and others had proposed which had been largely confirmed by later research; to the left side of the grid was a vertical column of consonants, and along the top a horizontal row of vowels, giving one in the boxes an array of CV (consonant-vowel) combinations. Grids of this nature had long ago been generated for the syllabic systems of early scripts elsewhere in the world – for Linear B in the Aegean, and Hieroglyphic Hittite in Turkey, for example – but this was an innovation for Maya studies. "We'll start with this," Dave told them, "now where do we go from here?"

One new path was provided by *polyvalence*, the writing principle long recognized by students of Mesopotamian cuneiform and Egyptian hieroglyphics, but until explored by the linguists James Fox and John Justeson[8] in the Albany conference, not really fully grasped by Mayanists; it was certainly not taken into account by Knorosov in his pioneering work. To recap, basically polyvalence is present (1) when a single sign has multiple values, and (2) when a sound is symbolized by more than one sign.

We find the first kind of polyvalence in English script – in fact, it is quite common. An example raised by Fox and Justeson is the compound sign *ch* in English: it has totally different values in the words *chart*, *chorus*, and *chivalry*. Just look at the sign *&* on your typewriter: this can be *and*, *ampersand*, and *et-* (in &c for "etcetera"). Cuneiform specialists call this kind of polyvalence "polyphony." Mayanists have known about polyphony for a long time. Take, for example, the well-established sign for the next-to-last in the list of twenty days: this is *Cauac*, given by Bishop Landa, but in Maya hieroglyphic writing it can also be *tun* or *haab* with the meaning "year," as well as acting as the phonetic-syllabic *cu*.

So how do the readers of this script know which of these polyphonic sound values is the right one? Exactly as they do with English-script polyphony – by context. To reduce further any possible ambiguity, the Maya scribes, just like their Mesopotamian and Egyptian counterparts, often added phonetic complements to reinforce the proper reading of the sign in question; for example postfixing the syllabic sign *n(i)* to show when the Cauac sign was to be read as *tun* and not *haab* or *Cauac*.

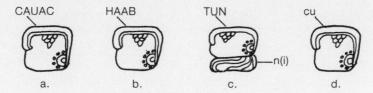

52 *Polyvalence: polyphony. Logograms are in upper case, phonetic signs in lower case. a. Cauac (day-sign). b. haab (365-day year). c. tun (360-day cycle). d. cu (syllabic sign).*

The converse of polyphony is *homophony*, by means of which multiple signs have the same sound value. This sometimes comes about historically when signs which once had distinctive pronunciations converge over time on the same sound – a situation well attested in Egyptian. Five years after the Albany meeting, Steve Houston presented a superb example of Maya homophony: the signs for "four," "snake," and "sky" all freely substituting for each other as logographs whenever the sound *can* (Yucatec) or *chan* (Cholan) was called for.[9]

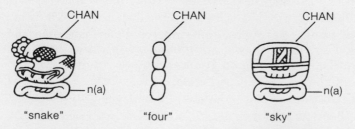

53 *Polyvalence: homophony. These glyphs are interchangeable.*

The significance of homophony was not lost on the young David Stuart. In future years, he would search out such substitution patterns to come up with many new readings that previous investigators, including Knorosov, had missed. This was the genesis of his important publication-to-be, "Ten Phonetic Syllables."

Fox and Justeson's paper proved to be enormously productive over the years. They themselves established several new glyphic decipherments, such as the glyph combinations standing for *uinic*, "man" in almost all Mayan languages, and *u bac*, "his prisoner," frequent on war monuments of the Classic period.

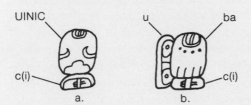

54 *Readings by James Fox and John Justeson. a.* uinic, *"man," "person." b.* u bac, *"his captive."*

The report on the Albany conference came out in 1984. In one appendix, Peter Mathews laid out – in published form for the first time – a reasonably complete syllabic grid for the Maya script, one in which the syllabic value of each sign was agreed upon by several speakers. This has been added to and modified over the subsequent years, but there was now little doubt at all that the Maya could and did write anything they wanted to with this syllabary. The logograms would prove a tougher nut to crack, but substitutions with purely phonetic signs would lead to their decipherment, too.

David Stuart didn't actually give a paper in Albany, but by this time he was already beginning to toy with the enigmatic Primary Standard Sequence, and submitted a short study of the second glyph in the sequence – a head of God N, which he felt was some kind of verb. In retrospect, we now know that he was right, but he was persuaded to withdraw it in favor of a short article on the reading of the bloodletting sign on Classic Maya reliefs.[10] David now disavows this reading, but in the paper (which came out with the volume in 1984), he made the important point that the ornate band which flows down from a ruler's hands during Period Ending rites is actually blood drawn from his own penis with a bone or stingray-spine perforator, an instrument previously identified by David Joralemon. It appeared that it was no light task to take on the kingship of a Classic Maya state.

I should imagine that being the son of a *National Geographic* editor, with endless possibilities for travel and adventure in foreign lands, would be every adolescent boy's dream. The reality is probably far from this, but it cannot be denied that David had an exciting youth as compared with mine (until I was of college age, I had never been to any place more exotic than Montreal).

Over Christmas vacation in the winter of 1980–81, the fifteen-year-old David had the opportunity to participate in a truly electrifying discovery that combined exploration, danger, and discomfort in about equal proportions.[11] It came about this way. The previous year, two Mopán Maya farmers had discovered an underground cavern in the southeastern Petén, near the border with Belize; it was subsequently visited by several Americans, including a young Yale graduate student, Pierre Ventur, who gave it its name: Naj Tunich, "the house of stone." Limestone caves are found in many parts of the Maya lowlands and in the hilly country of the Verapaz region, and everywhere they are venerated and feared by the Maya as the entrance to the dread Underworld. To enter them is considered an act of bravery, with the possibility of incurring the wrath of its Xibalban denizens, the lords of death – in fact, it was shortly after he had engaged on an extensive program of exploring Maya caves that the brilliant young archaeologist Dennis Puleston was struck down by a bolt of lightning atop the Castillo, the main pyramid of Chichén Itzá. The Maya would not have been surprised.

Reports had reached the *National Geographic* that Naj Tunich had a true treasure: its walls were covered with realistic drawings and long hieroglyphic texts of Classic age. The magazine decided that this would be a good story, and David flew down to Guatemala with his father, the chief editor, and a friend, reaching the cave site by helicopter. Establishing a small tent camp, they explored the cavern for several days, but even this was not sufficient time to survey all 1,200 meters of the cave's tortuous passages.

David was the expedition's epigrapher, and revelled in the several dozen long texts that were drawn in black pigment in single and double columns on the damp walls. There was much phonetic writing, and several dates in the Calendar Round which could be linked to the Long Count (one fell on 18 December AD 741, at the height of the Maya Late Classic). For him, the high point was when he came across a new way to write the month-sign Pax. The usual form is logographic, and seems to resemble a drum emitting sound (*pax* means "drum" in some Mayan languages); in its place, David found that the scribe had used two signs, the first being the well-known netted *pa* glyph used back in the sixteenth century by Bishop Landa as a phonetic indicator for his version of Pax, and in the name of God N or *Pauahtun, while the second was a sign that had never been read, an oval containing two parallel diagonal lines. Ergo, following Knorosov's Principle of Synharmony, the second sign must be *xa*, and together with the first, the reading would be *Pa-x(a)*. David had deciphered his first phonetic sign – the first in a long series – thanks to the fact that the ancient scribes had enjoyed playing with their script, shifting back and forth between logographic and phonetic writing, balancing sound and meaning.

pa

x(a)

55 *Phonetic spelling of the month Pax in Naj Tunich cave.*

The cavern walls, lit by their flashlights and photographic equipment, had many other surprises, not the least of which were realistic homoerotic encounters. But it was quite in character that there would have been a depiction of Hunahpu, the great Hero Twin, engaged in playing ball, for this cave was after all an extension of Xibalbá itself. What had brought the artist-scribes to Naj Tunich in the mid-eighth century? Today, throughout the lowlands, Maya shamans use the caverns for their most secret rites and divinations; but until the Naj Tunich texts have been fully deciphered and analyzed – this is now being done by Andrea Stone[12] – we can only guess what went on here by the light of pine torches.

All this took place while David was in high school. During summers he continued to go to Merle's Mesa Redonda conferences in Palenque. After his graduation in the spring of 1983, he gave a paper at the Mesa Redonda on the "count-of-captives" glyph, which he had discovered.[13] This is actually a complex of signs which previous generations of epigraphers had vainly attempted to make into something calendrical, since it always included a bar-and-dot number. David was able to show that it really meant "he of x captives," in line with the usual vainglorious claims of these warlike rulers. The phrase opened with the proclitic *ah*, "he of ——," then expressed the number, and concluded with the "bone" logograph which he showed was to be read *bac*, either "bone" or (in this case) "captive," a fine example of rebus writing in the Maya script. In a political milieu in which the taking of important prisoners validated royal power, Bird-Jaguar of Yaxchilán, a militarily successful king, often had the scribes interpose the phrase "he of the twenty captives" between his name and the Emblem Glyphs of his city.

By this time, David was becoming widely known in the Maya field, and had a large circle of acquaintances and friends who were working on

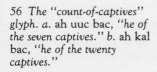 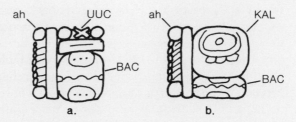

56 *The "count-of-captives" glyph. a.* ah uuc bac, *"he of the seven captives." b.* ah kal bac, *"he of the twenty captives."*

some of the same problems that he was. In spite of his youth, and regardless of the fact that he was not even a freshman in college, he was awarded a fellowship at Dumbarton Oaks for the academic year 1983–84. This meant that he could work in absolute tranquility in the beautiful setting of what is generally considered to be a scholar's paradise, with access to D.O.'s superb library and to its remarkable archive of photographs of Maya ceramics.

David then lived at home in Washington. One February day in 1984, he received a telephone call from Chicago; it was a representative from the MacArthur Fellowship: in recognition of his achievements as a Mayanist, he was to be made a Fellow and given an award of no less than $128,000. The wire services picked this one up right away, and the fairy-tale story that a boy of eighteen just out of high school had won a "genius prize" – as the journalists like to call this fellowship – was on the front pages of newspapers and in newsmagazines all across America. All of this publicity failed to turn his head, and it is generally agreed in the field that the MacArthur Fellow of eighteen was not much different from the self-contained, self-effacing small boy who had sat at Linda's elbow that long-ago summer in Palenque.

Between them, the two fellowships gave the young epigrapher two complete years to do nothing but to "play around with the glyphs," as he puts it. The MacArthur money was wisely invested, after setting aside part to fund travel to the Maya area and to buy a personal computer. His old mentor Linda came to Washington for two months during this time. "Those two years after high school were so productive, working with Linda. I really felt like I was in this for good."

It will be remembered that, thanks to the early research of Eric Thompson, we know that there are glyphic expressions associated with Distance Numbers that tell one whether one is to count backward (the Anterior Date Indicator or ADI) or forward (Posterior Date Indicator or PDI) from the base date to reach another date.[14] With considerable logic, Thompson had convinced most of his colleagues that the main sign in both the ADI and PDI, the head of a ferocious fish, was a rebus, playing on the homonyms *xoc*, "shark" and *xoc*, "count"; thus, he argued that one meant "count back to——" while the other was "count forward to——."

During his idyll at D.O., David noticed that the more abstract variant for this fish head could substitute for Landa's *u*-"bracket," the third person possessive pronoun, and he began entertaining the notion that perhaps both variants were really *u*. Since both the ADI and PDI were often followed by Landa's phonetic *ti*, he began to suspect that the fish head might even be *ut*, with *ti* as a phonetic complement. "I was pretty reluctant about this, because everybody was talking about *xoc*. I felt like I was being a heretic." But when he looked up *ut* and its Yucatec cognate *uchi* in dictionaries, he saw that it meant "to happen or to come to pass." He was obviously on a productive track.

David's decipherment of this glyph compound has been refined by several colleagues over the years, but the basic reading still stands. Four linguists – John Justeson, Will Norman, Kathryn Josserand, and Nicholas Hopkins – have found grammatical evidence in the Cholan languages (most Classic inscriptions are proto-Cholan) that the ADI reads *ut-iy* or *ut-ix*, "it had come to pass," and the PDI reads *iual ut*, "and then it came to pass."[15] This has recently allowed Linda Schele to paraphrase a text such as Lintel 21, a monument of Bird-Jaguar, ruler of Yaxchilán, as follows:

(On) 9.0.19.2.4 2 Kan
    G8 [Lord of the Night] ruled, Glyph Y
        7 days ago it arrived (the moon)
            Three moons had ended.
                3X [was the name] of the 29 [days of the lunar
                month].
2 Yax he dedicated the 4-bat place,
    it was his house
        "sky god lord," Moon-Skull
            the 7th successor, the lord of the title, Yat-Balam, Holy
            Lord of Yaxchilán.
(it was) 5 days, 16 uinals, 1 tun, 15 katuns
    and then 7 Muluc 17 Zec came to pass
        he dedicated the 4-bat place
            "sky god lord," Bird-Jaguar, 3 Katun Lord
            He of 20 Captives.

I find it ironic that even Maya calendrics have started yielding to the onslaught of phonetic analysis, considering that so many long-dead scholars (Seler, Goodman, and Morley, among others) had utterly

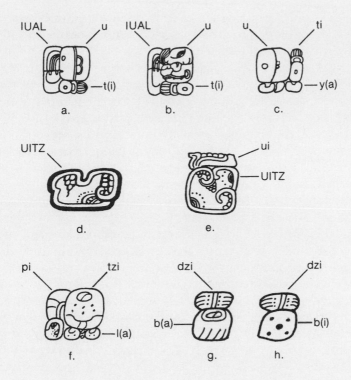

57 Readings by David Stuart. a, b. iual ut, "and then it came to
pass" (Posterior Date Indicator). c. utiy, "it had come to pass"
(Anterior Date Indicator). d, e. uitz, "mountain." f. pitzil, "play
ball." g, h. dzib, "writing."

rejected phoneticism while holding to the view that there was little else
than calendrical statements in the Classic inscriptions.

David's work on the *ut* glyph "really nailed home to me one of the
important workings of this writing system – the huge amount of free
substitutions. Despite all this graphic complexity, much of it was just
repetitive." The terrible morass that Floyd Lounsbury had found when
taking up Thompson's *Introduction* just didn't exist. During those
productive years from 1984 through 1987 (David entered Princeton as a
freshman in 1985), all sorts of new phonetic readings, he says, "exploded
right in front of me." To reiterate, this is *homophony* – phonetic signs
substituting for other phonetic signs or for logograms. The results of his
extraordinary findings, resting in part on collaboration with others like
Linda Schele, saw the light of day in a new series edited and published by
his father, *Research Reports on Ancient Maya Writing*. Number 14 in the

series was David's remarkable "Ten Phonetic Syllables," in which the kind of methodology pioneered by Floyd and continued by Fox and Justeson reached fruition.[16] The phonetic grid first presented in the Albany Conference was beginning to lose some of its blank spaces.

David's decipherments opened up many new lines of research. For me, the most significant was pinning down the glyph for the syllable *dzi* (written *ts'i* by linguists); with already identified signs for final *-b* – either *b(a)*, *b(i)*, or *b(e)* – this led to the stunning identification of the glyph compound for "writing" itself, *dzib*, and for the scribe, *ah dzib*, "he of the writing." The implications of this finding for our view of ancient Maya society and culture were enormous, as we shall see.

Puzzle after puzzle was solved in this slim, modest, carefully argued publication. The identification of the sign for the CV syllable *tzi* led David not only to the reading of the glyphic combination *utzil*, "good" (a frequent prognostication in the codices), but also to the discovery of the hieroglyphs for *uitz* or "mountain." When I was writing the Grolier catalog, I had noticed that a monstrous head with fringed eyes and Cauac markings on clay vessels had often served as a base or throne for individual gods, or had surrounded them like a cave; I called this the "Cauac Monster," for want of a better term. What David found was that the Cauac Monster logograph could have a phonetic substitute consisting of two signs, one to be read as *ui* (or *wi*), and the other as *tzi*; applying Knorosov's principles, this would be *uitz(i)*. Q.E.D.! As will later be seen, the *uitz* reading helped identify the toponyms or place-names within and without some Classic cities.

There was another dividend for the *tzi* reading: in conjunction with a sign deciphered by David as *pi*, it spelled out the name for "to play ball," *pitz* in the dictionaries. The great sacred game of the Maya elite had at last received its hieroglyphic name, and the title *ah pitz*, "he of the ballgame," began turning up among the titles or epithets of these Classic period emulators of Hunahpu and Xbalanque.

And one other god received his proper name in "Ten Phonetic Syllables." This was Schellhas' God K, a serpent-footed deity with a smoking tube or axe-blade protruding from his forehead. Ever since Late Pre-Classic times, before the beginning of our era, God K had functioned as a patron of royal lineages and royal power. His image was held in the right hand of the king as the so-called "mannikin scepter," the emblem of divine rulership, during Period Ending ceremonies. So who was he really? In a wonderful display of scholarship, around the turn of the century the formidable Eduard Seler had shown, by comparing the New Year ceremonies in the Dresden with those described by Landa for late pre-Conquest Yucatán, that God K must be the deity called Bolon Dzacab ("Nine Lineages") by the bishop's informants.[17] This seemed reasonable, but David found a phonetic substitution for the god's name when it was used in nominal phrases of important chiefs in the inscriptions of Chichén Itzá: *ka-ui-l(a)*, or Kauil, a supernatural mentioned in Colonial sources.

I should mention one further advance made by the young Stuart in this remarkable tour-de-force. So far, we have been dealing with words of the CVC or CVCVC sort, for which the final consonant is expressed by a syllabic sign in which the final vowel is silent. But the grammar of the Cholan and Yucatec languages often calls for a final vowel or weak consonant, such as in the Yucatec *ooc-ih*, "he entered," or *hantabi*, "was it eaten?" How was the reader to know when the final vowel was actually to be pronounced, rather than left mute? David came up with two signs, one of which was to be read as *hi* and the other as *yi*, which could be tacked on to grammatical endings to show that this vowel, indeed, had a sound.

By the mid-1980s, the trickle of decipherments that had started in the 1960s had increased to a mighty flood. A pilgrim attending one of Linda's Austin workshops might find him- or herself among not just a few dozen, but hundreds of eager participants, at least some of whom were beginning to make discoveries of their own. Yet among all these enthusiasts scattered across the land, there was a small handful of truly brilliant epigraphers, including David, who were on the very crest of the wave. They were all young, all were competent artists (a necessity for drawing the glyphs), and all had a working knowledge of at least one Mayan language. Their decipherments began to far outstrip possibilities for speedy publication, so they kept in touch by letter and word of mouth, only occasionally meeting at conferences or in the field. The hard core of these Young Turks consisted of Peter Mathews, David Stuart, Steve Houston, Karl Taube, Barbara MacLeod, and Nikolai Grube; all but Peter and Nikolai were Americans. Presiding over this closely-knit band were Linda and Floyd. About them, Floyd once wryly commented to me:

They're young and they just go too fast for me. I'm the slow type to begin with, and I don't have good visual memory, and that's a definite disadvantage for me. They can retain so much data in their heads, and this enables them to see things and make leaps ahead that just leave me trailing in the dust; whereas my pace would be to see just one such thing, and before going on to anything else, track it down and publish a proof, utilizing all the available occurrences of it anywhere. But if you go after it that way, you deny yourself the opportunity to learn as fast as possible.[18]

Like Peter Mathews, Steve Houston is a "faculty brat," born in 1958 in Chambersburg, Pennsylvania, to a college professor and a Swedish

mother. After his graduation *summa cum laude* from the University of
Pennsylvania, he came to Yale for his doctorate, studying under Floyd,
myself, and the young art historian Mary Miller. Karl Taube is also the
son of an academic, a Nobel Prize-winning chemist; only a year older
than Steve, he came to us from the University of California. Having once
been a graduate student myself, I am only too aware of the fact that as a
whole graduate students are far more difficult to teach than undergraduates: at one and the same time, they are your colleagues *and* your
subordinates. With students like Karl and Steve at Yale, I found myself
in a reversed situation – it was *they* who were teaching *me*, and not the
other way around. I always learn from students (this is why I prefer being
in an academic department rather than a pure museum curatorship), but
I doubt if I have ever learned so much as from these two.

The other two members of this extraordinary network – Barbara
MacLeod and Nikolai Grube – were not in the Yale orbit like Peter,
Steve, and Karl. Barbara was at the University of Texas as one of Linda's
burgeoning crop of graduate students, and Nikolai occupies a post at the
University of Hamburg, where there is a long and honorable tradition of
Mesoamerican studies. Nikolai's qualifications are unique in a way: for
several months of each year, he stays in a remote Maya village in
Quintana Roo and studies the esoteric language of a Maya *h-men* or
shaman; needless to say, he is as fluent in Yucatec as Champollion was in
Coptic.

Great epigraphic breakthroughs sometimes come from seemingly
insignificant decipherments, like the biblical storm that grew from a
cloud no bigger than a man's hand. It came about this way. My friend
David Pendergast of the Royal Ontario Museum was looking for an
epigrapher to handle the brief texts that he had found on jade and other
artifacts from Altún Ha, a small but rich site in Belize that he had
excavated.[19] I immediately suggested Peter Mathews, and he was hired.
While it did not take Peter long to find on an inscribed jade plaque that
Altun Ha had its own Emblem Glyph, of far greater import were the
glyphs that he found incised on a pair of beautiful, ground obsidian
earspools from a royal burial at the site.[20] The first glyphic compound on
each of these began with *u*, the familiar 3rd person possessive, then went
on to a *tu* sign (long ago pinned down by Thompson as *tu* through its use
as a numerical classifier in Yucatecan inscriptions), with Landa's netted
pa sign below. Peter read this as *u tup(a)*, "his earspool" in Maya;
following it were several glyphs of what seemed to be the owner's name,
presumably the man in the tomb. Thus came about the first attested case
in Maya epigraphy of "name-tagging."

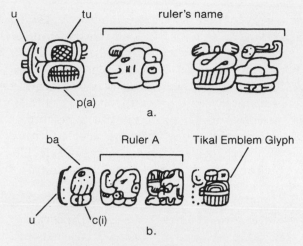

58 Name-tagging. a. u tup, "his earspool," incised on an
obsidian earspool from Altun Ha. b. u bac, "his bone,"
incised on a bone from the tomb of Ruler A at Tikal.

It was not long before David, on looking at the delicately incised texts
on a collection of bone strips placed with the body of the great king
under Tikal Temple I, noticed that several of them began with the phrase
u ba-c(i), that is, *u bac*, "his bone," followed by the king's name and the
Tikal Emblem Glyph.[21]

Here was an incredibly prosaic use of a script that Thompson and
others had always considered the domain of the purely esoteric and
supernatural. It was almost as though a communion cup would have a
large label, "the chalice of the Rev. John Doe." Thompson would have
been horrified, but name-tagging has turned out to be ubiquitous in the
world of the Classic scribes. The ancient Maya liked to name things, and
they liked to tell the world who owned these things. We shall find that
even temples, stelae, and altars had their own names.

That repetitive, almost ritualistic text that I had found on Maya pictorial
ceramics at the beginning of the 1970s, and which I thought might be a
funerary chant, lay dormant for many years, but at last began to attract
the attention of the young epigraphers – after all, the Primary Standard
Sequence was the most commonly written text in Classic Maya culture;
but it seemed impervious to decipherment. That is, until this new
generation came on the scene.

While working on the Grolier catalog, I had already noticed that there
were substitutions in the PSS, not only in what epigraphers call
"allographs" (minor variations in the same glyph), but substitutions in

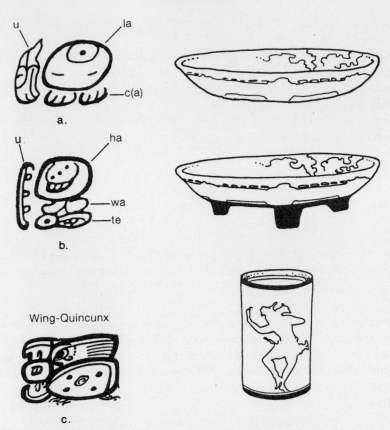

59 *Glyphs for vessel shapes in the Primary Standard Sequence. a.* u lac,
"*his plate.*" *b.* u hauante, "*his tripod dish.*" *c. Wing-Quincunx,*
representing cylindrical vases and round-bottomed bowls (beverage
containers).

whole signs which at times indicated polyvalence, and at times seemed to
change the meaning. This meant that the PSS could be subjected to
"distributional analysis," a study of the patterns of substitution between
signs in this highly codified, almost formulaic text. This is exactly what
Nikolai Grube set out to do in his Ph.D. dissertation, and what David,
Steve, and Karl began to work on at Yale and Princeton, and Barbara
MacLeod at the University of Texas.[22] Invaluable help was provided by
the ever-generous Justin Kerr, who made available to them hundreds of
rollouts of unpublished Maya vases, shot in his New York studio.

The results were extraordinary, and not exactly what I had expected. I
will take up later how David Stuart located the glyphic compound for
dzib, "writing," on these vessels, and the implications of this discovery.
What the PSS turned out to be, as Steve and Karl have pointed out, is a
gigantic case of name-tagging.[23] What they noted was that the compound

I had nicknamed "Wing-Quincunx" could alternate in some texts with another compound that was surely to be read as *u la-c(a)*. In many Mayan languages, and in reconstructed proto-Cholan, *lac* means "dish," and *u lac* would thus be "his dish." Confirmation comes from the fact that the phrase only occurs on wide pottery dishes. "Wing-Quincunx," on the other hand, occurs only on vessels that are higher than they are wide; their argument is complex, but Brian Stross, Steve Houston, and Barbara MacLeod have convinced their colleagues that this must be read *y-uch'ib*, "his drinking vessel."[24]

Maya archaeologists love to study pottery vessels. They revel in potsherds, which they dig up by the hundreds of thousands in their excavation trenches. But very few of them have thought about the *function* of all these ceramics. Iconography and epigraphy have begun to tell us what they were used for, at least as tomb furniture: elite Maya ceramics were containers for food and drink. Many palace scenes on painted pottery show that dishes or *laco'ob* were stacked high with maize tamales, and the tall vases were filled with a frothy liquid. This might have been *balche*, the native mead flavored with the bark of the *balche* tree, but it might have been something else.

What that "something else" was became clear with David Stuart's work on the PSS. I had called a glyph compound which follows the Wing-Quincunx glyph "fish," since that was its main sign. In a rush of inspiration, David saw that this fish, which is known to have the syllabic value of *ca*, was preceded by Landa's "comb" sign for *ca*, and followed by final *-u*, leading him to conclude that the compound must be read *ca-ca-u* – clearly cacao or chocolate.

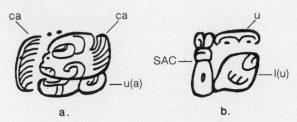

60 *Glyphs for beverages in the Primary Standard Sequence.*
a. cacau, *"cacao (chocolate)." b.* sac ul, *"white atole."*

An extraordinary confirmation of this reading came in 1984, when archaeologists found and excavated an Early Classic tomb in the heavily looted site of Río Azul in the northeastern Petén. In it was a strange vessel, finely painted over a layer of stucco; the lid of the pot could actually be screwed onto the vessel like a "lock-top" jar. Included in the hieroglyphic text were the owner's name or names and the *y-uch'ib*, "his drinking vessel" compound, as well as the newly identified cacao glyph.

Scrapings from the residue left inside the pot were sent to the Hershey Foods Corporation for laboratory identification. The verdict: it was chocolate![25]

It now looks as if every cylindrical vase with glyphic texts was used to hold cacao, and the magnificent Princeton Vase unmistakably shows a female attendant – perhaps one of God L's harem – pouring the chocolate drink from a height from one vase into another, to raise a good head of froth, which was highly prized among the Aztec and probably among the Maya as well. Yet there is one more beverage drunk by the Maya elite, for on rounded-bottom, open bowls, the chocolate "fish" glyph is replaced by another compound which reads *ul*; this is atole, a refreshing white gruel made from maize still imbibed today in Maya villages.[26]

So to whom did these dishes or these drinking vessels for chocolate or atole belong? The question must be asked, for we have seen this is a kind of name-tagging. The answer lies past the end of the PSS, in a position where names, titles, and Emblem Glyphs appear. This is where the noble owner comes in. Was he or she the one who had commissioned the vessel? And was it specifically potted and embellished, to go along with food and drink into the grave and Underworld with the body and soul of its patron or patroness (as I had long thought)? Or had the vessel had an existence of its own in the palace before its distinguished owner died? These are questions which have not yet been fully answered.

And what about the remainder of the PSS? The glyphs for vessel shape and the vessel's contents are only a fraction of the entire sequence, which might, if fully written out (it never is), contain up to thirty-five glyphs. One very large problem is that the PSS is an ancient formula, first appearing on carved stone vessels dating to the Late Pre-Classic. Much of its language, which is probably proto-Cholan, must be very archaic; one is reminded of the *e pluribus unum* written on American coins in a long-dead language, Latin. Nevertheless, in a 560-page Ph.D. thesis on the subject, Barbara MacLeod[27] has shown that the PSS falls into five parts: (1) a presentation or invocation, which calls the vessel into being; (2) a description of the surface treatment, whether painted or carved; (3) a naming of the shape of the vessel; (4) what she calls "recipes" – what is in the vessel; and (5) "closures," names and epithets relating to the individual in the afterlife. So is the PSS just a glorified case of name-tagging, of labeling an object and naming its owner? If so, then my older hypothesis that the PSS was some kind of funerary chant was downright wrong, as the Young Turks were quick to point out when they found *y-uch'ib*, *lac*, and *cacau* on the ceramics. But Barbara's findings suggest that both schools were right: this formulaic sentence served to dedicate the pot and its food or drink to the patron's soul on its journey to Xibalbá.

Most of the indigenous art of the Western Hemisphere prior to the European invasion seems quite anonymous and impersonal to us, and we have little or no information on who the artists were who produced all these masterpieces, or on what their status was within pre-Columbian societies. Throughout much of human prehistory and history, in fact, artists rarely signed their names. As the late Joseph Alsop made clear in his pioneering book, *The Rare Art Traditions*,[28] prior to the Greeks, only in ancient Egypt do we find signed works, and these rare examples have only architects' signatures. Yet, as Alsop has said,

In the larger context of the world history of art . . . a signature on a work of art must be seen as a deeply symbolic act. By signing, the artist says, in effect, "I made this and I have a right to put my name on it, because what I make is a bit different from what others have made or will make."[29]

Apart from the modern world (where even motel art is signed), the widespread use of signatures has generally been confined to only five art traditions: the Greco-Roman world, China, Japan, the Islamic world, and Europe from the Renaissance onwards.

That the Classic Maya were an exception to this rule began to be apparent from David Stuart's reading of *dzib* compounds on the clay vessels; the word means both "writing" and "painting," the Maya not distinguishing these perhaps because both were executed with a brush pen (there is evidence that the monumental texts were originally laid out on the stones as ink drawings, as in ancient Egypt). *Ah dzib* is "he of the writing," in other words "scribe." My own analysis of the scenes on the pots had already shown that the supernatural patrons of Classic Maya scribes and artists were the Monkey-man gods – One Monkey and One Artisan of the *Popol Vuh* – busily writing away with brush pens and conch-shell paint pots.[30]

U dzib, "his writing (or painting)," was revealed by David to occupy two positions in the PSS. The first was in Barbara's "surface treatment" section; David proved that this alternated with a compound in which syllabic *yu* preceded Landa's *lu* and a bat head. If the pot and its texts were painted, *u dzib* appeared; if it was carved or incised, "*lu*-Bat" was the appropriate compound. It was obvious that one compound referred to painting, while the other – still unread – had to do with carving.

The second position of *u dzib* is in the nominal phase section on some vases, where it is followed by a personal name. Since there is excellent reason to believe that one and the same person painted the pot and wrote the text, this can only be the artist's signature: "the writing of X." The question of the social status of these artists and scribes was answered by David in a study that he made of an extraordinary vase published in my Grolier catalog. This is a tall, white-background cylinder which almost surely comes from Naranjo, in the eastern Petén. The PSS appears in its

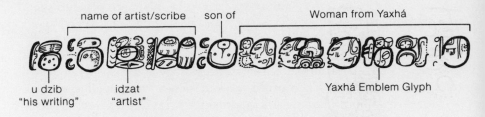

61 Text from a cylindrical vase from Naranjo, giving the artist/scribe's name and royal parentage.

usual place in a horizontal band just below the rim, but continues below in a band near the base. The *u dzib* glyph appears in the text at bottom, immediately followed by a personal name, then by a compound which David has deciphered as *i-dza-t(i)*; *idzat* is glossed in the dictionaries as "artist, learned one," a title that he has found elsewhere in signed works. Most astonishingly, after a compound which may give the artist's "home town," his mother and father are named in the glyph blocks which precede and follow his name: his mother is a lady from the city of Yaxhá, but the father is none other than a well-known *ahau*, a king of the mighty city of Naranjo.[31]

So, this artist-scribe not only signed his vase, but he was a prince, of royal descent on both sides. The Thompsonian view that these painters and carvers of ceramics were mere decorators, peasant-artists outside the orbit of the intellectual world of the Maya, has been consigned to oblivion by epigraphy (as it has been by archaeology). The *ah dzib*, the *ah idzat*, belonged to the very highest stratum of Maya society. Generations of Mayanists have claimed that the ancient Maya civilization was a theocracy, a culture run by priests, even after the discoveries of Proskouriakoff. But now the supposed priests have all but disappeared, to be replaced by warlike dynasts. The *real* repository of Maya learning in Classic times, then, may well have been the corps of these elite artists and calligraphers. As we shall see, the lofty status of the Maya scribe has been reaffirmed by the most recent excavations at Copán.

In the spring of 1989, David graduated from Princeton. His senior honors thesis was an epigraphic and iconographic study of the Maya artist.[32] Here he was able to delve much further into the implications for

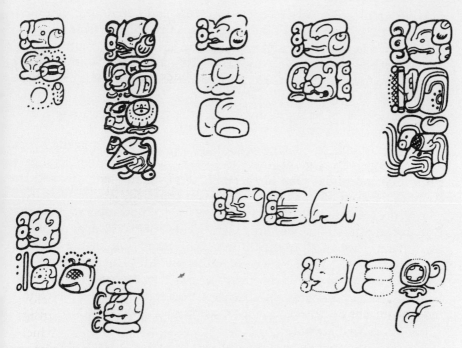

62 *Sculptors' signatures on Stela 31, El Perú, Guatemala. Each begins with the "lu-Bat" expression, and each is in a different "handwriting."*

Maya art and culture of the "to carve" glyph – "*lu*-Bat." As far back as 1916, Spinden had noted that this compound occurred with some frequency on Maya carved monuments, and he made the suggestion, astonishing at the time, that the glyphs written after it might contain personal names. But David knew from ceramics that "*lu*-Bat" introduces names of carvers, as *dzib* does for painters.

Thompson once jokingly told me that one of the texts on a stela from Piedras Negras might say "Epstein me fecit"; with the meaning of "*lu*-Bat" unraveled, this has turned out to be close to the truth, with a vengeance! For on Piedras Negras Stela 12, no fewer than eight artists claimed credit for the carving, each signing his name in a different "handwriting." One of these artists, Kin Chaac, put his signature on other monuments at Piedras Negras, such as the magnificent Throne 1, but he seems to have been as wide-ranging as some artists of the Italian Renaissance, for his signature appears on a panel in the Cleveland Museum of Art believed on good grounds to have been looted from a site located elsewhere in the Usumacinta drainage. This was a remarkable discovery, and ample testimony to the individuality which characterizes Classic Maya civilization. But the signature phenomenon is, to be frank, relatively restricted in time and space: it is confined mainly to the western part of the Maya lowlands, and to a time-frame of only about a hundred and fifty years, in the Late Classic. Yet it is a fine example of how the decipherment has let us at least in part lift the curtain of faceless anonymity which has shrouded the ancient Maya, to at last see some real people.

I can think of only two large-scale archaeological projects in the Maya lowlands in which epigraphy and art history have been an integral part from their inception. One of these is the program being directed by Arthur Demarest of Vanderbilt University (the same Arthur Demarest who wrote the youthful attack on Knorosov, but now repentant), in the Petexbatún region of the western Petén.[33] The other is at Copán, directed by William Fash of Northern Illinois University, one of the few dirt archaeologists whom I know who is able to read Maya hieroglyphs.[34] Bill has been at Copán for fifteen field seasons, having begun there even before finishing his doctorate at Harvard. As a consequence of his team's work (and that of his predecessors, to be sure), no other Maya city's history is so well known.

The site is located on the Copán River (which has over the years cut away part of its great Acropolis) and has been famed since Stephens' day for the beauty and deep carving of its trachyte monuments. David Stuart's introduction to the site, Stephens' "Valley of romance and wonder," came in the summer of 1986, following the Palenque Mesa Redonda. Linda, who was by then Bill's epigrapher and art historian, had invited David to join her for two weeks at the site, and he "had a blast with the Copán material," making many drawings of the inscriptions. While in Palenque, David had met the German epigrapher Nikolai Grube – "the only person significantly younger than Linda and the other people I had worked with." They hit it off right away, and these two, along with Linda, were to make significant strides with the decipherment using Copán data. Nikolai passed through Copán later that summer, and again the next year, by which time he was added to the epigraphic team. He and David, Steve Houston, and Karl Taube often interacted during those two years and, as David says, "the four of us became a new school of thought, or something like it."

In 1987, the tolerant Princeton authorities gave David the spring semester off, and he was back at Copán where he stayed for six months. It was then that he got his first real experience of field excavation, under the careful tutelage of Fash, a dark-bearded figure held in high esteem by his colleagues and by the local Copanecos. Now, some archaeologists can dig away for most of their lives without finding anything of note, but

David must have been born under a lucky star, for on 15 March (the Ides of March as he likes to point out) he hit upon a spectacular cache; placed as a dedicatory offering underneath the altar that forms the base of Copán's mighty Hieroglyphic Stairway, it included three finely chipped "eccentric flints," two heirloom jades, and paraphernalia used in ceremonial bloodletting.

The epigraphic team began putting out their findings in a new series, *Copán Notes*, which although occasionally showing the marks of undue editorial haste, nevertheless has made significant contributions to the decipherment. A major achievement was a complete list of Copán rulers with vital statistics for each, beginning with the founder of the dynasty, one Yax Kuk Mo' ("Green Quetzal-Macaw"), who flourished in the fifth century, and ending with the final great ruler, Yax Pac (or "New Dawn") who died in AD 820.[35] It was another German glyph specialist, Berthold Riese, also of the University of Hamburg, who had recognized that the famous, square Altar Q – thought by earlier Mayanists to depict an astronomical congress engaged in correlating the lunar and solar calendars – actually represented all sixteen dynastic rulers or *ahauo'ob* seated on their own name glyphs.[36] The details on their reigns unearthed by the epigraphers allowed Fash's archaeologists and art historians (including Mary Miller of Yale) to associate individual rulers and events of their reigns with specific monuments and architectural programs.

Much light has been thrown on the political history of the Copán kings and their relationship with the far smaller Quiriguá, a relatively small city over the hills in the Motagua Valley of Guatemala, well known since the visit of Stephens and Catherwood for its gigantic sandstone stelae and zoomorphic sculptures.[37] For much of the Classic, Copán had hegemony over its smaller neighbor, but on 3 May AD 738, the tables were turned, at least temporarily, for on that date one of Copán's most distinguished kings (18 Rabbit) had his head cut off by Quiriguá following his ignominious capture.

Yet this book is not about politics but decipherment. Which brings me again to the subject of name-tagging. It turned out that the Maya bestowed proper names not only on portable items like jewelry and ceramics, but on just about everything the elite considered important in their lives. In the very first *Copán Note*,[38] Linda and David showed that stelae were named as *te tun*, "tree stone," and demonstrated that the texts describing their erection said that they were "planted" (the Maya verb is *dzap-*, "to plant"); even further, individual stelae at Copán had their own proper names, just like people. By the time the next *Copán Note*[39] appeared, David Stuart had pinned down the Maya name for the stone incense burners uncovered by the archaeologists: *sac lac tun*, "white stone dish." As if this were not enough, he discovered the hieroglyphic

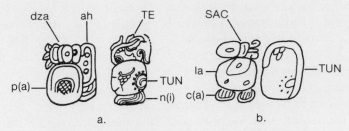

63 *Decipherments at Copán.* a. dzapah tetun, *"he planted the tree-stone (stela)."* b. sac lac tun, *"white stone dish (stone incense burner)."*

name of one of Copán's altars, Altar Q;[40] the stone represents a monster head with *kin* ("sun") signs in the eyes, and the yet incomplete reading for the proper name is, fittingly, *kinich* + unknown sign + *tun*, or "sun-eyed—— stone." "What's in a name?" Shakespeare asked; the Maya would have answered "Lots!," for so serious were they about nomenclature that it now seems probable every building, pyramid, and perhaps even plaza and tomb had a name in a major city like Copán. David picked up the names of temples in association with the verb for "house" (*otot*) dedication; such phrases read *u kaba y-otot*, "the name of his house is——."[41]

These Young Turk epigraphers have raised again the whole question of what Emblem Glyphs represent – are they the names of lineages or of places (Heinrich Berlin had left this question open)? While it is now generally accepted that Thompson's so-called "water group" prefix to the Emblem Glyphs is to be read as *kul* or *ch'ul*, "holy" – with the Ben-Ich and *ua* affixes, the Copán Emblem Glyph would be something like "holy lord of Copán" – it is nevertheless recognized that Emblem Glyphs sometimes apply to polities which include more than one city, and that there may be more than one Emblem Glyph in a particular polity (as in Yaxchilán and Palenque).[42]

64 *Reading of the affixes of the Copán Emblem Glyph as* ch'ul ahau, *"holy lord (of)." There is not yet agreement on how to read the main sign.*

David Stuart's discovery that the reading of the main sign in the Emblem Glyph for Yaxhá, a ruined Petén city, is actually *Yaxhá* and the name of a nearby body of water raised the possibility that at least in origin some Emblem Glyphs may have been place-names (toponyms).[43]

Bona fide toponyms have turned out to be quite common, as Steve Houston and David Stuart's recent research[44] has shown, the name of the place usually being introduced by David's *ut-i*, "it happened (at)."

Many of the toponyms include *uitz*, "hill" or "mountain," in the expression, a trait the Maya shared with the Aztec and Mixtec. In Copán texts, references to a *mo' uitz* ("Macaw Hill") are common; wherever it was, "Macaw Hill" was the location of a Period Ending rite celebrated by the unfortunate 18 Rabbit. Some place-names seem to refer to locations within a city, some to foreign places, while some are patently mythological. Included among the mythological names would be *matauil*, a place where deities mentioned on the tablets of Palenque's Cross Group were born. The most mysterious of these is a place of supernaturals translated by epigraphers as "black hole, black water," which may have existed at the beginning of creation.

One of the most astonishing discoveries at Copán, one that bears directly on the position of the scribes in Maya society, was made under the direction of William Sanders of Pennsylvania State University; this was in a large residential group known as "Sepulturas" lying to the northeast of the city's center.[45] The facade of the principal building (9N-82) was embellished with sculptures of scribes holding conch-shell inkpots in one hand, and the statue of one of my Monkey-men scribes was found in the fill, again with inkpot and brush pen. Inside the structure was a stone bench with Pauahtun gods carved on the supports, and with a magnificent full-figure hieroglyphic text across the front edge. This was in truth a scribal palace of great splendor, and its denizen was clearly patriarch of the entire compound.

Who was this scribe? The epigraphers soon found out that his name was Mac Chaanal, and that he had flourished during that last flowering of Copán, when decentralization and the passing of power into the hands of local satraps had taken place under *ahau* Yax Pac. So high was the status of Mac Chaanal that he was allowed to carve a dedication honoring his own ancestry, including the names of his mother and father.[46]

Equally exalted was an earlier scribe whose final resting place was a tomb deeply buried beneath the temple fronted by the Hieroglyphic Stairway. When this was discovered in 1989, the archaeologists thought that they had a royal burial, but when they found a hopelessly decayed codex next to the head, ten paint pots at the feet, and a bowl depicting a scribe, it became clear that this was indeed an *ah dzib* – but one of high rank, for he was accompanied into Xibalbá by a sacrificed child.[47] No one yet knows who this man was, but he lived about a century and a half before Mac Chaanal, in the seventh century; Bill Fash suggests he was a brother of the twelfth *ahau*, "Smoke Imix God K," but Linda deems it more likely he was the latter's non-ruling father and the younger brother of the previous *ahau*. Regardless, he was indeed a very important person. The Classic Maya took their intellectuals seriously.

The 1980s decade saw decipherments come at a dizzying pace. Often two or more of the new generation of Mayanists would hit upon the same reading totally independently of one another – perhaps this can happen, as Linda thinks, because things have now reached a "critical mass." By the end of the decade such a mass had clearly been reached as far as one puzzling glyph compound was concerned, and light was shed on a whole realm of beliefs and behaviors.

The main sign of this group is an Ahau glyph, the right half of which has been obscured by a jaguar pelt. Some epigraphers, including Linda, proposed that this should be read *balam ahau* with an approximate meaning of "hidden lord."[48] The glyph often appears in Secondary Texts on very fine pictorial vases; the texts as a whole are descriptive of individual supernatural figures in the scenes, which are named first, followed by the so-called *balam ahau* glyph with an Emblem Glyph bringing up the rear.

Near the end of October 1989, two letters, both written on the same day, reached Linda in Austin. One was from Nikolai Grube in Hamburg, the other from Steve Houston in Nashville, Tennessee (home of Vanderbilt, where he teaches). They had independently taken the affixes securely read as *ua* and *ya* as phonetic complements to the logographic main sign, and both proposed that it should thus be read as *ua-y(a)* (or *way* in the orthography used by linguists and most modern epigraphers). In his letter, after discussing a possible reading for another glyph, Nikolai says:

I am far more sure about the "Balam Ahau" title as WAY. This is a great thing! *Way* means "nagual" in all lowland languages, and "animal transformation" . . . The idea for this reading came to me when I talked with various Mayas in Quintana Roo who told me of a sorcerer who is able to transform himself into a cat or a spider monkey. They called the animals in which the sorcerer transformed himself *u way*, "his nagual."

For his part, Steve notes that in Yucatec, *way* is "to transform by enchantment," and in some other Mayan languages it can take the meaning "to sleep," "to dream."

What is the significance of all this? Throughout the indigenous cultures of the New World tropics, there is a widespread belief that shamans can transform themselves at will into dangerous animals, usually jaguars, and the anthropologist Peter Furst has been able to show that this notion can be traced back as far as the ancient Olmec civilization

Waterlily

Jaguar

u uay

Seibal Emblem
Glyph

ahau, "lord"

65 The uay *glyph. Detail from a codex-style vase, showing the Waterlily
Jaguar floating in the sea; the text identifies him as the* uay *of Seibal's king.*

of Mesoamerica.[49] More specifically for the Maya, ethnologists have
discovered a very similar principle in effect among the contemporary
Tzotzil of highland Chiapas. Among these Maya, every individual has an
animal counterpart called *wayhel* or *chanul*, in the form of a jaguar,
coyote, ocelot, owl, deer, hummingbird, and so on. According to my old
Harvard teacher, Evon Vogt, who has made a lifelong study of the
Tzotzil, these creatures live in a mythical corral inside a large volcanic
mountain. The kind of animal counterpart depends upon one's status: a
high-ranking Tzotzil might have a jaguar, while a lowly one might have a
mouse for *wayhel*. As Vogt has said: "A person's life depends upon that
of his animal counterpart which must be protected against evil or harm
to preserve life. All harm occurring to the *wayhel* is experienced by the
human body. The death of the body and that of its *wayhel* are
simultaneous."[50] When Nikolai was using the word *nagual* to describe
this "alter ego" concept, he was using a Nahuatl term, for the principle
was first described in the anthropological literature for peoples who
were once Aztec subjects; it is obviously pan-Mesoamerican.

In Classic times, as Steve Houston and David Stuart have noted in
their 1989 treatment of the subject,[51] the *way* or *uay* concept is most
striking on pictorial vases, particularly ones in the codex style. On these
painted surfaces, *uayo'ob* might take the form of the Waterlily Jaguar; or
of various "jaguarized" animals such as a Jaguar-Dog; or such mythological beasts as a monstrous toad, a monkey and a Deer-Monkey; or a
deer-horned, dragon-like serpent called *chi-chaan* in hieroglyphic texts.

But *uayo'ob* are not confined to the vases. In royal bloodletting rites so graphically depicted on the lintels of Yaxchilán, the "Vision Serpent" (Linda's term) that rises above the scene is identified in the texts as the *uay* of the personage shedding his or her own blood, or even as the *uay* of Kauil (God K). For even the gods had their own *uayo'ob*, and so did royal lineages. Entire structures are identified as *uaybil*, a term glossed in Tzotzil Maya as "sleeping place, dormitory." Was this a place where a great Yaxchilán *ahau* like the mighty Shield-Jaguar could commune with his *uay* (surely a jaguar) in dreams?

In summary, Steve and David look upon the *uay* as the "co-essence" of both humans and supernaturals. In a kick aimed at my own shins (in the same way that I had once kicked Thompson's) they claim that "much of the imagery on ceramics relates to Maya perceptions of self. As a result, death and the afterlife can no longer be regarded as the dominant theme of Maya pottery art."[52] Quite naturally, I don't exactly agree with this generalization: they admit that sleep is linked with death in the inscriptions, and the "percentage-sign" death glyph may substitute for the *uay* logograph, among other counter-arguments. Yet the discovery of *uay* by these new-generation epigraphers is a large step forward in the culminating age of the great Maya decipherment. In her reply to her young friends' letters, Linda spoke for many of us when she said: "Thanks to all of you for sharing this remarkable discovery with us. I am a little awestruck over this one."

So were we all!

11 A Look Backward, A View Forward

A glory attaches itself to a person who first deciphers an unknown script from the remote past, as Maurice Pope has told us.[1] The Maya inscriptions indeed come from the remote past, and have always been imbued with the aura of the exotic, but who first solved their mystery? Yes, it would have made a great story if the breaking of the Maya code had been the accomplishment of a single individual – or perhaps even a team of two, as James Watson and Francis Crick together discovered the double helix structure of DNA and in a way found the secret of all life. But there was no great race to the Maya decipherment on a par with this, rather, a century-long series of gropings and stumblings ending, at long last, with enlightenment.

John Lloyd Stephens had pleaded for a Champollion to materialize and read those mute texts at Copán, but one never appeared. And why not? As that curious "Constantinopolitan" Rafinesque had pointed out in the early nineteenth century, the language of the script was known and still in use; it could have been applied to the decipherment as the great Frenchman had brought his knowledge of Coptic to bear on the Egyptian hieroglyphics.

Unhappily, there were some almost insuperable stumbling blocks across the path of any one person who might have thought of making the great race, no matter how great his genius. No major decipherment has ever been made anywhere without the existence of a major body – a corpus – of texts, drawn and/or photographed in the greatest detail possible. Champollion's breakthrough was based upon really accurate renderings of the Egyptian monuments, beginning with the Rosetta Stone. I am far from being a Bonapartiste, but in a way it is too bad Napoleon never got around to invading Central America, for his corps of *savants* might have made the same wonderful record of Maya inscriptions that they had produced from his Egyptian campaign. No such corpus existed for Maya scholars until the close of the nineteenth century. Three books or codices were available, it is true, and these provided valuable grist for Förstemann's mill – his forays into Maya calendrics – but as far as *reading* the script was concerned, they were just not enough.

The second stumbling block was equally serious, not only for the pioneers of the last century, but for Mayanists in our own era. This is the mentalist, "ideographic" mindset that had served in a far earlier epoch to bog down would-be decipherers of the Egyptian monuments. Remember the Jesuit polymath Athanasius Kircher and his fantastic "readings" of the obelisks? The fallacy that hieroglyphic scripts largely consisted of symbols that communicate ideas *directly*, without the intervention of language, was held as an article of faith by generations of distinguished Maya scholars, including Seler, Schellhas, and Thompson, as well as the multitude of their lesser followers. I wonder whether they even were aware that this fallacy was dreamed up by the Neo-Platonists of the Classical world.

With his usual clarity of vision, in 1841 Stephens had made a prediction: "For centuries the hieroglyphics of Egypt were inscrutable, and, though not perhaps in our day, I feel persuaded that a key surer than that of the Rosetta Stone will be discovered."[2] Twenty-one years later that extraordinary discoverer, Brasseur de Bourbourg, came across the *Relación de Yucatán* in the dusty recesses of a Madrid library, and there it was: Landa's "A,B,C" of the Maya script. With their characteristic obduracy, Mayanists (excepting a few like Cyrus Thomas) spurned this precious document as a true key to the decipherment for about one hundred years; and this in spite of the fact that Bishop Landa actually provided many *more* readings for signs than the Rosetta Stone did for Egyptology.

For all of Eric Thompson's important findings in many areas of Maya studies, by the force of his character, bolstered by immense erudition and a sharp tongue, he singlehandedly held back the decipherment for four decades. Seler had previously crushed Thomas, and effectively finished the phonetic approach to the glyphs for a good long time; few ventured to resurrect Thomas' work while Thompson was still around. Linguists like Whorf who had the temerity to suggest that the script might express the Maya language were quickly sent to oblivion.

It seems that Thompson never believed that there was any system at all in what the Maya wrote down: it was a mere hodgepodge of various primitive attempts to write, inherited from the distant past and directed towards supernatural ends by the priests who supposedly ran the society. If he had been the slightest bit interested in comparative analysis, which he definitely was not, he would have found out that none of the "hieroglyphic" scripts of the Old World worked this way. Here he made a fatal mistake, for if anthropology teaches us anything, it is that at a given level of social and political evolution, different societies around the globe arrive at very similar solutions to similar problems – in this case, the need by early state societies to compile permanent, visual records of impermanent, spoken language.

Perhaps it was the terrible isolation imposed by Stalin's Russia that allowed Knorosov to achieve his great breakthrough, the trickle that started a flood. That may be true, but it is also true that from the beginning, whether as a Marxist or not, Knorosov had adopted a comparativist approach, and was as "at home" in Egyptian hieroglyphs and Chinese characters as he was in the signs of the Maya monuments and codices. I have often wondered whether it was by chance that the towering figures in the modern decipherment were both Russian-born: throughout Mother Russia's turbulent history, even in times of the most rigid repression, there have always been intellectuals who have dared challenge received wisdom. Yuri Knorosov showed that, far from being a hodgepodge, the Maya script was typically logographic, a discovery that eventually led to the reading of the Classic texts in the language spoken by the ancient scribes. Tatiana Proskouriakoff revealed the historical nature of these texts, not by linguistic methods, but by working out the structure of "published" Maya dates that had been in everyone's hands for generations, but not understood.

If it is a hero you are looking for, then it is Knorosov who most closely approximates Champollion. That being the case, then Thompson (apart from his affinity with Kircher) would be another Thomas Young, the brilliant innovator in Egyptology who, mired down by his mentalist and symbolist view of the script, never did achieve true decipherment. Both would bear this flawed burden to their deathbeds.

Well, you might say, why praise Champollion to the heavens? Didn't he have the advantage of the Rosetta Stone? Yes he did, but the Mayanists had their own all along and failed to recognize it for what it was. Champollion cracked the script in a mere two years, while it took the Mayanists what seems an eternity by comparison.

The snail's pace at which Maya decipherment proceeded before Knorosov's epochal article of 1952 also compares unfavorably with what happened with Hieroglyphic Hittite, the Bronze Age script of central Anatolia (modern Turkey) which is structurally almost identical with Maya writing.[3] Working without the benefit of a Rosetta Stone, and with only a few, extremely brief bilingual seals, an international team of scholars – all doing their research independently – had cracked the Hieroglyphic code within the space of the two decades preceding World War II. In contrast to the poor training of most Mayanists, these particular epigraphers were thoroughly familiar with Old World scripts like Assyrian cuneiform and Egyptian, and had a good idea of the structure of early systems. Ironically, for Hittitologists the "Rosetta

Stone" came *after* the decipherment had been made: this was the discovery in 1947 of the bilingual Phoenician and Hieroglyphic inscriptions at Kul Tepe, in the mountains of southeastern Turkey, which confirmed what this remarkable team had already found.

Is the Maya script really deciphered? How much of it can we now *read* (as opposed to simply knowing the meaning)? The answer to these questions pretty much depends on whether you are talking about the texts – on the monuments, codices, and ceramics – or only about the signary *per se*. I have seen modern estimates that about 85 percent of all *texts* can be read in one or another Mayan language, and certainly there are some monumental texts that can almost be read *in toto*; some of these are of respectable length, like the 96 Hieroglyphs tablet at Palenque.[4] But if one is dealing only with the signary as it appears in Thompson's catalog, that is another matter.

There are about 800 signs in Maya hieroglyphic script, but these include many archaic logograms, largely royal names, which were used only once and then dropped from general use. Many epigraphers would tell you that at any moment in Maya culture history, only about 200–300 glyphs were actually being utilized, and that some of these were surely allographic or homophonic. The signary is thus a great deal smaller than the one Egyptian scribes had to learn in school; if you glance back at the table on page 43, you will see that it is comparable to that of Sumerian cuneiform and Hieroglyphic Hittite. Figures of this sort should long ago have convinced Maya epigraphers that they were faced with a logophonemic or logosyllabic script.

More than 150 of these 800 or so signs are known to have a phonetic-syllabic function. Their phonetic values are overwhelmingly of the consonant-vowel sort, with the exception of signs standing for the pure vowels. As with many other early scripts, there is a great deal of polyvalence, including both homophony (several signs with the same reading) and polyphony (several readings for the same sign). Polyvalence could also result in a sign having both logographic and syllabic functions. Admittedly, there are still some blank spaces in the syllabic grid: out of the 90 possible boxes based on the phonemic structure of Cholan and Yucatecan Maya, 19 are yet blank, but I would predict that all will soon be filled.

As we have seen in Chapter 1, no writing system is really complete, in that it expresses visually every distinctive feature in the spoken language. Something is always left out, leaving the reader to fill in the gaps from the context. For instance, Yucatec Maya has two tones which are phonemic, but as far as I know these are not written in any way in the codices. Even though the glottal stop is important in all Mayan languages, rather than invent a special sign for it, the scribes wrote it by reduplicating the vowel after which it appears: thus, for *mo'*, "macaw," they wrote *m(o)-o-o*.

I can see no good evidence that the Maya used taxograms in their script – the "determinatives" or "radicals" that were used by Old World scribes to indicate the semantic class of phenomena into which their phonetically-written words belong. At one time, I suspected that the so-called "water group" sign prefixed to Emblem Glyphs would have served this function, but even this has fallen to the onslaught of phonetic analysis, and it must now be read as *kul* or *ch'ul*, "holy." Since it was not silent, it cannot have been a taxogram as this has been defined.

To satisfy their royal patrons – and their relatives, for they, too, belonged to this highest social stratum – the scribes played with the script, passing back and forth from the purely semantic dimension to the purely phonetic, with intermediary stages between. This playful aspect of the script is elegantly demonstrated by the different spellings for royal names like that of Pacal of Palenque or Yax Pac of Copán. To meet aesthetic demands, signs could occasionally be switched around within the glyph blocks, changing their order as Egyptian scribes had done millennia before along the banks of the Nile. And two contiguous signs could be conflated into one at the whim of the scribe, as in the glyph for the "seating" of a time-period. All this was predictable from Old World writing systems.

66 *Conflation of signs in Maya writing. All four examples spell* chum tun, *"seating of the* tun.*"*

The logograms, standing for entire morphemes, might have given the Maya reader trouble, but there was extensive use of phonetic complements before and/or behind the logograms to help in their reading, and it has often been these "props" which have led the epigrapher into the decipherment of these difficult signs. Phonetic-syllabic signs were also used to express grammatical endings of logographic roots. But there may always be a residue of logograms which will never be read, even though we can work out their approximate meaning; most of these, one can safely predict, will be name-signs of rulers which take the form of

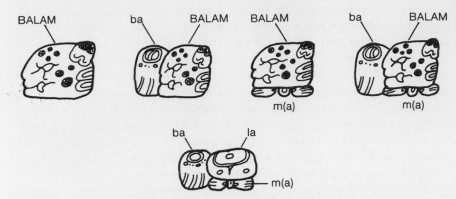

67 *Alternative spellings for* balam, *"jaguar." According to his whim, the scribe could write this purely logographically; logographically with phonetic complements; or purely syllabically.*

fantastic animal heads, difficult to match in nature, and which never appear spelled phonetically or with phonetic complements. Such "one-of-a-kind" glyphs defy analysis.

Now, the ancient Maya scribes could have written *everything* expressed in their language using only the syllabic signary – but they did not, any more than did the Japanese with their *kana* signs, or the Sumerians and Hittites with *their* syllabaries, or the Egyptians with their stock of consonantal signs. The logograms just had too much prestige to abolish. And why should they have done so? "One picture is worth a thousand words," as the saying goes, and Maya logograms, like their Egyptian equivalents, are often remarkably pictorial and thus more immediately informative than a series of abstract phonetic signs: for example, the Maya could, and sometimes did, write out *balam*, "jaguar," syllabically as *ba-la-m(a)*, but by using a jaguar's head for *balam*, the scribe could get his word across in a more dramatic fashion.

In fact, among the Classic and Post-Classic Maya, writing and pictorial representation were not distinct. Just as in ancient Egypt, texts have the tendency to fill all spaces which are not actually taken up with pictures, and may even appear as nominal phrases on the bodies of captive figures. Classic texts without pictures are relatively scarce – the tablets of the Temple of the Inscriptions and the 96 Hieroglyphs, both from Palenque, being notable exceptions. This is true both for the Classic monuments, and for the extant Post-Classic codices, hardly surprising when you consider that the artist and scribe were one and the same person.

And what do the now-deciphered texts say? Bear in mind that many thousands of bark-paper codices once in use among the Classic Maya have perished with hardly a trace. What we have been left with are four books in various states of completeness or delapidation, texts on ceramics and other portable objects (largely the result of the antiques trade), and monumental inscriptions, many weathered beyond recognition. These are surely a very skewed sample of what the ancient Maya actually wrote. Gone forever are purely literary compositions (which must have included historical epics and mythology), economic records, land transactions, and, I feel sure, personal and diplomatic correspondence. Books and other written documents must have freely circulated across the Maya lowlands, for how else could Classic Maya civilization have achieved such cultural and scientific unity in the face of such demonstrable political Balkanization? But thanks to the vicissitudes of time, and the horrors of the Spanish invasion, all those precious documents are gone. Even the burning of the library of Alexandria did not obliterate a civilization's heritage as completely as this.

The monumental inscriptions, on stone stelae, altars, lintels, panels, and the like, present public statements of royal deeds, descent, and other concerns (above all, warfare), and, like such permanent "billboards" in the Old World, tend to be quite parsimonious about what they say. They certainly keep adjectives and adverbs to a minimum, in good Hemingway style. Monumental statements almost always open with a chronological expression, and then go on to an event verb, an object (if the verb is transitive), and a subject; then, on to (or back to) another time expression, and another statement. *Fig. 68* overleaf gives an example of such an inscription from Piedras Negras.

As for the surviving codices, all from the Post-Classic, only three have texts of any length; these are short yet quite similar in structure to the Classic inscriptions – although in content they are not overtly historical but religious-astronomical. The Dresden Codex, for example, contains 77 almanacs based upon the 260-day calendar, in which specific days are associated with specific gods and appropriate auguries; New Year ceremonies; Venus and eclipse tables; and multiplication tables related to the calendar and the movements of the planets.[5]

We now realize that the ceramic texts are in a distinct class by themselves. Although much remains to be learned about it, the Primary Standard Sequence seems to be a kind of dedication statement for the vessel, naming its shape, its contents, and its owner, as name-tagging does for other kinds of objects from stelae to items of personal jewelry. For my part, I believe that the future study of the Secondary texts, which are directly linked to the scenes on the pots, will one day reveal an entire world of thought which may have been contained on the long-lost ritual codices of the Classic lowlands. The reading of the *uay* glyph described in the last chapter has indeed given Maya epigraphers, art historians, and students of religion something to ponder.

Reading in Chol Maya and Translation
courtesy Linda Schele

Synopsis

On 9.12.2.0.16 5 Cib 14 Yaxkin (7 July 674), Lady Katun Ahau was born in a place called *Man*, believed to lie between Piedras Negras and Yaxchilán. When only twelve years old, on 9.12.14.10.16 1 Cib 14 Yaxkin, she was married ("adorned") to the heir apparent to the Piedras Negras throne, Yo' Acnal, who succeeded to the rulership 44 days later. When she was 33, on 9.13.16.4.6 4 Cimi 14 Uo (22 March 708), Lady Katun Ahau gave birth to a daughter, Lady Kin Ahau, in the Turtle lineage of Piedras Negras. Three years after this, Lady Katun Ahau, a powerful queen throughout her life, celebrated a ceremony called "grasping the staff", on 9.13.19.13.1 11 Imix 14 Yax. The current katun ended, as the text notes, 99 days later on 9.14.0.0.0 6 Ahau 13 Muan (5 December 711). In the scene below, the queen and the 3 year old Lady Kin Ahau are shown seated on a throne.

A1 *tzic yaxkin*
The count is in Yaxkin.

B1 *bolon pih*
9 baktuns,

A2 *lahcham katun*
12 katuns,

B2 *cha tun*
2 tuns,

A3 *mi uinic*
0 uinals,

B3 *uacluhum kin*
16 kins

A4 *ho chibin*
5 Cib.

B4 *nah*
Nah [7th Lord of the Night]

A5 *ch'a hun*
tied on the headband.

B5 *uac kal huliy*
[It was] 27 days after [the moon] arrived,

A6 *cha tzuc (?) u*
two moons are worn out.

B6 *ux sac uitz ku*
Three White Mountain God [name of the lunation],

A7 *uinic bolon*
[with] 29 days.

B7 *chanluhum yaxkin*
14 Yaxkin.

A8 *sihi*
She was born,

A9 *na katun ahau*
Lady Katun Ahau,

A10 *nana man ahau*
Matron from *Man*.

C1 *mi, luhum uinicihi*
0 kins, 10 uinals,

D1 *lahcham tuni*
12 tuns.

C2 *iual ut hun chibin*
It came to pass [on] 1 Cib

D2 *chanlahum uniu, nauah*
14 Kankin, she was adorned,

C3 *na katun ahau*
Lady Katun Ahau,

D3 *nana man ahau, yichnal*
Matron of *Man*, in the company of

C4 *makina yo' acnal*
Great Sun Yo' Acnal.

D4 *luhum, buluch uinicihi, hun tuni*
10 kins, 11 uinals, 1 tun,

C5 *hun katun, iual ut*
1 katun. It came to pass

D5 *chan chamal*
[on] 4 Cimi

C6 *chanlahum icat*
14 Uo,

D6 *sihi*
she was born,

C7 *na hun tan ac*
she, the Cherished One of the Turtle [lineage],

D7 *na kin ahau*
Lady Kin Ahau.

E1 *holuhum, uaxac uinicihi, ux tuni*
15 kins, 8 uinals, 3 tur

F1 *iual ut*
It came to pass

E2 *buluch imix*
[on] 11 Imix

F2 *chanluhum yaxkin*
14 Yax

E3 *u ch'amua lom*
she grasped the staff,

F3 *na katun ahau*
Lady Katun Ahau,

E4 *nana man ahau*
Matron from *Man*.

F4 *homi u ho tun*
It ended, the 5th tun,

E5 *hun katun lati*
1 katun after

F5 *ti ahaule yo'*
his kingship, Yo'

E6 *acnal*
Acnal.

F6 *bolonluhum, chan uinicihi*
19 kins, 4 uinals.

E7 *iual ut*
It came to pass

F7 *uac ahau*
[on] 6 Ahau

F8 *uxluhum muan*
13 Muan,

F9 *homi*
it ended,

F10 *u chanluhum katun*
its 14th katun.

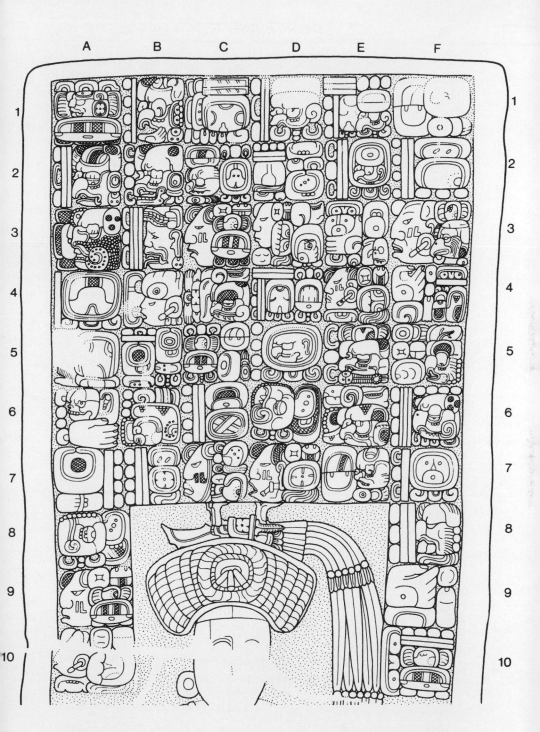

68 Stela 3, Piedras Negras: *an example of a complete text, its reading, and its translation.*

There is a Sumerian proverb four thousand years old that says, "A scribe whose hand matches the mouth, he is indeed a scribe."[6] There is now no question that Maya hieroglyphic writing "matches the mouth"; as linguists like Archibald Hill, Benjamin Whorf, and Floyd Lounsbury had been saying all along, the script is as much the visual form of spoken Maya as ours is of spoken English.

A meeting of about one-hundred-and-seventy-five linguists, art historians, epigraphers, archaeologists, and amateurs that took place in early 1989 at the University of California in Santa Barbara showed just what that means, and where the future of Maya decipherment may lie. As the monumental texts contain stories about real people and events, reported Sandra Blakeslee in the *New York Times*,[7] Maya linguists have reasoned that they should reflect real language. At this advanced stage in the decipherment, it has become clear that epigraphers are going to have to get down to the "nit-picking details of the language recorded," as David Stuart has put it.

At the Santa Barbara meeting, David himself came under some well-meant criticism from linguist Nicholas Hopkins, an expert on the Cholan languages, for not paying enough attention in his "Ten Phonetic Glyphs" to Knorosov's Principle of Synharmony. Hopkins pointed out that when the scribes apparently violate this rule, there is a good linguistic explanation for it; for example, when they write *mut*, "bird" or "omen," as *mu-t(i)*, instead of the predicted *mu-t(u)*, this is because the Western Mayan languages, including Chol, have high front vowels (like *i*) as echo vowels after an alveolar consonant (like *t*). When David wants to read both *u dzi-b(i)* and *u dzi-b(a)* as *u dzib*, "his writing," he is on target with the former reading but in violation with the latter, which may well be a verb, not a possessed noun: *u dziba*, "he wrote it."[8]

This brings us to discourse analysis, a specialty of Hopkins' linguist wife, Katheryn Josserand. A discourse is a connected text, not just a word or sentence, such as a conversation between two people, an oral narration, a prayer, or even a prophecy; these are all types of discourse in use among the contemporary Maya, and they have received increasing attention by the linguists. In addition, the Colonial period is rich in historical and prophetic texts from Yucatán – the famous Books of Chilam Balam, "the Jaguar Prophet"; and from the highlands we have such great epics as the *Popol Vuh*, analyzed and translated by Dennis Tedlock, a specialist in Native American literatures.[9]

What Josserand presented at Santa Barbara was the application of such analysis to long glyphic texts like those at Palenque, to "tease out meaning" as Sandra Blakeslee says. This consists of "participant tracking," trying to identify the protagonists of events where the names of the actors are not always expressed.

Here is how she solved the problem, according to Blakeslee:

Background information [placed chronologically by Anterior Date Indicators] is often marked with a suffix, a glyph whose phonetic value was -ix... A verb prefix, i-, indicates that the action relates to a main story line or new piece of information.

By dividing texts into chunks using these markers, she said, it is possible to find the peak event in the story. When Mayan scribes get to the most important part of the story ... they do not mention the name of the most important actor. The reader or listener must know the name from an earlier part of the story.

We already know that monumental and codical texts follow the peculiar (to us) rules of Maya grammar, but this kind of analysis is new and shows great promise for the future. One application might be to the thorny problems raised by the Terminal Classic carved lintels from Chichén Itzá in Yucatán, where as many as three actors, possibly co-ruling brothers, may appear in a single inscription.

Now for the question of literacy. Apart from the scribes and the rulers, who within the general population was actually capable of reading all these texts? The general opinion among Mayanists has always been that literacy was confined to a minute segment of the population.[10] That may have been true of the late pre-Conquest Maya of Yucatán, about whom Landa wrote, but their culture was then in a state of decline, and it may not necessarily be applicable to the Classic Maya.

Much scholarly speculation about this comes from a time when the script had not yet been deciphered, and from an intellectual milieu in which the difficulties and general awkwardness of logographic writing systems were greatly exaggerated. Epigraphers like Ignace Gelb[11] consistently denigrated such systems and saw the invention of the alphabet as the triggering mechanism for the spread of literacy around the world, a position subsequently embraced by the social anthropologist Jack Goody (who was convinced that the Maya had written with "knotted cords").[12] But the rate of literacy has little or nothing to do with the kind of writing system that you use, and lots to do with the culture you live in. The highest literacy rate in the world is Japan's, which uses a logosyllabic script, and one of the very lowest is Iraq's, which has the Arabic alphabet.

I suspect that the Maya script was not all that difficult to learn, at least to read: in her justly famed workshops, which last a single weekend each, Linda Schele has taught several thousand rank amateurs to scan Maya texts. I simply cannot imagine that the Maya man- or woman-in-the-street could not have looked at a carved and brightly painted stela in a plaza, and at least been able to read off the date, the events, and the names of the protagonists given on it, particularly when there was an accompanying picture, as there almost always was. Of course, all scripts are more difficult to write than to read, and there were probably precious few who were fully literate in this sense: small wonder that the scribes, the *ah dzib*, belonged to the royal caste.

Public exhibitions of pre-Columbian art have been held ever since the 1920s, but none have had the intellectual impact of the one entitled *The Blood of Kings*;[13] the splendid catalog resulting from this pioneering show revolutionized the way we think about the Classic Maya. Informed by the very latest research on the hieroglyphic script, for the very first time it allowed the ancient elite of the Maya cities to express their own concerns and goals through some of the most splendid objects ever assembled under one roof. In the highly critical museum world, this show was universally acknowledged as a blockbuster.

The exhibit was the brainchild of Linda Schele and Mary Miller, and opened in 1986 in Louis Kahn's splendid Kimbell Art Museum in Fort Worth, Texas. Just a word about my colleague Mary Miller, now Professor of the History of Art at Yale. It was Gillett Griffin who introduced her to the world of pre-Columbian art at Princeton, but her graduate career was at Yale, where she gained a Ph.D. in art history, writing her thesis on the murals of Bonampak. Thoroughly grounded in Maya glyphs, she was just the person to collaborate on a show of this sort, informed by the very latest advances in Maya epigraphy and iconography.

Basically, the picture of the Classic Maya that these two presented to the world was a series of kingly societies whose principal obsessions were royal blood (and descent) and bloody conquest. Through a host of the most beautiful Maya objects ever assembled under one roof, they spoke of penitential bloodletting of the most hair-raising sort, torture, and human sacrifice, all firmly based in what the Classic Maya actually said about themselves. These were certainly not the peaceful Maya about whom Morley and Thompson had rhapsodized. Thanks to Linda's numerous and informative drawings, the catalog is a mine of information about the art and life of the elite who ruled the Maya cities, while the exhibit itself, due to a tightly organized story line, was the first ever to present pre-Columbian art as something more than a collection of rather scary, barbaric masterpieces. The decipherment had made it all possible.

Accolades came from all (or almost all) sides. In a long essay in the *New York Review of Books*,[14] in which he chastized his compatriots for paying too little attention to the ancient Maya, the distinguished Mexican writer Octavio Paz praised the catalog in the warmest terms. On the other hand, one could hear the grumbling from the wings: all this was definitely *not* going over well with certain art historians whose noses had been put out of joint. One particularly sour reviewer even suggested that Schele and Miller had used the show to advance their own careers and make life more difficult for those pre-Columbian art historians who were not Mayanists.

But that was nothing compared to what was developing among our friends, the field archaeologists.

You might reasonably think that the decipherment of the Maya script would have been greeted with open arms by the archaeologists. Not a bit of it! The reaction of the digging fraternity (and sorority) to the most exciting development in New World archaeology this century has been ... rejection. It is not that they claim, like Champollion's opponents, that the decipherment has not taken place, they simply believe it is not worthy of notice (at least overtly).

In a way, today's Maya archaeologists are not to be blamed for their sad predicament. At the same time as excavation permits from foreign governments (particularly in Mexico) have become as scarce as the proverbial hens' teeth, sources of public funding to dig have been dwindling. As a result, competition for these scarce resources has reached fever pitch, and a kind of vindictive infighting has arisen among Mayanists that never existed in the Carnegie years. Lest this be thought a fiction on my part, allow me to mention a situation that arose a while back at Harvard. The plum position in Maya archaeology, the Charles Bowditch Professorship, was about to become vacant with the impending retirement of Gordon Willey, the acknowledged leader in the field. To fill it, a committee appointed by the President drew up a short list of candidates, and invited written evaluations of individuals on it from Mayanists. The results? It is widely reported that the President, shocked by the general nastiness and scurrility of the letters, remarked that he had never seen anything like this in his entire life. The respondents were like sharks in a feeding frenzy, and the academic waters were red with blood. The position was not filled, needless to say.

A situation had developed, thanks in part to an increasing number of new Ph.D.'s being turned out by American universities, that there were more and more archaeologists with less and less to study, and less and less to say about the Maya past. It began to look as though the age of archaeological discovery was over. With nothing better to do, the diggers would speculate about the Maya collapse. The new breed of archaeologists might control the funding process (they sat on all the right committees), publication (they made up the editorial boards of the journals), and academic promotions (they held tenure posts in the better departments); but they weren't finding much to gain public interest.

Contrast this with what was going on in epigraphy and iconography, and the pique of the field archaeologists is understandable. Here was a bunch of outsiders who were getting top coverage in the daily press and news magazines, who had never had to endure the heat, ticks, and gastrointestinal problems endemic to field excavation, who had never had to sort their way through mountains of drab potsherds and obsidian chips. Here was a person like Linda Schele, filling huge auditoriums to capacity wherever she went, and she didn't even have a degree in anthropology! It was unfair.

The wielders of trowels finally got their revenge, at Dumbarton Oaks in a conference held in early October 1989. It was called "On the Eve of the Collapse: Ancient Maya Societies in the Eighth Century, A.D." I (luckily) wasn't there, but there can be little doubt that the whole conference was a negative reaction to the decipherment and to *The Blood of Kings*. While Mary Miller and David Stuart were both put on the list of speakers, they were restricted to giving data only, and Linda – arguably the number one expert on the subject – was excluded from the rostrum (she came anyway and sat in the audience).

The hostility to the decipherment, and to the not illogical notion that the Classic Maya themselves might have had something interesting to say on this subject, was palpable. One well-known scholar managed to present a forty-four-page paper on ancient Maya political organization which never once mentioned the decipherment, or indicated that anything new had been found in the inscriptions beyond the work of Berlin and Proskouriakoff in the 1950s and 1960s. That was the cold-shoulder approach. But the prevalent attitude towards the demonstrable fact that we could now read the inscriptions was slightly different: yes, we can read the stuff, but it's all a pack of lies! Who can trust what these Classic politicos said, anyway?

The final blow was struck at the conference by its summarizer: the Maya inscriptions are "epiphenomenal," a ten-penny word meaning that Maya writing is only of marginal application since it is secondary to those more primary institutions – economy and society – so well studied by the dirt archaeologists.

In other words, sour grapes! Even if we card-carrying diggers bothered to learn how to read the texts, they wouldn't say anything of importance, and our valuable time would be wasted. But as one young epigrapher present at this D.O. meeting wrote me later,

These people have fundamentally misunderstood and underestimated historical and textual evidence. Haven't they heard of historiography? Aren't other lines of evidence equally equivocal? Shouldn't we be looking at how other scholars deal with other literate civilizations, such as those of Mesopotamia and China? There might be important lessons here.

These people are unable to criticize epigraphy on its own terms. Who denies that there are problems of interpretation? Yet a blanket dismissal of an entire set of data is both foolish and anti-intellectual. Learn first how epigraphers are reading the glyphs; then criticize.

I believe that the problem lies even deeper than that, in the inability or unwillingness of anthropologically-trained archaeologists to admit that they are dealing with the remains of real people, who once lived and spoke; that these ancient kings, queens, warriors, and scribes were actually Maya Indians, and that their words are worth listening to.

The ultimate stage in this rejection has now been reached in the journals controlled by the dirt archaeologists: even if all that epigraphy, art, and iconography is not just stuff and nonsense, even if the texts are not mendacious, they do not represent real Maya culture and social organization – as one conference participant put it, the "vast majority" of the Maya population is not even mentioned in the texts. Of course not! Neither are the millions of *fellahin* who built the pyramids and palaces of Egypt mentioned in the royal inscriptions of the Nile, nor do the swarms of peasants who worked the lands of the Hittite kings show up in *their* monumental reliefs.

What this populist viewpoint, so common among archaeologists, ignores is that in pre-industrial, non-democratic societies on a state level of organization, large chunks of the culture are indeed generated by royal courts and by the elite class in general. A Maya *ahau* could say with confidence, "*L'état, c'est moi,*" and I doubt whether the Maya peasantry would have disagreed. The concerns of a ruler like Pacal of Palenque were everybody's concerns, and Mayanists who choose to concentrate on Pacal instead of such topics as rural settlement patterns or the typology of utilitarian pottery are not wasting their time.

In my estimation, no amount of "circling the wagons," not even a conference like the one at D.O., is going to derail the continuing progress of the decipherment. As Linda Schele once told me, "The decipherment has occurred. There are two ways to react to it. One is to embrace it, and if you can't do it yourself, get someone on your side who bloody well can. The other is to ignore it, to try and destroy it, to basically dismiss it."

As we move into the third millennium, the way to do it properly has been shown by archaeologists like Bill Fash at Copán, Arthur Demarest at Dos Pilas and the sites of the Petexbatún, and by Diane and Arlen Chase at Caracol:[15] in those sites, epigraphy has been the handmaiden of field archaeology at almost every step of the project, as it has been since the last century in Egypt, Mesopotamia, and China.

But the kind of training Mayanists undergo will have to take a new direction, too. At present most field archaeologists, I am sorry to report, are almost totally illiterate in the Maya script, except for a possible ability to recognize Long Count dates in an inscription. Few if any have any knowledge of a Mayan tongue. Compare this with what an Assyriologist must know before he or she gets a Ph.D.: the candidate must have mastered both Sumerian and Akkadian cuneiform, and be well-grounded in one or more Semitic languages. Imagine someone calling himself an Egyptologist who couldn't read a hieroglyphic inscription, or a Sinologist tongue-tied in Chinese! How can illiterate scholars pretend to study a literate civilization? I will predict that all this is going to change, and for the better.

Certainly, linguistics is going to play an even greater role in the future, as readings are fine-tuned, and as we proceed with analysis of whole texts in place of individual glyphs or phrases. Maya epigraphers are going to have to work more closely with contemporary Maya story-tellers, shamans, and other specialists to better understand the ancient inscriptions. David Stuart is surely right when he says that even a few years ago, no one would have predicted the script was so phonetic – and it was heavily phonetic in the very earliest inscriptions. "We're just at the transition stage now," according to David, "I think we'll be able to read the stuff literally like we never imagined!"

My first visit to Yucatán, and my introduction to the ancient and modern Maya, took place in Christmas vacation of 1947, when I was still an English major at Harvard. I knew little or nothing of the Maya civilization, just what I'd gleaned from some trashy travel books borrowed from the Widener Library. Wandering around the ruins of Chichén Itzá, I came across the great Monjas complex to the south of the principal group, with its many stone lintels inscribed with those (to me) strange characters. As I was wondering in my innocence if the archaeologists could actually read what was written on them, there materialized an American, a movie photographer from Hollywood. Before my very eyes, he ran his hand over the glyphs on each lintel, and told me exactly what they said. I was dumbfounded with admiration – what a genius he must be! Only later, when I got back to Cambridge and actually met some real-life archaeologists, did I find out it was all balderdash. Every bit of it. Not even the specialists could then read those lintels.

Yet today, some forty-five years later, if you come across someone doing just that – reading those once-mute texts in authentic Yucatec Maya – you have no reason for disbelief. In one of the greatest intellectual achievements of our century, the Maya code has at last been broken.

Epilogue

Yuri Valentinovich Knorosov's blue eyes still gaze out across the Neva River, but he now finds himself not in Leningrad, but St. Petersburg – a lot of water has gone under the nearby bridge since we saw him last. His hero Peter the Great has been given back his city and his patron saint. And the man who let us read the Maya glyphs has at last stood in the shadows of Maya pyramids: late in 1990, he was invited to Guatemala to receive a gold medal from President Cerezo. After the ceremony, along with his young colleague Galina Yershova and her Guatemalan husband, he visited Tikal and Uaxactún. With characteristic Russian contrariness, he complained to his traveling companions that it was all no different from what he had read about in books.

Then, shortly after Cerezo left office, a sinister phone call came to them in Guatemala City: leave Guatemalan territory within seventy-two hours or be killed. Knorosov and his friends immediately went into hiding, then fled the country of the Maya – and of the right-wing death squads who have been engaged in extirpating all remaining Maya culture, and the Maya themselves. The man who had allowed the ancient Maya scribes to speak with their own voice was still unable to walk freely among the cities in which they had lived.

But who knows? Perhaps we are all headed for destruction. The Maya wise men all across Yucatán predict that the world will end in the year 2000 y pico – "and a little." How many years will that "a little" be? The Great Cycle of the Maya calendar which began in darkness on 13 August 3114 BC will come to an end after almost five millennia on 23 December AD 2012, when many of you who read this will still be alive. On that day, the ancient Maya scribes would say, it will be 13 cycles, 0 katuns, 0 tuns, 0 uinals, and 0 kins since the beginning of the Great Cycle. The day will be 4 Ahau 3 Kankin, and it will be ruled by the Sun God, the ninth Lord of the Night. The moon will be eight days old, and it will be the third lunation in a series of six. And what is to happen? A katun prophecy in the Book of Chilam Balam of Tizimín reads:[16]

Ca hualahom caan   Then the sky is divided
  Ca nocpahi peten   Then the land is raised,
Ca ix hopp i   And then there begins
  U hum ox lahun ti ku   The Book of the 13 Gods.
Ca uch i   Then occurs
  Noh hai cabil   The great flooding of the Earth
Ca lik i   Then arises
  Noh Itzam Cab Ain   The great Itzam Cab Ain.
Tz'ocebal u than   The ending of the word,
  U uutz' katun   The fold of the Katun:
Lai hun yeciil   That is a flood
  Bin tz'oce(ce)bal   Which will be the ending of
  u than katun   the word of the Katun.

APPENDIX A

Proskouriakoff's "Suggested Order of Discussion"

APPENDIX B

The Maya Syllabic Chart

Notes

Glossary

Sources of Illustrations

Further Reading and Bibliography

Index

Appendix A
Proskouriakoff's
"Suggested Order of Discussion"

Note: this outline was prepared by Tatiana Proskouriakoff for the student-run Mesa Cuadrada ("Square Table") held in the Peabody Museum, Harvard University, during the 1956–57 academic year. It is remarkable for its clear view of the future of Maya decipherment. Her "ideograms" would now be called "logograms."

SUGGESTED ORDER OF DISCUSSION
For Mesa Quadrada (sic) on decipherment of Maya writing

Introductory remarks

The structure of hieroglyphic systems as per Knorosov:
1. Essential similarity of all hieroglyphic systems.
2. Constituent elements:
   a. Ideograms: words
   b. Phonograms: syllabic, phonemic
   c. Determinatives: additional to above, referring to meaning only.
3. A given sign in different contexts may take on different functions.

Peculiarities of the Maya system, as per Knorosov:
1. Strong phonetic component.
2. Semantic indicator (not always present): Indicates whether sign is ideogram, phonogram or determinative. This is specific for a sign.
3. Most common particles have constant value.
4. Order of reading from left to right and from top to bottom, with occasional variations as follows:
   a. Determinatives have no fixed position.
   b. Rotation of signs 90 or 180 degrees.
   c. Inversions (of order of signs).
   d. Omissions of sounds (abbreviations?).
   e. Ligatures (one part common to two signs).
   f. Insertions of one sign in another (inserted sign to be read last).
   g. Additions of phonetic complement (usually repeated final phoneme).
5. Variation of vowel value in syllables
   a. Long and short vowels not differentiated.
   b. Discrepancies due to phonetic shifts.
   c. Apparently intrinsic interchangeability.
   d. Dropping of final vowel at end of word for consonant phoneme. Usually syllabic value repeats previous vowel (synharmonism).

Discussion

1. Theoretical structure of other proposed or implied systems:
   a. Pictographic and ideographic; no longer supported
   b. Whorf's system (phonetic emphasis) – (*Carroll)
   c. Thompson's (ideographic emphasis) – (Thompson?)
   d. Barthel – (Kelley). D. Kelley (Kelley)

2. Assuming Knorosov's premise that all hieroglyphic systems are basically similar, in what way can a knowledge of other writing (e.g. Chinese) help us in interpretation? Does Chinese roughly correspond to the outline given? Is a Chinese character read in one way only (linguistically)?
3. The language of the hieroglyphs.
   a. In what way can knowledge of phonemics, morphology and syntax be applied to decipherment of the Maya hieroglyphs?
   b. Are there strong syntactical differences between the Mayance languages which would tend to eliminate certain groups as inconsistent with the hieroglyphic structure (e.g. the frequency and position of particles?) (Carroll)
   c. Would such linguistic variations as between Chol and Yucatec, Yucatec and Mam, imply systematic changes in script? (Carroll)
   d. What are the specific indications the Chol or a Choloid language was the language of the hieroglyphs? (Kelley)
4. Approaches and demonstrations in decipherment.
   a. Selected examples:
   Thompson (Thompson?)
   Whorf (Carroll)
   Knorosov (Kelley)
   b. Do any or all of these fail to constitute sufficient proof? (open discussion) What are the weaknesses of each?

*John B. Carroll was then Associate Professor in the Graduate School of Education, Harvard University, and was Whorf's literary executor; David Kelley was then a graduate student in Harvard's Department of Anthropology; Eric Thompson refused our invitation to attend.

The Maya Syllabic Chart

	a	e	i	o	u
b					
ch					
ch'					
h					
c					
k					
l					
m					

The Maya writing system is a mix of logograms and syllabic signs; with the latter, they could and often did write words purely phonetically. This chart shows the Maya syllabary as it has been deciphered thus far. It should be kept in mind that, due to homophony, the same sound is usually represented by more than one sign; and that some of these signs may also act as logograms. With the exception of the top left row of boxes, in which each sign stands for a

	a	e	i	o	u
n					
p					
s					
t					
tz					
dz					
u					
x					
y					

syllable consisting of vowel only, each box contains one or more signs representing a consonant-vowel (CV) syllable; the consonants are at the left, and the vowels at the top. Thus all signs in the top right box would be pronounced *nu*.

As an example of syllabic writing, a Maya scribe would have written the word *pitz*, "to play ball," with the signs for *pi* and for *tzi*, combined thus:

Notes

Chapter 1 (*pp. 13–45*)

1 Tylor 1881: 179.
2 Plato 1973: 95–99.
3 Pope 1975: 30–31.
4 Pope 1975: 17.
5 Pope 1975: 19
6 Pope 1975: 21.
7 For the career of Athanasius Kircher, I have drawn on Godwin 1979 and Pope 1975: 28–33.
8 Quoted in Pope 1975: 31–32.
9 Gardiner 1957: 11–12.
10 Sampson 1985, 26–45 and figure 3.
11 Hill 1967.
12 Ascher and Ascher 1981.
13 Basso and Anderson 1973.
14 Trager 1974: 377.
15 North 1939.
16 DeFrancis 1989: 9.
17 Kramer 1963: 40–42
18 Morley 1946: 259–260.
19 Gelb 1952.
20 This script was first devised for the Cree language by the Methodist missionary James Evans (1801–1946).
21 Diringer 1962: 149–152.
22 The best analyses of Chinese writing are in Sampson 1985: 145–171 and DeFrancis 1989: 89–121.
23 DeFrancis 1989: 99.
24 DeFrancis 1989: 111.
25 For the Japanese script, see Sampson 1985: 172–193.
26 Wang 1981: 231.
27 Pope 1975: 9.
28 Kahn 1967: 21–22; there are numerous references to the careers of the Friedmans throughout this book.
29 The story of Champollion and the decipherment of Egyptian hieroglyphs is well told in Pope 1975: 60–84 and Gardiner 1957: 9–11.
30 Ray 1986: 316.
31 Gardiner 1957: 7–10. For good descriptions of the structure of Egyptian writing, see Ray 1986 and Schenkel 1976.
32 Gelb 1952: 79–81.
33 For a full biography of Champollion, see Hartleben 1906.
34 Quirke and Andrews 1989 is a complete and accessible treatment of the Rosetta Stone.
35 Stephens 1841 (1): 160.
36 See Powell 1981 for treatment of the earliest Sumerian.
37 Pope 1975: 136–145 and Hawkins 1986.
38 Pope 1975: 159–179 and Chadwick 1958.
39 I have adapted and enlarged a similar list appearing in Gelb 1952: 115.
40 For the Indus script, see Mahadevan 1977.

Chapter 2 (*pp. 47–72*)

1 A good account of the Mayan languages can be found in Morley, Brainerd, and Sharer 1983: 497–510.
2 Thompson 1950: 16.
3 Campbell 1984: 7–11.
4 Kaufman and Norman 1984.
5 My description of Mayan grammar and verb morphology is based upon Schele 1982; Bricker 1986; Morley, Brainerd, and Sharer op. cit.; and upon a Yucatec language course given by Paul Sullivan at Yale in 1989–90.
6 A very long list of classifiers is given in Pío Pérez 1898; most of these have fallen out of use.
7 Turner 1978.
8 White and Schwarz 1989.
9 MacNeish, Wilkerson, and Nelken-Turner 1980.
10 Coe 1968.
11 Thompson 1941.
12 Coe and Diehl 1980.
13 Marcus 1983.
14 Earle and Snow 1985.
15 See Coe 1976.
16 Matheny 1986.
17 Coe 1989: 162–164.
18 This is Stela 29; see Morley, Brainerd, and Sharer 1983: 276 and fig. 4.6.

19 Haviland 1970.
20 Schele and Freidel 1990: 171–183.
21 This has been detailed in Schele and Miller 1986.
22 The Bonampak murals are pictured in Ruppert, Thompson, and Proskouriakoff 1955.
23 Haviland op. cit.
24 Trik 1963.
25 Harrison 1970.
26 Unfortunately, there are no eye-witness accounts for the game as it was played among the Maya.
27 Coe 1988.
28 Speculations and hypotheses about the Maya collapse are covered in Culbert 1973.
29 These are stelae 8, 9, 10, and 11; see J. Graham 1990: 25–38.
30 Here I have followed the arguments put forward in Thompson 1970.
31 Diehl 1983.
32 Pollock et al. 1962.
33 Fox 1987.
34 The best English translation of the Popol Vuh is Tedlock 1985.

Chapter 3 (pp. 73–98)

1 Brunhouse 1973 is an excellent general treatment of early exploration in the Maya lowlands. Del Río's expedition to Palenque is described in Cabello Carro 1983.
2 Some of these drawings are reproduced in Cabello Carro 1983, but a facsimile edition has yet to be issued.
3 Del Río 1822.
4 G. Stuart n.d.: 8.
5 For details of Galindo's career, see I. Graham 1963 and Brunhouse 1973: 31–49.
6 For Waldeck's life, see Cline 1947 and Brunhouse 1973: 50–83. Waldeck deserves a full-length biography.
7 Quoted in Cline 1947: 282.
8 Cline 1947: 283.
9 Waldeck 1838.
10 Coe 1989.
11 Coe 1989: 1.
12 Translated in Coe 1989: 4.
13 Coe 1989: 4–5
14 The history of the Dresden Codex is given in Thompson 1972: 16–17.
15 Coe 1963.
16 Humboldt 1810.

17 Kingsborough 1830–48.
18 Norman 1843: 198.
19 Biographical and bibliographic details on this extraordinary figure can be found in Rafinesque 1987 and G. Stuart 1989.
20 Rafinesque 1954.
21 G. Stuart 1989: 21.
22 Rafinesque 1832: 43–44.
23 Rafinesque, ibid.
24 Stephens 1841 (1): 9.
25 Von Hagen 1947 is a good (although occasionally inaccurate) biography of Stephens.
26 G. Stuart n.d.: 16.
27 Stephens 1843.
28 Stephens 1841 (1): 137.
29 Stephens 1841 (1): 159.
30 Stephens 1841 (1): 152.
31 Von Hagen 1947: 187–188.
32 Stephens 1841 (2): 442–443.
33 Stephens 1841 (2): 343.
34 Norman 1843.
35 Stephens 1841 (2): 457.
36 Haggard 1896.
37 Kidder 1950: 94.

Chapter 4 (pp. 99–122)

1 Brunhouse 1973: 113–135 is an excellent, sympathetic treatment of Brasseur. See also Escalante Arce 1989.
2 Brunhouse 1973: 126–127.
3 Brasseur 1864.
4 Biographical material on Landa can be found in Pagden 1975: 11–17. Galina Yershova has completed a Russian-language biography of Landa, as yet unpublished.
5 For the Franciscan Inquisition in Yucatán, see Clendinnen 1987.
6 Personal communication, Galina Yershova.
7 Brasseur 1864; 1869–70, 1: 37–38.
8 I have translated this from the original Spanish. The translation of this critical passage in Pagden 1975: 124–126 is good; but the English version in Tozzer 1941: 169–170 is unreliable since it is based on a French translation of the Spanish.
9 Brasseur 1869–70.
10 For a modern facsimile edition of the codex, see Codex Madrid 1967.
11 Brunhouse 1973: 130.
12 The Atlantis myth was to have a long life

in Maya studies; among its adherents was Edward H. Thompson, the turn-of-the-century owner and excavator of Chichén Itzá.

13 For the life of Förstemann, see Reichert 1908 and Tozzer 1907.

14 A survey of Förstemann's achievements is in Thompson 1950: 29–30.

15 Codex Dresden 1880.

16 Charnay 1887; many of that book's engravings were based on Charnay's own photographs.

17 Brunhouse 1973: 136–165.

18 Rau 1979.

19 Thomas 1882.

20 For Maudslay's life, see Tozzer 1931.

21 Charnay 1887: 435–436.

22 Maudslay 1889–1902.

23 Goodman 1897.

24 Goodman 1905.

25 Thompson 1935.

26 Clemens 1924, 1: 277.

27 H. Hill 1978: 206.

28 Brunhouse 1975: 5–28 has an outline of Maler's life.

29 These great publications began with Maler 1901 and continued to be issued over the next ten years.

30 Pope 1975: 64.

31 For an appreciation of De Rosny, see Kelley 1962a: 7; see also de Rosny 1876, a pioneering work in Maya epigraphy.

32 For an obituary of Thomas, see Anonymous 1911.

33 Thomas 1882.

34 Thomas 1893.

35 Quoted in Brinton 1890: 234–235.

36 Brinton 1886.

37 Kelley 1976: 4.

38 Valentini 1880.

39 Pío Pérez 1898.

40 Thompson 1950: 31. Short biographies of Seler are to be found in Höpfner 1949 and Termer 1949.

41 Höpfner 1949: 63 (my translation).

42 Schellhas 1897.

43 Kelley 1976: 4.

44 See Thomas 1892a, 1892b; Seler 1892, 1893.

45 Thomas 1903.

46 Tozzer 1919: 445.

Chapter 5 (pp. 123–144)

1 For Eric Thompson's life, see Hammond 1977; I. Graham 1976; and Willey

1979. The autobiographical Thompson 1963 covers his early career in archaeology.

2 Thompson 1950.

3 Ruz Lhuillier 1976–77: 318 (my translation).

4 This theme has been explored in Villela n.d.

5 Morley 1915.

6 Thompson 1963a: 5–6.

7 Kidder 1950: 93–94. Brunhouse 1971 is a comprehensive biography of Morley.

8 Gordon 1896.

9 This famous story is well told in Brunhouse 1971: 63–78.

10 Thompson 1963a: 30.

11 Roys and Harrison 1949: 218.

12 Morley 1920.

13 Morley 1937–38.

14 Thompson 1963b.

15 Teeple 1925 is the first of these. Teeple's findings, which have never been seriously challenged, were summarized in Teeple 1930.

16 Morley 1910.

17 Thompson 1929.

18 Thompson 1943b.

19 Thompson 1934, 1943a.

20 Teeple 1930: 70–85.

21 A biographical sketch of Whorf can be found in Carroll 1956: 1–33.

22 Carroll 1956: 17.

23 Morley 1946.

24 Whorf 1933.

25 Teeple 1930: 31.

26 Houston 1989: 15.

27 Long 1935.

28 Whorf 1935.

29 Thompson 1950: 311–313.

30 Thompson 1941.

31 Thompson 1950; this went through two subsequent editions, unchanged except for the addition of new prefaces.

32 The analysis of Chichén Itzá dates was first presented in Thompson 1937.

33 Thompson 1944.

34 Thompson 1950: 295.

35 A. Hill 1952.

36 Thompson 1953a.

37 Morley 1940: 146–149.

38 Beyer 1937.

39 Schellhas 1936: 133.

40 Schellhas 1945.

Chapter 6 (*pp. 145–166*)

1 Knorosov 1952.
2 This section is based on my interviews with Y.V. Knorosov.
3 Knorosov 1955.
4 Thompson 1953b (in Spanish).
5 Ulving 1955. At that time, Ulving was head of the Chinese section of the University of Göteborg; he has Slavic languages in his academic degree, and reads Russian (letter to me of 22 August 1991).
6 Barthel 1958.
7 In my "Introduction" to the Schele and Miller 1986, this date is wrongly given as March 1956.
8 Knorosov 1954.
9 Coe and Coe 1957; Knorosov 1958a.
10 My account of David Kelley is based upon many years' acquaintance, and upon a taped interview of 12 December 1989.
11 Morris 1931.
12 Knorosov 1958a.
13 Kelley 1962b.
14 Knorosov's investigations were entirely confined to the codices.
15 Kelley 1976.
16 Thompson 1962.
17 These are Aztec gods.
18 Cottie Burland was then a clerk in the Ethnographic Department of the British Museum and a prolific author of books on Mexican religion. A political radical and eccentric mystic, he was often the butt of Thompson's humour. I had previously recounted to Eric my visit, in company with Burland, to the Abbey Art Center, a decommissioned church in the outskirts of London, where former nuns and priests worshiped amidst masks from New Guinea and other exotic places.
19 This was probably in response to our 1957 review of Knorosov's *Diego de Landa*.
20 Piedras Negras Stela 12 depicts a ruler above a group of prisoners; the body of each prisoner is marked with glyphs.
21 Knorosov 1958b.
22 Thompson 1958: 45.
23 Thompson 1959.
24 Thompson 1962: 29.
25 Thompson 1971a: vi.
26 Thompson 1972a.

27 Knorosov 1963.
28 Coe 1966: 166–169.
29 Demarest 1976.
30 Thompson 1950: figs. 16–19.

Chapter 7 (*pp. 167–192*)

1 Personal information from Y.V. Knorosov. Proskouriakoff visited the USSR in the early 1970s, and was warmly received by Knorosov and his colleagues.
2 For details of Proskouriakoff's life, I have relied on Marcus 1988 and I. Graham 1990.
3 Piedras Negras is not only in very dilapidated condition, it is threatened with flooding by a Mexican-Guatemalan dam project on the Usumacinta.
4 Satterthwaite 1947.
5 I. Graham 1990: 2.
6 Proskouriakoff 1946.
7 Proskouriakoff 1950.
8 Proskouriakoff 1960.
9 Proskouriakoff 1961a.
10 This theme is further explored in Proskouriakoff 1961b.
11 Proskouriakoff 1961a: 16.
12 Bowditch 1901: 13.
13 Kelley 1976: 214.
14 Spinden 1916.
15 Morley 1915: 36.
16 Thompson 1950: 64.
17 Personal information from Peter Mathews.
18 Berlin 1959.
19 Morley 1940: 148.
20 Berlin 1958.
21 Berlin 1963.
22 Berlin 1969.
23 Berlin 1977.
24 Proskouriakoff 1963, 1964.
25 The *sahalo'ob* have been established by recent research as subordinate war leaders, perhaps governors of subsidiary cities or towns.
26 The genesis of this project is described in I. Graham 1975: 7, but this fails to mention how the Guttman Foundation got involved in the first place. The ongoing series, *Corpus of Maya Hieroglyphic Inscriptions*, continues to be published by the Peabody Museum in Cambridge.

Chapter 8 (pp. 193–217)

1 Griffin 1974: 9.
2 Ruz Lhuillier 1954, 1973.
3 I am grateful to Elaine Kaplan for biographical data on Merle Greene Robertson.
4 Robertson 1974.
5 This section on Floyd Lounsbury is based upon a taped interview of 3 December 1989.
6 Published as Benson 1973.
7 Lounsbury 1973.
8 In modern linguistic orthography, -u(a) is spelled -w(a), but here and elsewhere I have held to the traditional Yucatec orthography.
9 For Linda Schele's life history, I have drawn upon my taped interviews of 11 and 28 November 1989.
10 This, as we shall see, was Pacal's tomb.
11 This and subsequent information were provided by Peter Mathews in telephone interviews.
12 See Berlin 1968.
13 Lounsbury letter of 12 February 1974 addressed to the "Palencophiles."
14 On an eighth century AD stone panel from the Palenque region, now in a regional museum at Emiliano Zapata, Tabasco, Chan-Bahlum's name is clearly preceded with the phonetic complement ca (T25); this implies that his name was Yucatec: Can-Balam.
15 Kelley 1976: 181.
16 Lounsbury 1974.
17 Schele and Freidel (1990: 223) state that Zac-Kuk actually did rule the city.
18 Information on Ruz was gathered over a period of years through conversations with colleagues.
19 Ruz Lhuillier 1981.
20 Ruz Lhuillier 1973.
21 Ruz Lhuillier 1975, 1977a, 1977b.
22 Schele interview of 28 November 1989.
23 Taped interview of 5 December 1989.
24 The continuing debate over the identification of these figures is examined in Schele and Freidel 1990: 470–471.
25 Lounsbury 1976.
26 Lounsbury 1980.
27 Schele 1982.
28 Jones 1977.
29 Schele and Miller 1986: 112, 114.
30 Schele and Freidel 1990: 492.
31 Trik (1963) and Jones (1988). This read-ing has been questioned by some epigraphers, since the glyph combination which begins the ruler's name may not be a reduplicated ca sign.
32 Thompson 1950: 161–162.
33 Schele 1978 marks the first of the Notebook series. These are indispensable for the student of Maya epigraphy.
34 Morley 1940: 148.

Chapter 9 (pp. 218–230)

1 Thompson 1962: 14–18 presents his views on ceramic texts.
2 Coe and Diehl 1980.
3 Meyer 1977.
4 Coe 1973.
5 Tedlock 1985 is the most recent translation into English, and is both readable and authoritative.
6 Thompson 1970b.
7 Taube 1989; this paper also provides confirmation for my Pauahtun reading of God N's name.
8 Coe 1973.
9 Justin Kerr describes his roll-out camera in Coe 1978: 138–139.
10 Coe 1978.
11 Coe 1982.
12 Hanson et al. n.d.
13 Coe 1976b.
14 Subsequently published in von Winning 1963: fig. 333.
15 Coe 1974.
16 The sample was processed by Teledyne Isotopes, Inc., of New Jersey, a highly regarded commercial laboratory.
17 Thompson 1976.
18 Carlson 1990: 99.
19 Taube and Bade 1991.
20 Some of this complex, supernatural world is described in Hellmuth 1987, which is largely based upon the iconography of Classic Maya ceramics.

Chapter 10 (pp. 231–258)

1 Pope 1975: 68.
2 My information about David Stuart is based on a taped interview of 10 December 1989.
3 Stuart and Stuart 1977.
4 D. Stuart 1979.
5 Justeson and Campbell 1984.
6 Campbell 1984: 11.
7 This was done for proto-Cholan in

Kaufman and Norman 1984.

8 Fox and Justeson 1984.
9 Houston 1984.
10 D. Stuart 1984.
11 For an account of the cave and its exploration, see G. Stuart 1981.
12 Andrea Stone, personal communication.
13 D. Stuart 1985a.
14 Thompson 1943a, 1944.
15 Schele 1991: 71–72.
16 D. Stuart 1987.
17 Seler 1902–23, 1: 377.
18 Lounsbury, taped interview of 3 December 1989.
19 Pendergast 1979.
20 Mathews 1979.
21 Described in Houston and Taube 1987.
22 Barbara MacLeod has taught Yucatec Maya, and done research on Yucatec and Cholan verb morphology.
23 Houston, Stuart, and Taube 1989.
24 MacLeod and Stross 1990.
25 D. Stuart 1988.
26 The *atole* drink also appears on ceramics as a glyph combination reading *sac ha*, "white water," one of its modern names in Yucatán.
27 MacLeod 1990.
28 Alsop 1982.
29 Alsop 1982: 181.
30 Coe 1976b.
31 D. Stuart 1989: 156–157.
32 D. Stuart n.d.
33 The early epigraphic research of this project is described in Houston n.d.
34 Fash 1991 is a popular but authoritative account of the Copán project.
35 Schele and Freidel 1990: 311.
36 Fash 1991: 142.
37 Schele and Freidel 1990: 317–319.
38 Schele and Stuart 1985.
39 D. Stuart 1986a.
40 D. Stuart 1986b.
41 See Schele 1991: 42, 56.
42 Schele 1991: 50–53. For a fairly complete list of Emblem Glyphs, see Mathews 1985: 25–26.
43 D. Stuart 1985.
44 Houston and Stuart n.d.
45 Webster 1989.
46 Fash 1991: 136–137
47 Fash 1991: 106–111.
48 Schele 1985.
49 Furst 1968.
50 Vogt 1971: 33–34.
51 Houston and Stuart 1989.
52 Houston and Stuart 1989: 13.

Chapter 11 (*pp. 259–274*)

1 Pope 1975: 11.
2 Stephens 1841 (2): 457.
3 Pope 1975: 136–145.
4 Peter Mathews does this regularly in his annual hieroglyphic seminars.
5 Thompson 1972 is a good description of the structure of these almanacs and tables, but as usual Thompson is misleading on the nature of the script.
6 Green 1981: 359.
7 Blakeslee 1989.
8 Hopkins n.d.
9 Tedlock 1985.
10 Cecil Brown (1991) believes that the Maya had a low rate of literacy. He bases this opinion on the fact that a single, basic word for "write" is widely diffused among the Mayan language groups, but the many words for "read" are heterogeneous and probably post-Conquest. I have reached a different conclusion.
11 See the chapter entitled "The future of writing" in Gelb 1950: 236–247.
12 Goody 1977: 82–83.
13 Schele and Miller 1986.
14 Paz 1987.
15 Chase and Chase 1987; in the last few years, Nikolai Grube has been epigrapher for the Caracol Project.
16 Edmundson 1982: 41.

Glossary

In compiling this list, I have benefited from the glossaries included in DeFrancis 1989, Kelley 1976, and Pope 1975.

affix In Maya writing, a smaller, usually flattened sign attached to the main sign (q.v.).

alphabet Defined narrowly, a more-or-less phonemic writing system in which some signs represent the consonants of a language, and others the vowels. More broadly defined, it would include consonantal alphabets like Arabic and Hebrew.

Anterior Date Indicator (A.D.I.) A glyph which indicates that a following date refers to an earlier time, in the Maya Long Count calendar.

baktun In the Maya Long Count, a period of 20 katuns or 144,000 days (394½ years).

bilingual text A text written in two languages and/or two different scripts with identical or very similar content.

Calendar Round A recurring Maya cycle based on the permutation of the Almanac of 260 days and the "vague year" of 365 days. Its length was slightly less than 52 years.

cartouche An oval line, sometimes in the form of a rope, surrounding royal names in Egyptian hieroglyphic texts.

character A term used by Sinologists to describe a single logogram or a compound sign in Chinese writing. Roughly equivalent to the term *glyph* in Maya epigraphy.

cuneiform The "nail-shaped" script of the ancient Near East, usually written on damp clay tablets with a stylus. Most cuneiform scripts were logographic (q.v.) and were used to record Sumerian, Akkadian, and other languages.

decipherment The process by which signs and texts in a previously unknown script are read and translated.

demotic A late, calligraphic variety of Egyptian hieroglyphic script, employed for everyday use, and generally written on papyrus scrolls.

determinative In logographic writing, an unpronounced sign conveying meaning only and indicating the class of words of related meaning to which the referent word belongs, e.g. in the Chinese script, all characters for objects related to "wood" take the "wood" determinative.

dialects Mutually intelligible varieties of spoken language; contrasted with *languages*, which are mutually unintelligible.

Distance Number A Long Count number giving the time interval between two dates on a Maya monument.

Emblem Glyph In Maya inscriptions, a compound glyph which indicates that a ruler or other important personage is identified with a particular city or polity.

epigraphy The study of ancient writing systems and texts.

glottal stop In speech, a consonant produced by the closing and opening of the glottis or vocal folds.

glyph A contraction of *hieroglyph*. In Maya epigraphy, it indicates a logogram, a phonetic sign, or a compound sign.

grammar The study of the structure of a spoken language.

head variant A Maya glyph substituting for a bar-and-dot coefficient in Initial Series (q.v.) texts; it takes the form of the head of the god presiding over that number.

hieratic An adaptation of the Egyptian hieroglyphic script, principally used for writing on papyrus scrolls. It is not as cursive as demotic (q.v.).

hieroglyphic Originally meaning "holy carving," it is now generally synonymous with logographic (q.v.).

homonym A word with the same pronunciation as another but with different meaning.

ideogram, ideograph An outmoded term once applied to a sign supposedly conveying meaning only; it was loosely used for logogram (q.v.) and semasiogram (q.v.).

infix In Maya script, an affix-like sign that can appear within a main sign.

Initial Series The first Long Count date which appears on a Maya monument; it is always preceded by an Introductory Glyph.

katun In the Maya Long Count (q.v.), a period of 20 tuns or 7,200 days (slightly less than 20 years).

kin In the Maya Long Count, a period of one day.

lintel A flat stone or piece of wood that spans a doorway.

logogram, logograph A written sign which represents a morpheme or, rarely, a whole word.

logographic script A mixed writing system consisting of logograms and phonetic signs, or semantic signs compounded with phonetic signs. Some logographic scripts incorporate determinatives (q.v.) as semantic signs. Synonymous with *hieroglyphic*.

main sign In Maya writing, the larger sign to which affixes are attached; main signs may also stand by themselves. There is no necessary functional difference between affixes and main signs.

morpheme The smallest meaningful unit of speech. For instance, the English word *cheerful* consists of the morphemes *cheer* and *ful*.

morphology The study of how morphemes are formed into words in speech.

name-tags Maya glyphs used to label objects; these objects may be as diverse as ceramic vessels, items of personal wear, monuments, or buildings.

phonetic signs In scripts, signs that indicate speech sounds, as opposed to *semantic signs* that convey meaning only.

phonetic complement Also called **phonetic indicator**. In a logographic script, a phonetic sign which signals the initial or final sound of the morpheme or word represented by a logogram; when a given logogram is polyphonic (q.v.), it acts to reduce ambiguity.

pictogram, pictograph A sign which pictures an object or thing in the real world.

polyphony, polyphonic A form of polyvalence (q.v.) in which more than one sound value is assigned to a given sign, e.g. in written English, the letter combination *gh* is highly polyphonic.

polysemy A form of polyvalence in which more than one meaning is assigned to a given sign.

polyvalence The assignment to a written sign of more than one value.

Posterior Date Indicator (P.D.I.) A Maya glyph which indicates that a following date refers to a later time.

Primary Standard Sequence (PSS) A formulaic Maya text which usually appears just below the rim of painted and carved Maya ceramics; it includes the name-tags for classes of vessels, and labels their contents.

quipu A group of connected, knotted cords of different colors, used for record-keeping by Inca bureaucrats.

reading In epigraphy, restricted to determining the spoken equivalent of a sign or text written in a hitherto unknown script.

rebus The principle of "puzzle-writing," in which a morpheme or word difficult to express by means of a picture is given by a pictograph of a homonym (q.v.).

semantic sign In scripts, signs that pertain to meaning.

semasiography, semasiographic Visual communication which indicates ideas directly, without being linked to a specific language. Formerly called ideographic (q.v.). Example: the "Arabic " numeration of the modern world.

sign In the study of writing systems, a unit of visual communication. For Mayanists, it is synonymous with *glyph*.

signary The total number of signs in a writing system.

stela A carved, freestanding stone monument, usually slab-shaped.

Supplementary Series In Maya writing, this was a series of glyphs following an Initial Series (q.v.), and bracketed by a Calendar Round date. It includes the glyph for the current Lord of the Night, and for lunar calculations.

syllabic script A writing system in which the signs stand for entire syllables. In most syllabic scripts, the signs stand for CV syllables, plus the vowels. Can be part of a logographic script, as in Maya and Hieroglyphic Hittite. The total list of syllabic signs comprises a **syllabary**.

syllable A vocal sound or set of sounds uttered with a single effort of articulation and forming a word or element of a word. It consists of a vowel (V) alone, or a vowel and one or more consonants (C).

synharmony A principle in syllabic writing among the Maya in which the last vowel in a pair of CV phonetic signs will echo the first, even though it is unpronounced.

syntax In speech, the way words are formed into sentences.

toponym A Maya glyph which indicates the name of a place, a geographic feature, or an important location within a city.

translation In epigraphy, a reading (q.v.) which has been put into the words of another language, such as English.

tun In the Maya Long Count, a period of 360 days.

tzolkin A modern term made up from Yucatec Maya, and used by some epigra-

phers to refer to the Almanac of 260 days.

uinal In the Maya Long Count, a period of 20 days.

water group In Maya writing, affixes accompanying the Emblem Glyph main sign and believed by J.E.S. Thompson to refer to water, but now known to mean "holy."

Sources of Illustrations

Text illustrations

1 Jean Blackburn. 2 From F. Guaman Poma de Ayala, *Nueva Corónica y Buen Gobierno* (Paris: Institut d'Ethnologie, 1936), p. 360. 3 M.D. Coe. 4 From H.A. Gleason, Jr., *An Introduction to Descriptive Linguistics*, (New York: Henry Holt, 1955), p. 307; by permission. 5 Vivian Wu. 6 From S. Elisseef, E.O. Reischauer, and T. Yoshihashi, *Elementary Japanese for College Students*, Pt. I (Cambridge: Harvard University Press, 1950), p. 149; by permission. 7–10 Jean Blackburn. 11 From J. Chadwick, *Linear B and Related Scripts* (Berkeley: University of California Press/British Museum Publications, 1987), fig. 23; by permission. 12 Jean Blackburn. 13 Anita Holland-Moritz. 14 Jean Blackburn and Annick Petersen. 15 Jean Zallinger. 16 From A. del Río 1822. 17 M.D. Coe. 18 From J.L. Stephens 1841, 2: 454. 19, 20 John Montgomery. 21 From Tozzer 1941 (Cambridge: Peabody Museum, Harvard University), p. 170; by permission. 22 John Montgomery. 23 From D. Charnay, *Les anciens villes du Nouveau Monde* (Paris, 1885), p. 427. 24 John Montgomery. 25 Anita Holland-Moritz. 26 After Brinton 1886: 9. 27–9 John Montgomery. 30 From Carroll 1956 (Cambridge: Massachusetts Institute of Technology), fig. 6; by permission. 31–2 M.D. Coe. 33 From Beyer 1937 (Washington: Carnegie Institute of Washington), p. 38; by permission. 34 M.D. Coe. 35–7 John Montgomery. 38 M.D. Coe. 39–41 John Montgomery. 42 From Proskouriakoff 1963, fig. 1. 43 M.D. Coe. 44–8 John Montgomery. 49–51 Diana Griffiths Peck. 52 M.D. Coe. 53 From Houston 1989 (London:

British Museum Publications), p. 38; by permission. 54 M.D. Coe. 55 From D. Stuart 1987 (Washington: Center for Maya Research), fig. 39a; by permission. 56 M.D. Coe. 57 Top, from Thompson 1971a (Norman, University of Oklahoma Press), figs. 30, 42, 45, 37; by permission. Middle, lower left, D. Stuart 1987, figs. 28, 34a; by permission. Lower right, M.D. Coe. 58 Top, from Mathews 1979 (Toronto: Royal Ontario Museum), p. 79; by permission. Bottom, from L. Satterthwaite, "Note on Hieroglyphs on Bone from the Tomb below Temple I, Tikal", *Expedition* 6.1:18–19; by permission. 59 From Houston, Stuart, and Taube 1989, fig. 2 (with modifications); by permission. 60 Left, from D. Stuart 1988, fig. 2; by permission. Right, M.D. Coe. 61 M.D. Coe. 62 From D. Stuart n.d., fig. 18c; by permission. 63 Left, from Schele and Stuart 1985:7; by permission. Right, M.D. Coe. 64 John Montgomery. 65 From Houston and Stuart 1989 (Washington: Center for Maya Research), fig. 3; by permission. 66–7 M.D. Coe. 68 John Montgomery.

Plates

1 From Godwin 1979 (London: Thames and Hudson), p. 4. 2 From Pope 1975 (London: Thames and Hudson), ill. 33. Painting by Léon Cogniet. Archives Photographiques, Paris. 3 From Pope 1975 (London: Thames and Hudson), ill. 109. Courtesy of Mrs L. Ventris. 4 Trustees of the British Museum. 5 Courtesy Peabody Museum, Harvard University. 6, 7 Nicholas Hellmuth; by permission. 8 From J. Winsor, *Aboriginal*

America (Boston: Houghton Mifflin, 1889), p. 186. **9** From W.J. Youmans, *Pioneers of Science in America* (New York: D. Appleton, 1896), p. 183 (engraving from *Analyse de la Nature*, 1815). **10** Anonymous portrait, courtesy Department of Library Services, American Museum of Natural History. **11, 12** From Stephens 1841, 2: facing p. 158. **13** From J. Winsor, *Aboriginal America* (Boston: Houghton Mifflin, 1889), p. 170. **14** From *Globus* 90:341. **15** From Förstemann 1880, pl. 49. **16** From A.P. Maudslay and A.C. Maudslay, *A Glimpse at Guatemala* (London, 1899). Photograph by H.N. Sweet, 1889. **17** From *Atlantis* 22:365 (Freiburg, Germany). **18** From J. Winsor, *Aboriginal America* (Boston: Houghton Mifflin, 1889), p. 202. **19** From W. Lehmann (ed.), *Festschrift Eduard Seler* (Stuttgart: Verlag von Strecker und Schröder, 1922), frontispiece drawing by Erich Heerman. **20** Courtesy Smithsonian Institution, National Anthropological Archives, Bureau of American Ethnology Collection. **21** From Brunhouse 1971 (Norman: University of Oklahoma Press), after p. 214; by permission. **22** Courtesy Peabody Museum, Harvard University. Photograph by Carnegie Institution of Washington. By permission. **23** From Carroll 1956 (Cambridge: Massachusetts Institute of Technology), frontispiece; by permission. **24** Courtesy Y.V. Knorosov. **25** Courtesy George Stuart and the National Geographic Society; photograph by Otis Imboden. **26** Courtesy D.H. Kelley. **27** From T. Proskouriakoff, *An Album of Maya Architecture* (reprinted Norman: University of Oklahoma Press, 1963); by permission. **28** Courtesy University Museum, Philadelphia. **29** Courtesy Peabody Museum, Harvard University. Photograph by Carnegie Institution of Washington. By permission. **30** Courtesy Peabody Museum, Harvard University. Photograph by Carnegie Institution of Washington. By permission. **31** From T. Proskouriakoff, *An Album of Maya Architecture* (reprinted Norman: University of Oklahoma Press, 1963); by permission. **32** Photograph by A. Ruz L. **33** Courtesy M.G. Robertson. **34** Courtesy George Stuart and the National Geographic Society. **35** Photograph by M.D. Coe. **36, 37** Courtesy Justin Kerr. **38** Courtesy George Stuart and the National Geographic Society. **39** Courtesy George Stuart and the National Geographic Society. Photograph by Ann Hawthorne. **40** Courtesy George Stuart and the National Geographic Society. **41** Photograph by M.D. Coe. **42** From Förstemann 1880, pl. 74. **43** Courtesy W.L. Fash, from Fash, *Scribes, Warriors and Kings* (London and New York, Thames and Hudson, 1991), p. 121.

Further Reading and Bibliography

For those wishing to delve deeper into the subject of writing systems in general, I highly recommend Sampson 1985 and DeFrancis 1989. Pope 1975 is the most complete and readable book on the decipherment of Old World scripts; the interested reader should also consult the British Museum series, *Reading the Past*. For a general introduction to Maya civilization, see Michael D. Coe, *The Maya* (4th edition), London and New York 1987; and Morley, Brainerd, and Sharer 1983. The history of Maya discovery is well presented in Brunhouse 1971, 1973, and 1975. Schele and Miller 1986 and Schele and Freidel 1990 present comprehensive treatments of elite Maya culture based on art and inscriptions. Those wishing to further their knowledge of Maya writing should consult Kelley 1976 (now a bit out of date), Houston 1989, and especially Schele 1991. Although seriously flawed, Thompson 1971a is still important; and anyone working with the Maya script must have Thompson 1962, the basic catalog of the glyphs. The most important series dealing with the script is *Research Reports on Ancient Maya Writing* (Center for Maya Research, Washington, D.C.). Maya pictorial ceramics and their texts are presented in Coe 1973, 1978, and 1982; and in Justin Kerr (ed.), *The Maya Vase Book*, 1 and 2 (New York 1989, 1990).

Alsop, Joseph 1982 *The Rare Art Traditions.* New York: Harper and Row.

Anonymous 1911 Cyrus Thomas. *American Anthropologist* n.s. 12: 337–393.

Ascher, Marcia, and Robert Ascher 1981 *Code of the Quipu.* Ann Arbor: University of Michigan Press.

Barthel, Thomas 1958 Die gegenwärtige Situation in der Erforschung der Mayaschrift. *Proceedings of the 32nd International Congress of Americanists, 1956:* 476–484. Copenhagen.

Basso, Keith, and Ned Anderson 1973 A Western Apache writing system: the symbols of Silas John. *Science* 180: 1013–1022.

Benson, Elizabeth P. (ed.) 1973 *Mesoamerican Writing Systems.* Washington: Dumbarton Oaks Research Library and Collections.

Berlin, Heinrich 1958 El glifo "emblema" en las inscripciones mayas. *Journal de la Société des Américanistes* n.s. 47: 111–119.

——1959 Glifos nominales en el sarcófago de Palenque. *Humanidades* 2 (10): 1–8.

——1963 The Palenque Triad. *Journal de la Société des Américanistes* n.s. 52: 91–99.

——1968 The Tablet of the 96 Glyphs at Palenque, Chiapas, Mexico. *Middle American Research Institute, Tulane University, Publ.* 26: 134–149.

——1969 Review of *The Maya* by Michael D. Coe. *American Antiquity* 34 (2): 194.

——1977 *Signos y significados en las inscripciones mayas.* Guatemala City: Instituto de Antropología e Historia.

Beyer, Hermann 1937 Studies on the inscriptions of Chichén Itzá. *Carnegie Institution of Washington, Publ.* 483, *Contrib.* 21.

Blakeslee, Sandra 1989 Linguists solve riddle of ancient Mayan language. *The New York Times,* 4 April 1989, Sect. C: 1, 14–15.

Bowditch, Charles P. 1901 Notes on the report of Teobert Maler (in Maler 1901).

Brasseur de Bourbourg, Charles Étienne 1864 *Relation des choses de Yucatán de Diego de Landa.* Paris.

——1869–70 *Manuscrit Troano. Études sur le système graphique et la langue des Mayas.* 2 vols. Paris.

Bricker, Victoria 1986 *A Grammar of Mayan Hieroglyphs.* New Orleans: Middle American Research Institute.

Brinton, Daniel G. 1886 *On the Ikonomatic Method of Phonetic Writing with Special Reference to American Archaeology.* Philadephia.

——1890 *Essays of an Americanist.* Philadelphia: David McKay.

Brown, Cecil H. 1991 Hieroglyphic literacy in ancient Mayaland: inferences from linguistic data. *Current Anthropology* 32 (4): 489–496.

Brunhouse, Robert L. 1971 *Sylvanus G. Morley and the World of the Ancient Maya*. Norman: University of Oklahoma Press.

——1973 *In Search of the Maya. The First Archaeologists*. Albuquerque: University of New Mexico Press.

——1975 *Pursuit of the Ancient Maya. Some Archaeologists of Yesterday*. Albuquerque: University of New Mexico Press.

Cabello Carro, Paz 1983 Palenque: primeras excavaciones sistemáticas. *Revista de Arqueología* 5 (38): 28–42.

Campbell, Lyle 1984 The implications of Mayan historical linguistics for glyphic research. In *Phoneticism in Mayan Hieroglyphic Writing*, ed. J.S. Justeson and L. Campbell, 1–16. Albany: Institute for Mesoamerican Studies.

Carlson, John B. 1990 America's ancient skywatchers. *National Geographic* 177 (3): 76–107.

Carroll, John B. 1956 Introduction. In *Language, Thought, and Reality. Selected Writings of Benjamin Lee Whorf*, ed. J.B. Carroll, 1–33. Cambridge: Technology Press and New York: John Wiley & Sons.

Chadwick, John 1958 *The Decipherment of Linear B*. Cambridge: Cambridge University Press.

Charnay, Desiré 1887 *Ancient Cities in the New World*. London.

Chase, Arlen F., and Diane Z. Chase 1987 Investigations at the Classic Maya city of Caracol, Belize: 1985–1987. *Pre-Columbian Art Research Institute, Monograph 3*. San Francisco.

Clemens, Samuel L. 1924 *Mark Twain's Autobiography*. 2 vols. New York and London: Harper and Bros.

Clendinnen, Inga 1987 *Ambivalent Conquests: Maya and Spaniard in Yucatán, 1517–1570*. Cambridge: Cambridge University Press.

Cline, Howard F. 1947 The apocryphal early career of J.F. Waldeck, pioneer Americanist. *Acta Americana* 5: 278–300.

Codex Dresden 1880 *Die Maya-Handschrift der Königlichen Bibliothek zu Dresden; herausgegeben von Prof. Dr. E. Förstemann*. Leipzig.

Codex Madrid 1967 *Codex Tro-Cortesianus (Codex Madrid)*. Introduction and summary by F. Anders. Graz: Akademische Druk- u. Verlagsanstalt.

Coe, Michael D. 1963 Una referencia antigua al códice de Dresden. *Estudios de Cultura Maya* 3: 37–40.

——1966 *The Maya*. London: Thames and Hudson (4th edition 1987. London & New York: Thames and Hudson).

——1968 *America's First Civilization*. New York: American Heritage.

——1973 *The Maya Scribe and His World*. New York: The Grolier Club.

——1974 A carved wooden box from the Classic Maya civilization. In *Primera Mesa Redonda de Palenque, Part II*, ed. Merle Greene Robertson, 51–58. Pebble Beach, Calif.: Robert Louis Stevenson School.

——1976a Early steps in the evolution of Maya writing. In *Origins of Religious Art and Iconography in Preclassic Mesoamerica*, ed. H.B. Nicholson, 107–122. Los Angeles: UCLA Latin American Center.

——1976b Supernatural patrons of Maya scribes and artists. In *Social Process in Maya Prehistory: Essays in Honour of Sir Eric Thompson*, ed. N. Hammond, 327–396. London, New York, and San Francisco: Academic Press.

——1978 *Lords of the Underworld: Masterpieces of Classic Maya Ceramics*. Princeton: Princeton University Press.

——1982 *Old Gods and Young Heroes: The Pearlman Collection of Maya Ceramics*. Jerusalem: The Israel Museum.

——1988 Ideology of the Maya tomb. In *Maya Iconography*, ed. E.P. Benson and G.G. Griffin, 222–235. Princeton: Princeton University Press.

——1989a The Hero Twins: myth and image. In *The Maya Vase Book, Volume 1*, ed. J. Kerr, 161–184. New York: Justin Kerr.

——1989b The Royal Fifth: earliest notices of Maya writing. *Research Reports on Ancient Maya Writing* 28. Washington.

Coe, Michael D., and Richard A. Diehl 1980 *In the Land of the Olmec*. 2 vols. Austin: University of Texas Press.

Coe, Sophie D., and Michael D. Coe 1957 Review of *Diego de Landa: Soobshchenie o delakh v Iukatani, 1566* by Y.V. Knorosov. *American Antiquity* 23 (2): 207–208.

Culbert, T. Patrick (ed.) 1973 *The Classic Maya Collapse*. Albuquerque: University of New Mexico Press.

DeFrancis, John 1989 *Visible Speech.* Honolulu: University of Hawaii Press.

Del Río, Antonio 1822 *Description of the Ruins of an Ancient City.* London: Henry Berthoud.

Demarest, Arthur 1976 A critical analysis of Yuri Knorosov's decipherment of the Maya hieroglyphics. *Middle American Research Institute, Studies in Middle American Anthropology* 22: 63–73.

Diehl, Richard A. 1983 *Tula. The Toltec Capital of Ancient Mexico.* London and New York: Thames and Hudson.

Diringer, David 1962 *Writing.* London: Thames and Hudson; New York: Praeger.

Earle, Duncan, and Dean Snow 1985 The origin of the 260-day calendar: the gestation hypothesis reconsidered in light of its use among the Quiché-Maya. In *Fifth Palenque Round Table,* ed. V. Fields, 241–244. San Francisco: Pre-Columbian Art Research Institute.

Edmundson, Munro S. 1982 *The Ancient Future of the Itzá.* Austin: University of Texas Press.

Escalante Arce, Pedro Antonio 1989 *Brasseur de Bourbourg. Esbozo biográfico.* San Salvador (El Salvador).

Fash, William L. 1991 *Scribes, Warriors and Kings: The City of Copán and the Ancient Maya.* London and New York: Thames and Hudson.

Fox, James A., and John S. Justeson 1984 Polyvalence in Mayan hieroglyphic writing. In *Phoneticism in Mayan Hieroglyphic Writing,* ed. J.S. Justeson and L. Campbell, 17–76. Albany: Institute for Mesoamerican Studies.

Fox, John W. 1987 *Maya Postclassic State Formation.* Cambridge: Cambridge University Press.

Furst, Peter T. 1968 The Olmec were-jaguar motif in the light of ethnographic reality. In *Dumbarton Oaks Conference on the Olmec,* ed. E.P. Benson, 143–174. Washington: Dumbarton Oaks Research Library and Collections.

Gardiner, Sir Alan 1957 *Egyptian Grammar.* 3rd edition. Oxford: Griffith Institute.

Gelb, Ignace J. 1952 *A Study of Writing.* Chicago: University of Chicago Press.

Godwin, Joscelyn 1979 *Athanasius Kircher.* London: Thames and Hudson.

Goodman, Joseph T. 1897 *The Archaic Maya Inscriptions.* (Appendix to Maudslay 1889–1902).

——1905 Maya dates. *American Anthropologist* 7: 642–647.

Goody, Jack 1977 *The Domestication of the Savage Mind.* London and New York: Cambridge University Press.

Gordon, George Byron 1896 Prehistoric ruins of Copán, Honduras. *Memoirs of the Peabody Museum of Archaeology and Ethnology, Harvard University* 1 (1).

Graham, Ian 1963 Juan Galindo, enthusiast. *Estudios de Cultura Maya* 3: 11–35.

——1975 Introduction to the Corpus. *Corpus of Maya Inscriptions* 1. Cambridge.

——1976 John Eric S. Thompson. *American Anthropologist* 78 (2): 317–320.

——1990 Tatiana Proskouriakoff, 1909–1985. *American Antiquity* 55 (1): 6–11.

Graham, John A. Monumental sculpture and hieroglyphic inscriptions. *Memoirs of the Peabody Museum of Archaeology and Ethnology, Harvard University* 17 (1).

Green, M.W. 1981 The construction and implementation of the cuneiform writing system. *Visible Language* 15 (4): 345–372.

Griffin, Gillett G. 1974 Early travellers to Palenque. In *Primera Mesa Redonda de Palenque, Part I,* ed. M.G. Robertson, 9–34. Pebble Beach, Calif.: Robert Louis Stevenson School.

Haggard, H. Rider 1896 *Heart of the World.* London: Longmans, Green, & Co.

Hammond, Norman 1977 Sir Eric Thompson, 1898–1975: a biographical sketch and bibliography. In *Social Process in Maya Prehistory: Essays in Honour of Sir Eric Thompson,* ed. N. Hammond, 1–17. London: Academic Press.

Hansen, Richard D., Ronald Bishop, and Federico Fahsen n.d. Notes on Maya Codex vessels from Nakbé, Petén, Guatemala.

Harrison, Peter 1970 *The Central Acropolis, Tikal, Guatemala: A Preliminary Study of the Functions of its Structural Components during the Late Classic Period.* Ph.D. dissertation, University of Pennsylvania. Philadelphia.

Hartleben, H. 1906 *Champollion: sein Leben und sein Werk.* 2 vols. Berlin.

Haviland, William A. 1970 Tikal, Guatemala, and Mesoamerican urbanism. *World Archaeology* 2: 186–198.

Hawkins, David 1986 Writing in Anatolia: imported and indigenous systems. *World Archaeology* 17: 363–376.

Hellmuth, Nicholas 1987 *Monster und*

Menschen in der Maya-Kunst. Graz: Akademische Druck- u. Verlagsanstalt.

Hill, Archibald A. 1952 Review of *Maya Hieroglyphic Writing: Introduction* by J. Eric S. Thompson, *International Journal of American Linguistics* 18 (3): 184–186.

——1967 The typology of writing systems. In *Papers in Linguistics in Honor of Léon Dostert,* ed. W.M. Austin, 92–99. The Hague: Mouton.

Hill, Hamlin L. 1973 *Mark Twain: God's Fool.* New York: Harper's.

Höpfner, Lotte 1949 De la vida de Eduard Seler. *El México Antiguo* 7: 58–74.

Hopkins, Nicholas A. n.d. Decipherment and the relationship between Mayan languages and Maya writing.

Houston, Stephen D. 1983 An example of homophony in Maya script. *American Antiquity* 49 (4): 790–808.

——1989 *Maya Glyphs.* London: British Museum Publications; Berkeley: University of California Press.

——n.d. *The Inscriptions and Monumental Art of Dos Pilas, Guatemala: A Study of Classic Maya History and Politics.* Ph.D. dissertation, Department of Anthropology, Yale University. New Haven.

Houston, Stephen D., and David Stuart 1989 The *way* glyph: evidence for "co-essence" among the Classic Maya. *Research Reports on Ancient Maya Writing* 30. Washington.

Houston, Stephen D., David Stuart, and Karl Taube 1989 Folk classification of Classic Maya pottery. *American Anthropologist* 9 (13): 720–726.

Houston, Stephen D., and Karl A. Taube 1987 "Name-tagging" in Classic Mayan script: implications for native classifications of ceramics and jade ornaments. *Mexicon* 9 (2): 38–41.

Humboldt, Alexander von 1816 *Vue des Cordillères, et monuments des peuples indigènes de l'Amérique.* Paris.

Jones, Christopher 1977 Inauguration dates of three Late Classic rulers of Tikal, Guatemala. *American Antiquity* 42 (1): 28–60.

——1988 The life and times of Ah Cacaw, ruler of Tikal. In *Primer Simposio Mundial Sobre Epigrafía Maya,* 107–120. Guatemala: Asociación Tikal.

Justeson, John S., and Lyle Campbell (eds.) 1984 *Phoneticism in Mayan Hieroglyphic Writing.* Albany: Institute for Mesoamerican Studies.

Kahn, David 1967 *The Codebreakers: The Story of Secret Writing.* New York: MacMillan.

Kaufman, Terence S., and William M. Norman 1984 An outline of proto-Cholan phonology, morphology, and vocabulary. In *Phoneticism in Mayan Hieroglyphic Writing,* ed. J.S. Justeson and L. Campbell, 77–166. Albany: Institute for Mesoamerican Studies.

Kelley, David H. 1962a A history of the decipherment of Maya script. *Anthropological Linguistics* 4 (8): 1–48.

——1962b Fonetismo en la escritura maya. *Estudios de Cultura Maya* 2: 277–317.

——1976 *Deciphering the Mayan Script.* Austin: University of Texas Press.

Kidder, Alfred V. 1950 Sylvanus Griswold Morley, 1883–1948. In *Morleyana,* ed. A.J.O. Anderson, 93–102. Santa Fe: The School of American Research and the Museum of New Mexico.

Kingsborough, Edward King, Viscount 1830–48 *Antiquities of Mexico.* 9 vols. London: James Moynes, and Colnaghi, Son, & Co.

Knorosov, Yuri V. 1952 Drevniaia pis'mennost' Tsentral'noi Ameriki. *Sovietskaya Etnografiya* 3 (2): 100–118.

——1954 *La antigua escritura de los pueblos de America Central.* Mexico City: Biblioteca Obrera.

——1955 *Diego de Landa: Soobshchenie o delakh v Yukatani, 1566.* Moscow: Akademia Nauk SSSR.

——1958a New data on the Maya written language. *Proceedings of the 32nd International Congress of Americanists, 1956,* 467–475. Copenhagen.

——1958b The problem of the study of the Maya hieroglyphic writing. *American Antiquity* 23: 248–291.

——1963 *Pis'mennost Indeitsev Maiia.* Moscow-Leningrad: Akademia Nauk SSSR.

——1967 Selected chapters from "The Writing of the Maya Indians." Transl. Sophie D. Coe, ed. Tatiana Proskouriakoff. *Peabody Museum of Archaeology and Ethnology, Harvard University, Russian Translation Series* 4.

Kramer, Samuel N. 1963 *The Sumerians.* Chicago: University of Chicago Press.

Long, Richard C.E. 1935 Maya and Mexican writing. *Maya Research* 2 (1). New Orleans.

Lounsbury, Floyd G. 1973 On the derivation and reading of the "Ben-Ich" prefix. In *Mesoamerican Writing Systems*, ed. E.P. Benson, 99–143. Washington: Dumbarton Oaks Research Library and Collections.

——1974 The inscriptions of the Sarcophagus Lid at Palenque. In *Primera Mesa Redonda de Palenque, Part II*, ed. M.G. Robertson, 5–19. Pebble Beach, Calif.: Robert Louis Stevenson School.

——1976 A rationale for the initial date of the Temple of the Cross at Palenque. In *The Art, Iconography, and Dynastic History of Palenque, Part III: Proceedings of the Segunda Mesa Redonda de Palenque*, ed. M.G. Robertson, 211–234. Pebble Beach, Calif.: Robert Louis Stevenson School.

——1980 Some problems in the interpretation of the mythological portion of the hieroglyphic text of the Temple of the Cross at Palenque. In *Third Palenque Round Table, 1978, Part 2*, ed. M.G. Robertson, 99–115. Austin: University of Texas Press.

MacLeod, Barbara 1990 *Deciphering the Primary Standard Sequence.* Ph.D. dissertation, Department of Anthropology, University of Texas. Austin.

MacLeod, Barbara, and Brian Stross 1990 The Wing-Quincunx. *Journal of Mayan Linguistics* 7: 14–32.

MacNeish, Richard S., S. Jeffrey K. Wilkerson, and Antoinette Nelken-Turner 1980 *First Annual Report of the Belize Archaic Archaeological Reconnaissance.* Andover, Mass.: R.S. Peabody Foundation.

Mahadevan, Iravatham 1977 *The Indus Script. Texts, Concordance and Tables.* New Delhi: Archaeological Survey of India.

Maler, Teobert 1901 Researches in the central portion of the Usumacinta Valley. *Memoirs of the Peabody Museum of Archaeology and Ethnology, Harvard University* 2 (1).

Marcus, Joyce 1983 The first appearance of Zapotec writing and calendrics. In *The Cloud People*, ed. K.V. Flannery and J. Marcus, 91–96. New York and London: Academic Press.

——1988 Tatiana Proskouriakoff (1909–1985). In *Women Anthropologists, a Biographical Dictionary*, ed. U. Gacs et al, 297–302. New York: Greenwood Press.

Matheny, Ray T. 1986 Early states in the Maya lowlands during the Late Preclassic Period: Edzná and El Mirador. In *City-States of the Maya*, ed. E.P. Benson, 1–44. Denver: Rocky Mountain Institute for Pre-Columbian Studies.

Mathews, Peter 1979 The glyphs on the ear ornaments from Tomb A-1/1. In *Excavations at Altún Ha, Belize, 1964–1970, Vol. I*, by David Pendergast, 79–80. Toronto: Royal Ontario Museum.

——1985 *Maya Hieroglyphic Workshop.* Los Angeles: Department of Anthropology, University of Southern California.

——1990 *The Proceedings of the Maya Hieroglyphic Weekend, October 27–28, 1990*, transcribed by Phil Wanyerka. Cleveland: Cleveland State University.

Maudslay, Alfred P. 1889–1902 *Archaeology. Biologia Centrali-Americana.* 5 vols. London.

Meyer, Karl E. 1977 *The Plundered Past.* New York: Atheneum.

Morley, Sylvanus G. 1910 The correlation of Maya and Christian chronology. *American Journal of Archaeology* 14: 193–204.

——1915 *An Introduction to the Study of the Maya Hieroglyphs.* Washington: Bureau of American Ethnology.

——1920 *The Inscriptions of Copán.* Washington: Carnegie Institution of Washington (Publ. 219).

——1932–38 *The Inscriptions of Petén.* 5 vols. Washington: Carnegie Institution of Washington (Publ. 437).

——1940 Maya epigraphy. In *The Maya and Their Neighbors*, ed. C.L. Hay et al, 139–149. New York: D. Appleton Century.

——1946 *The Ancient Maya.* Stanford: Stanford University Press.

Morley, Sylvanus G., George W. Brainerd, and Robert J. Sharer 1983 *The Ancient Maya.* 4th edition. Stanford: Stanford University Press.

Morris, Ann Axtell 1931 *Digging in Yucatán.* Garden City, New York: Doubleday, Doran & Co.

Norman, B.M. 1843 *Rambles in Yucatan Including a Visit to the Remarkable Ruins of Chichen, Kabah, Zayi, Uxmal.* New York: Henry G. Langley.

North, Eric M. (ed.) 1939 *The Book of a Thousand Tongues.* New York: American Bible Society.

Pagden, A.R. (ed. and transl.) 1975 *The Maya. Diego de Landa's Account of the Affairs of Yucatán.* Chicago: J. Philip O'Hara, Inc.

Paz, Octavio 1987 Food of the gods. *The New York Review of Books* 34 (3): 3–7.

Pendergast, David M. 1979 *Excavations at Altún Ha, Belize, 1964–1970, Vol. I.* Toronto: Royal Ontario Museum.

Pío Pérez, Juan 1898 *Coordinación alfabética de las voces del idioma maya.* Mérida.

Plato 1973 *Phaedrus and the Seventh and Eighth Letters.* Transl. W. Hamilton. Harmondsworth: Penguin Books.

Pollock, H.E.D., Ralph L. Roys, Tatiana Proskouriakoff, and A. Ledyard Smith 1962 *Mayapán, Yucatán, Mexico.* Washington: Carnegie Institution of Washington.

Pope, Maurice 1975 *The Story of Decipherment.* London: Thames and Hudson.

Powell, Marvin A. 1981 Three problems in the history of cuneiform writing: origins, direction of script, literacy. *Visible Language* 15 (4): 419–440.

Proskouriakoff, Tatiana 1946 *An Album of Maya Architecture.* Washington: Carnegie Institution of Washington.

——1950 *A Study of Classic Maya Sculpture.* Washington: Carnegie Institution of Washington (Publ. 593).

——1960 Historical implications of a pattern of dates at Piedras Negras, Guatemala. *American Antiquity* 25 (4): 454–475.

——1961a Lords of the Maya realm. *Expedition* 4 (1): 14–21.

——1961b Portraits of women in Maya art. In *Essays in Pre-Columbian Art and Archaeology,* ed. S.K. Lothrop et al, 81–90. Cambridge: Harvard University Press.

——1963 Historical data in the inscriptions of Yaxchilán. *Estudios de Cultura Maya* 3: 149–167.

——1964 Historical data in the inscriptions of Yaxchilán (part II). *Estudios de Cultura Maya* 4: 177–202.

Quirke, Stephen, and Carol Andrews 1989 *Rosetta Stone.* New York: Harry N. Abrams.

Rafinesque, Constantine Samuel 1832 Philology. Second letter to Mr. Champollion on the graphic systems of America, and the glyphs of Otulum, or Palenque, in Central America – elements of the glyphs. *Atlantic Journal, and Friend of Knowledge* 1 (2): 40–44. Philadelphia.

——1954 *Walum Olum or Red Score: The Migration Legend of the Lenni Lenape or Delaware Indians.* Indianapolis: Indiana Historical Society.

——1987 *Précis ou Abrégé des Voyages, Travaux, et Recherches de C.S. Rafinesque (1836),* ed. Charles Boewe, Georges Raynaud, and Beverley Seaton. Amsterdam/Oxford/New York: North-Holland Publishing Co.

Rau, Charles 1879 The Palenque Tablet, in the United States National Museum, Washington. *Smithsonian Institution, Contributions to Knowledge* 22 (5). Washington.

Ray, John D. 1986 The emergence of writing in Egypt. *World Archaeology* 17: 307–316.

Reichhardt, Alexander 1908 E.W. Förstemann. In *Biographisches Jahrbuch und Deutscher Nekrolog,* 177–180. Berlin.

Robertson, Merle Greene 1974 Preface. In *Primera Mesa Redonda de Palenque, Part I,* ed. M.G. Robertson, iii–iv. Pebble Beach, Calif.: Robert Louis Stevenson School.

de Rosny, Léon 1876 Essai sur le déchiffrement de l'écriture hiératique de l'Amérique Centrale. Paris.

Roys, Ralph L., and Margaret W. Harrison 1949 Sylvanus Griswold Morley, 1883–1948. *American Antiquity* 3: 215–219.

Ruppert, Karl, J. Eric S. Thompson, and Tatiana Proskouriakoff 1955 *Bonampak, Chiapas, Mexico,* Washington: Carnegie Institution of Washington.

Ruz Lhuillier, Alberto 1954 La pirámide-tumba de Palenque. *Cuadernos Americanos* 74: 141–159.

——1973 *El Templo de las Inscripciones, Palenque.* Mexico City: Instituto Nacional de Antropología e Historia.

——1975 Historia y fantasía en las inscripciones mayas. *Siete Días* 101. Mexico City.

——1976–77 Semblanza de John Eric Sidney [sic] Thompson (1898–1975). *Estudios de Cultura Maya* 10: 317–335.

——1977a Gerontocracy at Palenque? In *Social Process in Maya Prehistory: Essays in Honour of Sir Eric Thompson,* ed. N. Hammond, 287–295. London: Academic Press.

——1977b Lo que sabe y lo que no sabe de Palenque. *Revista del Sureste,* año 2 (5): 14–17.

——1981 El modo de producción tributario en el área maya. *Estudios de Cultura Maya* 13: 37–43.

Sampson, Geoffrey 1985 *Writing Systems.* London: Hutchinson.

Satterthwaite, Linton 1947 Concepts and structures of Maya calendrical arithmetic. *University Museum and Philadelphia Anth-*

ropological Society, Joint Publications 3. Philadelphia.

Schele, Linda 1978 *Notebook for the Maya Hieroglyphic Writing Workshop at Texas.* Austin: Institute of Latin American Studies, University of Texas.

——1982 *Maya Glyphs: The Verbs.* Austin: University of Texas Press.

——1985 Balan-Ahau: a possible reading of the Tikal Emblem Glyph and a title at Palenque. In *Fourth Palenque Round Table, 1980 (Vol.VII),* ed. M.G. Robertson and E.P. Benson, 59–65. San Francisco: The Pre-Columbian Art Research Institute.

——1991 *Notebook for the XVth Maya Hieroglyphic Workshop at Texas.* Austin: Art Department, University of Texas.

Schele, Linda, and David Freidel 1990 *A Forest of Kings.* New York: William Murrow and Co.

Schele, Linda, and Mary E. Miller 1986 *The Blood of Kings.* Fort Worth: Kimbell Art Museum; New York: George Braziller.

Schele, Linda, and David Stuart 1985 Tetun as the glyph for "Stela." *Copán Note* 1. Austin.

Schellhas, Paul 1897 *Die Göttergestalten der Mayahandschriften.* Dresden.

——1936 Fifty years of Maya research. *Maya Research* 3 (2): 129–139.

——1945 Die Entzifferung der Mayahieroglyphen ein unlösbares Problem? *Ethnos* 10: 44–53.

Schenkel, Wolfgang 1976 The structure of hieroglyphic script. *RAIN* 15: 4–7.

Seler, Eduard 1892 Does there really exist a phonetic key to the Maya hieroglyphic writing? *Science* 20 (499): 121–122.

——1893 Is the Maya hieroglyphic writing phonetic? *Science* 21 (518): 6–10.

——1902–03 *Gesammelte Abhandlungen zur Amerikanischen Sprach- und Alterthunskunde.* 5 vols. Berlin: Ascher & Co.

Spinden, Herbert J. 1916 Portraiture in Central American art. In *Holmes Anniversary Volume,* ed. F.W. Hodge, 434–450. Washington: J.W. Bryant Press.

Stephens, John L. 1841 *Incidents of Travel in Central America, Chiapas, and Yucatan.* 2 vols. London: John Murray.

——1843 *Incidents of Travel in Yucatan.* 2 vols. London: John Murray.

Stuart, David 1979 Some thoughts on certain occurrences of the T565 glyph element at Palenque. In *Tercera Mesa Redonda de Palenque, Vol.IV,* ed. M.G.

Robertson, 167–171. Pebble Beach, Calif.: Robert Louis Stevenson School.

——1984 A note on the "hand-scattering" glyph. In *Phoneticism in Mayan Hieroglyphic Writing,* ed. J.S. Justeson and L. Campbell, 307–310. Albany: Institute for Mesoamerican Studies.

——1985a The "count of captives" epithet in Classic Maya writing. In *Fifth Palenque Round Table, Vol. 7,* ed. V. Fields, 97–101. Austin: University of Texas Press.

——1985b The Yaxhá Emblem Glyph as *Yax-ha. Research Reports on Ancient Maya Writing* 1. Washington.

——1986a A glyph for "stone incensario." *Copán Note* 2. Austin.

——1986b The hieroglyphic name of Altar U. *Copán Note* 4. Austin.

——1987 Ten phonetic syllables. *Research Reports on Ancient Maya Writing* 14. Washington.

——1988 The Río Azul cacao pot: epigraphic observations on the function of a Maya ceramic vessel. *Antiquity* 62: 153–157.

——1989 Hieroglyphs on Maya vessels. In *The Maya Vase Book, Vol. 1,* ed. J. Kerr, 149–160. New York: Justin Kerr.

——n.d. *The Maya Artist. An Epigraphic and Iconographic Study.* Senior Thesis, Princeton University.

Stuart, David, and Stephen Houston n.d. Classic Maya place names.

Stuart, George E. 1981 Maya art treasures discovered in cave. *National Geographic* 160 (2): 220–235.

——1989 The beginning of Maya hieroglyphic study: contributions of Constantine S. Rafinesque and James H. McCulloch, Jr. *Research Reports on Ancient Maya Writing* 29. Washington.

——n.d. *Search and Research: A Historical and Bibliographical Survey.*

Stuart, George E., and Gene S. Stuart 1977 *The Mysterious Maya.* Washington: National Geographic Society.

Taube, Karl A. 1989 The maize tamale in Classic Maya diet, epigraphy, and art. *American Antiquity* 54 (1): 31–51.

Taube, Karl A., and Bonnie L. Bade 1991 An appearance of Xiuhtecuhtli in the Dresden Venus pages. *Research Reports on Ancient Maya Writing* 35. Washington.

Tedlock, Dennis 1985 *Popol Vuh.* New York: Simon and Schuster.

Teeple, John E. 1925 Maya inscriptions:

Glyphs C, D, and E of the Supplementary Series. *American Anthropologist* 27: 108–115.

——1930 Maya astronomy. *Carnegie Institution of Washington, Publ.* 403 (*Contrib.* 2). Washington.

Termer, Franz 1949 Eduard Seler. *El México Antiguo* 7: 29–57.

Thomas, Cyrus 1882 A study of the Manuscript Troano. *Contributions to North American Ethnology* 4: 1–237.

——1892a Key to the Maya hieroglyphs. *Science* 20 (494): 44–46.

——1892b Is the Maya hieroglyphic writing phonetic? *Science* 20 (505): 197–201.

——1893 Are the Maya hieroglyphics phonetic? *American Anthropologist* n.s. 6: 241–270.

——1903 Central American hieroglyphic writing. *Annual Report of the Smithsonian Institution for 1903*: 705–721.

Thompson, J. Eric S. 1929 Maya chronology: Glyph G of the Lunar Series. *American Anthropologist* 31: 223–231.

——1934 Maya chronology: the fifteen tun glyph. *Carnegie Institution of Washington, Publ.* 436 (*Contrib.* 11). Washington.

——1935 Maya chronology: the correlation question. *Carnegie Institution of Washington, Publ.* 456 (*Contrib.* 14). Washington.

——1937 A new method of deciphering Yucatecan dates with special reference to Chichén Itzá. *Carnegie Institution of Washington, Publ.* 483 (*Contrib.* 22). Washington.

——1941 Dating of certain inscriptions of non-Maya origin. *Carnegie Institution of Washington, Theoretical Approaches to Problems* 1. Cambridge.

——1943a Maya epigraphy: directional glyphs in counting. *Carnegie Institution of Washington, Notes on Middle American Archaeology and Ethnology* 20. Cambridge.

——1943b Maya epigraphy: a cycle of 819 days. *Carnegie Institution of Washington, Notes on Middle American Archaeology and Ethnology* 22. Cambridge.

——1944 The fish as a symbol for counting and further discussion of directional glyphs. *Carnegie Institution of Washington, Theoretical Approaches to Problems* 2. Cambridge.

——1950 *Maya Hieroglyphic Writing: An Introduction*. Washington: Carnegie Institution of Washington.

——1953a *Maya Hieroglyphic Writing*: a rejoinder. *International Journal of American Linguistics* 19 (2): 153–154.

——1953b Review of "La antigua escritura de los pueblos de America Central," *Etnografía Soviética*, octubre de 1952, by Y.V. Knorosov. *Yan* 2: 174–178. Mexico City.

——1958 Research in Maya hieroglyphic writing. *Pan American Union, Social Science Monographs* 5: 43–52. Washington.

——1959 Systems of hieroglyphic writing in Middle America and methods of deciphering them. *American Antiquity* 24 (1): 349–364.

——1962 *A Catalog of Maya Hieroglyphs*. Norman: University of Oklahoma Press.

——1963a *Maya Archaeologist*. Norman: University of Oklahoma Press.

——1963b *Rise and Fall of Maya Civilization*. Norman: University of Oklahoma Press.

——1970a *Maya History and Religion*. Norman: University of Oklahoma Press.

——1970b The Bacabs: their portraits and glyphs. *Papers of the Peabody Museum of Archaeology and Ethnology, Harvard University*, 61: 471–485.

——1971 *Maya Hieroglyphic Writing: An Introduction*. 3rd edition. Norman: University of Oklahoma Press.

——1972a *Maya Hieroglyphs Without Tears*. London: British Museum.

——1972b *A Commentary on the Dresden Codex*. Philadelphia: American Philosophical Society.

——1976 Review of *The Maya Scribe and His World* by Michael D. Coe. *The Book Collector* 26: 64–75. London.

Tozzer, Alfred M. 1907 Ernst Förstemann. *American Anthropologist* n.s., 9: 153–159.

——1919 Joseph Thompson Goodman. *American Anthropologist* n.s., 21: 441–445.

——1931 Alfred Percival Maudslay. *American Anthropologist* n.s., 33: 403–413.

——1941 Landa's Relación de las Cosas de Yucatán. *Papers of the Peabody Museum of Archaeology and Ethnology, Harvard University*, 18. Cambridge.

Trager, George L. 1974 Writing and writing systems. *Current Trends in Linguistics* 12: 373–496. The Hague.

Trik, Aubrey S. 1963 The splendid tomb of Temple I, Tikal, Guatemala. *Expedition* 6 (1): 2–18.

Turner, B.L. 1978 Ancient agricultural land use in the Maya lowlands. In *Pre-Hispanic Maya Agriculture*, 163–183. Austin: University of Texas Press.

Tylor, Edward B. 1881 *Anthropology*. New York: D. Appleton & Co.

Ulving, Tor 1955 A new decipherment of the Maya glyphs. *Ethnos* 20: 152–158.

Valentini, Philipp J.J. 1880 "The Landa alphabet," a Spanish fabrication. *Proceedings of the American Antiquarian Society* 75: 59–91. Worcester.

Villela, Khristaan n.d. J. Eric S. Thompson's first 25 years: Argentine politics and the Maya collapse. Class paper for *Topics in Pre-Columbian Art* (Prof. Mary Miller), Yale University, 1989.

Vogt, Evon Z. 1971 The genetic model and Maya cultural development. In *Desarollo cultural de los maya*, ed. E.Z. Vogt and A. Ruz L., 9–48. Mexico City: Universidad Nacional Autónoma, Centro de Estudios Mayas.

von Hagen, Victor Wolfgang 1947 *Maya Explorer: John Lloyd Stephens and the Lost Cities of Central America and Yucatan*. Norman: University of Oklahoma Press.

von Winning, Hasso 1963 *Pre-Columbian Art of Mexico and Central America*. New York: Harry N. Abrams Inc.

Waldeck, Jean Frédéric 1838 *Voyage pittoresque et archéologique dans de Province d'Yucatan pendant les années 1834 et 1836*. Paris.

Wang, William S.-Y. 1981 Language structure and optimal orthography. In *Perception of Print*. ed. O.J.L. Tzeng and H. Singer, 223–236. Hillside, N.J.: Lawrence Erlbaum Associates.

Webster, David (ed.) 1989 *House of the Bacabs, Copán, Honduras*. Washington: Dumbarton Oaks Research Library and Collections.

White, Christine D., and Henry P. Schwarcz 1989 Ancient Maya diet: as inferred from isotopic elemental analysis of human bone. *Journal of Archaeological Science* 16: 457–474.

Whorf, Benjamin L. 1933 The phonetic value of certain characters in Maya writing. *Papers of the Peabody Museum of Archaeology and Ethnology, Harvard University*, 13 (2).

——1935 Maya writing and its decipherment. *Maya Research* 2 (4): 367–382. New Orleans.

Willey, Gordon R. 1979 John Eric Sydney Thompson, 1898–1975. *Proceedings of the British Academy* 65: 783–798.

Index